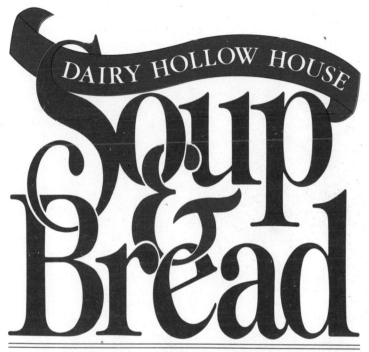

DAIRY HOLLOW HOUSE

Soup & Bread

A COUNTRY INN
C·O·O·K·B·O·O·K

DAIRY HOLLOW HOUSE

Soup & Bread

A COUNTRY INN
C·O·O·K·B·O·O·K

BY
CRESCENT DRAGONWAGON
ILLUSTRATIONS BY PAUL HOFFMAN

WORKMAN PUBLISHING ✦ NEW YORK

Library of Congress Cataloging-in-Publication Data
Dragonwagon, Crescent.
Dairy Hollow House soup & bread : a country inn cookbook / by
Crescent Dragonwagon.
p.   cm.
Includes index.
ISBN 1-56305-243-1 (cloth) : —ISBN 0-89480-751-X (paper)
1. Soups.   2. Bread.   3. Salads.   4.Dairy Hollow House (Inn :
Eureka Springs, Ark.)   I. Title.   II. Title: Dairy Hollow House
soup and bread.
TX757.D73   1992   91-50956
641.8′13—dc20   CIP

Cover illustration by Joyce Kitchell

Workman books are available at special discounts when purchased in
bulk for premiums and sales promotions as well as for fund-raising or
educational use. Special editions or book excerpts can also be created
to specification. For details, contact the Special Sales Director at the
address below.

Workman Publishing Company, Inc.
708 Broadway
New York, NY 10003

Manufactured in the United States of America
First printing August 1992
10 9 8 7 6 5 4 3

Acknowledgment is made to the following for permission to reprint
previously published material:

French Country Bread (page 328) adapted from Country-Style Bread from
THE COOKING OF SOUTH WESTERN FRANCE by Paula Wolfert. Copyright © 1983 by Paula Wolfert. Used by permission of Doubleday, a divi-
sion of Bantam Doubleday Dell Publishing Group, Inc.

The Jones's Country Loaves from Jan Brown (page 330) adapted from
Country Bread by Judith and Evan Jones, *Gourmet* magazine, February
1988. Used by permission of the author.

Betty Rosbottom's Cream of Artichoke Soup (page 250) from THE BETTY
ROSBOTTOM COOKING SCHOOL COOKBOOK by Betty Rosbottom.
Copyright © 1987 by Betty Rosbottom. Used by permission of Workman
Publishing Company, Inc.

For Steven Colvin,
with whom I hope to break the bread of life
for a long, long time.

ACKNOWLEDGMENTS

 book like this has many in-gredients, and simmers over a period of years. Do too many cooks spoil the broth? No, never! No amount of thank you's can be adequate to those who helped along the way:

Dairy Hollow cooks present: Sandy Allison and Rose Aparicio; Dairy Hollow cooks past: Rebecca Sisco, Wally Wood and Rowan Dougherty, Mark Dewitz, Tina Plowman, Rebecca Barden, and Ann Naumann.
Dairy Hollow occasional angel, seamstress, former innkeeper-collaborator, and person-just generally-in-a-class-all-by-her-own: Jan Brown.
Loyal recipe testers/tasters: Charlisa Cato Hattie Mae Cox, Marcia (Choux-Choo) Yearsley, Stephanie Yearsley, (and a special citation to Sag Harbor, New York, tester Julia Vandermade).
Waiter/garlic pickler, poke-finder, paw-paw slider "Does this have enough salt man": John Mitchell.
Assistant chef "She *can* stand the heat, that's why she's in the kitchen" garnish queen and ra-conteur: E. Rae Smith.

Front desk protectors-of-CD-during-her-incom-municado-writing-times: Paula Martin, Char-lisa Cato (again) Rebecca Sisco (again), Glenna Muse, Phyllis Poe; Carolyn "Well I can do *this*" Morgan; Edna "She be jammin' now" Apar-icio; And what-would-we-cook-*in*-if-it-wasn't-for-him daytime clean-meister: Roy White.

Miscellaneous bouquets of thanks also go to the following locals: Louis and Elsie Freund, for reasons beyond number but all boiling down to love, understanding, mutual ad-miration, and the pursuit of art; Bob Purvis, Eureka Springs Chamber of Commerce, for answering numerous fish questions; David Sisco, for answering numerous *other* fish questions, as well as hand-delivering us green peppers, letting us know when the artichokes are on sale, and treating me to ap-ple chips; Jim Long, passion-ate herbalist, adventurer, writer, lecturer, goose-and-guinea hen raiser, cartoonist, designer of edible landscapes, and occasional morel hunter; Susan and Bill Patton, who ar-rived in the nick of time.

And these celebrated non-locals: Mike "Roux the Day" Trimble; Ellen "Long May She" Fly; Shirley Abbott, generous reverse Arkansas/East Coast kindred spirit; Cynthia LaFerle, hugely supportive of DHH and the profession of innkeeping; JoAn Bell and Pat Hardy, and our colleagues in the Independent Innkeepers Association.

And for contributing recipes that added so much to this book, a golden whisk to: Jan Brown (again), Lyntha Wesner, Marquita Sorce, Jack Albert, Felicity Turner, Marge Parkhurst, Sally Williams Gorrell, and Peggy Pinkley.

Also contributing much—sometimes recipes, sometimes methods, sometimes quotes, always inspiration, are the following cookbook authors: John Thorne, Paula Wolfert, Judith and Evan Jones, Angelo Pellegrini, Adelle Davis, Louis P. DeGouy, Henri Charpentier, Leon Soniat, Betty Rosbottom, Michael McIlwraith, and John Egerton.

Further contributions of substance and spirit are made by several cherished fellow innkeepers: Deedy Marble of The Governor's Inn (Ludlow, Vermont); Katie and George Hoy of The Inn at Brandywine Falls (Sagamore Hills, Ohio); Laurie Anderson, David Campiche, and Chef Cheri Walker and the Kischners, of The Shelburne Inn and Shoalwater Restaurant (Seaview, Washington); Maureen and John Magee of the Rabbit Hill Inn (Lower Waterford, Vermont); Jack Coleman of The Inn at Long Last (Chester, Vermont); and Lindsay and Virginia Miller of Pentagoet Inn (Castine, Maine).

More thanks go to the Uncle Ben's folks—especially Marion Tripp and her associates—and Carolyn Oeben, for giving us recognition and praise so generous we had no choice but to live up to it.

A big, big thank you and a big, big box of Peanut Butter and Raisin Rafer-Wafers to Suzanne Rafer, my dear long-standing, long-suffering, hard-working editor—I've never had so much fun while being driven to distraction, and I certainly hope you feel the same. Let's do it again sometime, okay? Also, a big thank you to Lisa Hollander, for a good-looking book design and all those cows.

My mother, Charlotte Zolotow, has—as always—helped me, sometimes tracking down

quotes, sending clippings or cookbooks, and always just being *there*. There are no words for this kind of support and loving kindness.

And finally—it is customary for authors to thank their long-tormented spouses last in the acknowledgments (for they have been closest to the sometimes-agony and hassle of writing a book), but Ned Shank, my husband, Dairy Hollow House cohort and main-man, and general Darlin' Companion of fourteen-some years, deserves infinitely more than my thanks. My devotion, respect, and deepest, most heartfelt gratitude go to you for hanging out and hanging on through this, Ned—and to think you managed to chair term after term on the HDC this whole time, too!

THANK YOU ALL.

CD

CONTENTS

HOT, HEARTY BEAN SOUPS— LUSCIOUS, LUSTY LEGUMES

Black Beans ❖ Black-Eyed Peas ❖Chick-Peas (Garbanzos) ❖ Cranberry Beans ❖ Great Northern Beans ❖ Kidney Beans ❖ Lentils ❖ Lima Beans ❖ Navy Beans ❖ Peas ❖ Pinto Beans ❖ Red Beans ❖ Split Peas

GUMBO ZEB— HISTORY IN A BOWL AND MORE

Gumbo Zeb Base ❖ Completing the Gumbo Zeb Base

DELECTABLE DAIRY SOUPS FROM DAIRY HOLLOW

Cream- and Milk-Based Soups ❖ Yogurt- and Buttermilk-Based Soups ❖ Cheese Soups

SWEET HARVEST FRUIT SOUPS

Bananas ❖ Blackberries ❖ Blueberries ❖ Cherries ❖ Cranberries ❖ Melon ❖Oranges ❖ Peaches and Nectarines ❖ Strawberries

NUT SOUPS— FROM SOUP TO...

LOAVES, MUFFINS, AND MORE

Yeast Breads ❖ Rolls ❖ Quick Breads ❖ Biscuits ❖ Muffins

SALAD— THE GREEN PALETTE

Composed Salads ❖ Grain-Based Salads

Welcome

TO DAIRY HOLLOW HOUSE

elcome to Dairy Hollow House. We're glad you're here, and your room's all ready for you. Let's see, I think we have you here in the Main House. Let me check; yes, ma'am, right here in the Summer Meadows Suite. We've got some hot cider with cinnamon going for you in your room; we'll just take you upstairs to it. Did you have a pleasant drive over? Yes, the mountain roads can take longer than you expected, it's hard to quite believe how serious all those curves are when you see 'em on a map. Up these steps—what's that heavenly thing you're smelling? Well, right down there's the kitchen, so just at this point you get a lot of the aromas.

Oh, you mean what exactly? *Well, probably a combination of things. When I went through earlier Sandy was making chicken stock . . . and one of our soups tonight is black bean, and I was just sautéing onions and peppers for that a little while ago. Oh, and of course bread, you're smelling bread baking. What kind? Our yeast bread tonight is Country French, which is what's wafting up here. Of course we always have our Skillet-Sizzled Buttermilk Cornbread, too; but that doesn't get made until the last minute, so you wouldn't be smelling that quite yet. Ah, here we are, Summer Meadows. Oh, come on, it's only two hours to dinner, I know you can wait!*

And so it is at Dairy Hollow House, a country inn and restaurant in the Ozark Mountains started over a decade ago by me, Ned Shank (my husband), and Bill Haymes, a long-time friend.

The inn is in three buildings on either side of a green, wooded valley: an 1880s farmhouse, slightly secluded, now called by us "The Farmhouse"; our Main House, a rambling, welcoming 1950s "bungalow" with three guest suites, our check-in area, and our restaurant; and the Innkeeper's House, where Ned and I live. These structures are within the city limits of the mountain resort of Eureka Springs, Arkansas, year-round population 2,000, a quirky Victorian-era spa town built into the steep, up-and-down Ozark Mountain terrain. Our town motto since the 1880s has been "Where the Misfit Fits."

But an inn is about more than houses and more than locale, however pleasing those houses and that locale. An inn is about people taking care of people; expressing something intangible—something about life, love, service, caring—through the tangible. One of the tangibles we are best known for at Dairy Hollow House is our food, including our classic regional breads, always from scratch and fresh-baked, as well as our infinitely varied hot and cold soups, which range from classic to innovative, and which are also always from scratch.

This book is about these soups and breads (and also some of the glorious salads that round out a bread-and-soup-based meal). But I hope that as you make these very tangible recipes, some of the inn's intangibles will also reach you.

For besides cooking together—simmering soups, and placing clean towels over fat full bread doughs rising like pregnant moons in round bowls—you and I will become neighbors for a time. We will meet and explore how to make a really good vegetable stock or a nice brown roux for gumbo, or describe the best way to thicken a fruit soup or put together sesame-raisin vinaigrette, the best possible fall salad dressing.

But for you, until you come and stay with us, this territory, like the territory in all books as they are read, is imagined; you connect to the place partly by taking things on faith. You are my guest here, as much as if you were actually checking into the inn, perhaps in the Rose Room, with its Eastlake furniture and long, long clawfoot bathtub under the skylight; as much as if you were actually sitting on the front porch, sipping the long glass of iced herbal cooler garnished with lemon balm, if the day was hot, perhaps with one of the cats wandering over from the Innkeeper's House to weave against your legs.

With a cookbook, the border between imagined and here-and-now reality territory is handily breached. When you fix our cornbread—the baking soda dissolving in the buttermilk, the aroma as it bakes, the sweet grainy flavor, the moist crumb trembling on the tines of a fork—you cross its border. Here and there become elastic and reveal themselves, finally, as inseparable.

Our "here" is very personal, shaded by the influences I, and others, have brought to the inn. A good inn cannot be separated from the region in which that inn is located. It takes part in its region's history, and both built and natural environments. Being interconnected with its spiritual, social, and physical ecology is what makes an inn different from a chain motel, or even many very good hotels. As our world grows smaller and regional differences are eroded, accommodations often become airportlike; the bedspread and drapes and furnishings, the room layout, and sometimes even the view (if there is one) could be anywhere, just as most airports could be any airport.

But inns are absolutely unique to their site. When you wake up and see a white squirrel out your window skittering across the black walnut tree; when there's a knock on your door and there stands Sandy Allison with a big smile on her face, holding an even bigger split-oak basket and in it your breakfast; when you place that breakfast on the table (a kitchen table, antique, wooden, from a farmhouse near Golden, Missouri), where the very china and napkins set up

on the table match the room; well, you know you could only be in Dairy Hollow. The same panoply of utterly unique-to-that-place sights and sounds, aromas, decor, food (painted with local history), furnishings, climate, flora, fauna, is true of any really good inn— and meeting other innkeepers as colleagues, and occasionally visiting their places—has been one of the most wondrous and fascinating phases of our life in this profession, and has also brought home to us this quality of regional distinction.

As an inn cannot be separated from its natural and built environment, so it cannot be separated from its people: the innkeepers (in this case, me and my husband, our beloved colleagues and coworkers of the past and present, like unflappable, all-heart Sandy Allison, kitchen manager, mentioned above;

Paula Martin, our ever-organized, ever-resourceful business manager, who knows everything there is to know about American quilts and bookkeeping; or sweet Jan Brown, with whom I wrote the first *Dairy Hollow House Cookbook,* and who, to quote Zora Neale Hurston, "switches mean fanny around the kitchen." You will meet these people, and many others, in the "Inn Good Company" boxes here and there throughout this book.

Another part of our inn is undoubtedly, though indirectly, our townspeople—the locals who maybe eat here once a year on a birthday, but who refer business to us year-round; the shopkeepers and gallery-owners who wait on and chat with our guests downtown; the gardeners and farmers who supply us with fresh tomatoes, rabbit, lemon basil, shiitake mushrooms, pineapple sage,

The First Dairy Hollow House Cookbook

❦*Jan Brown, who early on cooked with me on a regular basis, loved to talk food. In the kitchen, we were Miles Davis and Thelonious Monk, jamming.*

We worked well together, with liveliness and mutual respect and just plain fun. This transferred itself to the Dairy Hollow House Cookbook, *written when guests began to query us for recipes. Originally published by* Macmillan, *it is still available from us; call us at (800)562-8650 for full info. Yes, we have an 800 number, but it's not "operators are standing by," it's Paula, Char, Becky, Phyllis, or occasionally me or Ned, and it's most certainly not one of those dorky machines where they say "I'm sorry, all lines are busy now, will you please hold for the next available operator" and then play stupid music for hours.*❦

and a hundred other good things; the carpenters who help us maintain the three garden-edged buildings that make up the physical side of Dairy Hollow House, the artists whose paintings add life, energy, beauty, and vision to our rooms. You'll meet some of them, too.

Inn people also include—of course!—our cherished guests. Some come like the Capistrano swallows, annually or twice annually, at certain times of year; some we meet only once; some we've known for years. Our guests come from every walk of life and every possible profession: we have not only doctors and lawyers and computer programmers and therapists, but actors and actresses, and many writers. We had a gentleman who was a naturalist for the American Weed Society, and could identify every single plant in the Hollow. We had Mrs. Arkansas 1989. We've had peace activists and Desert Storm vets; graduate students and tenured professors; veterinarians and couturiers and restaurateurs; artists who left drawings in our room diaries or sent watercolors after they left. We've had other innkeepers, chefs, and hoteliers; district attorneys and graphic designers; a casket salesman and a union organizer and a woman who teaches Lamaze-method childbirth and boutique-owners and natural-foods-store owners and orchid-growers and lily-hybridizers and musicians (orchestra violinists, Christian rock 'n' rollers, folksingers).

What do they have in common, our guests? People attracted specifically to inn travel seem to me open to new experiences, and filled with an expectation of the positive, like the Cincinnati couple who sent a letter with their initial deposit check which began "Dear Friends We Haven't Met Yet." (They've since stayed at least a dozen times, are indeed friends, and Frannie's Fast, Fabulous Buttermilk Bread is part of this book.)

Our guests frequently send us recipes (especially breads, I've noticed, perhaps because there's something so

INN GOOD COMPANY

❧ *The days when Ned and I could pull off everything from breakfast to dinner to bookkeeping to bed-making to gardening are long, long gone. These days we work with a dynamic and talented crew of staff—eighteen of us, to be exact, though only two of those eighteen are full-time staff. Eureka Springs being what it is, those who live here tend towards a multiplicity of talents and interests.*

Without them, this book would be missing a lot of key ingredients. So you will meet them here and there throughout the pages of this book, amidst the loaves and leaves and ladlefuls, under the heading "Inn Good Company." ❧

friendly about a golden loaf). But recipes are by no means our only communications with guests between visits. It is not uncommon for us to get birth announcements from guests or photos of the babies conceived here or anniversary pictures a year or five years after the wedding reception held in our dining room. And virtually any time a former Dairy Hollow guest sees a postcard with a cow (the DHH symbol) on it, he or she is likely to send it to us!

In all, innkeeping's a sweet and intimate way to become involved in the lives of others, and strangers become something much more in the process.

In addition to being an innkeeper and three-nights-a-week chef at our restaurant, I am a novelist and children's book writer, originally from New York. I have always loved to cook, entertain, and eat out, and I have lived in Eureka Springs since 1972. As a child, my parents took me to country inns in New England, especially Vermont, where my aunt spends half the year in a restored farmhouse.

Ned Shank, my husband, in addition to being an innkeeper, is an historic preservationist from Iowa, who met me at a potluck dinner in a Victorian "Steamboat Gothic" house in Little Rock in 1977 ("I came with a kipper salad and left with you," is one of the things he likes to say; it wasn't *quite* that fast, but almost). He is tall, blue-eyed, bearded, engaging, easygoing; he has been involved in the local and state preservation movement for over a decade. He also beats me at Scrabble roughly 50 percent of the time. (I know; we have a lifetime score tally written into the fly-leaf of our Scrabble dictionary.) At one time he had

his own preservation consulting business; he also marketed architectural services for an Atlanta architecture firm before coming home to Eureka and me and a life of full-time (and I do mean full) innkeeping and maître d'ing.

INN THE BEGINNING

Funky though it is, I've lived in the Innkeeper's House since I moved here as a nineteen-year-old, close to twenty years ago. It's in the wooded valley known as Dairy Hollow—we even got a street sign last year that actually *says* Dairy Hollow. In Ozark vernacular, a hollow, sometimes pronounced "holler," is a valley. Our particular green valley's name dates from when milk was not mass-produced, but came from real cows, with names like Bossy, Rosebud, and Lil, on small family dairy farms. At that time, in Eureka, there were several dairies along this valley. The last was still in existence when I moved to Eureka Springs from New York City, a story told in the beginning of the chapter on dairy-based soups.

My first few years here I admired, daily, the small, unpretentious farmhouse across the way. Here, in this town of elegant Victorian glamour-girls, it was a pure, simple Ozarks farm, sweet as a strain of fiddle music floating through the June air. It was *tiny*—three rooms—and it was owned by the family who had that last existing Dairy Hollow dairy, the Rhiel Dairy. Although not lived in, it was not for sale, but I begged Mrs. Rhiel's daughters to promise me that if they

UNFINISHED BUSINESS

❦ *I mentioned the three houses which make up the inn. The Farmhouse and the Main House are really beautifully kept up. Then there's Ned's and my home, the Innkeeper's House, which I frequently describe to guests as "the one that looks like Tobacco Road." There's always some piece of furniture on the front porch midway through being refinished, some boxes of Christmas decorations being readied to take out of or go into storage. I am trying to give up apologizing for the state of our house. One of our guests, Willie Miller, a doctor from Dexter, Missouri, once came over to borrow a videotape from me and I made some self-deprecatory remark to him about our house being trashed, saying it was due to some or another special event we had just gotten through. He smiled and said rather cheerfully, "Oh, it was just like this the last time I was here."*

"It was?" I said guiltily.

"Sure," he said, smiling at me. Obviously the kitchen table, armoire, and piles of sandpaper and steel-wool and boxes of notebooks didn't bother him.

"Well," I said, and took a deep and rueful breath. "Well, Willie, think of the inn as the finished work of art and our house as the studio."

True, and I hadn't known it until I said it to Willie! ❦

---

ever did consider selling it, they'd come to me first. Between the time I voiced this sentiment and when the sisters came to me with an offer, I married Ned, whose enthusiasm about starting an inn matched mine.

Up until that time, the only accommodations in Eureka Springs for visitors were contemporary motels and four old historic hotels which, though wonderful, had been allowed to fall into disrepair. Ned the preservationist was eager to demonstrate "adaptive reuse" in action; to show that tourism and saving old buildings could go hand in hand, and to point out that not only fancy-pants Victorians, but humbler vernacular homes, could have a new life. And I loved to cook and entertain and scrunch fabrics in my hand and shop at auctions and garden. (Now that I am an experienced innkeeper I wince at having gone into the profession knowing so little about it. It is a miracle that we made it through those first few years. I could write volumes about what we *didn't* know.)

Anyway, Ned, I, and a good friend, musician Bill Haymes, pooled our resources and got the building. We did all the work on its two, now three, guest rooms, each with private bath and private entrance, each furnished with antiques and enlivened with fresh flowers (usually a mix of wildflowers and garden flowers). In a later renovation, about the time Bill Haymes sold his interest in the inn to my brother, Stephen Zolotow, who has remained a nonactive but vital partner in the business, we enlarged the Farmhouse rooms slightly and added a fireplace to each.

From the first, we did breakfasts, and in 1982, with Jan Brown, began to serve dinner for room guests only. This started unofficially: Eureka Springs is a seasonal resort town, and in the winter restaurants tend to close, though it is lovely and peaceful and just beautiful as a walking-around-quiet-time-to-hang-out-with-each-other place. Well, what's an innkeeper to do, when two plaintive guests, who've been hiking all day, turn up at the doorstep of the Innkeeper's House, out of which wafts the steam of beany soup and baking bread, and they moan plaintively, "Could you *please* feed us? Something, anything? There isn't any other place *open!*" Eventually, our rooms began to sell out, and former guests, disgruntled at not having their accustomed room with us, would say, "Well, could you at least feed us dinner?" So began the first seeds of what would become the restaurant.

However, as Ned and I began to consider the possibility of a restaurant, we wanted a site nearby, with a greater presence on Spring Street. This led to the purchase of what's now our Main House, at the intersection of Spring and Dairy Hollow Road. Built in the late '40s as a retirement home for the very elderly parents of a neighbor, the house was rock solid (one of the few houses in Eureka Springs where, when you jump, nothing rattles), but it was plain and boxy, lacking in charm, and painted the color of a Band-Aid. We bought it in 1985 primarily for the location, but then we stripped acoustical tile and found knotty pine ceilings beneath it and hardwood floors under the turquoise carpeting and one of our carpenters broke a sledge hammer taking out a wall, and we gradually fell in love with it. By the time we added a windowboxed porch, landscaped the grounds, and painted, the Main House and its three suites had come to life.

After about three more years, we began putting on an addition—our first new construction. We added a check-in area with a huge, curved front desk—like a ship's prow, almost—an architectural antique, from the old, now defunct, Hotel Missouri in Springfield. And we added our restaurant.

After three years I still feel fondness, pride, and a lift of the heart when

I go through the French doors from the front desk area into the dining room. Ned did the overall design on the addition, beautifully tightened and codified by architect and friend Dan O'Connell. Since the inn's in a residential neighborhood, from the outside the addition looks small, indeed residential in scale, and the front desk area is pretty intimate. But you step through those French doors, and almost despite yourself you say "Oh!"

The cathedral ceiling soars to 18 feet in its highest part, there's a massive stone fireplace, the walls are pale yellow with an ivy stencil, dropped a foot from the ceiling, ribboning the room. There are two watercolors by Elsie Freund. One is a sweet-eyed brown Jersey cow, and the other is a dreamscape landscape painting of downtown Eureka, for which we traded Elsie and her husband, Louis, thirty-eight dinners at the restaurant. But undoubtedly the centerpiece of the dining room is a quilt, made by our own Jan Brown, entitled "Tea with Aunt Rose" (see page 176).

Then there's the heart of the house—the kitchen. Kitchens are exciting places. The four elements of the ancients (earth, as represented by the food substances born of it, water, fire, and air) co-mingle and re-combine. Sizzling, boiling, activity; the onions as they sauté, the wash of steam as the pasta is drained in the sink, the waft of baking bread, the pulsing white-veined heart of the deep purple cabbage, the transformation from liquid to solid of the cakes as they bake—these tasks and rhythms remain, for me, something both holy and fun. Cooking has alchemy and theater, the joy of creation; the sensual pleasure of touch-

ing and sniffing glorious foodstuffs; the pleasure of pleasing others; the adrenaline of turning out a great meal for forty in a timely fashion, despite the fact that the city street repair crew broke a gas main and left us without our stove and oven for four peak preparation hours. Can we pull it off? Yes!

INN REFLECTION

In fact, our lives as a whole are pretty seductive. Though like almost everyone I know, we are absurdly too busy (the disease of the era), I still marvel that Ned and I pulled it off. Such sweetness permeates life here. I love my husband, my town, our beautiful inn and restaurant, serving our guests. I love cooking, entertaining, writing about these and other matters. I love the joys of creative innovation and problem-solving, and I love as well the occasional periods of solitude I manage to wrest from all this (usually in the off-season, when I go away for a month or two, so as to stay in touch with the part of me that is "just" a writer, not a writer/innkeeper).

Dairy Hollow House has been a lot of firsts. We were the first bed-and-breakfast inn in the Ozarks and Eureka Springs, one of the first two in the state. We remain the first, and only, full-service country inn in a four-state area. We are the only inn within a ten- or twelve-state radius to have been named one of Uncle Ben's ten "Best Inns of the Year" (see page 154); we won this award three years in a row, the max that you *can* win

it, an honor we share with only one other inn in all the country (the Rabbit Hill Inn, Lower Waterford, Vermont, run by our dear colleagues, John and Maureen Magee). When I think that all this began with a dilapidated farmhouse along an unpaved road, three friends, two guest rooms and a cash stake of, I think, $2,000; with a lot of energy, good intentions, and very tolerant guests, well, I am simply amazed. Dairy Hollow House has taught me that anything is possible. You learn as you go along.

The kitchen is one of the places where I have learned the most. Our restaurant kitchen has no exterior windows, but it does have a window out to the front desk area, so guests can look in on us (and often smile or wave), and from that window we can see them, and also out to the front of the inn.

Ah, our food. We serve a six-course dinner, seven days a week except during the winter months, one seating nightly at 7:00 P.M. We call our style of cuisine, in soups and everything else, "Nouveau-'Zarks." Briefly, it is Jan's and my own very personal interpretation of contemporary regional cuisine—of using the ingredients, though rarely the techniques, of the Ozarks to create a new hybrid. Let me quote directly from our *Dairy Hollow House Cookbook:*

What do our soup-and-bread meals, our breakfasts, our elegant terrines, tortes and mousses have in common? What is the link between our straightforward honey-sweetened apple pies in whole-wheat crusts and our decadent chocolate wonders? Simple: everything is done attentively and from scratch; no

shortcuts, no convenience foods, the freshest and best possible seasonal ingredients.

And in this aspect, traditional French haute cuisine, nouvelle cuisine, real old-time Ozarks country cooking, well-done natural foods cooking, and good food preparation from many lands all come together.

We like to think of Dairy Hollow House, small though it is, tucked into an obscure Ozark hillside, as perched happily at this particular intersection.

An intersection, I would add, that extends from us here, in real time and space, to you, as you read the pages of this book.

Ten years ago, when Jan and I wrote the *Dairy Hollow House Cookbook,* we said being an innkeeper was like being a professional fairy godmother, and owning an inn was sending out a party invitation to the world, then waiting to see who arrived. I still feel this, and lovely people are still arriving.

I'm glad you have RSVPed. Pull up a chair. Soup's on; we have trout gumbo tonight, or asparagus and Cheddar cheese with white wine. There are daffodils in a white pitcher on the front desk. Ned's maître d'ing; Sandy and I are in the kitchen. The vinaigrette is bursting with three kinds of basil from Jim Long's herb garden, and the salad has the tenderest possible greens from the Millers. The cornbread, round and yellow like a sun, will be out of the oven in a minute. We've been expecting you.

Welcome.

Stocks

THE FOUNDATION

tock is that flavorful liquid in which meat, fowl, or vegetables have been cooked, and to which they have given their essence. It is this liquid component that makes soup soup and not casserole; that gives a "brothy" rather than watery consistency; that makes a potage spoonable or sippable but not forkable. Whatever the soup's featured players, it is stock that imbues the dish with its underlying substance of taste. With the exception of some cream- or milk-based soups, it's almost impossible to make good soup without good stock.

A stock's base may be animal or vegetable, but in most cases you won't notice the flavoring as such, only how good the soup is when it's present, or how pallid it is in its absence. A stock's presence makes the difference between "thin ... homeopathic soup that was made by boiling the shadow of a pigeon that had been starved to death," as described once by Abraham Lincoln, and the minestrone of Mrs. Mazza's 1947 *Herbs for the Kitchen:* "A plate of this pottage," she said, "and we have dined."

A stock may be enriched with wine or cream, thickened with starch or puréed vegetables, or thinned with milk or tomato juice. It may be seasoned with any number of things. A weak stock can be oomphed up by using a couple of tricks we'll touch on later in this chapter. But by hook or crook, when it becomes part of the soup, a stock must be flavorful and *there*.

With a good stock on hand, and some ordinary undistinguished kitchen staples, you can have a mighty passable homemade soup on the table, from start to finish, in fifteen minutes. Add another ten, and you could have a skillet of cornbread with it.

Such a soup (even using a few shortcuts we'll go into later) will be decisively homemade. Everyone, including yourself, will want seconds. You will marvel at how good it tastes—how quickly made and inexpensive it was; how good you felt sniffing, cooking, and eating it; how your husband, wife, neighbor, guest, or child poked his or her nose in the kitchen and said, "Mmmm, what smells so good?"

Although most stocks take a while to cook, they are not, as a rule, time consuming in active preparation nor are they incompatible with a full, busy life. They are not exacting—you usually put the stuff in the pot, add water, turn on the heat, and more or less leave it alone to fix itself. If you have never made stock on a regular basis, you'll be surprised to learn that if you're home at all, good, homemade stock can be yours with so little effort and such wonderful results that making it may easily become habitual, automatic, really. Stock-making happens easily around other things: while

you are watching the news, eating, or doing housework; reading the kids a bedtime story or catching up on office work at the kitchen table.

I do know people who make more of a production out of preparing stock simply because it makes them nervous to have something cooking unattended. Or they believe, with so casual an approach, that they're sure to forget some crucial point. So they plan a big prep cooking day once or twice a month, during which they just stay in the kitchen and happily putter. They make stocks and sauces, breads and casseroles, and stash everything in the freezer in portion- or recipe-size containers. My friends who organize their kitchen lives in such a fashion tell me they feel replete with satisfaction at the end of such a cooking morning, and more power to them. If this is your style, go to it. Just, please, do try stock-making a few times. See what a difference it makes to meals, those small measurements of our lives' quality.

On to some basic, vital principles of stock and stock-making, then the recipes. Lots of read-through-one-time instructional text; the actual recipes are quick and simple, so don't be put off.

In this book, I call stocks prepared specifically for use as stock "primary." I call all stocks created as beneficent side effects of cooking something else "secondary." And I call all stocks created primarily of trimmings that would otherwise be thrown out, but instead are saved for the stockpot, "found." Secondary and found stocks are less flavorful than primary, but they are still useful, and can always be enriched to bring them up to speed.

WATER PRINCIPLE (A)

When you drop an ingredient, whether animal or vegetable, into cold water, and cook it until it gives up its essence to the liquid, at the end of the cooking time, all that is left of the ingredient is tasteless fiber, to be strained out and discarded. The water, however, will have become a primary, flavorful stock.

When you drop an ingredient into hot water—either boiling or simmering—and cook it relatively briefly, the majority of the flavor will remain in the ingredient itself. When using chicken, fish, or beef, you'll still have a dividend of some nice, though mild, incidental or secondary stock; with vegetables, the cooking liquid will end up being more water than anything else, though it is worth saving to use instead of plain water the next time you prepare stock. It does have some nutrients and a ghost of flavor.

So, know before you start whether you intend the stock you're making to be the raison d'être, or whether you are merely using the water as the cooking vehicle for the chicken (or whatever), in which case any stock thereby created is incidental. This will tell you whether your cooking ingredients should be begun in hot or cold water, how long you should cook them for, and so on. This principle holds true for all stocks.

WATER PRINCIPLE (B)

Stock may be made from chicken, fish, vegetables, or miso (a fermented bean paste), but the main ingredient for each is identical, and one we think of as tasteless. Surprise! It's . . . water.

We think of water as tasteless, but actually it's not. Chlorine, fluoride, who-knows-what-all-and-you-probably-don't-even-*want*-to-know-what goes into your tap water. Yes, you can use tap water in your stock, and it will be perfectly acceptable; I do it often. But for refinement and clarity of taste in every detail, use spring or distilled water (flat, not sparkling, but *please* tell me you knew that!), both of which are available for home delivery in many areas. The difference this water makes is subtle, but unmistakable. I'm not going to specify "spring water" every time water's called for throughout this book, just in the stock recipes in this chapter. But know this is what I mean, ideally.

THE SAFE AND FRESH PRINCIPLE

Remember seventh- or eighth-grade science class, the unit before the frog one? The unit in which you grew mold and bacteria? Remember what the growing medium was, the culture used for the bacteria to multiply and be fruitful in?

Bouillon. Beef or chicken bouillon. So perfect a bacterial medium are these stocks that few kitchen basics can be considered as perishable and potentially dangerous as flesh-based stock.

But it is not at all difficult to practice, ahem, "safe stocks."

As soon as you complete making chicken or fish stocks, bring them to room temperature quickly, then immediately refrigerate or freeze them. *Do not, however, place hot stock in the fridge or freezer without cooling it somewhat.* This can raise the inside temperature of the refrigerator so that it won't cool properly for an hour or two, thereby creating a high-risk environment for any spoilage-prone foods.

In very hot weather, don't let the stock sit around during its cooling phase. Instead, after straining it into a stainless steel bowl (because this transmits heat or cold faster than glass, pottery, or plastic, allowing for quicker cooling), stir the stock a bit to get it past the steaming-hot point, then set the bowl in a sink full of cold water. The water should come well up the sides of the bowl. You may need to weight down the bowl of stock so it doesn't bobble in the water. To do so, place a plate on top of the bowl and on it put a large can or two or something else heavy. (If you have an ardent dishwasher in the house, a note taped to the top can might be helpful: *"Stock Cooling—Please Do Not Disturb".*)

The minute the stock is at room

temperature or coolish to lukewarm, transfer it to storage containers, cover it, and refrigerate or freeze it.

If you think there's a slight possibility that your stock may have been sitting out a little too long, give it a hard 5-minute reboil. If the possibility is more than slight, throw it out and start over again.

To thaw frozen stocks, begin the night before, if possible, moving the stock from freezer to fridge. The next day, enough stock should have thawed from the edges of the container so that you can shake all the stock out, emptying it (probably with a still-frozen chunk in the middle) into a heavy pot. Bring the stock to a boil quickly, and use it as soon as possible. If you forgot to move the frozen stock from freezer to fridge the night before, run hot water over the stock container, or set it in a bowl of hot water, until the edges have melted enough to remove the stock. Then heat it as described above.

This vigilance and caution need not be taken with vegetable stocks. Though somewhat perishable, they are not as prone to rapid bacterial development as are beef, fish, and chicken stocks.

Before moving on, one final suggestion: for best results do prepare your stock in a large, heavy enamel-clad cast-iron pot.

ADDING OOMPH, OR FLAVOR BOOSTERS

You've made a stock and it tastes insipid. Or you had leftover vegetable-cooking water, or some other secondary liquid with enough goodness in it to make you feel guilty about throwing it out, but not enough to be much more than faint on its own. What to do?

Every cook worth his or her sea salt has a few last-minute, seat-of-the-pants, up-the-sleeves tricks to turn up the volume of flavor which a person new to cooking wouldn't know, and which one rarely finds in a cookbook. There is something faintly dishonest, yet also praiseworthy, about this kind of last-minute silk-purse-from-a-sow's-ear (or "cow's ear," as Jan Brown used to say) salvaging. Here are some tricks of mine, but remember as you fool with these to *Taste, Taste, Taste*. With each new addition and revision, scoop up a little of the stock into your spoon. Sip and roll it around in your mouth. You will know when the soup is "there." Here goes:

❖ Boil the stock down to a quarter or half of its original quantity. This concentrates the flavor and often does the trick. Or boost the flavor with any, or several, of these:

❖ A Morga cube (see page 31)

❖ 1 teaspoon to 1 tablespoon of tomato paste

❖ 1 tablespoon or more of good brandy or cognac

❖ 1 teaspoon to a tablespoon of honey

❖ 1 teaspoon to a tablespoon of miso

❖ 1 teaspoon to a tablespoon of Pickapeppa or Worcestershire sauce

❖ ¼ teaspoon to 1 teaspoon of dark molasses

❖ Salt and/or freshly ground black or white pepper

❖ A little tamari/shoyu soy sauce

❖ Your favorite seasoning blend (we use one called BelleMystika; we also sell it at the inn and mail order it)

❖ 3 to 4 cloves of garlic, put through a garlic press and boiled in the stock for a few minutes; or, better yet, a tablespoon of Garlic Oil or Classic Basil Pesto (both page 41) which often work magic

❖ A few drops of lemon juice or vinegar (go easy)

❖ 2 or 3 tablespoons of dry white wine or dry vermouth (maybe more)

❖ Freshly grated nutmeg (particularly good with cream, onion, or mushroom soups; do not use in tomato soups, however)

❖ A tiny fleck of cinnamon and/or ground cloves (good with chili or spicy soups, often does the trick with tomato-based soups)

As you fool with these and grow more conversant with kitchen alchemy, you'll find certain of these secrets and certain combinations of them work better with some things than others. You may well need more than one. Tomato paste, cognac, and honey—just a little of each—work miracles on most vegetable or chicken soups and many fish soups (in fact, you'll run into several recipes here where I use just this triumvirate). Lemon juice and black pepper work to perk up a surprising variety of soups. Lemon or vinegar can be just the thing in a bean soup. (Bean soups in general, I find, usually need more salt than any other kind.) Start conservatively—especially with salty additions)—taste, then add a little more if necessary. And keep tasting!

CHICKEN STOCKS

What kind of chicken should you use for stock? As the good old *Joy of Cooking* says, "Stock-making is an exception to almost every other kind of cooking. Instead of calling for things young and tender, remember that meat from aged animals and mature vegetables will be most flavorsome."

Still, in my experience good stock can be made from birds of many ages: from the *Joy*-favored larger, older birds (sometimes sold as "stewing hens")

whose meat is most flavorful but too tough to eat as is; but also from the younger, fattier, and less richly flavored broiler-fryers. I've made stock, too, from less desirable pieces of chicken—the wings, necks, and backs of birds whose breasts and thighs were being used in other dishes. I've used farm-raised chickens ("free range" birds, although they weren't called anything so highfalutin; they were just chickens that scrabbled around in the barnyard of my friends' farm, and they absolutely *were* more flavorful than other birds) as well as mass-produced chickens. Although I could never quite bring myself to make it, because frankly, if irrationally, it gave me the creeps, I've eaten chicken broth made from chicken feet. The broth was flavorful, jelled exceptionally well, and cost next to nothing to make.

I'd have to give the edge for flavor to stocks made from a combination of a few chicken feet and the tough old birds (those weighing 4 to 5 pounds or more) which had led a happy, free-range life scrabbling for their dinners. We use 4-pound hens for our stock mostly, but rarely free-range; they're hard to get in quantity, expensive, and when available, too young and low in weight.

But since the ideal is not always available, know that all our stocks, from all the varieties of chicken mentioned, are very good. Certainly they are far ahead of their too-salty, preservative-laden canned counterparts, which, to my nose at least, always smell rank when their cans are opened. Use canned stock *only* if you are in a wild hurry. Otherwise, do your chicken stock from scratch from whatever hen, hens, or parts you can get hold of, with the flavor-deepen-

OF POULTRY AND POTENTATES

Though inexpensive, chicken is often equated with affluence. Queen Victoria's favorite soup was said to be a cream of chicken soup with potatoes, and Henry IV (Henry of Navarre) knew his symbols when he said, in the late 1500s, "I want there to be no peasant in my realm so poor that he will not have a chicken in his pot every Sunday." This sentiment was echoed centuries later by Herbert Hoover, who demanded "a chicken in every pot" for an impoverished America. And consider this sly backhanded axiom told to me by a Dairy Hollow guest from Lafayette, Louisiana: the difference between country Cajuns, and their city cousins, New Orleans' Creoles, is "a Creole uses three chickens to feed one family, but a Cajun feeds three families on one chicken."

ing vegetables, herbs, and spices called for. Possibly one reason our restaurant stocks are so flavorful is that we do use a few more herbs than are standard

issue in canned chicken stock. But the finished stock does not taste noticeably herby, just extra good.

DEFATTING CHICKEN BROTH

A tiny bit of fat in a soup is unobjectionable and, some feel, even pleasant. But anything more than the equivalent of, say, a half teaspoon or so per serving makes a soup greasy, caloric, and higher in cholesterol. It's unnecessary (because in many recipes calling for chicken stock, fat of one kind or another is also called for). There will be lots of fat floating on the surface of your stock, particularly if your chickens have been raised in a cage, and are fatty due to lack of exercise. If you wish, you can remove every trace of it from your broth. Here are two ways:

◆ Chill the finished stock. The fat will rise to the top in a solid sheet of yellow. Lift it off. Throw it out. Easy. Sayonara, fat.

◆ Or, should you find yourself needing to defat stock while it is still hot, go to any good cookware store and purchase a fat-separating device. Several are on the market; for home use I like the nifty little measuring cups with a slide-out stopper in the bottom. You pour the stock into the cup. The fat will rise immediately to the top of the cup. Holding the cup over a bowl, pull out the little stopper thing. The stock in the bottom of the cup will pour out into the waiting bowl below. Quick! As the cup drains you'll see the clear fat heading towards the hole. Slide the stopper back in before the fat can reach

> ### STOCK OPTIONS
>
> ❦ Short on freezer space, yet want to have good homemade stock on hand? Prepare any chicken stock, and after it has been strained and defatted, return it to the stockpot. Raise the heat and bring the stock to a hard boil. Allow it to evaporate by half. Bring the reduced stock to room temperature, then freeze it in an ice cube tray. When the cubes are frozen, pop them out of the tray and store in a sturdy plastic bag, such as a Ziploc.
>
> Use 1 cube at a time, diluting each cube with ¼ to ½ cup spring water, wine, vegetable cooking water, or tomato juice. Or use the cubes without diluting, as a flavor-booster any time a finished soup tastes a bit pallid. ❦

the exit. Discard the fat which remains in the cup. Repeat until all the stock has been done. Use only the defatted broth in the bowl. Obviously this method is a bit more troublesome than just lifting off congealed fat (though not nearly as troublesome as it sounds here).

Chicken Stock 1
A Primary Stock

The finished stock is what's important here. You will also be left with 1½ cups of meat, but this should be discarded; after all that simmering, it will be tasteless fiber, having given its goodness to the stock.

4 to 5 pounds chicken, preferably from 1
   stewing hen, or the necks, wings, backs,
   and feet from younger hens, or 2 whole
   or cut-up young broiler-fryers
Pam cooking spray
2 medium onions, unpeeled, quartered
8 whole cloves
3 ribs celery with leaves, each broken in 2
   or 3 big pieces
3 or 4 sprigs fresh parsley
1 medium leek, white part and several
   inches of green, split open lengthwise
   and well washed (optional)
1 medium parsnip, scrubbed and cut in a
   couple of pieces (optional)
2 medium carrots, scrubbed and cut in
   large chunks
2 bay leaves
3 cloves garlic, unpeeled
1½ teaspoons salt
6 to 8 black peppercorns
Large pinch each of dried rosemary, thyme,
   sweet basil, sage, and savory, or about 1
   tablespoon each chopped fresh herbs
Large pinch of celery seeds
3 to 3½ quarts spring water or leftover
   vegetable cooking water or any mild
   found or secondary stock
1 to 2 tablespoons distilled white or cider
   vinegar

1. Rinse the hen or chicken parts, leaving the skin on but removing any big lumps of fat. Spray a heavy soup pot with Pam. Place the chicken pieces in the pot.

2. Stud each onion quarter with a clove. Surround the chicken with the studded onions, and add all the other vegetables and seasonings (except the fresh herbs, if you're using them). Pour over all the cold water and vinegar.

3. Bring the liquids gradually to a boil over medium heat, then immediately turn down the heat and let simmer, uncovered, skimming any surface foam, for 2½ to 3 hours. Stir occasionally. You may replenish the water as it cooks down; otherwise, you will get a lesser amount of concentrated stock, which you can dilute later, if you wish. If you're using fresh rather than dry herbs, add them after about 1½ to 2 hours' cooking.

4. Remove the stock from the heat and strain into a clean container. Discard the solids. Let cool, uncovered, 30 minutes. If the weather is warm, speed up the cooling process by using a sink of cold water (see page 14). Refrigerate or freeze the cooled stock immediately. You may defat the broth before or after chilling (see page 18).

Makes about 3¼ quarts of strained stock if the water is replenished during the cooking time

Chicken Stock 2
A Secondary Stock

ere the cooked chicken pieces will be the featured players, to be used in a soup or another dish. Your resultant stock will still be good, but mild; if you plan to use it as a key ingredient, you will want to enrich it a little (see below).

3 to 3½ quarts spring water or leftover vegetable cooking water or any mild found or secondary stock
1 to 2 tablespoons distilled white or cider vinegar
4 pounds young chicken (about two 2½-pound broiler-fryers)
Pam cooking spray
2 medium onions, unpeeled, quartered
8 whole cloves
2 bay leaves
3 whole cloves garlic, unpeeled
1½ teaspoons salt
6 to 8 black peppercorns
3 ribs celery, with leaves, each broken in 2 or 3 big pieces
3 or 4 sprigs fresh parsley
1 medium leek, white part and several inches of green, split open lengthwise and well washed (optional)
1 medium parsnip, scrubbed and cut in a couple of pieces (optional)
2 medium carrots, scrubbed and cut in large chunks
Large pinch each of dried rosemary, thyme, sweet basil, sage, and savory, or 1 tablespoon each chopped fresh herbs
Large pinch of celery seeds

1. In a large pot—not the one in which you plan to cook the soup—bring the water or stock to a boil with the vinegar.

2. Meanwhile, stud each onion quarter with a clove. Spray a heavy soup pot with the Pam, and place the chicken in it.

3. Surround the chicken with the clove-studded onions, and add all the other vegetables and seasonings (except the fresh herbs, if using).

4. Pour over all the boiling water or stock. Bring the liquids back to a boil, then immediately turn down the heat, and let simmer, uncovered, skimming any surface foam, for about 20 minutes.

5. Cover the pot and cook. Check the chicken after about 30 minutes (add the fresh herbs now), and again after 45 minutes. The meat should be tender. If you poke it with a fork, you should be able to pull it from the bone with little effort. It should not have reached the point of completely falling off the bone on its own. Most likely, it will be ready after 1 hour of simmering over very low heat. Remove the pot from the heat when the chicken has reached this point.

6. Strain, reserving both the chicken and the stock. Discard the vegetables. Cool the chicken and stock, separately, for 30 minutes. If the weather is warm, speed up the cooling process by immersing the stock in a sink of cold water (see page 14). Refrigerate or freeze the cooled stock immediately. You may defat the broth before or after chilling (see page 18).

7. Pull the chicken from the bones in large pieces, discarding the skin. (Save the bones if you want to enjoy the smug feeling of canny frugality that comes from knowing you've wasted absolutely nothing. Return the stripped bones to the strained stock, and cook them a second time, uncovered, for another hour or so. Strain again. This stock will

WHERE THE CHICKEN STOCK COMES HOME TO ROOST

❦*Now, what do you do with all your delicious chicken stock? Well, in the case of Stock 2, you could cook a few carrots in the strained, finished stock, then serve a bowl of it with sliced carrots, large pieces of cooked chicken meat, and a tidy heap of cooked noodles. Garnish the whole with a long sprig of fresh dill and this is more or less Chicken Soup Jewish Sabbath-Style—simple, curative, and mighty good. You could replace the noodles with matzo balls (I always follow the recipe on the back of the matzo meal box), or make any of the dumplings found throughout these pages (see Index).*

Chicken soup is good with almost any vegetable cooked in the soup or stir-fried separately and then added. A chicken and vegetable soup is especially amenable to pairing with a starch—dumplings, rice, wild rice, diced potatoes, corn, noodles, or barley. These can be cooked in the soup itself (in which case they will thicken the soup a bit, clouding it and

making it quite hearty), or cooked separately. Add a handful of the chosen starch to each bowl. If you turn to the chapter "Chicken Soups to Crow Over" (page 57), you'll find four seasonal variations on the theme of chicken and vegetable soups with a starch.

At the restaurant, we sometimes do a wonderful, simple chicken and vegetable soup which we call Old-Fashioned Chicken Soup with Vegetables. It's made from homemade chicken stock, fresh onions, celery, green and red peppers, sliced carrots, okra, rice, and a liberal amount of fresh herbs. On those evenings when one of the soup choices is a little radical for local tastes, the Old-Fashioned Chicken Soup balances the menu nicely.

But if you want the chicken itself to star, turn again to the chicken soup chapter. There you'll find 8 entrée-type heartier soups; these are "cross-referenced" to other soups that take well to chicken and are easily "main-dishified."❦

have a little more body and oomph than it would have had otherwise.)

Makes 3¼ quarts stock, plus 1¼ cups cooked chicken meat

VARIATION:
Enrich this mild stock by using a vegetable stock (pages 27 to 34), or part white wine, or a combination of the two, to replace all or part of the water in cooking the chicken.

Chicken Stock 3
A Found Stock

hen you roast a chicken, duck, turkey, or goose, you have a leftover carcass—the bones of the fowl—to which a few shreds of meat still cling. Here's how to make some reasonably good stock with it.

1 carcass of a chicken, duck, turkey, or
    goose
1 pound chicken feet (optional)
Pam cooking spray
2 medium onions, unpeeled, quartered
8 whole cloves
2 bay leaves
3 whole cloves garlic, unpeeled
1½ teaspoons salt
6 to 8 black peppercorns
3 ribs celery, with leaves, each broken in 2
    or 3 big pieces
3 or 4 sprigs fresh parsley
1 medium leek, white part and several
    inches of green, split open lengthwise
    and well washed (optional)
1 medium parsnip, scrubbed and cut in a
    couple of pieces (optional)
2 medium carrots, scrubbed and cut in
    large chunks
Large pinch each of dried rosemary,
    thyme, sweet basil, sage, and savory,
    or 1 tablespoon each chopped
    fresh herbs
Large pinch of celery seeds
Spring water or leftover vegetable cooking
    water or any mild found or secondary
    stock to cover carcass and vegetables
1 to 2 tablespoons distilled white or cider
    vinegar

1. Spray a heavy soup pot with Pam. Place the carcass in the pot, cracking the bones here and there with your hands to help draw out any flavorful marrow. If the bones are particularly bare, add the chicken feet, if you can get them.

2. Stud each onion quarter with a clove. Surround the carcass with clove-studded onions, and add all the other vegetables and seasonings (except the fresh herbs, if using). Pour over all the cold water and vinegar.

3. Bring the liquids gradually to a boil over medium heat, then immediately turn down the heat and let simmer, uncovered, skimming any surface foam, for 2 to 2½ hours. Stir occasionally. You may replenish the water as it cooks down; otherwise, you will get a lesser amount of concentrated stock, which you can dilute later, if you wish. If you're using fresh rather than dry herbs, add them after about 1½ hours of cooking.

4. Remove the stock from the heat and strain into another container. Discard the solids. Let the stock cool, uncovered, 30 minutes. If the weather is warm, speed up the cooling process by using a sink of cold water (see page 14). Refrigerate or freeze the cooled stock immediately. You may defat the broth before or after chilling (see page 18).

This will be a mild stock, in need of enriching (see page 15).

Makes a variable quantity depending on the size of the bird's carcass

VARIATION:
Deepen the flavor of this mild stock by using a vegetable stock (pages 27 to 34) or part white wine or a combination of the two to replace all or part of the water in cooking the carcass.

FISH STOCKS

*T*he terms "fish stock" and "court bouillon" are sometimes used interchangeably, though incorrectly so; there's a marked difference between them. A court bouillon is a mixture of water, dry white wine, vinegar or lemon juice, herbs and other seasonings. A fish is poached in the mixture with an eye toward serving the fish as the centerpiece of the finished dish, *not* this poaching liquid. After the fish's bath in the court bouillon, the liquid will have picked up some fish flavor, though mildly so. Court bouillon left after poaching is well worth saving; it can serve as part of a memorable fish stock, and makes a good base for many fish sauces. In my own stock lexicon, I'd call court bouillon, after it's used for fish-poaching, an incidental stock.

A fish stock, also called a *fumet,* is a primary stock: a liquid which is vital to the finished dish. It's not the medium for another food to shine in; it's the star player (or the basis of a dish which, when finished, will be the star player). As such, it must be delicious, flavorful. A good fish stock supports the stew, soup, or sauce that will be built from it with character and strength.

Fish stock is composed of the same ingredients as court bouillon with three differences. First, instead of water, one may use a more full-bodied liquid: all or part chicken or vegetable stock; bottled (*not* canned) clam juice; or leftover post-poaching court bouillon—though if only water is available, that's okay too.

Second, the amount of vinegar or lemon juice required is less than that used in a court bouillon. (Classically, the acid would be omitted, but I always add some to take advantage of its calcium-dissolving abilities.) Third, and most important—most fish stocks use the often-discarded fish heads, tails, and backbones (called "frames," or "racks") of any non-oily fish which are simmered in it. Once the frames are added, the simmering *must* be fairly quick; cook a fish stock longer than 25 to 35 minutes, and you run the danger of a bitter or too-fishy taste.

To avoid the twin perils of fish bones and overcooked fish in the finished soups, you'll see that in many of our finny soup recipes the whole fish are first filleted. The bones are used to make the stock first, then strained out. Later, after the strained stock is seasoned and turned into soup by the addition of whatever ingredients may be called for, the boneless pieces of fillet are poached in the soup.

OF FISH AND FAT

🍎*In a fat- and calorie-conscious world, fish—whose fat content varies by species—do not escape scrutiny. There are culinary as well as nutritional reasons for knowing fish-fat contents; oily fishes do not make good stock, since fattiness tends to give it a pronounced fishy flavor. Thus the fattier fishes, as a rule, are not best used in soup at all. Here is a listing of lean, moderately lean, and fatty fish.*

Lean (non-oily) fish contain 5 percent fat or less, and have about 100 to 125 calories per 3- to 4-ounce serving. Catfish, cod, dover sole, and sole; flounder, grouper, lake white-fish, and halibut; haddock, hake, monkfish, and northern pike; rockfish, red snapper, shark,

and sea trout are among the fin fish in this category. Of the fin fish, cod, halibut, orange roughy, and pollock are exceptionally low in fat and calories. Moderately lean fish contain 6 to 9 percent fat, and have 125 to 150 calo-ries per 3- to 4-ounce serving. These include Atlantic herring, rainbow trout, mahi-mahi, ocean perch, yellow perch, and white sea bass.

Fatty fish contain 10 percent fat or more, and have 150 calories or more per 3- to 4-ounce serving. Herring, mackerel, salmon, and sablefish; lake trout, bluefish, and ocean pout; black sea bass and pompano are in this category.🍎

A second method—one we almost always use in the restaurant—calls for making and straining the stock, then poaching the fil-let pieces in the strained stock *before* turning the stock into soup. Stock and poached fish are reserved separately, the stock trans-formed into soup, and the poached pieces added to each bowl or cup of soup just before it is served. This guarantees that the fish pieces will be perfectly cooked, with a nice, firm texture.

Since the home cook is much less likely to have fish stock on hand than chicken or vegetable I usually begin most of our fish soup recipes with di-rections for making the stock from the specific fish frame used for the partic-ular soup. Even so, it's im-portant to know the general method.

Court Bouillon

ntended for poaching fish, with a little oomphing up, this liquid makes a good secondary stock. It's also an excellent base for a primary stock. You can use the court bouillon immediately to make fish stock (the recipe follows) or save it to poach your next batch of fish. If stock or more poached fish are not in your immediate future, by all means freeze this savory liquid to reuse later as either court bouillon or base for stock.

A court bouillon reused a couple or three times for poaching fish will be flavorful enough to use as fish stock proper. Among the freshwater fish commonly poached are trout of all varieties, bass, and pike; among the salt fishes, salmon, skate, haddock, and monkfish.

*4 cups water or Golden Vegetable Stock
    (page 28) or any mild-flavored
    vegetable stock*
2 cups dry white wine
*¼ cup cider vinegar or freshly squeezed
    lemon juice*
2 medium onions, unpeeled, thickly sliced
2 medium carrots, scrubbed and sliced
1 bay leaf
1 rib celery, sliced
2 sprigs fresh parsley (leaves and stems)
6 whole peppercorns
3 whole cloves
2 teaspoons salt
*Small pinch each of dried basil, thyme, and
    oregano or 1 tablespoon each chopped
    fresh herbs*
Fish for poaching

1. In a pan large enough to poach your chosen fish, combine all the ingredients except the fish. Bring to a boil, then turn down the heat and let barely simmer, uncovered, for 30 minutes. (Generally the vegetables and herbs are allowed to cook in the liquid 30 minutes or so before the fish is added, but if you're in a hurry, just lower the whole or filleted fish in the liquid as soon as the bouillon is hot.)

2. Poach the fish over low heat in the court bouillon until barely done. Figure on 8 to 10 minutes per inch of thickness for your cooking time. Remove the fish from the court bouillon.

3. Strain the court bouillon. Let it cool to room temperature, then quick-chill it, using the sink method (page 14) if necessary. Refrigerate or freeze.

Makes about 4 to 6 cups, depending on length of simmering time

Fish Stock
A Primary Stock (without court bouillon on hand)

he base for simply wonderful fish soups, with an amazing delicacy of flavor. Because fish loses so much flavor when overcooked, canned and frozen fish soups cannot come close to an attentively homemade fish soup with from-scratch fish stock.

Be sure to read the adjacent text, Of Fish and Fat.

2 pounds frames, heads, and tails from
   non-oily fish, such as catfish, red snapper,
   or lake whitefish
2 quarts water or, for a particularly heady
   stock, any of the chicken or vegetable
   stocks or part water and part bottled
   clam juice (not canned, please; it has an
   obnoxiously metallic off taste)
½ cup dry white wine
½ teaspoon salt
1 tablespoon freshly squeezed lemon juice
   or vinegar
2 medium onions, unpeeled, thickly sliced
2 medium carrots, scrubbed and sliced
1 bay leaf
1 medium rib celery, sliced
2 sprigs fresh parsley
6 whole peppercorns
3 whole cloves
½ teaspoon salt
Small pinch each of dried basil, thyme, and
   oregano or about 1 tablespoon each
   chopped fresh herbs

1. First prepare the fish frames. Because remnants of fish organs can be bitter when cooked for a stock, always clean each fish head, tail, and frame before using it. Wash, then cut away and discard any remains of viscera on the frame, as well as the pointy bottom part of the head. Also remove any organ remnants left in the upper part of the head. Rinse again. This removes any possible taint.

2. In a heavy soup pot, combine all the ingredients and bring swiftly to a boil. Turn down the heat to medium-low and let simmer about 25 to 30 minutes, no more. Push the pieces of fish frame down into the liquid with a wooden spoon 3 or 4 times as the stock cooks to help extract the flavorful juices from the bones.

3. Strain the cooked stock and discard the solids. Use immediately, or cool to room temperature (using the quick-chill sink trick, page 14, if necessary). Refrigerate or freeze.

Makes about 2 quarts

VARIATION:
Primary Fish Stock Made with Court Bouillon: Follow the above recipe, but substitute leftover court bouillon in which you've poached a fish for water and wine, you'll need 4½ cups of liquid altogether. If you don't have enough court bouillon on hand, make up the difference with water, vegetable or chicken stock, or clam juice. The slightly larger amount of vinegar or lemon juice in a court bouillon will not make any difference to a finished soup *unless you're making a milk-based fish soup,* in which case that bit of acidity might incline it towards curdling. See specific recipes for guidance on this. Makes about 1¼ quarts

VEGETABLE STOCKS

Vegetable stocks? In the good old bad old days, the very idea of a flavorful vegetable stock would have made a *laughing* stock out of the person suggesting it. That was when people who were health-conscious were fanatics and people who loved and cooked good food were gourmets, and the twain didn't meet. You simply didn't find recipes for vegetable-based stocks in any fine cuisine-oriented cookbook; only in cookbooks in which health was emphasized, usually at the expense of taste.

All this has changed markedly over the past twenty years. Vegetarianism has moved into the mainstream. "Fresh," "light," and "seasonal" no longer connote health food but *au courant*-ness. Of course, those of us who love good food are at least somewhat health-conscious—good (no preservatives, nothing artificial) food is, naturally, more healthful, and we want to be around to eat it for a while. What took us so long to get here?

Still, it's unusual to find good vegetable stocks in nonvegetarian cookbooks. This is a shame. Vegetable stocks are as varied in the flavors they can offer as chicken, beef, or fish stocks; they can easily be made 100 percent fat-free, without the bother of defatting; and they are highly economical. In fact, the one I make for home use is an almost entirely found stock, costing nothing. And vegetable stocks are less prone to spoilage than flesh-based stocks.

In addition to the above mentioned found stock which suits most soup purposes quite well, there are a number of primary vegetarian stocks in the Dairy Hollow repertoire. One is amazingly chickenlike; it has a golden color and a full, rich taste that mimics astonishingly a fine, primary chicken stock. Why use it instead of the real thing? Well, it's less expensive. It's less messy to prepare. It's quicker to cook. And you will absolutely make any vegetarians in the crowd melt with delight when they learn that, yes, they *can* partake of the soup. Golden-colored nutritional yeast, an entirely different product from the yeast used in bread-baking, is one of the secrets of this fine stock. I know when you read the recipe you won't believe the stock can taste as I've described it, but it does.

There are several vegetarian options that work as beef-style stocks—that is, they're hearty, dark brown, and rich in flavor.

But my very favorite of these brown vegetable stocks, which is sublimely well-flavored, is one developed in our restaurant by Chef Sandy Allison. It started out as a way to use up leftover "roasty - toasty" vegetables, simple, yes, but delectable combo of oven-browned

carrots, onions, and potatoes which we almost always serve as part of the side vegetable plate accompanying our entrées. But we have grown so devoted to this delicious and easily made stock that we now frequently prepare it from scratch, or fix "planned-over" roasty-toasties as a base for it. Here it appears as Browned Vegetable Stock.

I also do a vegetarian stock for which there is no ready equivalent in meat-based stock; it's a faintly sweet stock. Sometimes I do this from scratch; more often I simply include the sweet elements in one of the other stocks I have going. These elements include apple, sweet potato, tomato, and—surprise!—garlic.

In almost all vegetarian stocks, I use garlic—a lot of it. But because the garlic is simmered in water, an amazing alchemy takes place; its strong flavor is transmuted into a rich, savory sweetness, quite hearty but not in the least garlicky.

Golden Vegetable Stock
A Primary Stock

he chickenlike marvel described earlier. Getting two ingredients, light miso and nutritional yeast, will require a trip to the natural foods store.

1 large onion, unpeeled, quartered
1 large carrot, scrubbed and quartered
1 large sweet potato, scrubbed and
*   quartered*
1 large white potato, scrubbed and
*   quartered*
1 whole head garlic, papery skin left on,
*   halved*
3 ribs celery, with leaves, each broken in
*   half*
6 cups spring water
1 to 2 teaspoons salt
Small pinches of dried oregano, basil, sage,
*   and rosemary to taste (optional)*
½ cup Good Tasting or Red Star nutritional
*   yeast (not baking yeast or brewer's yeast)*
1 tablespoon light (white or golden) miso

1. In a soup pot, combine all the ingredients except the nutritional yeast and the miso. Bring to a boil, then turn down the heat to medium-low and let simmer gently until all the vegetables are quite soft, about 1 hour. Let cool, then strain, discarding the solids.

2. Whisk the nutritional yeast and miso into the lukewarm stock. Taste for seasoning; you may need a touch more miso. Use in any recipe where chicken broth is called for. Use immediately, or cool to room temperature, then refrigerate or freeze.

Makes about 5 cups

VARIATION:

Sweet Vegetable Stock: In many recipes, using a slightly sweet stock adds a surprising, pleasing dimension. Don't wait until I suggest this stock specifically to try it. It is particularly good in pumpkin, squash, or corn soups.

Follow the recipe for Golden Vegetable Stock, substituting another sweet potato for the white potato. Add, also, 1 tablespoon of raisins, a whole apple (or pear), quartered (or several apple cores and parings—I always make this stock on apple-pie days), and 1 tomato.

Simmer and strain as above. However, reserve the cooked garlic, and when it is cool enough to handle, squish the softened cloves out of their skins and back into the strained stock. Whisk the nutritional yeast and miso into the strained stock. Makes about 5 cups

Dark Vegetable Stock 1
A Primary Stock

 good substitute for beef stock, this is the darker-complexioned cousin of the previous stock.

2 large onions, unpeeled, quartered
1 large carrot, scrubbed and quartered
2 large white potatoes, scrubbed and
*   quartered*
1 whole head garlic, papery skin left on,
*   halved*
3 ribs celery, with leaves, each broken in
*   half*
6 cups spring water
1 tablespoon tamari/shoyu soy sauce
Small pinches of dried oregano, basil, sage,
*   and rosemary to taste (optional)*
¼ cup Good Tasting or Red Star brand
*   nutritional yeast (not baking yeast or*
*   brewer's yeast)*
1 tablespoon dark miso

1. In a soup pot, combine all the ingredients except the nutritional yeast and the miso. Bring to a boil, then turn down the heat to medium-low and let simmer gently, uncovered, until all the vegetables are quite soft, about 1 hour. Let cool, then strain, discarding the solids.

2. Whisk the nutritional yeast and miso into the lukewarm stock. Taste for seasoning; you may need a touch more miso. Use in any recipe where beef broth is called for. Use immediately, or cool to room temperature, then refrigerate or freeze.

Makes about 5 cups

Dark Vegetable Stock 2
A Primary Stock

 slightly richer "beefy"-style stock, due to the addition of a bit of butter and some lentils.

2 large onions, unpeeled, quartered
1 large carrot, scrubbed and quartered
2 large white potatoes, scrubbed and quartered
1 whole head garlic, papery skin left on, broken in half
3 ribs celery, with leaves, each broken in half
¾ cup lentils
6 cups spring water
1 to 2 tablespoons tamari/shoyu soy sauce
Small pinch each of dried oregano, basil, sage, and rosemary to taste (optional)
¼ cup Good Tasting or Red Star nutritional yeast (not baking yeast or brewer's yeast)
1 to 2 tablespoons dark miso
2 tablespoons butter or mild vegetable oil (or, if appropriate to the soup you'll be making with this, olive oil)

1. In a soup pot, combine all the ingredients except the nutritional yeast, miso, and butter or oil. Bring to a boil, then turn down the heat to medium-low and let simmer gently, uncovered, until all the vegetables and lentils are quite soft, about 1 hour. Stir in the butter or oil. Let cool, then strain.

2. Whisk the nutritional yeast and 1 tablespoon of the miso into the lukewarm stock. Taste for seasoning; you may need more miso. Use in any recipe where beef broth is called for. Use immediately, or cool to room temperature and refrigerate or freeze.

Makes about 5 cups

ABOUT A FEW SPECIAL STOCK-ENRICHING INGREDIENTS

❦ *Nutritional Yeast: Called "nutritional yeast" to distinguish it from the type of yeast used in leavening (it is an entirely different strain) and from brewer's yeast (the type used in making beer, of which it is a relative), this yeast, bought in natural food stores, can add a marvelous flavor to many stocks. Indeed, it is used in many bouillon cubes and powders. In these, it is tainted with an excess of salt, MSG, and so on, but you can take advantage of its wonderful richness unadulterated by using it in any of the vegetable stocks.*

Nutritional yeast was originally developed as a food supplement and is, therefore, quite good. Besides its use in stock, nutritional yeast is divine on popcorn.

Tamari/Shoyu Soy Sauce: Another natural foods store product, this hearty, strong, naturally fermented soy sauce, with no additives, can also be found at many Oriental markets. Tamari/shoyu (it may be called one or the other) bears little resemblance to supermarket soy sauce brands, which may be colored with caramel, preserved with sodium benzoate, and are unpleasant in flavor. A little tamari/shoyu goes a long way! Tamari is wheat-free; shoyu has wheat. Their flavors are identical and they may be used interchangeably.

Miso: This salty, fermented bean paste is used by the Japanese as we use bouillon cubes here: add boiling water to it, stir, and voilà!*—instant broth. But how much better and more full-bodied a miso broth is than a bouillon-cubed one!*

I use a straight miso-based stock rarely, though it does make a nice, quick, low-cal lunch when one's in the mood for something Oriental. In general, though, I prefer to mix it with other ingredients for stock, as in the recipes above. But it is nice to know that miso is a good, healthy, quick substitute for stock if you get into a time crunch. Its flavor is rather assertive on its own, but it still works well in a range of soups.

There are countless varieties of miso. Each miso is individual in its balance between sweetness and saltiness. Some are made from just soybeans, some mixed with rice or other grains. Each has its own character, but generally, dark *misos incline toward saltiness, with a meaty, hearty quality, while* light *(sometimes called white, yellow, or golden) misos have more sweetness playing off the saltiness, and tend towards more delicacy.*

Morga: This is my one major concession to convenience foods—Morga Vegetable Bouillon Cubes, the salt-free variety. Purchase them at a natural foods store. They are Swiss-made, and good. Always keep some on hand, but don't rely on them too often, or your soups will become monotonous. ❦

Browned Vegetable Stock

 ur favorite of all vegetable stocks, the richness of this stock belies its simplicity. Developed by our chef, Sandy Allison, it loans its full-bodied flavor to almost any soup. The variation which follows is sheer heaven: the ambrosia of soup stocks.

Pam cooking spray
3 onions, unpeeled, quartered
3 large carrots, unpeeled, halved, stem ends removed
8 ribs celery, with leaves, each broken in half
2 whole heads garlic, papery skin left on, cut in half across the middle (to expose each garlic clove)
3 tablespoons mild vegetable oil
¼ cup tamari/shoyu soy sauce
6 cups room temperature water, preferably spring, divided
2 bay leaves
2 sprigs fresh parsley
Salt to taste
1 teaspoon whole peppercorns

1. Preheat the oven to 350°F. Spray an 11 x 13-inch baking pan with Pam.

2. Place the onions, carrots, celery, and the garlic in the pan. Drizzle with the oil and toss to coat the vegetables. Pour over the soy sauce and bake until the vegetables are deeply browned, almost burnt-looking, 1 hour.

3. Transfer the vegetables to a large heavy soup pot. Add 4 cups of the water and the remaining ingredients.

4. Pour the remaining 2 cups of water into the baking pan, and using the blade of a spatula, scrape up all those wonderful browned, caramelized bits on the bottom. Add this to the soup pot.

5. Bring the water to a boil, then turn down the heat and simmer, partially covered, 30 minutes. Cool slightly and strain.

Makes about 4 cups

VARIATION:

Browned Vegetable Stock with Shiitake Mushrooms: We are most fortunate in living in a part of the world where quite a few people raise shiitake mushrooms. If you don't know this incredible fungus, whose full flavor some compare to lobster and others to beef, you have a treat in store.

The dark brown caps, wide and almost flat, sometimes marbled with white, are somewhere between tender and chewy. The stems, although full of flavor, are too tough to eat (except for hardcore shiitake freaks, like several of us in the kitchen; we call them "veggie-bones," and contentedly chew on them for 20 minutes at a time). They do, however, make extraordinarily flavorful stock. Simply add as many shiitake stems as you can get your hands on (say, 1 to 3 cups) to the browned vegetables with the water.

WHY SOUPS

❧At *Dairy Hollow House, cooking has always been regionally based, seasonal, innovative, ample, a little playful, pretty but not too frou-frou. And soup has always played a big part in it. Although we serve much more than soups at Dairy Hollow, I've always been a big soup fan, and the warmth and comfort good soups confer transfers easily to the sink-into-it kind of ambiance we strive for here.*

Soup, served with an overflowing basket of homemade breads, is the second course at our nightly dinners, with salad the third. When we serve lunches—for groups, by reservation only—soup is invariably on the menu. And at our "Table for Two" in-room suppers for guests in the winter months when the restaurant is closed, soup is also a featured player.

Soup was the very first non-breakfast dish we served all those years ago and soup is what I served last night: pumpkin and apple soup, with curry and cream, that same soup about which several different guests have commented, "This soup alone *is worth the price of the dinner!" And this is leaving aside the hundreds of pots of sustaining, homestyle soups that have nourished me and Ned and various carpenters, "Dairymaids," and miscellaneous staff through long days of gardening, renovation, cleaning, or kitchen prep.*

Some of these soups are peasanty complete-meal soups; some, more elegant, are pre-ludes to dinner; some are homey, some exotic. The soups in this book are drawn from our Peasant's Feasts and our Nouveau'Zarks Dinners. Some are cold and some are hot. Some are good any time, some are possible or appropriate only in certain seasons. Some are simple, quick; some are a big deal. Some you should eat by candlelight, with roses on the table, wearing a tea-length gown or tux, spooning up delicately with a silver spoon. Others will mend a broken heart, and call for nothing so much as the kitchen table, a stoneware bowl, your pajamas, a good book, or maybe a good friend. We have here healthy and/or low-calorie, low-cholesterol soups; we also have soups that are full-cream-ahead-and-damn-the-torpedoes. Vegetarian or chicken, built around grains or fish, fruit or nuts; classic, traditional-with-a-twist, or out-and-out innovative . . . you'll find all these and more soups here, along with perfect accompaniments and menus for many different occasions. ❧

CRUCIFEROUS VEGETABLES

❧In making a found stock from vegetable scraps, avoid using scraps from cruciferous vegetables, that is, from members of the cabbage family. These include Brussels sprouts, cabbage, broccoli, and cauliflower; all add a strong and objectionable flavor and odor if long-simmered.

Do be sure to eat your cruciferae though—they're delicious when quickly steamed or stir-fried, or added to soup at the last. They also have documented cancer preventative qualitites.❧

Basic Found Vegetable Stock

 he previous stocks are reliable because they use set, measured ingredients. I love them, and use them when I have to be absolutely certain of the flavor of my finished stock at the restaurant. But the truth is at home I make another kind of vegetable stock far more often: this found stock, made almost entirely from vegetable scraps. Though it changes character depending on what scraps are used, it is almost always good if you follow the guidelines given below. Despite its amenability to changes, it is rarely incompatible with a finished soup.

Accumulate ingredients over a few days to a week in a plastic bag in the fridge. Quantities are not remotely relevant to a stock like this.

8 to 10 cups of carrot tops, onion peels, pea pods or their trimmings, string bean ends, celery trimmings, stem ends of squash and tomatoes, insides of any sweet peppers, apple or pear cores, stems of greens and so on—anything except the cruciferous vegetables (see box)
1 whole head garlic, papery skin left on, broken in half
1 onion, quartered (unpeeled unless there are lots of onion ends and peels in your stock)
Spring water to cover
1 to 1½ teaspoons salt, approximately, per quart of water

1. Bring all the ingredients to a boil in a pot that will fit them. Turn down the heat to medium-low and let simmer gently, uncovered, for 1 hour or so.
2. Cool to lukewarm, then strain. Use immediately, or store in fridge or freezer.

Makes a variable quantity

Fillips, Flourishes

AND FINE POINTS

ood soup's underpinning is good stock, on which are laid dominant foundation ingredients: onions in onion soup, chicken in chicken soup, and so on. But many finished soups also have a special twist on flavor or texture, an indefinable, intriguing *je ne sais quoi*.

Except you, the cook, *sais quoi.*

Most often this twist is a matter of seasoning, but not in the sense of adding a pinch of this or that herb or spice. Rather, you somehow deepen the flavor.

Because of soup's liquid nature, it has its own special fillips, flourishes, and fine points, part technique, part recipe. The following simple twists recur not only throughout the recipes here, but in any good cook's entire kitchen life.

Assuming your stock is flavorful in its own right, we'll start with those additions used at the beginning of the soup-making which lend excellence and verve. We'll end with a number of finishing flourishes, last-minute additions, some of which also serve as garnishes. They can send soup's flavor soaring.

BEFORE-THE-SOUP FILLIPS

MIREPOIX

The basic beginning-of-the-soup twist is mirepoix, the best possible start to many, many soups. It's simply a savory sauté of diced vegetables and aromatics, done before liquid is added.

What vegetables go into a mirepoix? The classic French version consists of about half onion and one-quarter each carrots and celery, sautéed until limp, possibly allowed to brown slightly, in the amount of *heated* butter or oil called for by the recipe. (Or dictated by the cook's conscience, and willingness

to use Pam cooking spray.) The heating is important; if the substance being sautéed goes into a cold skillet, with fat that hasn't yet been heated, it will absorb the fat and not be seared.

The sauté generally takes place in a good-size heavy cast-iron skillet, at least 8 inches across, but 10 or 12 inches if possible; at the restaurant we often work with several 16-inch skillets mirepoixing at the same time. In any case, the skillet must be large enough so there is space around the vegetables as they are tossed in the fat. If too many vegetables are crowded into one skillet so that they

lie on top of each other, they will steam rather than being properly seared. (If you're doubling a recipe which calls for a mirepoix, bear this in mind and do it in two batches or two skillets.) Only *after* these aromatics have been sautéed are liquids added.

But although this classic onion-celery-carrot mix is the start of an unlimited number of good soups, many other aromatics and vegetables will benefit a soup if given the mirepoix treatment. First, don't worry too much about the precise proportions; a soup mirepoix is forgiving and malleable. Leeks or shallots can be added to or substituted altogether for the onions; diced mushrooms, or even better shiitake mushrooms, can be added and sautéed in amounts roughly equal to the carrots and celery. A diced sweet or hot pepper, added with the carrots and celery, is quite good in a mirepoix for some soups, and sautéing a bay leaf along with the vegetables brings out the bay flavor pleasantly. Parsnip, a wonderfully sweet and aromatic root underutilized in this country, is just great if peeled and diced finely and used instead of, or in addition to, the carrot. And a little minced garlic is heavenly added at the last.

A great tip I learned from Jan Brown—she with whom I wrote the first Dairy Hollow House Cookbook—is to add a little tamari/shoyu soy sauce late in the sautéing of almost any mirepoix. Continue to sauté the mixture until the liquid has evaporated and the vegetables are glazed a deep, slightly sticky brown. Don't think of this as Oriental; the soy sauce adds a remarkable depth of flavor to a wide range of soups, and is not at all Chinese restaurant-y.

DEGLAZING

❧*Deglazing is an important part of the mirepoix-making or sautéing process. When the sautéed vegetables have been removed from the skillet, some of their savory essential juices, slightly browned now, will remain stuck to the bottom of the skillet. These are full of flavor. Add 1 cup or so of hot stock to the skillet and heat quickly, swirling around to get these flavory essences up. Use this as part of the stock requirement in your recipe.*❧

Basic Mirepoix

4 tablespoons (½ stick) butter, or ¼ cup mild vegetable oil, such as corn or peanut, or half of each (less if you use Pam and/or are calorie/fat watching)
1 medium onion, diced
½ cup finely diced carrot
½ cup finely diced celery with leaves
Other aromatics or vegetables if desired

1. In an 8-inch skillet, melt the butter or heat the oil over medium heat. Add the onion. If the skillet's at the proper temperature, it'll sizzle slightly as it goes in. Stir with a wooden spoon until the onion begins to go limp and translucent, losing its rawness, about 5 minutes.

2. Add the carrot and celery, stirring frequently. When the carrot and celery are limp, and the onion pieces are just on the point of being a little browned at the edges in about 5 more minutes, the mirepoix is done and ready to be used in soup.

3. Deglaze as necessary, using the liquid called for in individual recipes.

Enough for 4 to 6 cups stock

VARIATION:

Mirepoix Jan Brown: Follow the above recipe, adding 1 tablespoon of tamari/shoyu soy sauce after the carrot and celery have begun to soften. Stir more often and use slightly lower heat, or the mixture will stick. Continue sautéing until the liquid has evaporated and the vegetables are glazed. Be sure to deglaze the pan with a little stock.

BAGHAR

One of the most interesting uses of the mirepoix technique is in making *baghar,* a blend of Indian aromatics, which always includes dry spices, and is again sautéed in hot oil or fat to bring out the flavor before any liquid is added. Used in India for thousands of years, and no doubt long predating French cookery techniques, baghars add savor and fire to the plainest, simplest of ingredients— beans or lentils, potatoes or other vegetables. They're mixtures of dry aromatics (black mustard seeds, turmeric, cayenne, coriander, cumin seed, and possibly others); and fresh ones (onions, garlic, and fresh gingerroot). All are sautéed together in clarified butter or oil until browned. A degenerate version of the dry mixture is what we call curry powder. Now, some curry powders are perfectly good spice mixes, but they are certainly not authentic to Indian cookery, nor are they nearly so dimensional as the true Indian family of spices and flavorings, where the ingredients change with each dish and season. Because this exotic cuisine is to me not at all "Dairy Hollow House-y," I almost never use baghars and dishes made with them at the restaurant. But I do at home, and you should, too, if you enjoy tastes that surprise your mouth.

Even if you do use ready-made curry powder, try sautéing it baghar-style before adding it to a dish next time. The powder's flavor will be heightened and mellowed, its rawness tamed. This is particularly true if the curry powder is going into a dish that won't be cooked further, such as a dip.

A Medium Spicy Baghar
Indian Mirepoix

An Indian cook prepares a different baghar for every dish. Once you get the hang of this you can play with the spices and quantities. You'll probably need to take a trip to the spice

store, Indian market, or natural foods store before undertaking this.

¼ cup mild vegetable oil, such as peanut or untoasted sesame, or clarified butter (see box, right)

3 tablespoons black mustard seeds (omit if not available; do not substitute yellow mustard seeds)

1 medium onion, diced

1 teaspoon peeled, finely chopped fresh gingerroot

2 to 3 teaspoons cumin seeds

2 to 3 teaspoons ground turmeric

2 to 3 teaspoons ground coriander

Cayenne pepper to taste (start with ⅛ teaspoon and increase if you wish)

1. In a heavy 8- to 10-inch skillet heat the oil or clarified butter to the point of fragrance.

2. Add the mustard seeds and stir about 30 seconds.

3. Add the onion and cook, stirring constantly, until it begins to wilt, about 3 minutes.

4. Add the gingerroot, and cook 30 seconds, stirring often.

5. Add the remaining spices, stirring. The idea is that the spices should cook a bit, roasting in the heat while absorbing a bit of the fat. Cook for about 3 more minutes, stirring often, until the spices deepen in color without actually browning, and are very fragrant. The mustard seeds will pop—not out of the pan, like popcorn, but audibly.

6. Deglaze as necessary, using the liquid called for in individual recipes.

Makes about ½ cup

VARIATION:
For Western tastes, this makes enough to season 4 to 5 cups of stock, soup, or cooked beans or lentils. If you are fond of spicy foods, double the quantities of the ginger and spices, keeping the amount of oil or clarified butter the same.

CLARIFYING BUTTER

To clarify butter, you remove its milk solids—a simple process. Why bother? Because clarified butter has a light, pure taste, can be heated to a higher temperature than regular melted butter without burning, and keeps beautifully. Its texture, unrefrigerated, is that of an oil. In India, where many homes lack refrigeration and the temperature is hot, clarified butter (called "ghee") is the only type used.

1 pound unsalted butter

▶ In a saucepan, melt the butter over medium-low heat. Using a spoon, carefully skim any froth from the top. Carefully pour off the golden liquid, stopping before you reach the white, milky solids at the bottom of the pan. Clarified butter keeps indefinitely when refrigerated.

Makes about ¾ cup

AFTER-THE-SOUP FILLIPS

A number of concoctions that add savor to soup can be added after cooking, or passed at table. Each of the following will make a soup transcend itself. We are not talking about garnishes per se here, though some additions are pretty to look at. Rather, this collection of quickly made herb pastes, sauces, and vividly flavored vegetable purées please the palate as much as the eye. A few hot-hot options follow, as well as delicious dabs of dairy products like crème fraîche, yogurt, and so on. These flourishes are as simple to prepare as they are marvelous to eat.

THE GARLICKY GREATS

Most garlic finishes are kissing cousins. Well, non-kissing if you feel *that* way about garlic—but really, given the uninhibited and sensual nature of those who love this reprobate of the lily family, it is probably in your best interest to drop this prissiness. I have found garlic lovers as a group to be lusty lovers of life, not bound by what others think, given to celebrating the joys of the senses with abandon. What's a little, or a lot, of garlic on the breath compared with such delicious openness in the kitchen or elsewhere? When I was single, I kissed many garlic eaters. When I married, I married one. (Of course, so did he.)

At any rate, the following recipes are all related by garlic, and are all from adjacent parts of the garlic-loving Mediterranean. Even simpler, and starting off our review of finishes, is the one we use most often, Garlic Oil.

A SLIGHTLY EASIER WAY TO PEEL GARLIC

❦ There's no way to peel garlic that's exactly easy, I should know— we peel enough of it. But try this, which is much quicker than picking off each papery skin from each clove by hand (and much less residually garlicky on the fingers). Separate the garlic cloves, laying them out on a cutting board. One by one, lay the flat side of a broad knife on each garlic clove. With the heel of your hand press down hard on the knife until you feel the clove give slightly. Then pick up each clove and slip off its skin. It comes off, comparatively speaking, much more easily. ❦

Garlic Oil

 f you make one garlic preparation, it should be this. We always have a couple of cups of this in the fridge at the restaurant, and during busy times of the year go through several quarts a week. It is *so* handy, and virtually a secret weapon in seasoning. We brush fish with Garlic Oil before baking them; we stir it into soups at the last minute; we add it to meat and chicken marinades; to sauces and vinaigrettes; to everything you might imagine and more. Once you get the garlic cloves peeled, this is a breeze to prepare, provided you have a food processor. See the adjacent notes on peeling.

25 medium cloves garlic, peeled
1 cup olive oil

▶ Buzz the garlic cloves and oil together in a food processor until an almost-smooth paste is formed. Store, covered, in the refrigerator, in a glass jar. When you use the Garlic Oil, stir it well, since garlic tends to settle.

Makes 1 generous cup

Important Note: Garlic and oil are a botulism-prone combination if left at room temperature. Of course there's a food horror story every time you turn around, but we do keep Garlic Oil refrigerated when not scooping a bit out of the jar. We remake it every few days at the restaurant, but at home I have kept it under refrigeration for as long as two weeks. If you're wondering about buying premade garlic paste or minced garlic as a substitute, don't. Preservatives are added to these preparations, sometimes including vinegar. And because the finished product is pasteurized, the flavor just isn't there.

Classic Basil Pesto

 here has been more than one summer when the deer ate everything in our vegetable garden except the basil. Perhaps they were just being considerate, knowing how much we love basil. We make pestos, pastas, dressings, butters, and even jelly from this wonderful herb, of which we grow several varieties. We pot up a few plants, too, and bring them in for the winter. They don't exactly thrive, though their window is sunny, but they do hang in there, giving us enough basil for an occasional fix through the winter.

Basil with garlic is food for the angels—the nonfastidious angels, at least—and the herb paste called pesto is essentially garlic and basil. Added to these two ingredients, traditionally, are a little Parmesan cheese, enough olive oil to smooth things out, and some nuts. What follows is more or less the classic preparation, though don't you know every housewife in Genoa surely prepares it her own way!

I love the way such a pesto smells, but I have to say that classic pesto is too oily for my taste, especially on pasta. But it's wonderful stirred into many different kinds of soup, most especially tomatoey minestrone soups with beans, just before serving. Pass additional pesto at the table. It's also quite good spread over a rolled out batch of bread dough, to make a fragrant herb bread. (Fold the dough up jelly roll-style, put it in a loaf pan, and bake.) Or brush pesto (or its cousin, Gremolata, facing page) on baked chicken or fish halfway through the cooking process. Add it to marinades or scrambled eggs or use it in omelet fillings.

This, like all pestos, should be made at least 30 minutes before serving, and may be prepared several days in advance if refrigerated. It freezes well, too.

2 cups moderately packed fresh basil leaves
2 to 4 large cloves garlic, peeled
 (more to taste; for my taste, lots more!)
2 tablespoons grated Parmesan cheese,
 preferably freshly grated (even better, use
 1 tablespoon Parmesan and 1
 tablespoon Pecorino/Romano)
¼ cup walnuts or pine nuts, toasted (page 316)
½ cup fruity extra-virgin olive oil
Salt and freshly ground pepper to taste

▶ Buzz together everything but the olive oil and salt and pepper in a food processor until a thick paste is formed. With the machine on, add the oil tablespoon by tablespoon. Season to taste with salt and pepper, using plenty of the latter.

Makes about 1¼ cups

VARIATIONS:

I usually omit the nuts and reduce the oil to about 1 or 2 tablespoons, which results in a thick paste rather than a saucelike purée. I prefer the pesto chunky, so I process with quick on-off bursts, thus retaining the texture of the leaves. For use on pasta I'll add an egg to this paste (or, if the salmonella-in-egg stories have gotten to you, a finely diced hard-cooked egg is also acceptable and good), 1 teaspoon of butter, garlic to the max, a lot of freshly ground black pepper, and more Parmesan. I toss the resulting paste with hot pasta. If I want nuts, I'll usually sprinkle just a few, toasted, atop the finished pasta or soup for texture rather than puréeing them into the paste. I do, however, confess to a fondness for the green, green pistachio pesto I've made a few times when I was feeling devil-may-care about fat grams—shelled pistachios replace the pine nuts in the basic recipe and are sprinkled over the top of the cooked pasta.

Of course, there are also herb pestos beyond number. Experimentation and availability are the names of the game here. For example, substitute fresh parsley for all or part of the basil, then add 1 to 3 sprigs of rosemary, thyme, marjoram, and sage (all these in fairly small quantities; sage and rosemary in particular can be strong). You can use a larger amount of oregano or—surprisingly but very good—fresh mint.

From time to time I've also puréed pitted Greek olives and/or sundried tomatoes and added them to these pastes. These purées have wonderful flavors that sing when combined with garlic, and are excellent

stirred into a surprising range of soups. They're also stunning in omelets with feta cheese and sliced tomatoes, or on pasta or crackers.

HOT STUFF

❦ *To me, garlic is the ultimate way to awaken the palate, but hot stuff ranks a close second. My home spice cabinet has a whole shelf devoted just to various things: hot green chilies, Szechuan chilies, chilies tepine, chilies ancho, half a dozen other dried red chilies, pink, green, black, and white peppercorns, ground cayenne, chili oil, Chinese chili-garlic paste, and home-canned jalapeños from the garden (jalapeños, like basil, are another thing the deer marauding in our garden leave). It gives me pleasure just to look at this palette of heat!*

Three not-for-the-wimpy preparations to pass at table, guaranteed to wake up any soup, are Harissa, a Moroccan chili paste, Harira (page 231), and our own dear Arkansalsa, a fresh, zingy, Mexican-style salsa cruda (page 199). ❦

Gremolata

 light, delicious herb mixture, Italian in origin, enlivened with a bit of finely grated lemon zest. Summery, delicious, and very fresh tasting. Follow the preceding recipe for Classic Basil Pesto, omitting the cheese and nuts, and adding ½ cup Italian (flat-leaf) parsley leaves and 2 teaspoons grated lemon zest.

Makes a scant ½ cup

VARIATION:
Gremolata is often made with about ½ cup grated Parmesan, and/or Pecorino/Romano. You can always add additional garlic, too. The more garlic you use, of course, the more garlicky the flavor; Parmesan, in addition to adding flavor, makes the gremolata even thicker.

Pistou

 esto goes to France. Specifically, Provence. Use pistou as a last-minute add-in to almost any vegetable soup or plain brothy soup if you want to give it a kick. Since pistou's fairly thick, ladle a scoop of your soup into the pistou to thin it, stirring to combine, then add this thinned-down pistou to the entire pot. It's good in any soup with beans or vegetables; it also turns a good

but plain homemade chicken stock into something fragrant and very special. Top a pistou'd soup with grated Parmesan and/or Romano and or Gruyère; serve some good bread, salad, and sorbet and maybe some good cookies for dessert. And invite me for dinner!

½ cup moderately packed fresh basil leaves
*1 bunch fresh Italian (flat-leaf) parsley,
    leaves only (save the stems for the stock
    pot or herb bread)*
2 to 4 cloves garlic (more to taste)
*2 fresh tomatoes, peeled, seeded, and diced,
    or 1 to 2 teaspoons tomato paste*
*Small slice of bread (French bread is
    traditional, naturally)*
⅓ cup freshly grated Parmesan cheese
1 to 2 tablespoons olive oil
Salt and freshly ground pepper to taste
*Soup broth (from whatever soup you're
    making)*

1. Place the ingredients through the olive oil in a food processor, and pulse-chop, stopping and scraping down sides of the work bowl with a plastic spatula, until a smooth paste is formed. Season with salt and pepper.

2. Ladle in a little of the broth from your soup, give everything a buzz in the processor, and return the resulting mixture to the pot.

*Makes about
⅔ cup*

CONTEMPORARY COLORATIONS— PART GARNISH, PURE ZAP

A palette of vivid and easily made purées of herbs, fruits, and vegetables, and some forty-nine-cent squeeze bottles—the type that you buy at the supermarket to put ketchup and mustard in— can change the way your special-occasion soups look and taste forever. Not only will they take a quantum leap forward in flavor in an entirely different, much more subtle and sophisticated way

than the previous garlicky and spicy fillips, but they will look as though they could be photographed for the cover of *Gourmet* or *Bon Appétit.*

The method: Prepare brilliantly colored and flavored vegetables, fruits, and herbs, simply, in ways that do not mask their flavor but allow them to cook to complete softness while maintaining their color and taste. Then purée each separately, and, after puréeing, strain the vegetable or run through a power strainer (a food processor attachment—mine is a Cuisinart) to make it absolutely satin-smooth. Place each in a squeeze bottle, yes, the ones with the tacky mustard-yellow and blood-red colors. (If you're working with a number of different-colored purées, you'll want to label the bottles, or better yet make a trip to a restaurant supply house where you can buy clear or translucent plastic squeeze bottles.)

So. You take your soup. It must be on the dense side and smooth rather than chunky; if it is brothy, this kind of garnishing won't work. Maybe your soup is a bland, pale, creamy one with a potato, cheese, or navy bean base. Maybe it's a dark, mysterious mushroom potage or a soft yellow-gold pumpkin soup. Maybe it's a deep green zucchini-spinach purée or a pale fuchsia borscht that has been lightened with cream or yogurt. It may be hot or cold. Whatever your soup, ladle it carefully into serving bowls. (The simpler the bowl, the better. A bowl of plain white will show off the finished work of art that will be your soup.)

Now take in hand your squeeze bottle filled with bright purée. Perhaps it's a shockingly purple beet or raspberry or dark blackberry purée. Perhaps

it's a purée of bright red pepper or tomato; verdant green basil or spinach. Or a festival-vibrant purée of golden-yellow pumpkin, butternut squash, or yellow pepper. Or it might be an ivory purée of turnips, dramatic on a darker soup.

Using the squeeze bottle, squiggle an irregular line or two of purée of contrasting color and flavor across the surface of your soup. You can use two different-colored purées, even three. You simply won't believe how easy this is to do for such a spectacular effect. The food processor makes such quick work of the purées, too.

The only potential glitch is a soup or purée that's too thin. Both soup and purée cannot be watery. They must be decidedly thick, but not too much so— the thickness, say, of applesauce, rather than of tomato paste. When the consistency is right, the purées are a tad too thin to pipe through a decorating bag. But with a squeeze bottle, they'll work perfectly. And so will your soups.

A few recipes for specific purées follow, and specific combinations using those purées are suggested throughout this book. But do take the concept and play with it. Here are some ideas, to get you imagining:

❖ A cream of corn soup with a southwestern flavor, squiggled with red pepper purée, yellow pepper purée, and green chili purée

❖ A sweet, ivory-colored parsnip soup, with ruby beet purée and golden rutabaga purée

❖ A pale green cream of avocado soup with a dark green, garlic-basil purée

❖ A puréed pale white bean and vegetable

soup with the same vivid green garlic-basil purée

❖ A curried pumpkin or squash soup with sweet red pepper purée

❖ A dark, dark black bean soup, with one purée of butternut squash and a second of green chili

Beet Purée

his purée must be made with fresh beets; the canned kind are too watery. I like beet purée squiggled on the Cream of Cauliflower and Carrot Soup with Fontina Cheese, on Deep December Cream of Root Soup, or in Tomato Soup with Cognac (see Index). Beautiful, faintly sweet beet purée adds extraordinary life and beauty to old favorites and new.

1 bunch (3 or 4 large) fresh beets, greens removed

1. Bake and peel the beets as for the borscht on page 112.

2. Purée in a food processor, adding any liquid which collects in the aluminum foil. You may need to add a few tablespoons of additional liquid—water or stock. If desired, put the beets through a food mill, strainer, or—best yet—use a power strainer for absolute smoothness.

Makes 2 to 3 cups

Bell Pepper Purée

or the forty-nine-cent squeeze bottle trick (see page 44), peppers are perhaps the single best vegetable. The pepper purées—the whole palette of them—are compatible with a wide range of soups. I love red pepper purées floated over pumpkin soups of all kinds, but no matter what your choice of pepper, you get incredibly vivid color and dimensional taste.

You may have made recipes for which a pepper is roasted first. Its skin is charred, giving it a wonderful, dusky, indefinable flavor, unlike anything else. The problem is, after the skin chars and the pepper is popped in a paper bag to steam, its charred skin must be peeled. This is the worst kind of nitpicky kitchen work in the world, though the results are delicious. Of course, if you own a power strainer, the roasted peppers need not be skinned at all. Roasting, peeling, and puréeing peppers is described in detail in Roasted Red Pepper Soup with Roasted Yellow Pepper Ribbons (page 262).

Occasionally you get some red peppers that are beautiful but not all they might be tastewise; if your finished red pepper purée is at all bland, add a few drops of fresh lemon juice and a heaping teaspoon of tomato paste to the finished purée.

Depending on the pepper, purée made for soup is sometimes too watery.

If your purée seems drippy, cook it down a little (in a skillet sprayed with Pam over high heat, stirring constantly) to evaporate some of the liquid.

Broccoli Purée

roccoli purée is lovely over a creamy potato soup, or a thick, smooth tomato soup.

1 head broccoli, thick stems trimmed
Pam cooking spray
2 tablespoons butter
½ cup boiling water
½ cup fresh parsley leaves
1 teaspoon fresh lemon juice
Salt and freshly ground black pepper to
* taste*

1. Separate the flowerets from the broccoli stalks; peel and dice the stalks.

2. Spray a 10-inch skillet with the Pam, and in it melt the butter. Add the stalks and flowerets and quickly stir-fry for 3 minutes. Add the boiling water, cover, and let steam until crisp-tender.

3. Transfer the broccoli and cooking liquid to a food processor. Add the parsley (to rebrighten the green color) and lemon juice. Season with salt and pepper. Purée. If desired, put the purée through a food mill, strainer, or for absolute smoothness, a power strainer.

Makes 1½ to 2½ cups

DELICIOUS DAIRY DABS THAT MAKE A DIFFERENCE

There is no garnish easier than a spoonful of sour cream, crème fraîche, or one of its dairy cousins placed atop a bowl of steaming soup. Some stir the garnish in, lightening and enriching the soup; some leave the spoonful distinct, chipping off a tiny bit with each bite. Either way, these thickened milk products make divine eating. Some are higher in fat than others; this list proceeds roughly from high to low. (For a fuller discussion of this topic, and suggestions for "light" substitutions, see page 51.)

WHIPPED CREAM

Whipped heavy (whipping) cream, unsweetened, is the ultimate delicious dab. Reserve it for special occasions.

To whip cream, simply chill beaters, bowl, and cream deeply, and whip the cream until it is almost, but not quite stiff. Use as is, barely salted, or seasoned with any one of the following. To each cup of whipped cream, add either:

❖ 1 teaspoon Dijon mustard

❖ 1 teaspoon curry powder (toast for 3 minutes over medium-low heat, stirring constantly, in a small cast-iron skillet; cool before using)

❖ 1 teaspoon grated horseradish

❖ 1 teaspoon tomato paste

❖ 1 teaspoon of any of the purées described in Contemporary Colorations, above (red pepper is especially wonderful)

Add the seasonings when the cream has just started to thicken. Each lends a subtle flavor and (except horseradish) pastel shade to the whipped cream.

As for the amount of cream to use, a half-pint (1 cup) of cream, whipped, is 2 to 2½ cups in volume—enough, theoretically, to give a 1 tablespoon–size dollop to 32 servings. Less than ½ pint is hard to whip, unfortunately, so you'll likely have to whip more, leaving some

OF DABS AND DOLLOPS AND "SOUR CREAM OR . . . ."

❦ *When I say—and I do, often— "dab (or dollop) each serving with a spoonful of sour cream or..." what am I talking about?*

A "dab" when applied to dairy products is to me about 1 rounded teaspoon. A "dollop" is about 1 to 2 tablespoons, well rounded.

And "sour cream or..." means sour cream or crème fraîche or Cottage Cream or kefir cheese. It could also mean, if you don't mind a slight moderation in taste and texture, plain, unsweetened yogurt. Actually, I prefer several of these to sour cream proper, but since that is the ingredient most people are most familiar with, I've headed the list with it. ❦

left over. Extra whipped cream may be stirred into the soup itself, or if unflavored, used for other purposes. Or divide it in two, flavor one half with a half-quantity of any of the seasonings listed above (for soup) and save the other half for dessert, adding to it a drop of vanilla

and 2 tablespoons of sifted confectioner's sugar.

One further refinement, done by me only very occasionally, but wonderful to know about for state occasions: When the garden or market is full of fresh herbs, make herb cream. Start the night before, heating the cream to a shade under the boil, then pour it hot over 4 tablespoons of minced fresh herbs. Let the mixture steep, refrigerated, overnight. Next day, strain out every bit of the herbs, which will have imparted their flavor subtly, but indescribably wonderfully, to the cream. They will also have colored it a bit. Whip the chilled, strained herb cream, and use as described above.

A puff of sweet basil cream on chilled tomato soup is sublime; the kind of dish gazebos were made for.

The next three dabs, as well as Cottage Cream (page 52) can be used interchangeably as dabbers in every single recipe in this book which calls for a dollop of sour cream. All are delicious. Flavors differ, but subtly; textures differ more so. Fat and cholesterol counts vary drastically.

SOUR CREAM

This is cultured heavy cream, luscious and traditionally dabbed on many soups, especially those of European origin. Try to find some that is *just* sour cream—it is a revelation if all you've tasted is guar-gummed and sodium-benzoated. If I can't have the real stuff, I'll just do without, especially as the following two options are just as delicious, though less widely available. You cannot cook with sour cream—it is very curdle-prone when heated—but you can stir it into something off the heat just before serving.

CREME FRAICHE

Crème fraîche is another cultured milk product, second cousin to sour cream, buttermilk, or yogurt. I just love its rich taste and texture: thicker than commercial sour cream, a bit tangy, yet still retaining sweetness. Those angels not inclined towards garlic and basil probably eat crème fraîche made with certified raw cream—cream not ultra- or otherwise pasteurized—from Jersey cows. They eat it with strawberries and raspberries and meringues, or possibly tiny heart-shaped scones.

Crème fraîche has the added advantage of being able to withstand heat beautifully without curdling, though it does thin a bit when warmed.

SOUR HALF-AND-HALF

This is a fine, useful way to instantly cut your dab calories by half. In some regions of the country, commercially made sour half-and-half (sometimes called "lite sour cream") is available. Or follow the crème fraîche recipe above, simply substituting half-and-half for whipping cream. This will likely take a bit longer to thicken, nor will it have that totally dreamy, spreadable texture of crème fraîche, even after its sojourn in the fridge. But it is plenty dreamy still: delicious, easily made, and

CRÈME FRAÎCHE

I understand that commercially made crème fraîche is starting to become available in the larger cities, but we certainly haven't seen it around here yet. However, making it at home is simplicity itself. If possible use cream that has not been ultra-pasteurized. This is for reasons of wanting the absolute finest flavor and avoiding additives. But ultra-pasteurized cream will sour just fine, and its flavor is nothing to sneeze at; in fact, it is delectable.

I have read that crème fraîche can take as long as 36 hours to thicken, particularly if ultra-pasteurized cream is used, but that has never been my experience. I think it is warmth, not ultra- or regular pasteurization, that determines how long the cream mixture will take to thicken.

Crème fraîche keeps for a week or so, beautifully. And how nice it is to have—the culinary equivalent of mad money.

2 cups (2 half-pint containers) heavy (whipping) cream
2 tablespoons cultured buttermilk, preferably Bulgarian-style, or unsweetened, plain, additive-free yogurt (I prefer the latter, but both are good and work equally well; buttermilk's traditional)

1. In a quart glass jar with a tightly fitting lid combine the cream and the buttermilk or yogurt. The cream does not need to be warmed or even brought to room temperature; it can be used straight from the fridge.

2. Shake the cream and the buttermilk or yogurt hard for about 30 seconds to combine. Let it stand in a warm place, such as near the stove, on an upper kitchen shelf (remember, heat rises) or in a turned-off oven with a pilot light on (but be sure to put a "Crème Fraîche In Progress" note on the oven door lest someone decide to whip up a batch of corn bread and blithely preheat the oven to 400°F).

3. Leave the cream mixture until thickened but still a little liquidy, about 12 hours. It sets up as it chills. It can be used right away, but is best after aging overnight in the refrigerator.

Makes about 2 cups

thick enough to dab satisfactorily. Excellent, too, on baked potatoes. About 20 calories a tablespoon. Hey—that's a *level* tablespoon! I know you!

KEFIR CHEESE

Kefir is a cultured milk product like yogurt; kefir *cheese* is kefir that has had some of its water removed. This is delectable stuff—similar in flavor to a slightly tangier commercial sour cream, but with a creamier, richer taste and a slightly thicker consistency which makes it ideal for garnishing. Although it is marketed as a cheese, its flavor and texture are not what most people would consider cheeselike (except as a very soft cream cheese, perhaps). To me,

kefir cheese is most like crème fraîche. You'll find it in health food stores. The most widely available brand is made by the California-based natural foods dairy, Alta Dena, a company whose products are always astonishingly good.

Oddly, considering its gorgeous taste and consistency, kefir cheese is made of more whole milk than cream, making it lower in calories than most of the above—33 a tablespoon.

Listen: this is really good stuff; maybe what the sub-angels eat before they graduate to crème fraîche. It's *not* health-foody. Try it and fall in love.

DELICIOUS LOW-FAT DAIRY DABS

PLAIN UNSWEETENED YOGURT

There are as many variables in flavor and calorie count for this great, versatile cultured dairy product as there are different brands. Be sure to avoid any brands that have additives, such as gelatin. Yogurt that's entirely fat-free is rather disappointing in taste and texture, but several low-fat yogurts, of which Dannon is the best known and certainly the most widely available yogurt of quality, are very good. (Dannon has a mere 8¾ calories per tablespoon—you can really go to town!) Full-fat yogurts, such as Brown Cow, or some of Alta Dena's, are made from whole milk and are extra good in flavor. Even with whole milk, these yogurts are still lower in calories than are sour cream or crème fraîche.

Yogurt has a softer texture than sour cream, crème fraîche, or kefir cheese; this hurts its dabbing appearance a little (with most brands the edges of the dab will disintegrate rather than hold together when scooped onto hot soup). But the tangy-creamy taste is quite similar to the richer stuff, and just delicious as an everyday, at-home staple (save the full-fat dabbers for company fare or special occasions).

COTTAGE CREAM

This easy, very versatile recipe—nothing more than buttermilk, cottage cheese, and a bit of lemon juice buzzed together in the processor or blender—has been around for several decades, at least since the fifties, when people first began in earnest to seek ways to spare calories. Versions of it appear in virtually every health-conscious cookbook since the 1956 *Complete Book of Low Calorie Cooking* (advertised as "The book that takes your breadth away") on up to *Jane*

A RECIPE FOR COTTAGE CREAM

3 tablespoons milk, buttermilk, or unsweetened plain yogurt
1 tablespoon fresh lemon juice, or more to taste
1 cup low-fat cottage cheese

1. Buzz together in a food processor until very, very smooth, 2 to 4 minutes.

2. Refrigerate. It will get thicker as it chills.

Makes about 1 cup

Brody's Good Food Book. It is usually called "mock sour cream," an offensive and precious designation I detest. We've always called it "cottage cream" around our house, since cottage cheese is one of its ingredients, I live more or less in a cottage, and because we love the sort of English, Devonshire sound of it. I was delighted to see that Jane Brody calls it the same thing. "I'm not a fan of imitation anything," she writes.

It cannot be heated, for it will separate, but it is a dabber *par excellence*.

Be sure to buzz the ingredients together for the full time, so the texture will be absolutely smooth. Alta Dena is the preferred brand of cottage cheese.

ITALIAN COTTAGE CREAM

Yum. Substitute part-skim ricotta cheese (360 calories a cup) for cottage cheese following the above recipe. A little sweeter in flavor than plain cottage cream, a little richer, and very pleasant. (I sometimes mix Italian Cottage Cream with a dab of honey and a dash of cinnamon, and spread it on breakfast toast—a sort of low-fat cheese danish.)

A FEW NOTES ON COOKING FROM THIS BOOK

RECIPE YIELDS

The question of how many servings any given recipe yields depends entirely on how the cook is using the soup in the meal, and whether he or she is serving it in cups or bowls (which, oddly enough, only contain about a cup and a half of soup; wouldn't you think they'd hold more?).

If you're serving a soup as a starter, you'll most likely serve it in a cup, and requests for seconds are unlikely. If you allow 1 cup per person, plus extra (for tasting as you go along), you'll be fine.

If you're planning to serve the soup in bowls as a main dish, however, allow a minimum of 2 cups per person. This will allow some to have full seconds, as well as satisfy those "I'll-just-take-a-*little*-more" folks. But, to me, having fed my six foot four Ned for many years, 2 cups borders on just plain stingy. Unless you are certain your crew are all dainty eaters, I'd plan on 3 cups per person, plus another 2 or 3 "for the pot." Probably many people would say these are overly generous amounts, but I can't tell you how often I've seen guests and friends put away two, three bowls of soup, sometimes four.

Besides, the host should always err on the side of too generous.

Besides, you can always have the leftovers for lunch.

IMPROVISATIONAL NOTES

Most soups are not exacting. Unlike cake or bread recipes, it's pretty hard to mess up soups by fooling with the proportions, assuming you have good basic ingredients and rudimentary cooking know-how. If you make a soup from this book as written and you decide you want it more brothy, hey, feel free to add more liquid. The recipe calls for green beans and all you've got is zucchini? No problem, zucchini it is. While I give fairly precise and detailed recipes, you are hereby granted dispensation to play with them as much as you like. We do, here in the inn's kitchen, and at home all the time.

WHICH STOCK TO USE

Okay—I like to cook. I like good homemade from-scratch stocks of many kinds, and at the restaurant we keep a variety on hand. I virtually never use canned stock or what is called euphemistically "beef base" (or chicken, lobster, or whatever base). I can taste a fresh homemade stock versus a "base" stock in a spoonful, and I think the fresh is infinitely better.

But—I know in the real world many people are, one, not as fanatical as I am, and, two, short on time.

Now, I know that in the stock chapter you'll see this whole array of from-scratch stocks we make at the restaurant: three different chicken stocks, four different vegetable stocks, and numerous variations on each of those. And here I'm going to contradict myself: while I think ideally you should make and use these stock recipes, you don't *have* to to

INN GOOD COMPANY: E. RAE SMITH

❧ *One especially bright star of our restaurant galaxy is E. Rae Smith, who steps in for special events, busy weekends, and any above-and-beyond decorating projects. With a background that ranges geographically from Memphis to Denver to New York, and professionally from world-class party planner to interior and floral designer, E. Rae preps,* *garnishes, takes the lead on most of our holiday decorating, and does it all with a sly smile and a good story or two . . . or three. To see her garnish tray, with its assemblages of counted-out herb bouquets, one kind for each of the evening's four or five entrées, is to sigh with pleasure. And, oh, her pie crusts!* ❧

make a perfectly respectable soup. If you can take the time to do a stock from scratch, sure, that's the best; but an avenging soup angel is not going to fly down and beat you with its wings if you use canned or cubed stocks.

For most recipes I'll list the ultimate, ideal stock you should use—Chicken Stock 1 for instance—and then I'll add, as an alternative, "or any well-flavored chicken stock." You just give it your best shot.

ABOUT "PAM"

I love this stuff—a basically tasteless cooking spray, virtually non-caloric and made of lecithin, which you use to coat pans and prevent sticking.

I use Pam at home all the time to save fat grams. Once it's sprayed on, a mere teaspoon of butter or oil will do the trick when sautéing most foodstuffs. And I use it all the time at the restaurant to prevent sticking, which can easily happen, especially when simmering something starchy in a large pot.

Know that if you use a spray of Pam when sautéing something, you can get by with a minimal amount of fat, just enough to give a little of the fat's characteristic flavor. It won't be 100 percent as wonderful as if made with full fat—

this is the sad truth of the low-fat life—but it'll be, say, 80 percent there.

What does this mean in practical terms? If a recipe calls for 3 tablespoons oil, I'd make it that way at the restaurant or for company. But for myself and Ned, at home, I'd use a spray of Pam and maybe 1 teaspoon of oil.

Do use plain Pam, not butter-flavored, which is repellently fake tasting.

ABOUT SEASONING "TO TASTE"

I generally undersalt dishes at home, and have encouraged everyone who cooks in the restaurant kitchen to do the same. To some extent, many of the recipes in this book could also be considered undersalted. This is less for reasons of health than because I think most dishes are oversalted to make up for a lack of balanced, intense, natural flavors and good ingredients. Too, it's always easy to add salt later, but impossible to remove it. Besides, personal preferences vary.

Non-salt seasonings vary, too. The dried herbs we get from Mary Wagner's Bleumarie Farms here in Eureka or from Jim Long at Long Creek Herbs are more intensely flavored, because fresher, than any we've ever bought commercially. A cookbook writer not only has no way of knowing where in the spectrum of how-highly-flavored-I-like-it a cookbook user's tastebuds are, but also where his or her bottle of basil is. How fresh is it? How close to the stove has it been sitting? How long has it been in the cupboard?

DAIRYMAIDS

🍎 *Other inns have maids. We have Dairymaids (and in one case, a Dairydude). The word has become a verb around here, as in "Who's dairymaiding today, Cheryl or Carolyn?"*

Ex-Dairymaid Donna made the ruffled embroidered pillows that say "Privacy Please," and may be hung over the door-knobs—so much more gracious than "Do Not Disturb." The Rose Room's pillow has roses, the Iris Room's—well, you get the drift.

Almost everywhere you look you see Carolyn's handiwork. Carolyn made: Iris Room curtains and dust-ruffle; Peach Blos-som Suite pillow shams (complete with appliqued cows); Spring Gardens canopy bed curtains.

"You know," one guest told me, "I stay in hotels and inns a lot, and I always hate seeing the maids. You just feel they're so oppressed and demoralized. And exploited. Cleaning rooms; why would anyone do it if they had a choice? But when Donna knocked at my door with those flowers and said, 'Sorry to disturb you, I'm your nuisance Dairymaid,' I just said to myself, no way is she oppressed. That woman has a life!" 🍎

So use our seasoning amounts as mere guidelines; your discrimination is the final measurement.

HERBS AND SPICES

When an herb is called for in the recipes that follow, a *dry* herb is meant, unless otherwise specified. I also assume the use of leaf, flake, or whole dried herbs; almost never, and then only if explicitly specified, the prepowdered or ground kind, which generally have the seasoning power of sawdust. However, to get the utmost flavor from herbs, do "grind" them yourself immediately before using by rubbing them between your thumb and forefinger as you sprinkle them into the pot. This brings out their essential oils, besides letting you know how fresh they are (the more fragrant, the fresher). It's also one of the kitchen's small sensual pleasures.

Spices, though, like cinnamon and cloves, maintain good flavor even when ground; for those, you can assume I *do* mean ground, unless I specifically state "2 whole cloves, 1 cinnamon stick," and so on.

Since gingerroot is used in both fresh and dry forms, I always specify which is meant.

Chicken Soups

TO CROW OVER

olden, comforting, and redolent of home cooking, chicken soup is one of the perfect, longed-for foods of childhood. It's a legendary folk-cure and a classic expression of mother-love. As soothing and homey as it is, basic chicken soup, dressed up, is a frequent guest at the finest tables in the world. Good chicken stock is neutral yet full-flavored, friendly to a thousand different ingredients and a thousand different soups. It's fundamental—as welcome in the palace as the nursery; and, of course, welcome here at the inn.

Our restaurant menu changes all the time, but I doubt a week goes by that we don't make gallons and gallons of chicken stock: for soups throughout the year, for sauces and glazes, sometimes even for our breakfasts. (One regular breakfast item, a homemade chicken hash baked in ramekins and served piping hot is essentially fresh-poached chicken in a well-seasoned, thickened chicken stock.) And when that stock or one of the dozens of soups we make from it is simmering in the kitchen, and the smell drifts up the stone steps to street level, I can't tell you how often passers-by come down those same steps, to ask Paula, Char, Ned, or me, "Excuse me, but what smells so good?"

Chicken soups of one kind and another appear on the inn's dinner menu frequently. The six-course dinners we serve do mean a lot of food, especially to an eating-light-oriented world, so while each portion we serve is generous, we try not to make it so ample that guests become too full to enjoy every course. In a meal where the entrées are particularly rich, you might well find that the lightest possible chicken soup—such as our Chicken Broth Supreme—is one of the soup choices on our evening's menu. Simple, refreshing, and slightly acidic from the addition of white wine, you could sip from the cup just as easily as spoon it. It's very good, but not in itself, totally, *outrageously* good. Instead, it's the perfect balance to many formal or rich meals. It's a favorite of our waiter, John Mitchell.

Another balance we strive for—more so because the inn's in a part of the country where there are many conservative eaters—is between adventurous dishes and reassuringly recognizable ones (taken, of course, to their highest level). If one of the evening's soup choices is at all exotic—a chilled blackberry-burgundy soup, for instance, or something particularly spicy or curried—you can be sure the alternative choice will be in the line of Old-Fashioned Chicken Soup with Vegetables. Brunch is another meal for which our customer's tastes do not run to the exotic, and when we do it, a good chicken soup almost always fills the now-now-this-isn't-so-weird-after-all role. (At one brunch a lady who'd ordered one of our chicken soups as a starter told the kitchen via John to cancel her omelet—she'd decided she wanted a second bowl of soup for her entrée instead!)

Hearty or light, homey or exotic, you will find many soups here that will bring your chickens home, happily, to roost. P.S.: At the end of the chapter is a fine recipe for duck soup—don't miss it.

ENTREE-STYLE HEARTY CHICKEN SOUPS

These, along with Chicken Gumbo Zeb (page 240) are our basic main-dish chicken soups at the inn. We vary them with each season, different starches and different vegetables predominating accordingly. All are delicious and satisfying, of-the-moment without being far-out, any time of year.

Chicken and Corn Soup with Late Summer Vegetables

Many people know the creamy chicken and corn soup of Pennsylvania Dutch origin. This is a different, delicious take: a white wine-enriched broth with a touch of tomato, tender pieces of chicken, corn cut from the cob, and still-a-bit-crisp zucchini pieces. Perfumed by basil fresh from the garden, this soup is savory, dimensional, and far lower in calories and fat grams than the cream version.

2½ quarts Chicken Stock 1 (page 19) or any well-flavored chicken stock
3 cups dry white wine
1 tablespoon tomato paste
1½ teaspoons Pickapeppa sauce
3 cups corn kernels cut from 4 to 6 ears of corn on the cob (or 3 cups frozen corn kernels)
1 tablespoon butter
1 tablespoon mild vegetable oil, such as corn or safflower
2 large onions, diced
3 fresh tomatoes, roughly chopped (peeled and seeded if you find having bits of skin and seeds in the finished soup offensive)
2 small zucchini, quartered lengthwise, then cut into strips about 1½ inches long (or slice into rounds or half-rounds, though strips are more interesting)
1 cup lightly packed fresh basil leaves
Salt and freshly ground black pepper to taste
1 tablespoon Garlic Oil (page 41; optional, but awfully good)
2 tablespoons cornstarch (optional)
3 tablespoons additional chicken stock or wine (optional)
1¼ to 2 cups boned and skinned cooked chicken, cut into spoonable pieces

1. In a heavy soup pot combine the chicken stock and wine and bring to a boil.

Turn down the heat to medium-low and simmer. Whisk in the tomato paste and Pickapeppa sauce. Drop the corn kernels into the simmering stock. Cover and let cook about 15 minutes.

2. Meanwhile, in an 8- or 9-inch skillet, heat the butter and oil over medium heat. Add the onions and sauté until translucent, 3 to 4 minutes. Add the tomatoes and toss in the hot fat, another 3 minutes or so. Scrape the tomatoes and onions from the skillet into the stock mixture. Deglaze the pan with a bit of the stock mixture, and add the pan contents to the soup pot. Continue to simmer the soup, covered.

3. Now, barely blanch the zucchini pieces: Put them into a colander. Bring a tea kettle of water to a boil and pour the boiling water slowly over the zucchini. Refresh in cold water.

4. If using fresh basil: Stack 8 to 10 basil leaves with one hand, and with the other gently slice the basil into thin ribbons. Repeat until all the basil has been ribboned.

5. Add the basil ribbons, the salt and pepper, and the optional garlic oil to the soup. Taste. *Bueno?* Keep seasoning until it's there.

6. Now decide if you want the soup brothy or slightly thickened. If you decide on brothy, skip to the next step. If you want it thickened, mix the optional cornstarch and stock or wine to a smooth paste with your fingers. Drizzle a little hot stock into this mixture, then pour it into the simmering soup, stirring. It should thicken almost immediately.

7. Stir the barely blanched zucchini and the chicken into the soup. Heat through quickly, and serve very hot, immediately.

Serves 4 to 6 as an entrée, with bread and salad

Chicken and Vegetable Soup with Tiny Meatballs

In this very pleasant main-dish soup, meant for fall or winter, a selection of vegetables and wonderful, garlicky balls of ground chicken and ham bobble agreeably in a savory broth. We rarely use beef or pork in our recipes; these meatballs, delicious exceptions to the rule, were invented following our catering of a wedding reception. An Ozark smoked ham had been specifically requested, and we had a bit left over. The soup and meatballs were so popular we've periodically bought ham ever since. Adults love the soup, but it's a great favorite with kids, especially if cooked elbow macaroni is added.

Other vegetables, according to the season, can easily be added. A handful of shredded fresh greens, for instance, is always good.

3 quarts Chicken Stock 1 or 2 (pages 19
  and 20) or any well-flavored chicken
  stock
1 tablespoon olive oil
1 tablespoon butter
2 medium onions, diced
2 ribs celery, diced
1 medium carrot, scrubbed and diced
2 tablespoons tomato paste
1 tablespoon brandy
1 large turnip, peeled and diced
¼ large butternut squash, peeled, seeded,
  and diced
1 thick slice crusty French or Italian bread
  (French Country Bread, page 328, is
  ideal)
3 small cloves garlic
1 egg
12 ounces boned and skinned cooked
  chicken, coarsely diced
4 ounces best-quality smoked ham, coarsely
  diced
Freshly ground black pepper
A few small sprigs fresh basil and/or parsley
Unbleached all-purpose flour
Salt to taste

1. In a large soup pot, bring the stock
to a boil. Turn the heat down to medium-
low and let simmer, uncovered, while you
continue.

2. In a skillet, heat the oil and butter
over medium heat. Add the onions and sauté
2 or 3 minutes. Add the celery and carrot,
sauté another 5 minutes, then add the vegetables to the simmering chicken stock with
the tomato paste, brandy, turnip, and butternut squash. Cover, and let simmer gently until
the vegetables are tender, about 15 minutes.

3. Meanwhile, make the meatballs: In
a food processor buzz together the bread,
garlic, and egg until a smooth paste is
formed, about 30 seconds. Add the chicken

and ham, pepper, and the basil and/or parsley. Pulse-chop 10 or 15 times, then buzz until
a smooth, very thick paste is formed.

4. Roll the ham-chicken paste into balls
the size of a large marble. Roll the balls in
the flour so that they are lightly dusted all
over.

5. When the vegetables are tender,
raise the heat on the soup ever so slightly,
so that it simmers with a little more intensity.
Drop the meatballs into the soup, and let
cook 5 to 7 minutes. Taste for seasoning and
adjust, being careful not to oversalt as the
ham is salty. Serve immediately.

*Serves 6 to 8 as an entrée, with bread and
salad*

Note: This is even better the next day, but
first fish out the meatballs and wrap them up
separately, rather than storing them overnight in the broth.

Chicken and Rice Soup with Fresh Spring Vegetables

his is a light soup, thickened
only by the rice that is cooked
in it. It's deliciously springy.

2½ quarts Chicken Stock 1 (page 19) or
  any well-flavored chicken stock
3 cups dry white wine
½ cup long-grain rice
Good pinch of dried sweet basil or 1
  tablespoon chopped fresh basil or dill
1 tablespoon butter
1 tablespoon mild vegetable oil, such as
  corn or safflower
2 large onions, diced
2 ribs celery, diced
2 carrots, scrubbed and diced
2 scallions, thinly sliced crosswise
8 ounces snow peas, strings and stems
  removed, cut crosswise in halves or, if
  large, in thirds or quarters
Salt and freshly ground black pepper to
  taste
1¼ to 2 cups boned and skinned cooked
  chicken, cut into spoonable pieces
Paper-thin slices of lemon, seeds removed,
  for garnish

1. In a heavy soup pot combine the chicken stock and wine and bring to a boil. Add the rice and dried basil, if using, and stir. Turn down the heat to medium-low and let simmer, covered, about 15 minutes.

2. Meanwhile, in an 8- to 9-inch skillet, heat the butter and oil over medium heat. Add the onions, and sauté until translucent, 3 to 4 minutes. Add the celery, carrots, and scallions, and toss in the hot fat, another 3 minutes or so. Scrape the vegetables from the skillet into the stock mixture. Deglaze the pan with a bit of the stock mixture, and add the pan contents to the pot. Continue to simmer the soup, covered.

3. Now, barely blanch the snow peas: Put them into a colander. Bring a tea kettle of water to a boil and pour the boiling water slowly over the peas. Refresh in cold water.

4. Add the fresh basil, if using, and the

AN ALTERNATIVE PREP METHOD

❦Both rice and snow peas get mushy if held too long. If you're not sure when all those dining will arrive, or if you've made enough for leftovers, try this restaurant service trick: finish the soup by the serving, not by the pot. That is, cook the rice separately (ideally in equal parts chicken stock and white wine) and reserve it, as well as the half-blanched snow peas. When ready to serve, spoon a bit of rice and a scattering of snow peas into each bowl or cup, and ladle on the hot soup.❦

salt and pepper to the soup. Taste. Keep seasoning until it's there.

5. Stir in the barely blanched snow peas and the cut-up chicken. Heat through quickly, and serve very hot. Don't permit it to wait; snow peas lose their charm if they sit around. Garnish with the lemon slices.

Serves 5 to 6 as an entrée, with bread and salad

VARIATION:
Chicken and Rice Soup with Vegetables Oriental-Style: Cook the rice separately, as in the Alternative Prep Method. Use 2 table-

spoons toasted sesame oil to replace the butter and oil. Add 2 teaspoons peeled, finely chopped fresh gingerroot with the carrots and celery. Spoon the rice and snow peas into each bowl; ladle on the hot soup. A nice garnish here: sliced scallions and a sprinkle of toasted sesame seeds. Or substitute 1 pound of fresh asparagus for the snow peas. The asparagus should be of small- to medium-size diameter (large is also fine, but allow a few more minutes of cooking time). Cut the asparagus on an angle into 1-inch pieces and drop them directly into the soup the last 3 to 5 minutes of cooking time.

Wintery Chicken and Pasta Soup

articularly hearty and warming version of chicken and vegetable soup, almost a chickeny minestrone but with a bit of sweetness from the butternut squash. Just perfect for cold weather. There are so many interesting flavors in this that the white wine is superfluous; use straight chicken stock.

3¼ quarts Chicken Stock 1 (page 19) or any well-flavored chicken stock
1 tablespoon tomato paste
1½ teaspoons Pickapeppa sauce
1 teaspoon dried oregano
1 teaspoon dried thyme
½ teaspoon dried rosemary
1 teaspoon dried basil or, preferably, 1 cup lightly packed fresh basil leaves
1½ cups peeled, seeded, and diced butternut squash
1 tablespoon butter
1 tablespoon mild vegetable oil, such as corn or safflower
2 large onions, diced
3 fresh tomatoes, roughly chopped (peeled and seeded if you find having bits of skin and seeds in the finished soup offensive)
½ pound greens such as turnip, spinach, romaine, collard, or cabbage, washed very well, tough stems or cores removed, leaves sliced into thin ribbons
1 can (15 ounces) chick-peas (garbanzo beans), with liquid
Salt and freshly ground black pepper to taste
1 tablespoon Garlic Oil, (page 41; optional)
1¼ to 2 cups boned and skinned cooked chicken, cut into spoonable pieces
4 to 6 ounces (dry weight) bowtie noodles or ziti, cooked
Grated Parmesan cheese, to pass at the table

1. In a heavy soup pot, bring the chicken stock to a boil. Turn down the heat to medium-low and simmer. Whisk in the tomato paste, Pickapeppa sauce, and dried herbs including dried basil, if using. Drop the butternut squash pieces into the simmering stock. Cover and let cook until the squash starts to soften, about 10 minutes.

2. Meanwhile, in an 8- to 9-inch skillet, heat the butter and oil over medium heat.

Add the onions and sauté until translucent, 3 to 4 minutes. Add the tomatoes, and toss in the hot fat for another 3 minutes or so. Scrape the tomatoes and onions from the skillet into the stock mixture. Deglaze the pan with a bit of the stock mixture, and add the pan contents to the soup pot, along with the shredded greens and chick-peas. Continue to simmer the soup, covered.

3. If using fresh basil: Stack 8 to 10 basil leaves with one hand, and with the other gently slice the basil into thin ribbons. Repeat until all the basil has been ribboned.

4. Add the salt and pepper, the optional garlic oil, and the basil ribbons to the soup. Taste. Keep seasoning until it's there.

5. Stir in the chicken and get the soup good and hot. Place a handful of the cooked pasta in each serving bowl, and ladle the steaming soup over it. Serve hot, immediately. Pass the Parmesan cheese at the table.

Serves 6 to 8 as an entrée, with bread and salad

Chicken and Potato Soup with Fall Vegetables

his is an exceptionally full-flavored soup. It practically says "bountiful harvest."

2½ quarts Chicken Stock 1 (page 19) or
    any well-flavored chicken stock
3 cups dry white wine
1 tablespoon tomato paste
1½ teaspoons Pickapeppa Sauce
2 teaspoons dried basil or, preferably, 1 cup
    lightly packed fresh basil leaves
3 medium potatoes, scrubbed or peeled, as
    you prefer, cut into ½-inch dice
1 to 2 cups peeled, seeded, and diced
    butternut squash (1 small to medium
    squash)
1 tablespoon butter
1 tablespoon mild vegetable oil, such as
    corn or safflower
2 large onions, diced
1 large red bell pepper, cored, seeded, and
    diced
1 fresh tomato, roughly chopped (peeled
    and seeded if you find having bits of skin
    and seeds in the finished soup offensive)
½ pound fresh green beans, stems removed,
    sliced crosswise into very thin ¼-inch
    slices
Salt and freshly ground black pepper to
    taste
1 tablespoon Garlic Oil (page 41; optional,
    but great)
1¼ to 2 cups skinned and boned cooked
    chicken, cut into spoonable pieces

1. In a heavy soup pot combine the chicken stock and wine and bring to a boil. Turn down the heat to medium-low and simmer. Whisk in the tomato paste and Pickapeppa Sauce. Add the dried basil, if using. Drop the potatoes into the simmering stock, cover, and let cook 10 minutes. Uncover, and drop in the butternut squash.

2. Meanwhile, in an 8- to 9-inch skillet, heat the butter and oil over medium heat. Add the onion and sauté until translucent, 3 to 4 minutes. Add the pepper, stir-fry 1 minute, then add the tomato. Toss the vegetables in the hot fat until slightly softened, another 3 minutes or so. Scrape the vegetables from the skillet into the stock mixture. Deglaze the pan with a bit of the stock mixture and add the pan contents to the soup pot. Continue to simmer the soup, covered, for 5 minutes.

3. Uncover the pot, and drop in the sliced green beans. Cover.

4. If using fresh basil: Stack 8 to 10 basil leaves with one hand, and with the other gently slice the basil into thin ribbons. Repeat until all the basil has been ribboned.

5. Add the basil ribbons to the soup. Then add salt and pepper, and the optional garlic oil. Taste. Keep seasoning until it's just right, then add the chicken. Continue cooking until the green beans and butternut squash are tender but not mushy, about 5 minutes. Serve hot, immediately.

Serves 5 to 6 as an entrée, with bread and salad

Mulligatawny

ulligatawny's a spicy curried chicken soup with rice and vegetables, supposedly of Indian origin, though I suspect its ancestry is more Anglo-Indian than true Indian. I've always read in American cookbooks that the word "mulligatawny" is Tamil for "pepper water"; but throughout Tamil-Nadu and Kerala, pepper water is called "rasam," a thin soup so hot it makes your sinuses sadomasochistically cry "More! Stop! More! Stop!" Yowza!

Mulligatawny's calmer. Wonderfully warming, seasoned enough so you wouldn't want to spring it on those with extremely conservative tastes, but mild enough to please most, it's hearty main-dish fare—and a fine way to feed a lot of people well on little money. It should be served with a fork and knife as well as spoon, since the chicken's on the bone (although you may bone it if you like). I add lentils to my version, because to me lentils are magic with Indian spices.

You may double the quantities of all spices if you like the soup really spicy; I do at home, but not at the restaurant.

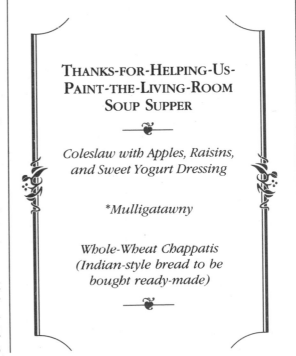

THANKS-FOR-HELPING-US-PAINT-THE-LIVING-ROOM SOUP SUPPER

Coleslaw with Apples, Raisins, and Sweet Yogurt Dressing

*Mulligatawny

Whole-Wheat Chappatis (Indian-style bread to be bought ready-made)

3 quarts Chicken Stock 1 (page 19) or
Golden Vegetable or Browned Vegetable
Stock (pages 28 and 32) or any well-
flavored chicken or vegetable stock
1 cup lentils
¼ cup mild vegetable oil, such as peanut
2 pounds chicken pieces (thighs serve up
particularly neatly)
1 bay leaf
2 medium carrots, scrubbed and sliced
1 large onion, diced
2 ribs celery, diced
1 Granny Smith or other tart apple,
unpeeled, cored and diced
1 tablespoon black mustard seeds (purchase
at a spice shop; do not substitute yellow
mustard seeds; omit if unavailable)
2 teaspoons finely chopped fresh gingerroot
2 teaspoons ground cumin seeds
2 teaspoons ground turmeric
2 teaspoons ground coriander
1 tablespoon good prepared curry powder
⅛ teaspoon cayenne pepper
2 tablespoons all-purpose flour
4 cups hot cooked rice, cooked separately
during the last 30 minutes of the soup's
simmering time
Salt and freshly ground black pepper to
taste

1. In a medium-sized soup pot, bring 2 quarts of the stock to a boil. Then add the lentils. Return to the boil, turn down the heat to medium-low, and let simmer, covered, until the lentils are quite soft, 45 minutes to 1 hour. (If the stock is especially fatty or heavily salted, it will take longer for the lentils to get tender.)

2. Meanwhile, in a large cast-iron skillet, heat the oil over medium heat. Add the chicken pieces and brown lightly on all sides; transfer to a heavy soup pot. Pour the remaining quart of the chicken stock over them

---

OTHER ENTRÉE-STYLE CHICKEN SOUPS

❦You won't want to miss the chicken variation of Gumbo Zeb (page 240). This greens-filled, herbed, spicy gumbo will almost surely be the best you've ever eaten. Also, turn to Greens and Pot Likker Soup Nouveau 'Zarks Style (page 134), an updated version of heart-and-soul Ozarks food. It can be made more hearty easily, becoming, with a few changes, Chicken and Greens Soup-Stew with Cornmeal Dumplings (page 135), a substantial meal for four to six.❦

---

and bring to a boil. Turn down the heat to medium-low, add the bay leaf and the carrots, and continue to simmer, covered.

3. In the oil in which you browned the chicken, sauté the onion until translucent, 3 to 5 minutes. Add the celery and apple. When they have softened slightly, stir in the spices and cook over medium-low heat until the spices are fragrant and on the edge of browning, another 3 minutes. Sprinkle with the flour, and smooth it in. Then gradually stir in 1 cup of the stock dipped from the simmering-chicken pot. Stir to smooth the flour and spices into the stock, scraping the flavorful chicken bits from the bottom of the

skillet. Raise the heat to medium, and cook, stirring, about 2 minutes. Pour this spicy blend over the chicken.

4. By now the lentils should be done or close to it. Add to the chicken pot. Continue to cook over low heat, covered, until the chicken is very tender and the lentils are extremely soft, about 1 hour. (Don't forget to cook the rice 30 minutes before completion.)

5. When the chicken and lentils are tender, taste for seasoning and correct with salt and pepper. Serve hot, over the rice.

Serves 6 to 8, with the rice

Note: If you want to serve the chicken off the bone, prepare the soup in advance, cool to room temperature, and pick all the meat off the bones. This dish freezes superbly, but always freeze the rice separately.

Supreme Of Chicken and Olive Soup Eureka

o me, this is classic country inn fare—a little old-fashioned, not hip or bizarre or nouvelle, devoid of fat gram consciousness, yet just delicious—and interesting enough to be out of the ordinary. The good flavors of chicken and white wine are zapped with green and black olives; half-and-half makes it creamily unctuous; and it just seems to say "celebratory and special" to guests, who request the recipe often (it was in the *Dairy Hollow House Cookbook,* too). This is our annual offering at the Eureka Springs Historical Museum's annual fundraiser, to which local restaurants each donate a kettle of soup. One year we gave a different kind of soup, and there were howls of protest. We learned our lesson, "Supreme" it is!

4 cups Chicken Stock 1 (page 19) or any
*   well-flavored chicken stock*
1 cup dry white wine
4 tablespoons (½ stick) butter
1 medium onion, diced
1 medium carrot, peeled and diced
1 rib celery, diced
5 tablespoons unbleached all-purpose
*   flour*
½ cup fresh or frozen peas
1½ cups half-and-half
½ cup cooked rice
¼ cup fat black olives, pitted and sliced
*   in thickish rounds (regular old*
*   supermarket-style California black*
*   olives, nothing fancy or imported)*
¼ cup pimento-stuffed green olives, sliced
*   in thickish rounds*
3 cups chunked cooked chicken
Salt and freshly ground black pepper to
*   taste*
Finely chopped fresh parsley, for garnish

1. In a soup pot, combine the chicken stock and wine and bring to a boil. Turn down the heat to medium-low and let simmer while you continue.

2. In an 8- to 9-inch skillet, melt the butter over medium heat. Add the onion and sauté until slightly softened, about 5 minutes.

Add the carrot and celery and sauté, stirring, another 5 or 6 minutes.

3. Sprinkle the vegetables with the flour, and lower the heat. Cook 2 minutes more, stirring. Gradually stir in a ladleful of the stock-wine mixture, then add the thickened pan contents to the remainder of the stock and wine mixture. Let this barely simmer at a very low heat for 20 minutes, uncovered. If using fresh peas, add during the last 5 minutes of cooking time.

4. Add half-and-half to the soup. If using frozen peas, put them into a strainer and "cook" briefly by running hot tap water over them for 20 seconds or so. Add the peas to the soup along with the remaining ingredients except the salt, pepper, and parsley. Heat through; add salt and pepper and garnish with the parsley.

Serves 4 to 6 as an entrée

Chicken and Cheese Soup with Green Chilies

exas, Arkansas's due-South neighbor, has made Tex-Mex one of our state's most popular foreign, or foreign-influenced, cuisines. This outstanding, hearty, chowderlike soup is full of that cooking idiom's bursting flavors. It was inspired by the taste of chicken and green chili enchi-

ladas (concomitant with the wish that, just for once, I could indulge in Mexican food without feeling stuffed to the gills and starched-out immediately after). This very popular full-meal soup fits the bill. It's medium-spicy; turn the heat up or down according to taste. Serve the soup proudly in some pretty, peasanty bowls, with a skillet of corn bread (page 352) or your favorite Spanish rice recipe. Add a green salad with Mexican Vinaigrette (page 379), a few slices of avocado and tomato, or some chips and guacamole.

DINNER FOR BILLY AFTER HE DROVE THROUGH THE SNOW TO GET HERE

Salad of Sliced Tomatoes, Avocados, and Red Onions on a Bed of Greens with Creamy Mexican Vinaigrette

*Chicken and Cheese Soup with Green Chilies

Spanish Rice

Orange Pound Cake

Coffee and/or Hot Chocolate with Cinnamon Stick

6 cups Chicken Stock 1 (page 19) or any
    well-flavored chicken stock
3 fresh tomatoes, chopped
2 tablespoons butter
2 tablespoons mild vegetable oil, such as
    corn or peanut
1 large onion, diced
2 to 3 fresh green chilies, to taste, stems and
    seeds removed, diced (faintly sweet
    poblano chilies, which are greenish-black
    triangular peppers, intriguingly sweet-
    hot, are great here)
½ to 1 whole fresh jalapeño pepper, stem
    and seeds removed, diced
2 teaspoons ground cumin seeds
2 teaspoons good Mexican chili powder
½ cup unbleached all-purpose flour
2 cups milk (half-and-half if you're feeling
    indulgent; low-fat if you're feeling
    prudent)
12 ounces sharp Cheddar cheese, grated
½ cup Crème Fraîche (page 50) or kefir
    cheese
1¼ to 2 cups diced, boned and skinned
    cooked chicken
Chopped fresh cilantro leaves to taste
Salt and freshly ground black pepper to
    taste
Tabasco or similar hot sauce (optional)
Finely chopped fresh cilantro or parsley
    and crushed tortilla chips, made,
        preferably, from both blue
            and yellow cornmeal,
                for garnish

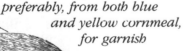

1. In a large soup pot, bring the
chicken stock to a boil. Add the tomatoes,
turn down the heat to low, and let simmer,
covered, while you continue.

2. In a large skillet, heat the butter and
oil together. Add the onion and sauté until
translucent, about 4 minutes. Add the chilies
(be prepared to cough a bit as the spicy odors
permeate the air), and after they have softened slightly, another 2 to 3 minutes, the
cumin and chili powder. Stir, then sprinkle
in the flour, blending it in with a spoon.
Gradually add the milk or half-and-half, stirring to smooth. Let cook a few moments until
thickened and free of all the raw flour taste.

3. Ladle 1 cup or so of the stock mixture into the thickened milk mixture and stir
to thin it a little. Pour the entire contents of
the skillet into the soup pot and let cook at
a bare simmer over very, very low heat, stirring often, about 15 minutes.

4. Very slowly stir in the grated Cheddar and crème fraîche or kefir cheese. Cook
5 minutes, stirring often. Add the chicken and
chopped cilantro. Taste and season with the
salt and pepper. If it's not spicy enough for
you, make the soup hotter with a judicious
application of Tabasco. Serve hot immediately, garnished with the additional cilantro
and crushed tortilla chips. (I like to make a
stripe of blue corn chip crumbles flanked by
a stripe of yellow. The rest of the chips go
in a bowl to the table, along with a bowl of
guacamole, natch.)

*Serves 4 to 6 as an entrée, with rice or bread
and a salad*

VARIATIONS:
**Wintertime Green Chili and Chicken
Soup with Crème Fraîche:** If fresh jalapeños and chili poblanos are not available,
or if fresh tomatoes are pale and flavorless,

you can still make this fine soup. To the simmering stock add half a 10-ounce can of Ro-Tel Diced Tomatoes and Green Chilies (usually kept with the canned tomatoes in the supermarket), thereby replacing both the tomatoes and jalapeño. In place of the chilies, add a 4-ounce can of diced green chilies to the cream sauce.

Elegant Green Chili Chicken Soup with Crème Fraîche: Follow either version of the soup, but make a green chili purée of reconstituted dried green chilies in your blender or food processor. Pipe a bit atop the soup. This is wonderful—pretty, delicious, and very Santa Fe.

LIGHTER CHICKEN SOUPS

*H*ere are a few less hearty chicken-based soups, more frequently used as starters. "Less hearty" does not necessarily mean less caloric; some of these soups are rich with cream, to be served in small cups. Some also have main-dish variations.

chicken broth, are sublime with cream, white wine, sherry, or brandy. These layers of compatible flavors make a rich, wonderful soup, perfect for a soigné occasion. Or try the main-dish variation which follows.

Fresh shiitake mushrooms are a born-again ingredient of New American Cooking. Long prized in the Orient, they are now being grown on small family farms all over the country, including here in the Ozarks (we get ours from Shinola Farms in Durham, Arkansas, and Persimmon Hill Farms in Blue Eye, Missouri). Delectable shiitakes are a high-ticket item, and are helping many such farms get back on their feet. What a transition—from corn, milo, and soybeans to shiitakes!

Wild morels, perhaps the most sought-after native American mushroom, come in the spring. Most years there are just a few, and, precious morsels that they are, we simply sauté them

Chicken Soup with Forest Mushrooms

he uncultivated earthy tastes of wild mushrooms and wild rice, partnered by ever-congenial in butter and garlic, and bar the door until the feast is finished. But every so often there's a bumper season for morels, as spring 1988 was. At such times, there's enough to share, and this soup becomes a must.

4 cups Chicken Stock 1 (page 19) or
    Golden or Browned Vegetable Stock
    (pages 28 and 32) or any well-flavored
    chicken stock
1 ounce dried porcini mushrooms
¼ to ½ pound fresh shiitake mushrooms,
    tough stems removed, caps and tender
    parts of stems diced, 1½ ounces dried
2 cups dry white wine
¾ cup wild rice, rinsed
2 tablespoons butter
2 tablespoons mild vegetable oil, such as
    corn or peanut
1 large onion, diced
¼ pound domestic white mushrooms,
    coarsely diced
¼ pound any other exotic seasonal edible
    mushrooms, such as morels, tree ears, or
    oyster mushrooms, cleaned, tough stems
    removed, caps sliced
¼ cup unbleached all-purpose flour
1 cup heavy (whipping) cream (or
    evaporated skim milk, if you must save
    calories and fat grams and/or watch
    cholesterol)
¼ teaspoon dried thyme
Several gratings of fresh nutmeg
Salt and lots of freshly ground white pepper
2 tablespoons dry sherry or brandy
1 teaspoon, approximately, Garlic Oil (page
    41; optional)
Minced fresh parsley or sprigs of fresh
    thyme, for garnish

1. In a soup pot, bring the chicken stock to a boil.

2. In a small bowl, put the dried porcini and the dried shiitakes, if using. Pour 1 cup of the boiling chicken stock over them to cover, weighing the mushrooms down with a plate so they remain submerged.

3. Add the white wine to the stock remaining in the pot and bring to a boil. Stir in the wild rice. Turn down the heat to medium-low and simmer, covered, until the rice is tender and split open, 45 minutes to 1 hour.

4. Meanwhile, in an 8- or 9-inch skillet, heat the butter and oil over medium heat. Add the onion and sauté until translucent, about 5 minutes. Add the fresh mushrooms of all types, including the fresh shiitakes, if using, and sauté, stirring often, until the mushrooms soften, are fragrant, and on the edge of browning, 5 to 10 minutes. Sprinkle the flour over the sauté mixture, and gradually add the cream, stirring and cooking until the flour is smoothed in, the cream thickens, and all delicious mushroom and onion bits are scraped up. Season with the thyme, nutmeg, and salt and pepper. When the wild rice is done, add this mushroom-cream mixture to the barely simmering stock.

5. Remove the reconstituted mushrooms from their broth. Wash them very well if they are at all dirty, cut them up fairly fine, and add them to the soup. Strain the mushroom soaking liquid through a paper coffee filter to remove any dirt or grit, and add it to the soup. Add the sherry or brandy. Let the soup simmer over the lowest possible heat about 20 minutes to blend the flavors. Taste, and if it's not quite there, sneak in a little garlic oil. Do not boil; stir often. Taste for seasoning. You got it? Oh! Divine! Garnish with the minced parsley or sprigs of thyme.

Serves 4 to 6 as a starter (smallish portions; this is quite rich)

VARIATIONS:

For an entrée version: Add 2 cups or so of cooked chicken. If you like, omit the rice and ladle the soup over cooked fettuccine noodles.

INNECDOTE

Back maybe eight years ago, in the pre-restaurant days when we served meals to inn guests only, I prepared dinner one night for newlyweds. It was served, as all meals were then, in the little tiny Farmhouse parlor/breakfast room. My friend Gina Meadows was serving, and I was in the kitchen. Because the kitchen opened right onto the parlor, I could hear every word the honeymoon couple was saying—or rather not *saying. The quiet was deafening. Through the starter, the soup, bread, salad, the entrée, not a word did they speak to each other, and only the most rudimentary, if polite, "Thank you" and "This is delicious" to Gina. The awkwardness was palpable.*

Gina, an aspiring actress rich in social skills, kept trying to make conversation and lighten the atmosphere. A timbre of manic cheerfulness rose in her voice each time she brought something: "And this is our pear-ginger marmalade, we made it ourselves from pears grown just up the road." When she came back to the kitchen, we'd exchange I-don't-know-what-can-you-do looks and shrugs, wordlessly, of course, since we were within earshot of them, too. Through dinner the intense silence continued.

Then, suddenly, as Gina leaned down to take away the entrée plate, the new bride broke it. She reached up suddenly, grabbed Gina's forearm, and without preface said, "I don't know what happened, we dated for eight years before we got married and we always had plenty to say to each other before!"

P.S. Two days later, the new bride—with a big smile—waved to me from the garden, "Oh by the way, everything is good now."

Turkey and Wild Rice Soup with Forest Mushrooms: The day after Thanksgiving is made brighter by this soup. Reserve and dice any leftover turkey. Make a good strong found stock from the carcass, oomphing it up if necessary by reducing it, or doing any of the other tricks described on page 22. Make the soup with this turkey stock, stirring in the cooked turkey just before serving.

Mark's Version: Mark, our co-chef one year, made this or any other mushroom soup without adding the brandy or sherry directly to the pot. Instead he drizzled a teaspoon or so into each serving. Nice.

Déjà Food: If you have even a tad of this soup, any version, left over, save it for the most delicious omelet filling you can imagine. Or thicken the soup with just a bit more flour, omit the rice, and add pieces of chicken. This makes a crêpe filling luscious beyond belief.

Cock-a-Leekie

he British Isles equivalent of French onion soup, this is a simple and delectable beginning to many kinds of meals. There's little to it but onions (these are the "leekies") and chicken stock (the "cock") so make sure your stock is the best.

The first time people eat this they are startled: what *is* that black thing on the bottom of the bowl? That, my dear, is a prune, and yes, it does belong there. Try this soup once and you'll become a convert.

6 to 8 pitted prunes
1 tablespoon butter
1 tablespoon mild vegetable oil, such as corn or peanut
1 large onion, finely diced
3 to 4 leeks, white part only, split open lengthwise, well washed, and thinly sliced
2 quarts Chicken Stock 1 (page 19) or any well-flavored chicken stock
Salt and freshly ground black pepper to taste
1 tablespoon Garlic Oil (page 41; optional)

1. The night before you plan to make the soup, put the prunes in a small bowl and pour boiling water to cover over them. Let them soak overnight.

2. Next day, in an 8- to 9-inch skillet, heat the butter and oil together over medium-low heat. Add the onion and leeks and slowly sauté until very limp and well browned, but not burnt. Take your time; 30 minutes or so is fine. Much of the flavor is given by the browning-to-the-point-of-near-caramelization of the onion and leeks.

3. In a soup pot, bring the chicken stock to a boil. Scoop out a ladleful, and pour it over the well-browned onions and leeks to deglaze the pan. Add the pan contents to the remainder of the stock. Turn down the heat to medium-low and let simmer, partially covered, 30 minutes. Taste for seasoning, adding salt and pepper. If your stock had a good solid flavor, the soup will be perfect as is, but if it's at all pallid, add the garlic oil,

stir, and taste again. Amazing what that garlic oil does, isn't it?

4. At serving time, drain the prunes. Place 1 prune in each bowl or cup, and ladle the cock-a-leekie over it. Serve very hot, immediately.

Serves 6 to 8 as a starter

Chicken Broth Supreme

A fabulous quickie, this is a light lunch or starter *par excellence*. We almost always serve it clear, as a very light soup choice when a dinner has an entrée or two with exceptionally rich sauces. But you could add a little cooked rice, noodles, or barley stirred in at the last. Or try a few of the tiny meatballs (page 60) or the cornmeal dumplings (pages 136 and 138), made tiny. Because of the tomato, the tomato juice, and the wine, the soup has a slightly acidic quality that is quite refreshing. Here is one of the few recipes for which we do not sauté the onion first, mirepoix-style. Also here, a most delicious use of the odds and ends that may be lurking around the bottom of the vegetable bin.

This was inspired by, and is close kin to, Wine Broth Supreme, from the intriguing *Blue Strawberry Cookbook* by James Haller.

1 medium onion, peeled and quartered
1 medium carrot, scrubbed and coarsely chopped
1 rib celery, coarsely chopped
1 ripe apple or ripe pear, unpeeled, cored, and cut up, or ⅓ cup unsweetened applesauce
1 tomato, or 2 teaspoons tomato paste
2 scallions, coarsely chopped
3 bay leaves
1 whole head garlic, papery skin left on, halved crosswise and cut coarsely into eighths
¾ cup good-quality natural-foods-store tomato juice
1 tablespoon honey
4 cups Chicken Stock 1 (page 19) or any well-flavored chicken stock (rich, delicious broth is really essential here)
3 cups medium-dry white wine, such as a Chablis
Minced fresh parsley, for garnish

1. In a food processor, place the onion, carrot, celery, apple or pear, tomato or tomato paste, scallions, bay leaves, and garlic. Pour in the tomato juice and pulse-chop 15 or 20 times to make a thick, chunky purée.

2. Place the purée in a soup pot, add the honey, stock, and wine, and bring to a boil. Turn down the heat to medium-low and let simmer briskly, uncovered, for 30 minutes. Strain and serve immediately.

Serves 5 to 6 as a starter

INN GOOD COMPANY: JOHN MITCHELL

John Mitchell, our headwaiter, has been with us since the restaurant's first night of operation. Although born in the Arkansas delta in the town of Marianna, John's pure Eureka. He's lived here about twenty years, runs an antique shop, restores old Jaguars, runs a small pickled garlic side-business, and is known for his bon mots *and a style of service that is warm, professional, but not fawning.*

The restaurant's very first night, we had a big table of doctors and state legislators and John was serving.

Turns out that one of the legislators was from Marianna.

Turns out some 15 years earlier John was in a tiny village in Mexico, on a garlic run, and ran out of money. His frantic family attempted to wire him some cash.

Turns out there are some places, as John says, "That even Western Union cannot reach. I waited."

While he waited he bartended in a cantina, and slept in his truck (with the garlic, of course). "It wasn't all bad," says John. "My Spanish improved, certainly."

By now his family was really frantic and convinced he was in jail. "I think my mother still thinks I was," says John. John's family called the Arkansas governor, senators, and congressmen to prevail on them to get money to him. It was the congressman from Marianna that finally sprang John.

And our very first night at the restaurant, here is the very same congressman who liberated John Mitchell from Mexico.

And here is John, crisp and totally presentable in his tuxedo. "How nice to see you again, sir. May I tell you about our specials?"

Chicken Soup Marengo

he inn's restaurant is open for one 7:00 seating seven nights a week, but by reservation only. If on a given night there are no reservations by six, we go home. Of course, during the season, we almost never get a night off. But in the off-season, especially when the weather's bad, there are some nights we close for lack of reservations. This is especially true as Eureka Springs is so hilly ice storms in particular can leave it impossible to get around for days at a time in some cases. So it was in December, 1990, when two weeks of ice led to scads of cancellations, and to Mark and Sandy (then co-chef and prep chef, respectively) being stranded at their homes outside of town.

But even if the hills are covered with ice, as long as we have even *one* reservation by 6:00, we're open for dinner an hour later, fire crackling cheerfully and with food every bit as "right there" as if we had a full dining room. Which happened five days into that uncharacteristic two weeks of ice, when we got a reservation which came in at *one minute before six.* Of course, since Sandy and Mark hadn't been there, and since there'd been no reservations for days, almost nothing was prepped. Ned and I, ever game for a challenge, flung ourselves madly into preparations. We reached John, our eternally loyal waiter, and he trudged/slid in from town.

But by the time our two dinner guests arrived (and, I have to say, any couple who manages to come out in that kind of weather is so committed to eating with you that they deserve the best), we had pulled off a very nice meal indeed for them. Their soup was this, invented-on-the-spot, seat-of-the-pants Chicken Soup Marengo, made from a little leftover sauce from our Chicken Marengo (originally reserved in the fridge for the chef to enjoy for lunch over rice), then thinned down with some good chicken broth.

It was wonderful, and has periodically appeared, in two versions, by intent instead of accident, on our menu ever since.

6 cups Chicken Stock 1 (page 19) or any
    well-flavored chicken stock
2 cups dry white wine
1 1/4 cups coarsely chopped fresh tomatoes,
    or canned whole tomatoes with their
    juice
1 tablespoon butter
1 tablespoon olive oil
1 medium onion, chopped
1 medium carrot, scrubbed and
    sliced
1/4 pound domestic white mushrooms,
    sliced
2 ribs celery, diced
2 tablespoons Garlic Oil (page 41)
1/4 cup unbleached all-purpose flour
2 tablespoons raisins
3 whole peppercorns
1 teaspoon dried basil
1 teaspoon dried thyme
1/2 teaspoon dried rosemary
2 bay leaves
Assorted chopped fresh herbs, for garnish:
    Italian parsley, celery leaves, basil

1. In a large soup pot, combine the chicken stock, white wine, and tomatoes. Bring to a boil, then turn down the heat to medium-low and let simmer, partially covered, while you continue.

2. In an 8- or 9-inch skillet, heat the butter and oil over medium heat. Add the onion and sauté until softened, about 5 minutes. Add the carrot, mushrooms, and celery and sauté, stirring, another 5 minutes. Lower

the heat and add the garlic oil. Stir about 30 seconds, add the flour, and cook for about 1 minute, stirring.

3. Ladle out 1 cup or so of the wine-stock mixture, and gradually whisk it into the skillet mixture. Cook, stirring, for 3 to 4 minutes. When smooth and thick, transfer the mixture to the soup pot. Add the raisins, peppercorns, basil, thyme, rosemary, and bay leaves. Let simmer, uncovered, over very low heat for about 1 hour, stirring every so often.

4. Cool slightly and strain out all the solids. You should have a very flavorful, slightly thickened soup. Taste for seasoning. Reheat and serve very hot, garnished with a sprinkle of the chopped fresh herbs.

Serves 6 to 8 as a starter

VARIATION:
Sandy's Entrée-Style Chicken Marengo Soup: Sandy prefers this soup chunky and full meal style. She doesn't strain out the vegetables, and after the soup has simmered adds ½ cup of black olives, sliced into rounds, and 1 to 2 cups chunked boned and skinned cooked chicken. Serves 4 to 6 as an entrée

Duck Soup with Sweet Potatoes

his is a fabulous duck soup that's perfect for fall—the combination of duck and sweet potatoes couldn't be more autumnal. The taste of the sweet potatoes is heightened by a touch of orange, which is indiscernible to the tongue, as is a tiny bit of tomato paste.

The meatiness of this soup depends on whether you use the carcass of an already roasted duck, or cook a duck solely for the purpose, or something in between. We usually opt for the something in between: cutting up a whole raw duck, roasting the breasts (with Arkansas pears, as a restaurant entrée), and making soup from the rest of the bird. Whatever you do, save the duck liver for the soup; it's essential. This soup is a celebration of rich, plush colors and taste: ladle it up fondly to those you love.

1 whole duck, or 1 duck carcass left
    over from a roasted duck with some
    meat still on it, or 1 whole duck,
    breasts removed (if using whole duck,
    reserve the liver)
2 quarts Chicken Stock 1 (page 19) or any
    well-flavored chicken stock
3 tablespoons sweet vermouth
1 tablespoon tomato paste
Grated zest and juice of 1 orange
1 teaspoon honey
BelleMystika seasoned salt to taste or a
    mixture of salt, a pinch of cayenne,
    and a fleck of dried dill and
    dried basil
Freshly ground white pepper
3 medium to large sweet potatoes, peeled
    and diced
1 tablespoon butter
2 tablespoons mild vegetable oil, such as
    corn or peanut
1 onion, chopped
2 ribs celery, chopped
3 tablespoons unbleached all-purpose
    flour

1. Make a stock using the duck or duck carcass and the chicken stock (see page 22). Bring the stock to a boil, then turn down the heat to medium-low and let simmer, gently, partially covered, until the duck meat is tender. If using a raw duck, this will take 1½ hours or so; if using a duck carcass, about 40 minutes.

2. Strain the stock. Remove the meat from the bones, discarding the bones (unless you want to use the reboil trick to make the stock stronger; see page 15), and the skin. Reserve the duck meat. Defat the stock, and measure it. You'll need about 2 quarts duck stock. If you're short, add water plus a Morga cube, vegetable stock, or additional chicken stock to make up the difference. If you have a little extra stock, boil it down to reduce it.

3. Bring the strained, defatted stock to a boil, and add the vermouth, tomato paste, orange zest and juice, honey, and seasonings. Taste. Turn down the heat to medium-low, and drop in the sweet potato pieces. Let simmer gently, partially covered, until the potatoes are tender but not falling apart, 15 to 20 minutes.

4. Meanwhile, in an 8- or 9-inch skillet heat the butter and oil over medium heat. Add the onion and sauté until softened, 5 or 6 minutes. Add the celery and sauté 1 or 2 minutes. Add the reserved duck liver (if using), mashing it into the vegetables with a fork. Cook for 1 or 2 minutes, stirring often, until the liver changes from red to gray-brown.

5. Sprinkle the flour over the vegetables and liver. Avoiding the sweet potatoes, ladle in 1 cup or so of the simmering stock, whisk until smooth, then add a little more stock. Cook, stirring, until the mixture is smooth (except for the vegetable and liver pieces, of course!) and thick. Pour the thickened liver-vegetable mixture into the soup.

Add the reserved pieces of duck meat. Let simmer a few minutes to blend flavors, and serve.

Serves 4 as an entrée, 6 as a starter

Déjà Food: Make a lot out of any leftovers of this scrumptious soup by thinning it down with good chicken stock and adding 1 cup of cooked wild rice.

LAST-OF-THE-CHRYSANTHEMUMS OCTOBER SOUP SUPPER FOR MARGARET VAN STAVERN

*Salade Automne:
Greens and purple onion with slivered apple, toasted walnuts, blue cheese and *Sesame-Raisin Vinaigrette*

*Duck Soup with Sweet Potatoes

*Felicity Turner's Slightly Fanatic Dream Whole-Grain Bread

Baked Apple with Custard Sauce and Molasses Crisps

Fine Fish Soups

FROM CREEK AND LAKE

lexibility is one of soup's most endearing qualities, but fish soups are flexible only to a point.

The cook at work on a wondrous creamy fish chowder, a saffron- or fennel-scented Provençale fish soup, or a garlicky rouille can be as playfully free-form with ingredients, seasonings, and the proportion of liquid to solid as when making any other potage, but he or she cannot be cavalier about time and temperature. Five or ten minutes here or there makes a big difference with fish. Cook fish too long or at too high a heat, and it will (depending on the cooking medium or fish type) toughen, disintegrate, become bitter or fishy in taste and smell. These limitations explain why most cookbooks have fewer fish soups than any other kind; they're more exacting than most other soups.

But if you pay attention to cooking time and temperature, you can make some truly great fish soups, with great adaptability of ingredients and flavors.

The exigencies of restaurant service—that food be top quality over several hours and able to be prepared ahead of time—means good things for you the home cook using this book. Because we've had to come up with ways to work around fish's only-for-a-moment perfection, you'll find most of our recipes have a much-easier-to-do-in-advance modus operandi, perfect for entertaining. This not only allows for the convenience of cooking ahead but also lessens the possibility of overcooking the fish. In this method the fish is poached in stock until barely cooked. The stock then serves as the base, or part of the base, for the soup, and the poached fish is added to each bowl or cup at the last minute. This way it's cooked to perfection, and everyone gets an equal amount of savory poached fish morsels. As long as the two components, the brothy part and the poached fish, are kept separate until serving, any leftovers will be as good, as fresh, as the original.

LANDLOCKED IN THE MOUNTAINS

Arkansas is one of only three Southern states that does not touch a coast, but our creeks, rivers, lakes, and (in the southeastern part of the state) bayous make us rich in a profusion of freshwater fish. Here at the inn, when it comes to fish, we adhere even more strictly than usual to our rule of "fresh and regional," working almost exclusively with local freshwater fish. That's what I've done in the fish recipes here, too, especially since freshwater fish, and especially soups made from them, are underrepresented in most cookbooks anyway.

Because our state's game and fish commission prohibits the sale of game fish, the fish soups at the inn, with rare exception, are made with local "farmed" trout or catfish. (Our local trout are "farmed" in cold water springs that more closely simulate their natural habitat and give them, many people feel, a somewhat wilder taste than most other cultivated trout.) Occasionally we break down and buy a flown-in fresh order of shrimp, lobster, crab, crawdad, or finned ocean fish, but, delicious though they are, the "fit" isn't quite right for us.

Though the inland crawdad and shrimp farming industry is in its infancy, it will surely be as successful as catfish and trout farming are now. These farmed creatures will undoubtedly lack somewhat the full flavor and texture of the wild, but they will make such delicacies accessible to those of us who are landlocked. More importantly, they will keep natural reserves from becoming depleted, which is what those cumbersome regulations are all about and why they're so necessary.

LITTLE FISH MAKE BIG SOUPS

If there were a way for us to legally serve other local fish, we would in a minute. Our local fresh fish are so good, and many are unknown to those without a freshwater fisherman in the family. Even those who know and love crappie, bream, black or white or striped bass, walleyed pike, bluegill, and the various sweet sunfishes think of them almost exclusively as "pan fish"—that is, small enough to fit comfortably in a skillet, preferably after being breaded in cornmeal and fried in butter, oil, or bacon fat over an open fire. They are mighty good that way, especially if just caught. But if you have more than one meal's worth or must wait until you get home to cook and eat your catch, you'll find they're every bit as good in soup, if quickly and discerningly cooked. If you have an off day at the stream and only catch a couple of fish, remember that with soup, as opposed to pan frying, you can still feed a multitude, and deliciously.

For home cooks, then, I've included some notes on and recipes featuring these game fish. Although the game fish and farmed fish flavors are distinct, most are interchangeable in recipes.

In addition to the well-loved pan fish, we have numerous other interesting-to-delectable lake and river fish (which, again, we are forbidden to buy) which are, for no good reason, despised. Carp and freshwater eels are among those outcasts known disparagingly as "trash fish." They've been eaten for centuries the world over, including right here in America, by our own forefathers and people today. I've tried to give them their due.

Fish, like everything else, go in and out of fashion. Twenty years ago, who on either American coast outside of fish dealers ate monkfish or tilefish or skate? Now all are common to fish cognoscenti. Food prejudices like this are as hard to break as they are inexplicable. *Madame Prunier's Fish Cook Book,* written in 1938 and considered the subject's classic, contains no fewer than sixteen ways of preparing freshwater eel! Only to a few does it even occur to gather river mussels; yet they are not only edible but "tol'able good eating" as one old-timer told me, and there for the taking.

Freshwater Fish Soup Provençale

This is the fish soup we serve most often at the restaurant, almost always making it with trout or a combination of trout and catfish. Guests comment on the freshness and unusual flavors all the time. Substantial, filling but not hearty, this soup proves that the good south of France flavors of herbs, tomatoes, and garlic do as well in freshwater fish soups as in bouillabaisse and other seaside soups. Best of all, it's one of those rare low-calorie, low-cholesterol dishes that is honestly delicious.

Because the danger of overcooking the fish in a fish soup is even greater in a restaurant kitchen than at home, I've developed an easy, foolproof method that assures the fish will be done perfectly every time. The whole fish is poached in a wine-stock mixture, then picked from the bones and set aside. The fish stock is combined with a luscious tomato sauce scented with a delectable, indefinable bit of orange zest. When ready to serve, you simply heat this mixture, and ladle it over some cooked rice and the reserved poached fish pieces. *Voilà!*

STOCK AND FISH:
4 cups Fish Stock (page 25) or Chicken Stock 1 (page 19) or any well-flavored chicken stock or bottled clam juice
1½ cups dry white wine
Juice of 1 lemon
3 cloves
3 black peppercorns
3 allspice berries
1 bay leaf
1 teaspoon fennel seeds
Skin of 1 large onion
½ teaspoon salt
⅛ teaspoon cayenne pepper
¼ teaspoon dried dill
2 to 2½ pounds whole bass, catfish, or trout, cleaned and cut into pieces that will fit into a 9- or 10-inch skillet

TOMATO SAUCE:
¼ cup olive oil
1 large onion, finely chopped
2 medium carrots, scrubbed and finely chopped
2 ribs celery with leaves, finely chopped
5 ripe garden tomatoes (peeled first if you find having bits of skin in the finished soup offensive) or 2 cups canned plum tomatoes, drained and coarsely chopped
Grated zest of ¼ orange
3 cloves garlic, peeled
4 to 5 large fresh basil leaves
Tiny pinch of cayenne pepper
1 teaspoon honey or sugar
1 tablespoon tomato paste
1 cup dry white wine
Salt and freshly ground black pepper to taste

FOR SERVING:
2½ cups cooked rice
Finely chopped fresh Italian (flat-leaf) parsley and/or fresh basil leaves, for garnish

1. In a large skillet, combine all the ingredients in the first list except the fish and bring to a boil. Add the fish, turn the heat down to low, and barely simmer, covered. Poach the fish until it is firm and done, 6 to 8 minutes unless the fish pieces are thicker than ¾ to 1 inch (in which case, cooking will take a little longer; keep checking).

2. Pour the stock and fish into a colander set over a bowl; reserve both stock and fish. Discard the whole spices and the onion skin. When the fish is cool enough to handle, skin the pieces and pull out the bones. Discard the skin, head, tail, and bones; reserve the flesh.

3. Prepare the tomato sauce: In a large skillet, heat the oil over medium heat. Add the onion and sauté until slightly softened, about 3 minutes. Add the carrots and celery and sauté another 3 minutes. Put the tomatoes, orange zest, garlic, basil, cayenne, honey, and tomato paste in a food processor and process until the leaves are fairly chopped and the tomatoes are a chunky purée. Add this mixture, plus the wine, to the sautéed vegetables. Cook, stirring often, over medium-high heat for 10 minutes.

4. Fifteen to 20 minutes before serving, combine the broth and tomato sauce and simmer gently for 5 to 10 minutes. Taste; correct the seasoning with salt and pepper. Meanwhile, have your soup bowls or cups ready, heated, if possible. In each bowl place a serving of the rice, and a generous amount of the poached fish pieces. Ladle the piping hot soup over the rice and fish (if the soup is hot enough, you won't have to worry about reheating the fish or rice). Garnish with the chopped parsley or basil and serve at once.

Serves 6 to 8 as an entrée or 10 to 12 as a starter

FRIDAY NIGHT SUPPER WHEN THE LEAVES CHANGE

*Freshwater Fish Soup Provençale

*Skillet-Sizzled Buttermilk Corn Bread and *Buttermilk Biscuits

Watermelon Jelly and Peach Preserves

*The Salad

Persimmon Pudding with Whipped Cream

Menu note: Wild persimmons grow along every fence-row in the Ozarks, and the trees are heavy with the small, sweet, purple-orange globes through well after first frost. If you have access only to the larger, bright orange cultivated Japanese persimmons, you will have to wait until around Christmastime to have your pudding.

Matelote

adame Prunier, the French fish authority, says, "A matelote of river fish is a charming dish." Enriched fish stock is thickened and then refined with flamed brandy. The fish chunks poach in this heady brew. Although this freshwater fish stew isn't for the novice cook, it's not all that time consuming.

Pike, perch, bream, sunfish, grass carp, white or black crappie, eel, or—with a bit more preparation trouble but delicious results, common carp—make the soup with any of these or, as is more usual, a combination of several.

3 pounds whole freshwater fish
6 cups Golden Vegetable Stock (page 28)
*   or Chicken Stock 1 (page 19) or any*
*   well-flavored chicken stock or bottled*
*   clam juice*
2 cups dry white wine
6 black peppercorns
3 whole cloves
1 bay leaf
Pinch of dried rosemary
Salt and freshly ground black pepper to
*   taste*
4 tablespoons (½ stick) butter
2 onions, finely chopped
8 ounces domestic white mushrooms,
*   stems finely chopped, caps halved*
*   and sliced*
3 tablespoons unbleached all-purpose flour
1 tablespoon Garlic Oil (page 41; optional)
⅓ cup brandy
Finely minced fresh parsley, for garnish
1 hard-cooked egg, minced, for garnish

1. Fillet and skin the fish (or have your fishmonger do it). Cut the fillets into large pieces, and refrigerate. Clean the fish heads, tails, and frames (page 26, step 1) and place them in a heavy soup pot. Add the stock, wine, peppercorns, cloves, bay leaf, and rosemary. Bring quickly to a boil, then turn down the heat to medium-low and let simmer, uncovered, 25 to 30 minutes, pushing down on the fish bones with a wooden spoon several times. Strain the stock and discard all the solids. Season with salt and plenty of pepper. Pour the stock into a clean soup pot and heat until hot.

2. In a medium-size skillet, melt the butter over medium heat. Add the onions and sauté until beginning to soften, about 3 minutes, or until translucent. Add the mushrooms and sauté another 3 minutes. Sprinkle with the flour and stir in. Gradually add 1 cup of the hot stock, stirring to smooth any lumps, then stir in 1 more cup of the stock. Cook 3 minutes, or until thickened. Transfer the thickened mixture to the remaining stock in the soup pot. Stir until blended. Bring to a boil, then immediately turn down the heat so that the liquid simmers.

3. Add the fish fillets and the garlic oil to the soup. In a small saucepan, warm the brandy over medium heat. Remove the brandy from the heat and ignite it. Wait until the flames subside, 1 minute or less. Pour the brandy over the fish. Cover the pot and simmer until the fish is just done, 10 to 15 minutes. Ladle the soup into bowls and garnish with the minced parsley and egg.

Serves 4 or 5 as an entrée or 6 to 8 as a starter

VARIATIONS:
Meurette: Many people think that because common carp is relatively assertive in flavor, it does even better in a *meurette,* the red

wine version of a matelote. Simply substitute dry red wine for the white.

Matelote Normande: Substitute hard cider for the wine and Calvados for the brandy. Omit the mushrooms, and sauté 1 celery rib, 1 carrot, 1 peeled and cored apple, all diced, with the onion. Matelote Normande is especially wonderful with an assortment of any of the on-the-large-side sweet pan fish: bright sunfish such as pumpkin seed, bluegill, and so on. But it's also great with common carp, since they have an affinity for the sweetness in the preparation.

For a less fussy do-ahead preparation: Poach the whole fish in the stock until just done (for the method, see Freshwater Fish Soup Provençale, page 82). Remove the fish from the stock and let cool. Discard the head and tail, then skin and bone the fish, making sure to remove all the bones. Separate the meat into large chunks. Proceed as directed above and ladle the hot soup over the fish pieces.

Pine Bark Stew

 n the Carolinas and Georgia, where this spicy fish stew is best known," writes John Egerton, "there are almost as many explanations for the name as there are ways to make it." Egerton lists four: that the soup was originally seasoned with small, tender pine shoots; that the stew's color is that of pine bark; that pine was the dominant wood used in the stew's cooking fires; and that "early backwoodsmen who got the dish from the Indians made it thick enough to be served on slabs of pine bark." However it got named, it's a good, hearty soup-stew of fish, potatoes, tomatoes, and herbs—the simple American cousin to the preceding Provençale soup. Here's my version.

3 pounds whole freshwater fish, such as bass, catfish, trout, bream, or perch, or a combination, cleaned

4 to 6 cups Fish Stock to be made with the heads, tails, and frames of the fish (see step 1)

2 to 4 tablespoons corn oil

1 large onion, finely chopped

1 rib celery with leaves, finely chopped

3 or 4 fist-sized potatoes, scrubbed and sliced

3 or 4 large ripe tomatoes, chopped (peeled first if you find having bits of skin in the finished soup offensive), or 2 cups canned whole plum tomatoes, chopped

1 tablespoon Worcestershire sauce or Pickapeppa sauce (or similar savory sauce)

Pinch each of dried basil, thyme, oregano, and celery seeds

Cayenne pepper to taste (tiny fleck to ½ teaspoon)

Salt and freshly ground black pepper to taste

1 tablespoon Garlic Oil (page 41; optional)

1. Fillet and skin the fish (or have your fishmonger do it). Cut the fillets into large pieces, and refrigerate. Clean the fish heads, tails, and frames and use them to make the stock (page 25).

ABOUT TROUT

❦*Trout is one of our most delicious and sought-after fish. Rainbow trout (Salmo gairdnerii) is a native of the Pacific Coast and is the trout that is farmed in America. Indeed, rainbows have been stocked successfully all over the world. They like clear cold water, between 50 and 60° F, get unhappy at around 70° F, and cannot live in water warmer than 80° F. Their white to pale pink-orange flesh is slightly fatty, that of the farmed fish more so than that of the wild, and has a sweet, mild, unfishy flavor. The fish's texture is moist and slightly gelatinous. Some say the wild trout is far more flavorful than the farmed; others contend there's a drop in flavor only if the trout are raised in too-warm water. Related trout which can be used interchangeably with the rainbows are brown (harder to catch), cutthroat, lake, and brook trout.*❦

2. In a 9- or 10-inch skillet, heat the oil over medium heat. Add the onion and sauté until translucent, about 3 minutes. Add the celery and sauté a few minutes more. Add the potatoes and toss them until coated with the oil and barely beginning to cook, about 5 minutes.

3. Pour the fish stock over the vegetables and add the remaining ingredients except the garlic oil. Bring to a boil, then turn down the heat so that the liquid simmers. Add the filleted fish, cover the pan, and barely simmer until the fish is just done, 10 to 15 minutes. Taste, and adjust the seasonings, stirring in the garlic oil if using. Serve at once.

Serves 4 to 6 as an entrée or 6 to 8 as a starter

VARIATIONS:

Fry 6 slices of bacon until crisp. Drain on paper towels and coarsely crumble. Substitute 2 tablespoons of the bacon fat for the corn oil. Just before serving the soup, sprinkle it with the bacon.

For a less fussy do-ahead preparation, poach the whole fish in chicken, vegetable, or fish stock or bottled clam juice, until just done. Remove the fish from the stock and let it cool. Discard the heads and tails, then skin and bone the fish, making sure to remove all the bones. Separate the meat into large chunks and add them to the soup at the last moment.

Native American-Style Pine Bark Stew: Use indigenous North American vegetables for this variation—green pepper instead of the celery, 1½ to 2 cups corn kernels instead of, or replacing part of, the potatoes, and 2 cups or so of peeled butternut squash cut into small dice. Add the corn and squash to the soup with the fillets. The sweetness of the squash is a pleasant note indeed.

Fishysoisse

hat do you call a potato- and cream-based soup, heightened with leeks and fish stock, buzzed to smoothness in the food processor, and then enlivened with dreamy chunks of just-poached fish? *Fishysoisse,* of course! We serve this soup hot unlike vichysoisse, the conceptual starting point of this creamily comforting potage.

4 cups Fish Stock (page 25) or bottled clam
   juice
2 pounds skinned freshwater fish fillets
   (trout is nice here), cut into large pieces
2 to 3 tablespoons butter
2 large leeks, white part and 1 inch green,
   split open lengthwise, well rinsed, and
   thinly sliced
1 medium onion, finely chopped
1 medium carrot, scrubbed or peeled and
   sliced
4 or 5 medium potatoes, peeled and sliced
3 cloves garlic, peeled and put through a
   garlic press
1 teaspoon honey
1 cup heavy (whipping) cream
1½ cups milk or half-and-half
Salt and freshly ground white pepper to
   taste
Finely minced fresh chives or scallions, for
   garnish

1. In a medium-size skillet, heat the fish stock to boiling, then turn down the heat so that the liquid barely simmers. Add the fish fillets, cover, and let simmer until the fish is just done, no longer than 5 minutes. Remove the fish, strain, and reserve the stock.

2. In a medium-size heavy skillet, melt the butter over medium heat. Add the leeks and onion and sauté until translucent, about 4 minutes. Add the carrot and sauté 1 minute, then add the potatoes, fish stock, garlic, and honey. Simmer, uncovered, until the potatoes are quite tender. Let cool slightly, then transfer the mixture to a food processor. Process the soup until smooth. If you want an extra velvety texture, strain after puréeing.

3. Just before serving, heat the soup. Combine the cream and milk in a separate saucepan, heat, and stir this mixture into the soup. Season with salt and pepper, add the fish, and heat through. Garnish with the chives.

Serves 4 to 6 as an entrée or 6 to 8 as a starter

VARIATION:
For a low-calorie, low-cholesterol version, spray a skillet with Pam, and use 1 tablespoon of any mild vegetable oil to sauté the leeks and onion. Substitute evaporated skim milk for the cream and milk, or use low-fat milk thickened with 1 tablespoon cornstarch.

White River Chowder

any fish chowders are made with either a cream or tomato base. This savory potage, inspired by Louis P. De Gouy's Hudson

River Chowder (in *The Gold Cookbook,* 1947), has both, along with a pleasing blend of seasonings and a heavenly enrichment of cream and egg yolks. *White River Chowder* is excellent with striped bass, eel, walleyed pike, catfish, trout, or any combination of these.

2 to 2½ pounds whole freshwater fish (see above for suggestions)
3 cups Fish Stock, to be made with the heads, tails, and frames of the fish (see step 1)
¼ cup corn oil
1 large onion, finely chopped
1 medium carrot, scrubbed and diced
1 rib celery with leaves, very thinly sliced
1 green bell pepper, stemmed, seeded, and diced
1 red bell pepper, stemmed, seeded, and diced
2 large potatoes, peeled and diced
2 tablespoons all-purpose flour
2 cups dry white wine
2 tomatoes, chopped (peeled and seeded if you find having skin and seeds in the finished soup offensive)
1 bay leaf
2 tablespoons chopped fresh parsley
1 tablespoon chopped fresh basil leaves or 1 teaspoon dried
2 teaspoons fresh thyme leaves (minced if large-leafed) or ½ teaspoon dried
2 fresh sage leaves, finely chopped, or ½ teaspoon dried
1 sprig fresh marjoram, stemmed and finely chopped, or ½ teaspoon dried
Several gratings of nutmeg
Small pinch of ground allspice
Several grindings of black pepper
1 cup heavy (whipping) cream
2 large egg yolks
Minced fresh parsley, for garnish

SUNDAY SUPPER BACK HOME AFTER A FISHING WEEKEND

*White River Chowder

*Frannie's Fast, Fabulous Buttermilk Bread

Sliced Garden Tomatoes with Basil, Chives, and Freshly Cracked Pepper

Sliced Garden Cucumbers

Apple Crisp*

1. Fillet and skin the fish (or have your fishmonger do it). Cut the fillets into large pieces, and refrigerate. Clean the fish heads, tails, and frames and use them to make the stock (page 25).

2. In a large skillet, heat the oil over medium heat. Add the onion and sauté until softened, about 6 minutes. Add the carrot, celery, and bell peppers and sauté, tossing them in the hot oil until limp. Stir in the potatoes and sauté 1 minute or so. Sprinkle with the flour and stir in. Gradually add the wine, stirring to smooth any lumps. Transfer the thickened mixture to a soup pot, then stir in the tomatoes, herbs, and spices. Simmer, covered, until the flavors are blended and the potatoes are tender, 20 to 30 minutes.

3. Add the fish stock and fish pieces to the vegetable mixture, turn the heat down to very low, and let barely simmer, covered, 15 minutes.

4. Meanwhile, in a small saucepan, heat the cream until hot. Add a little hot cream to the yolks, stir, then whisk the egg-yolk mixture back into the hot cream. Whisk 1 cup of the chowder into the cream, stir, then whisk this into the remaining chowder. Heat through, stirring well and taking care not to let the chowder boil. Serve hot, garnished with the parsley.

Serves 4 as an entrée or 6 as a starter

VARIATION:
For a low-calorie, low-cholesterol version, substitute low-fat milk thickened with 2 tablespoons cornstarch, or evaporated skim milk alone, for the cream and egg yolks. Not as rich and flavorful, but mighty good.

Mussel Chowder Shelburne-Shoalwater

rom fellow Uncle Ben's Best Inn of the Year (see page 154) winner, The Shelburne Inn, in the state of Washington. Located in a town named Seaview and featuring a restaurant called The Shoalwater, you'd expect the menu to include soups rich in shellfish—and you'd be right. We include here the succulent mussel chowder conceived by innkeeper David Campiche and served at The Shoalwater by restaurateurs Tony and Ann Kischner and their chef, Cheri Walker. (Another Shelburne-Shoalwater recipe, Cioppino, is featured on page 94.)

Thick with mussels, rich with cream, this soup is given delicious intrigue by the addition of both tomato and curry. The Kischners note, "Be sure to taste and correct the seasoning. Mussels vary greatly in saltiness."

1 cup dry white wine
2 ribs celery, chopped
2 medium onions, chopped
5 pounds live mussels in the shell,
 preferably Penn Cove or other Northwest mussels, cleaned (page 92) and bearded if necessary
2 medium potatoes, peeled and cut into
 ½-inch dice
2 tablespoons butter
3½ cups tomato sauce
2 cups heavy (whipping) cream
1 tablespoon chopped fresh basil leaves or
 1½ teaspoons dried
2 teaspoons mild curry powder
Salt and freshly ground black pepper to taste

1. Place the white wine, half the celery, half the onions, and all the mussels in a large stockpot. Simmer gently until the mussels open, 6 to 7 minutes. Remove the mussels to a colander, discarding any that haven't opened. Strain the liquid through cheesecloth or a very fine strainer as it may be sandy. Set aside the liquid. Remove the mussels from their shells when they are cool enough to handle. Discard any stray pieces of beard you find inside the shells.

2. Meanwhile, bring to a boil a small pot of water. Add the potatoes, parboil for about 5 minutes, then drain well.

3. Melt the butter in a large (4- or 5-quart) saucepan. In it, sauté the remaining celery and onions until the onions are translucent, about 6 minutes. Add the potatoes, and toss to coat them with the butter.

4. To the vegetable mixture, add the tomato sauce, cream, and reserved mussel liquid. Season with the basil, curry powder, salt, and pepper. Let simmer over low-medium heat, stirring frequently, about 30 minutes.

5. Add the reserved mussel meat and serve.

Serves 3 to 4 as an entrée

Moules à la Marinière

he classic way with mussels is French, simple as it is sublime, and stewlike in its proportion of liquid to solid. The savory liquid is not thickened, however. Please note that when steaming mussels, you start them in *cold or room temperature liquid* which you gradually bring to a bare boil over medium heat. This way, the steam develops gradually and opens the shells. Liquid that is quickly brought to a hard boil may clamp those shells shut.

3 pounds live mussels in the shell, cleaned (page 92) and bearded if necessary
2 cups good-quality dry white wine (Pinot Blanc, Chardonnay, or Sauvignon Blanc are all fine choices)
1 medium carrot, scrubbed and chopped
1 medium onion, chopped
1 bay leaf
1 sprig fresh thyme leaves (minced if large-leafed) or 1 teaspoon dried
3 cloves garlic, peeled and put through a garlic press
2 tablespoons butter
Juice from ¼ to 1 whole lemon
Salt and freshly ground black pepper to taste

1. In a large soup pot, combine the mussels, ½ cup of the wine, the carrot, onion, bay leaf, and thyme. Bring to a simmer and cook gently, covered, until the mussels open, 6 to 8 minutes. Discard any mussels that have not opened. Remove the mussels to a warm platter and keep warm. Strain the liquid through cheesecloth or a very fine strainer as it may be sandy. Return just the liquid to the rinsed-out soup pot. Add the remaining wine to the pot and boil, covered, several minutes. Meanwhile, remove the top shell from each mussel.

2. Stir in the garlic and butter. Taste and season with lemon juice, salt, and pepper. Divide the mussels among wide soup bowls, then ladle the liquid into the bowls. Diners spoon out the mussel from each shell, scooping up some of the fine winey broth as well; some say you should use a mussel shell for a spoon. Of course you will want to serve this with the best crusty French bread you can buy or make (see page 328).

Serves 2 to 4 as an entrée or 4 to 6 as a starter

Mussel Soup Dublin

his soup, like most Ozark natives, is of Scots-Irish origin. It's excellent on a chilly night. The cider adds a pleasant, subtle note that tastes right from the first soothing, swooningly good bite, especially with the mellowing touch of whiskey. Remember Molly Malone who lived "in Dublin's fair city, where girls are so pretty, crying 'Cockles and Mussels, alive, alive-o' "? The mussels must be alive, alive-o, to make this or any other mussel soup. (Cockles, by the way, are members of the clam clan.)

3 pounds live mussels in the shell, cleaned
   (page 92) and bearded if necessary
4 cups unsweetened cider, flat or sparkling
   (such as Martinelli), or dry hard cider if
   you can get one that is high quality
¼ cup Irish whiskey
2 sprigs fresh parsley
2 tablespoons butter
1 medium onion, chopped
1 medium carrot, scrubbed or peeled and
   chopped
1 rib celery with leaves, chopped
1 red bell pepper, stemmed, seeded, and
   diced (optional)
¼ cup unbleached all-purpose flour
4½ cups milk, heated
Grating of fresh nutmeg
Salt and freshly ground white pepper to
   taste
½ cup heavy (whipping) cream (see
   Note)

1. In a large pot, combine the mussels, 2 cups of the cider, the whiskey, and parsley. Simmer gently, covered, until the mussels open, 6 to 8 minutes. Discard any mussels that have not opened. Remove the mussels to a colander, reserving the cooking liquid. Strain it through cheesecloth or a very fine strainer as it may be sandy. Remove the mussels from their shells when they are cool enough to handle.

2. In a large skillet, heat the butter over medium heat. Add the onion and sauté until softened, about 4 minutes. Add the carrot, celery, and bell pepper and sauté until softened, 2 minutes more. Sprinkle the flour over the vegetables and stir it in, cooking for a minute or so. Gradually whisk in the hot milk and season with the nutmeg, and salt and pepper. Simmer, stirring frequently, over very low heat about 10 minutes, then stir in the remaining 2 cups cider and the mussel cooking liquid. Heat through gently. At this point you may strain the soup or leave it chunky (I prefer the latter).

3. Add the mussels and cream to the soup. Heat through slowly and serve very hot.

Serves 6 as an entrée or 8 as a starter

Note: You may substitute milk thickened with cornstarch or evaporated skim milk for the cream or simply omit it. As always, the cream does make the soup more delicious, but it's also good without.

OF MUD, MUSSELS, AND MONKEY FACES

🍎 Ocean mussels are among the most delicious of shellfish. In Europe they have been farmed seaside for over 300 years, and they play a starring role in many soups, especially in France. In America mussels are also farmed along the coast of Maine and Rhode Island.

But did you know there are also edible mussels in many of America's rivers? All of our many varieties of river mussel are edible. They have picturesque vernacular names—pistol grip, maple leaf, grandmaw, pig toe, monkey face—which usually have to do with the distinctive look of the variety's shell (but grandmaw?). Both river and ocean mussels were prized by many Americans—Native Americans, Pilgrims, and waves of early settlers.

My friend Billy Jo Tatum is a wild-foods authority and forager, as well as the author of several cookbooks. She has eaten river and ocean mussels and delights in both. The two taste much the same, she says, although river mussels sometimes have a faint muddiness in flavor. She finds this not disagreeable but rather part of their characteristic flavor. The muddiness can be removed, however, through the cleaning process described at right.

When BJ was a child, she and her family would float the Black, Mulberry, and Arkansas Rivers regularly in a john-boat, a long, flatbottomed boat used for shallow navigating. They would bring a net and, when they saw mussels, simply throw the net out and dredge the bottom, bringing up mussels by the score. As an adult, she did the same thing with her own children in a canoe on the White River. These days, of course, you need to be sure the river you dredge is relatively clean. Submerged mussels, whether in salt or fresh water, are tastiest, for they've been feeding most recently. (Mussels haven't been feeding recently when they're found along rocky banks or only half submerged.)

As with all seafood it's best to eat mussels the same day you bring them home, but they can be stored in the refrigerator (in a plastic bag or on a tray with a damp cloth over them) up to 2 days. Rinse them quickly before refrigerating them, but don't clean them thoroughly until right before you intend to cook them.

CLEANING MUSSELS: To clean mussels, first discard any that are exceptionally heavy—they are probably filled with mud. Next pour an amount of cold water, measured in quarts, into a large bowl, and add 1½ teaspoons salt for every quart. Swish the mussels around in the water and let them sit a few minutes. Remove the mussels and pour away the water. If there's any grit, mud, or sand in the bottom of the bowl, repeat with clean salted water. Give the mussels one last wash with more water and salt if grit is

still visible in the bowl. Drain.

Next, feed the mussels. Mix ¼ cup flour with 4½ quarts cold water and pour this into the clean mussel bowl. Add the mussels and let them sit for 30 minutes. They will eat the flour and disgorge the last of their mud or sand.

After the de-mudding and feeding, scrub the shells well with a plastic scouring pad. Ocean mussels have tiny tough threads with an almost Brillo-like consistency, called "byssus," but commonly known as beards, by which they attach themselves to rocks and piers. Leave the beards on until ready to cook the mussels, then remove. River mussels are beardless.

Before cooking the mussels, check to make sure that all the shells are closed, or that they close easily if you tap the shell. Discard any that do not. And after cooking and shucking the mussels, check for any stray pieces of beard that may have found their way inside the mussel. Remove and discard before going any further with the recipe.

On the average, 1 quart (commercial) mussels equals about 25 mussels equals 1½ pounds equals 1 cup shelled mussel meats. 🌿

Lyntha's Friend's Great Cioppino

ou might wonder how a luscious cioppino—the famous Italian-American seafood stew created by Genoan fishermen settling in the San Francisco area—found its way to Norman, Oklahoma, and from there to Eureka Springs, Arkansas. Easy—through Lyntha Wesner, a devoted home cook who, with two close friends, cooked her way through Julia Child over a four-year period. Her friends eventually left Oklahoma, one moving to San Diego, and the other to just outside Princeton, but they stayed in touch, and kept cooking. Their correspondence often included recipes, like this one, from Lyntha's San Diego friend.

When the Wesners stayed at Dairy Hollow in May of '90, our Freshwater Fish Soup Provençale happened to be on the menu. "I've got this cioppino recipe I've *got* to send you," Lyntha told me. When she did, she noted, "It doesn't quite fit in with the philosophy of 'Nouveau'Zarks,' being too dependent on ingredients from an ocean close by. But it remains a great recipe and you can take it along the next time you visit relatives in New York." It is! I did!

The herbs really must be fresh, and so must the seafood and fish. Strip the herb leaves from the stem and chop finely before measuring. Don't be put off by the long list of ingredients; preparation is incredibly simple.

¼ cup finely chopped fresh marjoram

¼ cup finely chopped fresh basil leaves

2 tablespoons finely chopped fresh rosemary

2 tablespoons finely chopped fresh sage

2 tablespoons finely chopped fresh thyme

½ cup finely chopped fresh parsley

4 to 6 cloves garlic, peeled and put through a garlic press

4 red bell peppers, stemmed, seeded, and finely chopped

4 cups well washed, coarsely chopped Swiss chard

40 fresh cockles or any very small clams

2 large cooked crabs, such as Dungeness, cracked

2 pounds fresh shrimp

2 pounds firm-fleshed white fish fillets, such as red snapper or sea bass

2 cans (28 ounces each) plum tomatoes, coarsely chopped

1 can (6 ounces) tomato paste

¾ cup olive oil

2 tablespoons salt, or to taste

2 teaspoons freshly cracked black pepper, or to taste

1 cup dry white wine

1. In a bowl, combine the herbs, garlic, peppers, and chard, tossing all together. Arrange the clams in the bottom of a heavy 8-quart soup pot with a tightly fitting lid. Sprinkle the clams with one-third of the herb mixture. Next, layer in the cracked crab, and sprinkle with another third of the herb mixture. Layer the shrimp on next, and sprinkle with the last of the herbs. Arrange the fish on top.

2. In another bowl, combine the tomatoes, tomato paste, olive oil, and salt and pepper. Pour the tomato mixture into the seafood pot. Bring to a simmer, cover, turn down the heat slightly, and let simmer 30 minutes. Uncover, pour in the wine, and sim-

mer 10 minutes longer. Serve immediately, preceded by a peppery, garlicky salad with some bitter Italian greens, and accompanied by the best sourdough bread you can put your hands on.

Serves 8 to 10 as an entrée

Cioppino Shelburne-Shoalwater

 his wonderfully flavorful, aromatic cioppino from the Shelburne Inn's Shoalwater Restaurant in Seaview, Washington, is quite different from the preceding one. Though some of the ingredients are identical, others are very different and the preparation is entirely distinct. Instead of the unusual layering technique Lyntha's friend's cioppino employs, this version calls for first making a lusty herb-infused tomato sauce, drenched with red (not white) wine, then combining it with an assortment of lightly sautéed seafood and fish.

The sixteen-room Shelburne, furnished in antiques, was founded in 1896, making it the oldest continuously-running hotel in the state of Washington. The gracious old Victorian was given new life in 1977 when David Campiche and his wife Laurie Anderson purchased it. The glorious Art Nouveau stained-glass windows that now front the building with its pub are real showstoppers. They were imported from Morcambe, England, by David and Laurie.

I met this congenial innkeeping couple at the 1990 Uncle Ben's Best Inn of the Year ceremony, when their inn and ours were winners, and can't wait to visit them, especially after perusing their luscious *Shelburne Breakfasts,* a seasonal and regionally oriented cookbook with recipes that would start anybody's day off right. In it I learned that David prepares his own caviar! Now that's impressive. He and Laurie do the breakfasts, their friends Tony and Ann Kischner run the restaurant. The Kischners, with their chef, Cheri Walker, have recently published a cookbook called *The Shoalwater's Finest Dinners,* which features recipes from the monthly wine-tasting dinners they do. According to chef Cheri, Northwest Cioppino is one of the restaurant's most requested recipes.

Do give the Shelburne a call at (206) 642-2442, if you're heading to the Northwest, or if you want the book ($22.50 postage included) mail-ordered.

½ cup olive oil
2 medium onions, chopped
4 cloves garlic, peeled and put through a garlic press
12 sprigs fresh parsley, minced
6 cups peeled, seeded, and chopped fresh plum tomatoes (substitute canned tomatoes in the winter)
3½ cups tomato sauce
2 cups burgundy wine
2 cups water
¼ cup red wine vinegar
1½ teaspoons dried basil
1½ teaspoons dried rosemary
1½ teaspoons dried marjoram
1½ teaspoons dried oregano
1½ cups Fish Stock (page 25) or bottled clam juice
Salt and freshly ground black pepper to taste
¼ cup clarified butter (page 39)
24 steamer clams, cleaned
24 large scallops (about ¾ pound)
24 medium shrimp (about 1 pound), peeled and deveined
1½ pounds fresh fish fillets, carefully checked over for bones and cut into 1-inch cubes (a firm meaty variety, or a combination of same, is best; Cheri suggests halibut, sturgeon, or cod)
8 to 16 slices toasted Garlic Bread Croûtes (optional; recipe follows)

1. In a large (6-quart) stockpot, heat the olive oil over medium heat. Add the onions and sauté until translucent, about 6 minutes. Add the garlic and parsley, and cook 1 minute more.

2. Add the tomatoes, tomato sauce, wine, water, vinegar, herbs, and fish stock. Bring to a boil, reduce the heat to low, and let simmer gently, stirring occasionally, for 40 minutes. Add salt and pepper to taste. This tomato sauce is the cioppino base (it makes a great spaghetti sauce, says Cheri). Set the base aside and wash and dry the stockpot.

3. Melt the clarified butter in the stockpot over medium heat. Add the clams and sauté until they pop open, barely 30 seconds. (Remove and discard any clams that remain closed.) Lower the heat, and add the rest of the seafood and fish, all at once. Sauté lightly, pushing the fish and seafood around gently, until barely cooked, about 1 minute.

4. Add the cioppino base to the seafood, raise the heat slightly, and bring to a boil to heat through. This will also finish cooking the fish.

5. Then, to quote the Shoalwater folks, "Dish into 8 bowls, making sure to give everyone some of everything!" Accompany with Garlic Bread Croûtes.

Serves 8 as an entrée

Garlic Bread Croûtes

1 loaf any good French bread (try the French Country, page 328)
8 tablespoons (1 stick) butter, softened
5 cloves garlic, peeled and put through a garlic press
¾ cup freshly grated Parmesan cheese

1. Preheat the broiler.

2. Slice the bread into 16 fat slices. Lay the slices out on a baking sheet.

3. Combine the butter and garlic. Spread each slice of bread with the garlic butter and sprinkle with the Parmesan.

4. Place the baking sheet under the broiler until the slices are lightly browned, 3 to 5 minutes.

Makes 16 croûtes

Mussel Soup Suggin-Style

ere mussel soup takes on an American/Arkansawyer coloration while remaining faithful to its Irish roots. While signing *The Dairy Hollow House Cookbook* at the Arkansas Territorial Restoration at Little Rock, an energetic lady appeared seemingly from nowhere, pressed a book into my hands, and disappeared. The book was called the *Suggin Cookbook*. I never again met its author, Josus, an artist and archivist whose real name is Josephine Hutson Graham, but I have enjoyed her book since. Her delightful block prints and prose enliven this collection of handwritten 1829 "receipts" from three northeastern Arkansas counties: Jackson, Independence, and Woodruff.

The early settlers of these counties were called Suggins. "The word is Gaelic, very old," writes Josus, who believes it came to America in 1719 from Derry County in Ireland when several families began their migration to Jacksonport, Arkansas. Their descendants are still called Suggins, though the word is now pejorative in some circles according to Josus. "Today [it] means a somewhat uncouth and unsophisticated person living in a rural area along the White River watershed in the three named counties," she writes. "Nobody would ever admit to being a Suggin. Fact was everybody was Suggins."

This variation of Josus's White River mussel stew is homey, savory, and good.

3 to 5 pounds live river mussels in the shell (the amount depends on what you've gathered. Ocean mussels work as well, but then the soup wouldn't be Suggin), cleaned (page 92)
Equal parts water or any well-flavored vegetable stock, plus beer to cover
3 tablespoons butter
1 bunch scallions, chopped, or 1 leek, white and light green parts, split open lengthwise, well cleaned, and chopped
1 medium carrot, scrubbed and chopped
1 rib celery with leaves, chopped
4 tablespoons finely chopped fresh parsley
3 tablespoons unbleached all-purpose flour
3 cups milk, heated
1 tablespoon Worcestershire or Pickapeppa sauce
2 dashes Tabasco, or similar hot pepper sauce
Salt and freshly ground black pepper to taste
2 tablespoons fresh lemon juice
Garlic Oil (page 41; optional) to taste (start with 2 teaspoons)

1. Put the mussels in a stockpot and add water or stock and the beer to cover. Simmer gently, covered, until the mussels open, 6 to 7 minutes. Discard any mussels that have not opened. Remove the mussels to a colander, reserving the cooking liquid. Strain it through cheesecloth or a very fine strainer as it may be sandy. Remove the mussels from their shells when they are cool enough to handle and coarsely chop them.

2. In an 8- or 9-inch skillet, heat the butter over medium heat. Add the scallions or leek and sauté until softened, about 4 minutes. Add the carrot, celery, and half the parsley; sauté 2 minutes more. Sprinkle with the flour, stir it in, cooking for a minute or so. Then whisk in the hot milk, ½ cup at a time. Transfer the mixture to a stockpot. Stir in the strained mussel cooking liquid, the Worcestershire, pepper sauce, salt, and pepper. Let barely simmer 10 minutes, then add the mussels.

3. Remove the soup from the heat and stir in the lemon juice. Taste and adjust the seasoning; stir in the garlic oil if using. Garnish with the remaining parsley and serve.

Makes 6 to 7 cups (more with the larger amount of mussels); serves 3 or 4 as an entrée

Crabmeat Soup Pentagoet Inn

 e haven't seen the Millers' Pentagoet Inn yet, but it looks beautiful in the brochure: wide-porched and inviting, on a crest looking down towards the sea, in the historic village of Castine, Maine. Castine is on the eastern shore of Penobscot Bay, and so, of course, lots of the famous Maine seafood is featured in the dining room. According to the Millers, guests frequently comment on this delectable, creamy curry-and-apple sparked crabmeat soup. It's the perfect starter for a special-occasion dinner. The Pentagoet's number is (207) 326-8616.

3 tablespoons butter
1 medium onion, finely chopped
2 medium apples, cored, peeled, and
    coarsely chopped
3 tablespoons unbleached all-purpose flour
2 tablespoons curry powder
2 quarts Chicken Stock 1 (page 19) or any
    well-flavored chicken stock
2 cloves garlic, peeled and put through a
    garlic press
1 pound crabmeat, preferably Maine,
    carefully picked over
½ pint heavy (whipping) cream
Salt and fresh cracked black pepper to taste

1. In an 8- or 9-inch skillet, melt the butter over medium heat. Add the onion and sauté until translucent, about 4 minutes. Add the apples, flour, and curry, and sauté stirring, 3 to 5 minutes longer.

2. Transfer the sauté mixture to a soup pot, deglazing the skillet with a little of the chicken broth and scraping up any of the browned bits that have stuck to the pan. Add this and the rest of the chicken stock to the soup pot, along with the garlic and half the crabmeat. Simmer gently, partially covered, for 30 minutes.

3. Stir in the cream and the remainder of the crabmeat. Let cook over low heat another 5 to 10 minutes stirring occasionally. When heated through, season to taste and serve piping hot.

Serves 8 to 9 as a starter

MUSSEL BEACH

A substantial river-mussel industry existed in Arkansas, and many other states, from the late 1800s until just prior to World War II. In those days the mussel shells, with their pearly interiors, were made into buttons. The shellfish themselves were eaten, but only by people who lived in the little river towns where mussel fishing was an important source of income. The technology for safely shipping the mussel meat once the shells had been removed did not then exist. Plastic gradually replaced mussel shells for button-making, and the mussel industry gradually died away, except by river families here and there, who went on to scratch out a living in other ways.

Currently there's a resurgence of mussel fishing, for now the pearly lining of the shells is used in Japan for manufacturing cultured pearls. There is even talk of a cultured-pearl factory starting up in Arkansas or Tennessee. Maybe this time someone can figure out how to process the mussel meat as well and market it successfully.

Vegetable Soups

FOR MARKET-DAY

arly mornings, spring through fall, one day a week, a dozen or so different Eureka Springs area farmers display their produce somewhere in town.

Dripping Springs Garden has the prettiest displays; Mark and Michael grow flowers as well as dozens of greens, onions, berries, beans, exotics like burdock and daikon, baby beets, herbs galore, garlic (which, in fall, they braid into gorgeous garlands, interspersed with dried flowers, herbs, and peppers). All this bounty's wonderfully turned out in baskets and pottery bowls.

Others may arrange their offerings less artfully, but, ah, the stuff itself. Win saves me tiny, marble-size potatoes: delectable whole, stir-fried, or added to soup (one restaurant patron asked, "I've heard of cherry tomatoes, but where on earth did you find cherry *potatoes?*"). Paul and his wife always have something you simply won't find elsewhere: fresh, organic blue cornmeal, from home-grown, hand-ground blue corn, brought to market refrigerated. Cornbread made from it is an epiphany—essence of corn. Jewell has the standbys in the trunk of her Pontiac—plump tomatoes, heavy with juice, zucchinis, green beans, peppers, and of course, in high summer, fresh corn. Yo-anka has herbs, greens, and, in fall, the most extraordinarily sweet pears, bumpy and funny-looking but with a deep, almost burnt-sugar, saturated-in-sweetness flavor. The Millers have a few vegetables—sweet potatoes, red peppers, maybe—and sometimes they bring the best homemade whole-wheat bread; you can also place orders for fresh rabbit with them.

Throughout the year, these and many other purveyors come and go, bringing what they have in season: raspberries, fresh local eggs, wild mushrooms, blueberries. But great produce and chit-chat and recipe-exchanging with those who grow it are only part of the farmer's market experience. In small-town Eureka, a person can also count on running into fellow shoppers he or she knows and loves at the market: the motel owner and the local astrologer, the librarian, the playwright from New York who lives here six months a year, the chef from one of the town's Best Westerns. "How *are* you!" we exclaim to each other, as if we hadn't seen each other in months—as if we didn't know that, despite the way we like to gossip about each other and carp about Eureka's latest scandal, we are all, essentially, happy to be here.

Not that I don't like "there," too. Off-seasons (in Eureka, January through March) are made for travel. When I travel, I hit the markets. For the sweetness of buying produce in season, often from those who grow it, is a story that is told and retold on market day the world over. It is universal, yet colored precisely by place. It is a story about connection.

Until I traveled internationally, I thought that all national traits were stereotypes. But the French, though abrupt, really *are* sensualists; I found fresh Tunisian dates at the Paris markets, plump, intense, still on the stem, and beets sold already cooked, and *christa-marine,* a sea vegetable that looks like a pencil-lead-thin asparagus, and—I was told with French hauteur—has a two-week season; "And we are at the very end of the two weeks, Madame, so you see you are most fortunate." In Zurich, on the balmiest of spring days, I saw the strawberries compulsively but beautifully, precisely, lined up in rows, like-sized berries in the same row, perfect points standing proudly upright. But not only the strawberries—the greens, the asparagus, the oranges, even the onions were arranged in neat lines, roots up, at precisely the same angle, waiting like good little Swiss school children.

How different was this from the messy, teeming South Indian market I'd visited one market day, years earlier. It was a perfect *National Geographic* photograph, rich with color and exoticism: the vivid-sareed housewives, dripping gold, poking at the piles of produce laid out on large straw mats: red chili peppers and green-going-to-black peppercorns, still on the stem, from nearby Alleppy; shopkeepers and stall-men in dhotis, wrapping up a kilo of sugar or mustard seeds in a quickly-made cone of newspaper, tied with white string.

VEGETABLE SOUP DEFINED

❦*In this chapter, "vegetable soup" means soups whose* base and dominant flavors *are vegetable, as opposed to dairy, legume, chicken, or fish. The liquid component is usually vegetable stock (though I have listed chicken stock as an option, since the two can always be used interchangeably, unless you're cooking for vegetarians). The solid components, too, are vegetable—the flavor and texture of one specific vegetable, or a mix of vegetables, predominate. Other vegetable soups in other chapters are by my subjective reckoning cream soups with vegetables, chicken soups with vegetables, and so on.*

There are two exceptional mixed vegetable soups for which I feel such fondness and respect that I gave each its own chapter. These soups are Gumbo Zeb (the stuff of legend) and The Soup (a comfortable, loyal, low-calorie, low-fat friend, which will not only stick with you through thick and thin, but help take you from thick *to* thin*).*

Also, I've cross-referenced in this chapter, so that, for example, when someone gives you a bushel of yellow squash (how nice—as if your own garden wasn't producing more than enough yellow squash on its own, thank you very much), you'll have many options (probably not as many, however, as you have yellow squash). ❦

Wandering the Chenganacherry market, I suddenly knew why I had never really liked such photographs; they distance, rather than bring closer, the experience. The heat and dust, the sweat; the co-mingled smells of frying spices, cooking fires, and jasmine blossoms at a flower stall; photographs sanitize the experience, making it more pleasant in some ways, perhaps, but infinitely less. It was the same reason, I decided, that so often museums made me want to go back to the hotel and nap while markets energize me. Objects taken from their context, captioned and explained, are embalmed, their essence lost. Still-life versus *active*-life.

As expressive of local character as markets are, I have never visited one anywhere that did not have certain constants: humble, earthy carrots, potatoes, garlic; fat lovely green cabbages resting sedate· and rose-like in their curved leaves. Nor have I ever gone to a produce market without either becoming acquainted with a new vegetable, or a new way of preparing a vegetable with which I was already familiar—regardless of whether or not I spoke the tongue of the vendors and my fellow shoppers, had ever met them before or would ever meet them again. Cooks speak a universal language. Gestures, expressions, enthusiasm can communicate volumes.

Market displays are alive, present tense. They invite you to touch, bite, taste; to buy, take home, prepare. They are practical, not abstract. They require no explanation. They change. They are easy and uncomplicated to understand, even love—to love in the way I love vegetable soups, including the one that waits for me in the kitchen today, bubbling as I write these words (tomatoes, garlic, green beans, yellow and zucchini squash, some canned kidney beans, a snip of fresh basil from last years' garden, growing, potted, on my living room windowsill). This soup smells good. It will feed me, and feed me well.

Yet as one sniffs the simmering soup, or the market's damp, vegetal odors, for a moment, the veil lifts. Common sense departs; a different sense takes over. One moment a person's negotiating the price of tomatoes, or washing leeks for soup under a stream of cold water, the next, unpredictably, taken out of him or herself. There's a certain taking note. The seasons, the earth, those who labor in gardens and fields, those who ship and can, truck and sell, buy, cook and feed; the long, awesome chain extending back to when men and women first learned to participate in that great miracle—seed in ground, cultivation, harvest. Suddenly, one is both deeply involved, yet standing outside, watching. It is sweet and poignant: lives (of vegetables, of men and women) come and go; life itself goes on. The harvest celebrates that life, every single bowl of vegetable soup is sacrament. Eternity resides in a cabbage leaf.

ARTICHOKES

Quickly surveying a pan of steamed, halved artichokes, Ned asked E. Rae Smith, assistant chef on weekends, "Now, did you get out all the stickery parts?"

"Of course," E. Rae said. "All that's left is the *art.*"

The *stickery part* is called the choke, but properly prepared, these edible thistles won't choke anyone. They do look intimidating, though, the first time you meet up with a whole one on your plate. Artichokes are so delicious, however, that after a little instruction, and the first bite, they are old friends. As much as we love them, they are more of a home favorite than a frequent restaurant ingredient; they are so very non-Ozark.

The frozen hearts (frozen plain, that is, with no butter sauce) make a fine soup, but the fresh are so much better that, pesky prep work or no, you really ought to try the recipes with them at least once in your life as a special indulgence. When you decide on this undertaking (and it *is* an undertaking), please read the accompanying artichoke anatomy and preparation information.

Although available year-round, their price, as well as their flavor, make artichokes a luxury. But sometimes in April to May, at the height of their season, you can find a bargain on them. Load up!

ARTICHOKE ANATOMY

Large, mature artichokes are about fist-sized, though the edible portion, when disinterred, is smaller than palm-sized.

Artichokes consist of the stem, the fully formed leaves, the immature leaves, the choke, and the heart, or bottom. After cooking, the heart of the artichoke is fully edible, the leaves and stem partially so. Only the choke, a fuzzy, tasteless middle core, is inedible (strictly for reasons of texture; it's not poisonous). The edible part of the leaves is near their base, which is attached to the rich-meated heart, or bottom.

The meat of an artichoke is hard until it is thoroughly cooked; this is not a "cook until tender-crisp" vegetable. The artichoke reaches full flavor only when its heart is meltingly soft (though the upper part of the leaves will still be tough). At this point, a leaf can be plucked easily from the artichoke. (In Europe, I saw leeeetle tiny cute baby artichokes which are supposedly entirely edible. But I've never cooked one, so I can't tell you a thing about them.) The artichokes I refer to here are the great big California ones, probably from Castroville, where I will someday attend that town's famous artichoke festival, I hope.

THE ABC'S OF THE ARTICHOKE

🍂 ***How to Cook an Artichoke:*** *It is possible to remove the choke before cooking, but I almost never do.*

Cut the stems off the artichokes, so they are flat on the bottom. Reserve the stems (see information in the How to Eat an Artichoke section). Wedge the artichokes, stem side down, into a nonaluminum pot. Heat a tea kettle full of water, then pour it over the artichokes until they are about halfway covered. Bring the water back to a boil, turn the heat down to medium-low, and simmer, covered, for about 25 minutes. Drop the reserved stems into the pot, cover, and continue cooking until done, about 20 minutes (40 to 50 minutes total cooking time for good-sized artichokes). A leaf will pull off easily from the heart when they are done. Drain well in a colander.

How to Remove the Choke: *There are two post-cooking ways to remove the choke, that hairy fortress guarding the delicious nucleus, the princess heart locked in the castle of the artichoke.*

1. For an artichoke which is to be served whole, first cool it enough to handle. You can facilitate this by running cold water over it. Look! It opens like a blossom as you do this! Reach down into the center, opening the closed mature leaves slightly (they will open easily).

When you come to the immature leaves—soft, usually purple-tipped, and a bit pointy-sharp on the end—just reach in and pull them out. These leaves are partially edible; nibble on their delicious bottoms yourself, a cook's dividend. Now you have a straight shot at the fuzzy choke. Just reach in and scrape it out with a spoon, preferably a serrated grapefruit spoon. Discard the choke and the tiniest of the sharp immature leaves.

2. When an artichoke is to be used in a soup and thus its appearance as a whole vegetable is not important, simply pull off all the leaves in one conelike, witches' hat-shaped clump. Set these leaves aside (more on how to handle these in the How to Get at the Edible Parts section). Now the choke is easily visible. It may be scraped out easily with a spoon or, once you get the knack, carefully pulled off with the fingers, which leaves the most artichoke meat. Behold! A perfectly concave artichoke heart, or bottom.

And by the way, which is it, heart or bottom? Well, when canned, the cuplike treasure of artichoke flesh you're looking at is called an "artichoke bottom." But when fresh, people generally refer to the center of the artichoke as the "heart." What, then, are canned, frozen, or bottled marinated artichoke "hearts?" Something entirely different: a section of heart or bottom

flesh with a few edible leaves. I think these canned and frozen "hearts" must be from the baby artichokes I mentioned earlier. Are you suitably confused yet? At any rate, discard the choke after removing it, reserving the whatshamacallit (heart, or bottom).

How to Eat an Artichoke: *Hot or cold, plain or stuffed, with pleasure. With an herbed, garlicky vinaigrette to which the minced tender parts of the cooked artichoke's stem have been added. With melted butter (if you take no heed of cholesterol or calories), or with yogurt into which you've stirred a little Dijon mustard. With aïoli or rouille. Eat your artichoke leaf by leaf, dipping each in your butter or yogurt, then scraping off the little mound of edible deliciousness at the inside bottom with your teeth. Discard the inedible portion.*

When you come to the heart, have at it with your fingers (if you're by yourself) or with knife and fork (if with company), dipping it, too, into the sauce of choice.

The stem is not generally served, which is a shame. It is eminently edible, usually, though it must be peeled. Remove the tough base of the stem along with any especially fibrous parts. If not using the stem immediately for soup, I sometimes purée or fine-chop it for use in a vinaigrette as mentioned above. More often I save it, and after peeling freeze it. A stash of these will eventually add up to enough to make an artichoke

soup, or will supplement the one or two whole artichokes needed for a soup with less trouble than following the process described below.

How to Get at the Edible Parts of the Artichoke for Use in Soup: *Don't bother to remove the choke ahead of time. When you're ready to remove the artichoke meat, use the second or "soup" method of choke and leaf removal described above. Next, dice the revealed heart, or bottom, and the peeled stem. Then take the cone of smaller, immature leaves and, with a sharp knife, carefully slice off the bottom of the cone— the edible portion of the leaves. This is a matter of a few seconds.*

Now, here's the picky part. Take the mature leaves, two, three, maybe four at a time and lay them out, overlapping slightly, on a cutting board. Hold the leaves down with one hand at their sharp inedible tip ends, with their meaty sides facing up. Now, using a sharpish paring knife, scrape the flesh, one by one, from the base of the leaves. Reserve the flesh along with the diced hearts and stems. Once you've done your first batch of leaves and get the hang of it, you'll find you can do an artichoke's worth in less than a minute.

Okay, yes, it's easy to see why people would use frozen artichoke hearts. But you've got to try the from-scratch way at least once in your life. The results are too good not to! 🦃

Artichoke Soup Avgolemono

his is a delectable soup. Avgolemono is Greek for "egg and lemon"; if you've traveled to Greece, or eaten much in Greek restaurants, these bright flavors—sometimes used in sauces, sometimes in soup—will be familiar to you. Here, egg yolks give slight thickening to a flavorful broth, supplying a velvet smoothness; fresh lemon enlivens the whole.

Artichokes, much loved by the Greeks, are often served with lemon juice. It's a wonder someone didn't cut up artichokes into avgolemono soup a long time ago, and I feel sure they must have; but to my knowledge, this is an original pairing, and the ingredients are soulmates. This soup's exquisite hot, refreshing cold. Its one drawback is its unattractive beige color. Compensate with a simple, colorful garnish–finely chopped parsley or mint, diced red pepper, or a lemon slice.

This is quick work once you have the artichokes done.

6 cups Chicken Stock 1 (page 19) or Golden Vegetable Stock (page 28) or any well-flavored chicken or vegetable stock
½ cup long-grain white or brown rice
3 to 5 egg yolks (larger number if you wish it thicker)
¼ cup freshly squeezed lemon juice, strained to remove seeds
2½ to 3 cups cooked artichoke hearts or bottoms and leaf scrapings, as well as any tender, peeled stems, coarsely chopped into uniform pieces (about 4 or 5 large artichokes or two 10-ounce packages frozen artichoke hearts, thawed)
Chopped fresh parsley or mint, for garnish
Sliced red bell pepper, for garnish
1 lemon, sliced paper thin, seeds removed, for garnish

1. In a soup pot, bring the stock to a boil and stir in the rice. Turn down the heat to medium-low and let simmer, covered, until the rice is done, 20 to 25 minutes for white rice, 30 to 45 minutes for brown.

2. Whisk together the egg yolks and lemon juice. When the rice is tender, ladle 1 or 2 scoops of the hot stock into the yolk mixture, whisking to blend. Pour the yolk-stock mixture back into the pot and blend. Barely simmer over very low heat, stirring constantly; the egg yolks will cook and slightly thicken the soup, about 2 minutes. Don't let the soup boil.

3. Remove the soup from the heat. Stir in the cooked artichokes. Serve the soup hot immediately, or let it cool, chill deeply, and serve it cold the next day. In either case, ladle the soup into white bowls, sprinkle it with fresh parsley or mint (or a combination of the two), a scattering of red pepper, and float a slice of lemon on top. And life is good, isn't it? Excellent served with a savory phyllo pastry triangle.

Serves 6 as a starter

Artichoke Soup-Stew Paysanne

he liquid left over from cooking artichokes is not generally used for stock; its faint, sweetish taste is off-putting in combination with most other flavors. But in this rustic, unusual, and excellent soup—kind of a vegetable "boiled dinner"—it becomes a delicious broth. Each bowl of soup is an earthy, primitive still life: a half artichoke, a small new potato or two, a length of carrot, with the broth ladled over them. One can imagine shepherds cooking something like this over an open fire, with some good local wine, and whatever wild herbs were at hand. Like oven-roasted vegetables, everything here tastes like itself. The result is so unsophisticated it's chic—and with only 2 tablespoons fat included, this is a superb calorie bargain. Serve this, in nice rustic pottery bowls, to your friends who've just gotten back from Tuscany or Provence. (Your Aunt Clara from Des Moines might think it's a little weird.) Add a hearty, peasanty bread, a board with a couple of cheeses, and a fruit tart for dessert. My oh my.

Pam cooking spray
3 artichokes, uncooked, stems cut flush with bottom of leaves, cut-off stems reserved
2 cups dry white wine
4 to 6 cups Chicken Stock 1 (page 19) or Golden Vegetable Stock (page 28) or any well-flavored chicken or vegetable stock
1 tablespoon olive oil
1 tablespoon butter
2 bay leaves
6 medium or 12 small new potatoes, unpeeled
3 large carrots, scrubbed and halved crosswise
12 pearl onions, peeled
3 sprigs each (about 3 inches long) fresh thyme, dill, and savory, or as many as are available
1 sprig (about 3 inches long) fresh rosemary
3 ribs celery, halved lengthwise and crosswise
6 cherry tomatoes, stemmed
Garlic Oil (page 41; optional)
Salt and freshly ground black pepper to taste

1. Spray a large, heavy soup pot (an enameled cast-iron dutch oven is ideal) with the Pam. Place the artichokes in it, reserving the stems. Pour the wine and just enough boiling stock over the artichokes that, were they not bobbing around, they would be covered. Bring to a boil. Drizzle the olive oil over the artichokes, then chip the butter over them. Add the bay leaves. Turn down the heat to medium-low and let simmer, covered, for 20 minutes.

2. Add the potatoes, nestling them around the artichokes. Let simmer another 10 minutes, covered. Add the artichoke stems, carrots, onions, and herbs. Let simmer,

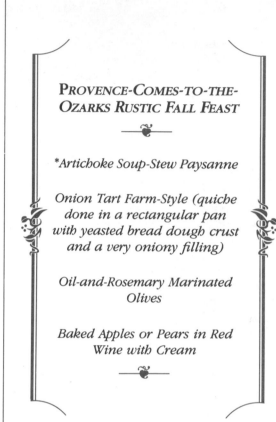

PROVENCE-COMES-TO-THE-OZARKS RUSTIC FALL FEAST

Artichoke Soup-Stew Paysanne

Onion Tart Farm-Style (quiche done in a rectangular pan with yeasted bread dough crust and a very oniony filling)

Oil-and-Rosemary Marinated Olives

Baked Apples or Pears in Red Wine with Cream

covered, 10 minutes more. Add the celery and let simmer, uncovered, 10 minutes. Add the tomatoes and let simmer, covered, for 5 minutes only. The tomatoes should not be allowed to lose their shape.

3. Drain the broth from the vegetables into a second pot. Have ready the bowls in which the soup will be served. When the artichokes are cool enough to handle, cut them in half (the halves won't be neat but never mind), and scoop out the chokes. Bring the stock back to the boil while you arrange in each bowl, as for a still-life, a half artichoke (including leaves and half of the heart), a strand of cooked herb, a cherry tomato, a potato (or 2 small potatoes), a half rib of celery, a half carrot, and 2 pearl onions.

4. Taste the boiling broth, and season

with the optional garlic oil, and salt and pepper. Ladle the soup, very hot, over the vegetables in the bowls. Serve immediately, with a soup spoon and a knife and fork at each place. Your guests will probably use all three—plus their fingers.

Serves 4 to 6 as an entrée, when accompanied by a hearty bread and cheese

VARIATION:

Make a richer, more substantial (and more caloric) version of this soup by thickening the broth with 3 to 4 egg yolks before ladling it over the vegetables. To do so, beat the yolks, then ladle 1 or 2 scoops of the hot stock, strained, into them. Whisk to blend, then whisk all back into the pot. Barely simmer over very low heat, stirring constantly. The egg yolks will cook and slightly thicken the soup, about 2 minutes. Don't let the soup boil.

For another soup recipe using artichokes, see Betty Rosbottom's Cream of Artichoke Soup (page 250).

ASPARAGUS

❦*I am a fresh asparagus fiend, and I eat it by the pound in the spring. But I only make one soup out of it: Asparagus and White Wine Soup (page 251). Don't miss it!*❦

AVOCADOS

Like fruit soups, avocado soups have been around for a while, yet they remain unfamiliar to many. There's something a bit shocking, faintly titillating, about soup made from these pear-shaped, sweetly nutty tropical vegetables with their dense, rich, oily flesh of pale green. When they are hard they are unripe. When they yield to the gentle pressure of a finger, they are perfect.

Avocados must never be cooked beyond the time it takes to heat them through or they become bitter and unpleasant. Most avocado soups avoid this by using the precious "alligator pear" raw.

Chilled Avocado Soup Mexique Bay

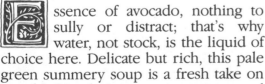

Essence of avocado, nothing to sully or distract; that's why water, not stock, is the liquid of choice here. Delicate but rich, this pale green summery soup is a fresh take on an old friend. Its taste is creamy and fresh, simple and uncomplicated. Better yet, it's made in a flash—handy, since it does not keep well.

4 large or 6 to 7 small, ripe avocados, preferably Haas, peeled and pitted
3 to 4 tablespoons lime or lemon juice
3 to 4 cloves garlic, peeled
1 tablespoon picante sauce or salsa, either commercial, such as Pace's, or homemade, such as Arkansalsa (page 199)
3 scallions, trimmed, coarsely chopped
2 tablespoons coarsely chopped fresh parsley
½ cup plain yogurt
¼ cup Crème Fraîche (page 50)
4 to 5 cups water, preferably spring water
Salt and freshly ground black pepper to taste
1 cucumber, peeled, halved lengthwise, seeded, and cut into ¼-inch slices
½ red bell pepper, diced, for garnish

1. Put the avocados, 3 tablespoons of the lemon or lime juice, garlic, and 1 tablespoon or so of picante sauce in a food processor, and buzz until smooth. Add the scallions and parsley, and pulse-chop a few times. Add the yogurt, crème fraîche, and 3 cups of the water. Buzz again until the parsley and scallions are chopped fine. If the texture seems too thick—more like a dip than a soup—continue to add water. Taste for salt and pepper (this takes quite a bit of salt). You may also need a little extra lemon or lime juice.

2. Transfer the soup from the food processor to a bowl. Chill for 1 hour or so. At the same time chill 6 to 8 soup cups.

3. Just before serving, taste again for salt, pepper, and lime or lemon juice, adding any that seem needed. Stir in the cucumber slices. Serve the soup (within a few hours of making it) in the chilled cups, garnished with the diced red pepper.

Serves 4 to 6 as a small starter

VARIATION:
Add to the soup a cup of fresh, ripe tomato, peeled, seeded, and chopped with the cucumber.

MEXICAN BIRTHDAY LUNCHEON FOR THE LEO LADIES

❧

*Chilled Avocado Soup Mexique Bay

Nachos
(made with blue corn chips, black beans, sharp Cheddar, tomatoes, red onion, jalapeños, and alfalfa sprouts)

Ice Cold Coffee-Chocolate-Cinnamon Smoothies

❧

Avocado Consommé

Pure, elegant simplicity. This is that rare *hot* avocado soup. If you can taste mentally, you'll know how exquisite this is when you read the recipe.

Because I first had this topped with a puff of unsweetened whipped cream, I can't imagine it without, or with a replacement, though a thin slice of lemon wouldn't be bad. But what the hey, you're already in deep with the avocado calories; might as well go for it. This begins a sophisticated dinner, or a seduction supper *par excellence*.

6½ cups Chicken Stock 1 (page 19) or Golden Vegetable Stock (page 28) or any well-flavored chicken or vegetable stock (the stock must *be flavorful in itself for this to work)*
½ cup dry sherry
3 large avocados, preferably Hass, ripe but not overripe, diced (about 2 cups)
¼ cup frozen petit peas, thawed (optional)
½ cup cooked long-grain white rice (optional)
Salt and freshly ground black pepper to taste
Unsweetened whipped cream, for garnish (optional)
2 to 3 tablespoons freshly grated Parmesan cheese, for garnish
6 to 8 small sprigs fresh parsley or dill or small basil leaves, for garnish

1. In a soup pot, combine the stock and sherry, and bring to a full boil.

2. Divide the avocados, peas, and rice among 6 to 8 heated serving cups.

3. Taste the stock and correct the sea-

soning. Ladle the piping hot broth into the cups, topping each with a puff of the optional whipped cream, a delicate sprinkle of Parmesan, and a parsley or dill sprig or basil leaf.

Serves 6 to 8 as a starter

VARIATION:

Seaside Avocado Consommé: Substitute fish stock and/or bottled clam juice for all or part of the chicken or vegetable stock. Add 1 to 3 shelled, deveined cooked shrimp to each bowl or cup.

BEETS

Beet soup is not something a person would want to eat day in, day out, nor would you spring it on a guest unless you know someone to be a lover of beets. But, oh my, how warming and good is that savory Russian soup of beets, cabbage, and dill, topped with a bit of sour cream, known as borscht. It "ranks with all the aristocracy of the soup tureen," says Louis P. De Gouy, "[and] cheer[s] the wayworn traveler . . .; a taste for it is not hard to cultivate." Indeed, once you know borscht, two or three or four times a winter you'll positively crave it, with good dark homemade bread on the side. This may be biological; beets are iron-rich, and they *feel* as tonic as they are. When I have this on a dark November day I can practically measure the vitamins and minerals in this intensely colored, delicious potage coursing through my blood. For those of us of Russian-Jewish ancestry, this is soul food on an almost cellular level.

Quick, chilled light beet soups are sublime summer offerings; as refreshing in the heat as good hot borschts are nourishing in February.

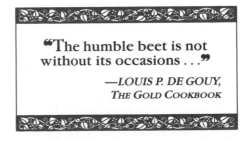

❝The humble beet is not without its occasions . . .❞

—LOUIS P. DE GOUY,
THE GOLD COOKBOOK

Winter Borscht à la Vielle Russe

erved to great acclaim at the Glasnost Dinner we hosted at the restaurant. The fundraiser helped send nine Eureka Springs teen-agers to Samantha Smith World Peace Camp, an exchange program with the then Soviet Union teens.

3 or 4 large fresh beets, greens removed
Vegetable oil for rubbing beets
3 to 4 tablespoons butter
2 large onions, chopped
4 or 5 cloves garlic, peeled and put through
  a garlic press
2 medium carrots, peeled and sliced
1 parsnip, peeled and sliced very thinly
1 can (16 ounces) tomatoes with their
  juice, buzzed to a chunky purée in the
  food processor
4 cups Chicken Stock 1 (page 19) or
  Golden or Browned Vegetable Stock
  (pages 28 and 32) or any well-flavored
  chicken or vegetable stock
2 tablespoons honey
½ cup loosely packed fresh young dill,
  feathery leaves only
2 bay leaves
1 teaspoon dried oregano
1 teaspoon dried basil
1 teaspoon salt
½ head cabbage, cut into thin ribbons
12 to 15 small red-skinned new potatoes,
  scrubbed and boiled until tender
Sour cream
Additional dill sprigs, for garnish

1. Preheat the oven to 350°F.

2. Scrub the beets, leaving the "tail" and top cluster of the stems on. Rub each beet with a little vegetable oil. Wrap each individually in aluminum foil, and bake until barely tender, about 1 hour. Smaller beets will cook more quickly. (Baking the beets, rather than boiling or steaming them, con-centrates their flavor, leaves them cooked through yet firm, and prevents wateriness.)

3. Meanwhile, in a heavy soup pot, melt the butter over medium heat. Add the onions and sauté until softened a bit, about 4 minutes. Add the garlic, carrots, and par-snip. Lower the heat slightly. When the veg-etables are slightly limp, about 6 minutes more, add the tomatoes with their juice, the stock, honey, fresh and dried herbs, and the salt. Bring to a boil, turn down the heat to medium-low, and let simmer gently, covered, about 40 minutes.

4. Remove the beets from the oven and poke them with a fork; they should be barely tender. Let them cool until you can handle them, rinse them quickly in cold water, and slip off and discard their skins. Dice the beet flesh and add it to the soup along with the cabbage. Continue to simmer, covered, until the cabbage is tender and fla-vors are blended, another 15 to 20 minutes.

5. Taste and adjust the seasoning. Serve very hot with 1 or 2 whole potatoes in each bowl. Dollop sour cream or any dairy options atop the borscht, and add a sprig of dill. Accompany the soup with big chunky slices of toasted dark bread—of course, rye's traditional, but any whole-grain, hearty bread will do well.

Serves 4 to 6 as an entrée or 6 to 8 as a starter

Gazpacho Rosa

've never been a fan of classic tomato gazpacho, though I like every one of its ingredients, it's amiably low-cal, and I *ought* to. But Gazpacho Rosa—well, *here's* a summertime soup to revel in! Its raspberry-pink color couldn't be prettier or more festive, and its mild sweet-tartness makes it refreshing. The secret? An improbable one—beets and cranberry juice! Given that people are funny about both beets and chilled soups—either they love or are appalled by them—you should probably exercise caution about whom you serve this to, or at least to whom you tell what's in it. But I hate to warn you off something so sensational.

This is a real quickie—I almost always cheat with canned beets. In the summer, a lapse from purity is forgivable, especially if it means the cook can steal out to Beaver Lake for an hour in the afternoon.

1 can (20 ounces) whole beets with
   liquid or 2 cups cooked fresh beets,
   plus 1 cup of the liquid in which they
   were cooked
1 cup buttermilk, preferably
   Bulgarian-style
1 cup plain yogurt or, if you want
   your soup extra rich, ¼ cup kefir
   cheese or Crème Fraîche (page 50)
   mixed with ¾ cup yogurt
1 cup Chicken Stock 1 (page 19) or
   Golden Vegetable Stock (page 28) or
   any well flavored chicken or
   vegetable stock
½ cup cranberry juice—yes!
1½ tablespoons raspberry vinegar
1 teaspoon sugar (quite a bit more—2
   tablespoons to ¼ cup—if cranberry juice
   is the unsweetened, health-food-store
   kind)
⅛ teaspoon cayenne pepper
Salt to taste
1 large, red ripe tomato, unpeeled, cut into
   small dice
¼ small red onion, finely chopped
1 cucumber, peeled, seeded, and finely
   diced
1 red bell pepper, stemmed, seeded, and
   diced
1 green bell pepper, stemmed, seeded, and
   diced
2 tablespoons chopped fresh dill or 1 scant
   tablespoon dried
Sour cream, kefir cheese, crème fraîche, or
   yogurt, for garnish (optional)
Dill sprigs, for garnish (optional)

1. In a food processor, combine all the beet juice and half of the beets with the buttermilk, yogurt, and kefir or crème fraîche if using, stock, cranberry juice, vinegar, sugar, cayenne, and salt. Buzz until smooth. Transfer to a bowl.

2. Dice the remaining beets, and stir them into the soup mixture. Stir in the remaining vegetables and the dill. Chill deeply, for at least 4 hours. Serve, ideally in iced glass cups, garnished with a dollop of sour cream or other dairy choice and a sprig of dill.

Serves 4 as a starter

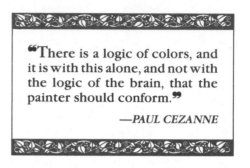

> **"**There is a logic of colors, and it is with this alone, and not with the logic of the brain, that the painter should conform.**"**
>
> —*PAUL CEZANNE*

BROCCOLI

*P*oor broccoli. Especially since George Bush trounced it. Well! For the record, *I* feel it's very unlucky when Hart's Family Center, our local supermarket, or our restaurant purveyor is out of broccoli. Broccoli's in the cabbage family, and, like all the cabbage kin, is said to be a cancer preventative. But I eat it because I like it, day in and day out (often stir-fried and then tossed with pasta and Parmesan cheese). It's also on the vegetable side plate that accompanies our restaurant entrées. If cooked right, broccoli's such a bright, pretty green, and its flowerets are, well, so *floral;* it really adds a lively note to the plate.

Our ways with it are many. Sometimes we simply blanch it beforehand, then stir-fry it at the last minute with butter and lemon juice, or olive oil and garlic, or fresh ginger and sesame oil. Sometimes we'll purée it, combine it with eggs and cream or milk, and bake it in a timbale. A purée of peeled, tender cooked broccoli stems with a bit of yogurt and dijon mustard is excellent and admirably low fat!

Of course, some of those ways are soup, like the wonderful hot and sweet curried broccoli soup which follows. It may be a little exotic for some tastes, but not yours or mine, right? Hey, we're sophisticated eaters!

Broccoli and Potato Curry Soup Primo

roccoli and potatoes are natural soupmates, appearing together, happily, in many recipes. Often they're combined in creamy, cheesy chowders—pleasing, but sometimes, well, bland. No one could accuse this captivating, spicy-sweet soup of being bland. It's nice and thick and hot; it can be a great vegetarian entrée (assuming you use vegetable stock), if served piping hot over a larger portion of rice than the few tablespoonsful per serving called for here.

This is *not* a quick one-two-three soup. Here's the concept: an aromatic, spiced purée of broccoli and potatoes in which distinct pieces of sautéed broccoli and carrots float. The purée and the sauté are done separately, then combined at the last minute. It is worth the fuss. And here's one useful prep note to make it easier: Do the seasoned spiced purée the day before. This method is handy when preparing the soup for a company dinner; it makes less of a production out of things.

I dedicate this soup fondly to Charlisa Cato, who has for years worked our front desk a couple of days a week, and once called it (the soup) "primo."

PUREE:
Broccoli stems, from 1 head (bunch) broccoli, tough bottom 2 inches removed (see step 1)
3 tablespoons butter
1 onion, diced
Fresh gingerroot, about the size of a thumb, peeled and very finely diced
2 teaspoons black mustard seeds (omit if black are not available; don't use yellow)
2 to 3 teaspoons ground cumin
2 to 3 teaspoons ground coriander
2 to 3 teaspoons good-quality curry powder
2 to 3 teaspoons ground turmeric
⅛ teaspoon cayenne pepper, or to taste
4 cups Chicken Stock 1 (page 19) or Golden or Browned Vegetable Stock (pages 28 and 32) or any well-flavored chicken or vegetable stock
2 medium red-skinned new potatoes, scrubbed and diced
2 medium parsnips, peeled and sliced
2 cloves garlic, peeled and put through a garlic press
3 tablespoons raisins
1 cinnamon stick (about 2 inches)
Salt and freshly ground black pepper to taste
½ cup Crème Fraîche (page 50)

SAUTE:
Broccoli flowerets from 1 head (bunch) broccoli (see step 1)
2 tablespoons butter
2 medium carrots, peeled and sliced
2 ribs celery, sliced

FOR SERVING:
1½ cups cooked long-grain rice
2 tomatoes, chopped
1 cup plain yogurt
½ cup minced fresh mint

1. Divide the broccoli. Cut off the flower heads leaving about 1 inch of the stems and coarsely chop; these will be used for the sauté. Peel the remainder of the stems and carefully slice into matchsticks. These will be used for the purée.

2. Make the purée: In a 10-inch skillet, melt the butter over medium heat. Add the onion, and sauté until it starts to soften, about 3 minutes. Add the gingerroot and all spices. Cook, stirring constantly, over medium heat, about 5 minutes. Pour in the stock—it will sizzle dramatically—then scrape the pan contents into a soup pot. Add the remaining purée ingredients except the crème fraîche or kefir cheese.

3. Cover the soup pot and let simmer about 30 minutes, or until the vegetables are quite tender. Remove the cinnamon stick, and purée the mixture in a food processor with the crème fraîche or kefir cheese. Return the purée to the soup pot, and reserve.

4. While the purée cooks, make the sauté: In a 10-inch skillet, melt the additional 2 tablespoons of butter over medium heat and stir-fry the floweretted broccoli for about 3 minutes. Add the carrots, and stir-fry for 2 minutes more. Cover. Lower the heat slightly and let the broccoli steam for about 3 minutes. Remove the cover, add the celery, and stir-fry another 3 minutes.

5. Reheat the spicy broccoli purée, stirring often. Add the sautéed vegetables to the purée. Heat thoroughly, stirring; do not allow to boil. Taste for seasoning; adjust the spiciness, salt, and pepper. Place ¼ cup of cooked rice in each bowl, and ladle the very hot soup over it. Accompany with the remaining rice, a big bowl of chopped fresh tomatoes, and the yogurt lightly blended with the minced mint.

Serves 4 to 6 as an entrée, with the rice

Déjà Food: A little bit of this soup re-spiced with some extra cayenne and spelled out with a few additional vegetables, makes a great sauce for a bowl of couscous. Or, instead of rice or couscous, eat it with warmed whole-wheat chappatis (Indian bread, not unlike tortillas, which you can buy at a natural foods store).

CABBAGE

At times I've felt my fondness for cabbage doomed me in the eyes of the terminally hip the way my choice to live in Arkansas did. I used to try to explain my love for Eureka Springs to my New York cronies and colleagues—it was safe, beautiful, eccentric, an artist's colony. But the prevalent geographic chauvinism always ensured that this was met with some cute remark like "Oh, yeah, you're a *writer* and you live in Arkansas; I didn't know they could *read* in Arkansas." Finally I got tough: "Well," I'd say mildly, "You know, I *did* own two houses

in Eureka Springs before I was twenty-one on a freelancer's income." This rejoinder finishes the condescension pronto. Someday I will find the analogous thing to say about cabbage.

There is much good, and little bad, to be said. It's healthy, being one of the anti-carcinogenic cruciferae. It's inexpensive, and it's universally available. It's diverse: There's standard green cabbage and the savoy, and Chinese varieties, and there's red cabbage. Cabbage is wonderful raw, not only as the dominant vegetable in dozens and dozens of different slaws, but as a team player in many salads. Its outer leaves do the most gorgeous decorative things on a buffet table. Try covering a board or flat basket on which cheeses will be placed with cabbage leaves, or lining a basket with them, then filling it to overflowing with crudités for a beautifully abundant garden-y display. These same outer leaves can be arranged around a whole cored cabbage which, with most of its insides scooped out, serves as a bowl for a dip or spread. And its inner leaves, blanched briefly, can be stuffed with any one of countless savory fillings. Stuff the leaves individually to make cabbage rolls, or reassemble them into one huge rococo stuffed cabbage ball. Wrap the ball in cheesecloth, slowly steam it, and slice to serve—an amazing creation.

This leaves cabbage as a side vegetable, which is how we often use it at the restaurant. A quickly stir-fried, sweet-and-sour green cabbage, with the "sour" provided by raspberry vinegar, is a revelation. Mark Dewitz, who worked for us one year, did a great classic red cabbage sauté with caraway seeds. But cabbage as a simple stir-fry is best of all.

Just loads of shredded cabbage quickly tossed around in butter and vegetable oil over medium-high heat, covered to steam for a minute or two, then uncovered to finish. A tiny bit of salt and that's it. You can't believe how good this is; the cabbage is neither too crisp nor sodden—and astonishingly sweet.

How did cabbage get so bad a rep? For years in much of America it was boiled, and boiled in large pieces. Wrong! This makes its texture soggy, its flavor blah, and its cooking odors lingeringly, sulphurously unpleasant. No other single vegetable is as resentful of mistreatment as cabbage (though its kin—brussels sprouts, broccoli, and cauliflower—come close). Also, because cabbage was inexpensive, it was often eaten by immigrants. So to the list of bad cabbage associations was added one more item: poverty. Have you ever, anywhere in fiction, read a description of a tenement hall that did *not* portray it as smelling of overcooked cabbage?

When *quick* cooked, by steam or stir-frying, cabbage tastes and smells delectable. In order to cook it this speedily, it *must* be cut into thin ribbons. In many of our soup recipes the cabbage is cooked separately and added to the soup at the very end. Then, too, the cut is all-important. Cut your cabbage for soup in fine ribbons and *simmer* it. Never boil. That way, even when it is cooked longer, there is no obnoxious odor. Promise.

Joseph Saltzman's Shchi
(Russian Cabbage Soup)

 oseph Saltzman, a family friend, is a Russian émigré who remembers visiting his well-off grandparents as a child in the Crimea. But rather than eating with them, he and his brother begged to eat with the servants. They ate the simple food the boys much preferred: dark bread, kasha (cooked buckwheat), and shchi.

Like borscht, another Russian soup of a thousand spellings, shchi is transliterated into English many different ways. However you spell it, it's a Russian cabbage soup that is not unrelated to borscht. It is Slavic soul food; perfect wintertime peasant fare. Its pleasant, intriguing sweet-sourness is due to a bit of cider vinegar and sometimes sauerkraut, raisins, a few prunes, and honey.

Shchi is sometimes made with fresh cabbage, or sometimes a combination of sauerkraut and cabbage. I like the combo. When it's made with sauerkraut, Russians call it day-old shchi. Actually, the soup does get even better the next day.

To make this an entrée, serve the soup over potatoes; omit them if the soup is to be used as a starter.

3 tablespoons butter
1 large onion, diced
1 medium carrot, scrubbed or peeled and diced
1 medium turnip, scrubbed or peeled and diced
1 parsnip, scrubbed or peeled and diced
1½ to 2 quarts Chicken Stock 1 (page 19) or Browned Vegetable Stock (page 32) or any well-flavored chicken or vegetable stock
1½ cups green cabbage, cut into fine ribbons
1½ cups fresh sauerkraut, bagged or jarred, but never canned, well drained
1 cup canned whole tomatoes with their juice, mashed or buzzed to a chunky purée in a food processor
3 cloves garlic, put through a garlic press
¼ cup dark raisins
¼ cup yellow raisins
10 pitted prunes, diced
2 tablespoons honey, or more, to taste
1 to 2 tablespoons cider vinegar, or more, to taste
1 bay leaf
Salt and freshly ground black pepper to taste
6 to 8 small red-skinned new potatoes (optional)
1 cup sour cream or other dairy option (page 47), for garnish

1. In a 10-inch skillet, melt the butter over medium heat. Add the onion and sauté until it starts to soften, about 3 minutes. Add the carrot, turnip, and parsnip. Continue sautéing until the vegetables start to soften, about 4 minutes. Transfer the vegetables to a large soup pot and add all the remaining ingredients except the potatoes and sour cream. Use a little of the stock to deglaze the skillet, then add the pan contents to the soup pot.

2. Bring to a boil, turn down the heat to medium-low, and let simmer, covered,

until the vegetables are quite soft and the dried fruits have almost disintegrated into the broth, 1 hour or so. Taste for seasoning; the soup should be decidedly sweet and sour, but not sharply so. Adjust with the vinegar and honey.

3. Towards the end of the cooking period, boil or steam the potatoes if using, separately, until tender.

4. Serve the shchi very hot, dividing the cooked potatoes among each serving bowl and ladling the soup over them. Dollop 1 tablespoon of sour cream, or the dairy option of your choice, over the soup; pass extra at the table.

Serves 6 to 8 as a starter, 4 to 6 as an entrée

VARIATIONS:

Shchi with Kasha: Preferred by Joseph Saltzman. Omit the potatoes. Cook 1½ cups kasha according to the package directions. Put a few spoonfuls of the cooked kasha in the bottom of each soup bowl before ladling the shchi over it. Pass the extra kasha at the table.

Jack Albert's Sweet and Sour Cabbage Soup: Jack staked his claim in Eureka Springs some years ago, using money from the sale of a natural foods restaurant he started in New York called Angelica's Kitchen. He is a fine cook, with a natural-foods orientation. Jack has been associated with several restaurants around town, most recently the Oasis, his tiny, funky Mexican/Jewish café. It's an inexpensive, tasty hangout for alternative types, as well as for the occasional astonished tourist. Where else in the world can you get your *huevos rancheros* with a bagel?

Jack makes a glorious, super-duper shchi. It follows the recipe above using vegetarian stock, with these changes: Substitute 3 tablespoons oil for the butter, and at the end of the sauté period, drizzle the vegetables with 2 tablespoons of tamari/shoyu soy sauce. Omit the tomatoes and parsnip. Replace the sauerkraut with 1½ cups additional shredded cabbage. Use very little salt; tamari/shoyu is salty. Since the sauerkraut is omitted, add a little extra vinegar to make it sour enough to balance the sweet.

CARROT

Carrots, second only to onions, are real seasoning workhorses in any cook's stable. Whether diced and sautéed in a mirepoix (page 37) or in a mixed vegetable dish like The Soup (page 167), their cheerful color and slight sweetness is always agreeable.

They really do best in collaboration with lots of other vegetables; while "just" carrot soup is delicious, it's less dimensional, a once-in-a-while thing to fill a spot on a specific menu. Given this, our carrot soup is nonetheless something very special.

Younger carrots are much sweeter and more tender than their aged kin. Here's how to tell the difference: young carrots are thinner and bright orange, older are bigger, paler, and often cracked.

Carrot-Orange Soup with a Toasted Cashew Garnish

his soup is *gorgeous* in pale yellow cups. I know; I've ladled it into them enough times at our restaurant. And it's as refreshing as it is pretty. The grated orange zest used here works magic, adding indefinable freshness and surprise. (We use this trick in our Freshwater Fish Soup Provençale with its tomato and white wine base.)

This is essentially a purée of carrots and sautéed onions enriched with cream, brightened with a tad of tomato paste, and, of course, sparked with orange zest. Toasted cashews add crunch and contrast.

The carrots called for here are peeled; this adds to the smoothness of the finished purée. Puréed rice provides a slight thickening, an easy (and calorie-light) trick I've used here and there in the recipes.

2 tablespoons butter
1 large onion, chopped
4 to 5 cups Chicken Stock 1(page 19) or Golden Vegetable Stock (page 28) or any well-flavored chicken or vegetable stock
1 tablespoon honey, more to taste, if needed
14 to 16 young, sweet, thin carrots (about 1½ pounds), peeled and chopped
2 tablespoons tomato paste
2 tablespoons long-grain rice
Grated zest of 1 orange
1 cup fresh orange juice
½ cup heavy (whipping) cream, evaporated skim milk, or Crème Fraîche (page 50)
Salt and freshly ground black pepper to taste
⅛ teaspoon or so freshly grated nutmeg (optional)
1 tablespoon brandy (optional)
¼ cup freshly toasted cashews (see page 316), coarsely chopped, for garnish

1. In a 10-inch skillet, melt the butter over medium heat. Add the onion and sauté until it starts to soften, about 3 minutes. Transfer the sauté to a soup pot with 4 cups of the stock, the honey, carrots, tomato paste, and rice. Bring to a boil, then turn down the heat to medium-low and let simmer, covered, for 30 minutes or until the rice is quite soft.

2. Transfer the soup to a food processor and purée with the orange zest and juice, cream, and salt and pepper. Taste. If the carrots are flavorful enough, you won't need anything else, but if it's not quite there, add the nutmeg (to taste) and the brandy. For extra smoothness, you may strain the soup after puréeing.

3. Return the soup to the pot and reheat, watching closely to prevent burning. Taste. If it's too thick for your liking, thin it with additional stock. Serve very hot in

cups, garnished with a sprinkle of the toasted cashews.

Serves 4 to 6 as a starter

Note: The purée is rich enough in texture so that you could get away with using evaporated milk here; still, the larger amount of heavy cream is my preference for good taste—alas.

VARIATIONS:

Height of Summer Soup: Add 3 red bell peppers, diced, to the onions after they've sautéed for 3 minutes; sauté the peppers and onions 5 minutes more. This addition enriches both the color and flavor of the soup beautifully. You may even want to omit the cream and just let the pure vegetable flavors speak for themselves.

Or, to dress up this essentially unpretentious and inexpensive soup, squiggle the

---

CAULIFLOWER

❦*I love cauliflower, but because it's both mild and easily overcooked, it's not a vegetable that naturally whispers "soup" to me, except when combined with cream or milk or cheese as in the Blushing Cream of Cauliflower Soup (page 252). Please note the sidebar there about selecting a good cauliflower.*❦

---

soup with red pepper purée before you add the cashews. Use the forty-nine-cent squeeze bottle trick (see page 44).

CELERY

Celery's many virtues (crispness, low-calorie content, mild flavor, universal supermarket availability) give it a familiarity that has too often led to contempt. This contempt intensifies if it is so associated with "diet" that it becomes, ergo, hateful. Too, celery's crisp texture keeps well and it is frequently kept long past its prime flavorwise. We overlook its delightful crunch; complain about its stringiness; and never realize that its relative lack of flavor is due to its keeping qualities. If you ever get to have young, fresh-out-of-the-ground celery, you'll discover that it is actually sweet.

Even ordinary supermarket celery, if seen and tasted anew, without prejudice, has charm. Pretend it is something exotic or one-season-a-year, like asparagus, then have a bite. You might be surprised.

APPLES: THE SECRET INGREDIENT

❦*What are apples doing in Celery and Tomato Soup Aurore and numerous other offerings here and there in other chapters? They (and sometimes pears) are adding a subtle sweetness and an even subtler tang; they're adding a little body and a smooth, velvety texture when a soup is puréed; they're gently rounding out an amazing variety of other flavors. Then, too, we have some local apples that are inspirational.*

Many of Arkansas's apples are excellent, especially two old varieties I've not seen elsewhere: the Arkansas Black, and the Black Twigg. Both are superlative apples—very, very firm, flavorful, and tart. Another old apple, the Stayman Winesap, is not uncommon, but to me the locally grown Stayman Winesaps are superior to any I've tasted elsewhere except in British Columbia. The Quindell is another Arkansas original, though I'm not as fond of it as the others; it's a very pretty Red Delicious-type apple, but soft-textured and bland for my taste. Its sport was discovered at Banta's, an apple orchard in Alpena, about forty minutes from Eureka Springs.❦

Celery and Tomato Soup Aurore

If you think of the canned, bland, faintly pasty "cream ofs" when you think of celery soup, think again. This feisty soup is light, refreshing, and without even a trace of cream or milk.

The color is a sunrise golden-orange; tomato adds an acidic zing and apple a sweetness. Yet the celery flavor remains strong and clean, underscored by the use of celery seeds. I like this best hot, but it's good cold, too. If you plan to serve it chilled, use vegetable oil instead of butter.

A fine-mesh strainer is best here— well, you could do it by hand, but it's a lot of work.

Pam cooking spray
2 tablespoons butter or mild oil, such as
corn or peanut
1 large onion, chopped
1 teaspoon celery seeds
1 bunch celery plus leaves from a second
bunch, washed well and coarsely
chopped (reserve a few whole leaf sprigs
for garnish)
2 ripe tomatoes, coarsely chopped
2 tart apples, unpeeled, cored, and coarsely
chopped
3 to 4 cups Chicken Stock 1 (page 19) or
Golden Vegetable Stock (page 28) or any
well-flavored chicken or vegetable stock
¼ cup brandy
1 tablespoon honey
Salt and freshly ground black pepper to
taste
3 tablespoons cornstarch
3 tablespoons water
Sour cream, yogurt, kefir cheese, or Crème
Fraîche (optional; page 50), for garnish
Sprigs of celery leaf, for garnish

1. Spray a heavy 10-inch skillet (or the largest pan you have) with Pam, and in it melt the butter or heat the oil over medium heat. Add the onion and sauté until slightly softened, about 3 minutes. Add the celery seeds, and sauté another 2 minutes. Add the celery and celery leaves and stir-fry just until coated with butter, about 1 minute. Add the tomatoes and apples and raise the heat slightly, cooking and stirring until the tomatoes have begun to give up their juice, about 5 minutes.

2. Spray a large heavy enameled pot with Pam and transfer the sauté to it. Add the stock, brandy, and honey. Deglaze the skillet with a little stock, and scrape the pan contents into the pot. Bring to a boil, turn down the heat to medium-low, and let simmer, covered, until the vegetables are quite soft, about

30 minutes. Let the soup cool slightly, then drain, reserving both the solids and liquids.

3. Put the solids in a food processor and purée, then strain the purée. Return this very smooth purée to the strained liquid, and reheat to a near boil. Add salt and freshly ground black pepper to taste.

4. Combine the cornstarch with the water, smushing the mixture with your fingers until it's absolutely smooth. Ladle a bit of the hot soup into the cornstarch paste, whisk, then whisk the mixture into the hot soup. Cook, stirring constantly, until the soup is slightly thickened and all the raw cornstarch flavor is gone. If the soup is very hot, thickening may take place almost instantly; otherwise, it will take 2 to 3 minutes.

5. If you're serving the soup hot, do so immediately, garnished with the optional sour cream and a sprig of celery leaf. Or let it chill overnight and serve cold. It's a good starter for a curried entrée.

Serves 6 to 8 as a starter

For another refreshing celery soup, see Marge Parkhurst's Yogurt Cream of Celery Soup (page 273).

CORN, CUKES, AND EGGPLANT

🍒*Nothing could be better than a good corn-filled soup, and you'll find several recipes in the book. There's a full-meal Chicken and Corn Soup with Late Summer Vegetables (page 59); it's a great basic soup. Then, there's the delectable, spicy New World Corn Chowder (page 253). This is five-star; don't miss it or any of its variations if you're a fan of things caliente.*

If, however, you have access to the best height-of-summer sweet corn, as well as some really good made-from-scratch chicken stock, try this Simplest of Corn Soups: Cut fresh corn from the cob, allowing 1 ear per diner and per cup of chicken stock. Cook the corn in the stock, then purée the corn and stock in a food processor. If desired, strain. Reheat, add salt and freshly ground black pepper (and if you like, ½ teaspoon of sugar or honey, though you won't need it if the corn is fresh enough). Serve with just a sprinkle of chopped parsley as a garnish.

Just as simple, though much richer and less good for you, is this Creamy Simple Corn Soup: Follow the above method, but substitute heavy cream for part of the chicken stock—say, ¼ cup heavy cream per cup of stock. Add it when puréeing the soup. Even just 1 tablespoon of heavy cream per cup of stock adds a most pleasant creaminess.

With or without cream, these are both di-vine simplicity. But because there are so few in-gredients, the freshness and full flavor of each must be impeccable.

CUCUMBER: *Some people cook cucumbers; I don't, since I'm usually inundated enough as it is by other members of the ever-prolific squash family, many of which have to be cooked to be good eating. Since cucumbers are delicious raw, I say use them and enjoy them that way. Several of our summery chilled soups do: crisp cukes in a smooth soup which is served in a frosty glass cup on a sweltering day elevates the phrase "cool as a cucumber."*

Chill out with Gazpacho Rosa (page 113), as well as the luscious "Good Foods" Cucumber Yogurt Soup (page 274); all are delicious, and incredibly refreshing.

EGGPLANT: *Eggplant is one of our favorite veg-etables. We use it a lot, but rarely in soups. How-ever, see Curried Cream of Eggplant Soup-Stew (page 256) for a wonderful exception to the rule.* 🍒

FENNEL

*T*his faintly licorice-flavored bulb, beloved by the Italians, is just starting to be widely available in America. The greens which top it look much like dill, and Jim Long of Long Creek Herbs brings them to us all summer long and into the fall, for garnishes. The feathery, dark, brilliantly green foliage is so pretty, as are the sunburst-yellow flowers, which look like an explosion of fireworks.

The bulb we get less often, but several local gardeners have promised to grow us more this coming year, since we like it so much. Sometimes we slice and quick-sauté it as a side vegetable; sometimes we make it into one of the two soups included here. It is delicious, faintly sweet with a subtle but pervasive anise taste. Fennel is not a flavor common to the America palate; on first bite you might be a little dubious, but by the last, you want more. It is haunting, addictive. In soups that use fennel bulbs, I also usually sauté fennel seeds to emphasize and strengthen the flavor, but you may omit them until you're certain that you are a fennel lover.

To prepare the bulb, slice it perpendicular to the stem end. The bulb is actually a bunch of tightly gathered stems attached to a central core, not unlike a bunch of celery, though short and round and fist-sized. But when you slice the bulb, you'll see; what you expected to be one round slice falls into crescent shapes, just like sliced celery ribs.

The slices should be about ¼ inch thick. Discard any outer segments of the fennel if they feel tough and fibrous as you cut through them.

Italian-Style Fennel Soup with White Wine and Tomatoes

I n Italy, fennel is often served raw, as a crudité, or lightly cooked, then marinated in oil and vinegar. But to my mind it also mixes well with these classic Mediterrean flavors. Bright colors echo the bright, clear tastes.

5 cups Chicken Stock 1 (page 19) or
    Golden Vegetable Stock (page 28) or any
    well-flavored chicken or vegetable stock
3 medium bulbs fennel, sliced
2 cups dry white wine
2 cups seeded and chopped fresh tomatoes
    (peeled if you find tomato skin in the
    finished soup offensive) or 1 can (15
    ounces) whole tomatoes with their juice
Pam cooking spray
1 to 2 tablespoons olive oil
2 large red onions, chopped
1 teaspoon fennel seeds (optional)
4 cloves garlic, peeled and put through a
    garlic press
2 teaspoons honey
Salt and freshly ground black pepper to
    taste
1 cup coarsely chopped fennel leaves, any
    tough stems removed before chopping

1. In a large soup pot, bring the stock to a boil. Drop in the sliced fennel and blanch it over medium-high heat just until tender-crisp, about 3 minutes. Remove from the heat and strain out the fennel using a slotted spoon. Set the fennel aside.

2. Add the wine to the stock. Bring back to a boil, and let boil over high heat 5 minutes. Then add the tomatoes. Turn down the heat to medium-low and let simmer for 10 minutes.

3. Meanwhile, spray a large skillet with Pam. Add the olive oil, and heat over medium-high heat. Add the onions and sauté until starting to soften, 4 to 5 minutes. Add the fennel seeds if you wish a more pronounced fennel flavor in the finished soup, and continue stirring and sautéing for another 5 minutes. Add the garlic, and stir for 1 minute more.

4. Scrape the contents of the skillet into the soup pot, deglazing the pan with a little of the soup and adding the deglaze to the pot as well. Add the honey. Let the soup simmer 5 minutes, then season to taste with salt and pepper.

5. When ready to serve, return the blanched fennel to the pot, and heat through. Remove from the heat, stir in half the fennel leaves, and serve. Pass additional fennel leaves at the table.

*Serves 6 to 8 as
a starter*

Fennel Soup Finished with Cream

 f you know you like the flavor of fennel, you'll find this soup heavenly, as I do. Without the acidic wine or tomatoes, you get pure, unadulterated fennel, in all its sweet, elusive glory. As in the Italian-Style Fennel Soup, a touch of honey brings out fennel's innate sweetness. Make sure you use a good, flavorful chicken broth here, as the seasonings are so simple.

5 cups Chicken Stock 1 (page 19) or
    Golden Vegetable Stock (page 28) or any
    well-flavored chicken or vegetable stock
2 medium bulbs fennel, sliced
Pam cooking spray
1 to 2 tablespoons butter
2 large yellow onions, chopped
1 to 2 teaspoons fennel seeds, optional
4 cloves garlic, peeled and put through a
    garlic press
2 teaspoons honey
½ cup heavy (whipping) cream
Salt and freshly ground black pepper to
    taste
1 cup coarsely chopped fennel leaves, any
    tough stems removed before chopping

1. In a large soup pot, bring the stock to a boil. Drop in the sliced fennel and blanch it over medium-high heat just until tender-crisp, about 3 minutes. Remove from the heat and strain out the fennel using a slotted spoon. Set the fennel and stock aside.

2. Spray a large skillet with Pam. Add the butter, and melt over medium-high heat. Add the onions, and sauté until they start to soften, 4 or 5 minutes. Add the fennel seeds if you wish a more pronounced fennel flavor in the finished soup, and continue stirring and sautéing for another 5 minutes. Add the garlic and stir for 1 minute more.

3. Bring the stock to a boil. Then turn down the heat to medium-low and let simmer. Scrape the contents of the skillet into the simmering stock, deglazing the pan with a little of the stock and adding the deglaze as well. Add the honey and cream. Let the soup simmer 5 minutes more, then season with salt and pepper.

4. When ready to serve, return the blanched fennel to the pot, and heat through. Remove from the heat, stir in half the fennel leaves, and serve. Pass additional fennel leaves at the table.

Serves 6 to 8 as a starter

GARLIC

❝*I am the garlic lady, six pressed cloves on my spaghetti and those bulbs as raw as myself
on this blustery day, which I shall spend at home, entertaining myself...***❞**

I wrote these words on a blustery day. I was single, proud of it, satisfied with my solitary life and ecstatic over my newly devised recipe for Garlic Spaghetti, the recipe I have sometimes said

I want chipped on my tombstone as an epitaph.

When I think about how different though equally rich my life now is as a very married innkeeper/chef/writer/

teacher, my head spins. But there's one constant: I still love garlic. Papery-skinned, beautifully fragrant, no-messing-around: still reeking after all these years.

Shortly after Ned and I married we went to the Bank of Eureka Springs for Ned to co-sign my notes. John Cross, the then-president, eyed him skeptically and said, "Well, she's got you signed up for the liabilities, I hope she's letting you in on the assets." Love of garlic may be the greatest asset I let Ned in on. (Lesser men might have thought it a liability.) Fortunately, he was a willing convert.

I have three entirely different garlic soups in this book, and it was hard to stop there. A rich, creamy, elegant one (yes, garlic can be elegant) is in the dairy chapter. Another, a tomato-based soup filled with good things—pasta, a few vegetables, all thickened with a bit of egg yolk. It's called Hangover Soup, although I have more often used it to chase away colds or sorrow than hangovers. And below is the very simplest, pleasantest most-shrouded-in-legend one, *aïgo bouïdo,* in Provençal dialect, "boiled water." *"Boiled water?"* you ask. Well, not hardly. And yet . . . sort of. You'll see in a moment.

Hangover Soup

his garlic soup differs from the other: it's hearty but also elegant, fussier than Aïgo Bouïdo. It is the kind of soup a person craves when recovering from a cold or a broken heart. Not being a drinker myself I can't swear to this, but it's reputedly a good hangover cure. The combination of garlic, herbs, and cloves is magic, the tomato juice adds zip, and the unctuous egg yolk enrichment is balanced by the pasta's pleasant, soothing note.

2 large heads garlic, separated into cloves, unpeeled
6 cups Chicken Stock 1 (page 19) or Golden or Browned Vegetable Stock (pages 28 and 32) or any well-flavored chicken or vegetable stock
3 whole cloves
Good-sized pinch dried leaf sage
Good-sized pinch dried leaf thyme
Several sprigs fresh parsley
Salt and freshly ground black pepper to taste
2 cups tomato juice or V8 vegetable juice
¾ cup or so uncooked smallish pasta, like baby shells, small elbows, or alphabets
3 egg yolks
6 to 8 whole-wheat bread croûtes (page 96), small if using soup as a starter
4 to 6 ounces sharp Cheddar or Monterey Jack cheese, or a combination of both, grated
Finely minced fresh parsley or cilantro, for garnish
1 ripe avocado, pitted, peeled, and sliced, for garnish

1. In a large soup pot, combine the garlic, stock, cloves, sage, thyme, parsley, and salt (go easy; some of the later additions to the soup are salty). Bring to a boil, lower the heat to medium-low, and let simmer gently, uncovered, for 45 to 60 minutes. Strain the soup, pressing down the solids with the back of a wooden spoon to extract most of the garlic from the peels. Scrape any garlic purée from the underside of the strainer into the broth. Discard the garlic peels and the spent herbs.

2. Add the tomato or V8 juice to the strained soup and bring it to a boil. Drop in the pasta and let it cook until done—5 minutes for alphabets, 8 to 10 minutes for the larger shapes.

3. Meanwhile beat the egg yolks in a small bowl.

4. Put a croûte in each soup bowl and top with a handful of grated cheese (the cheese is not melted beforehand in this recipe).

5. When the pasta is done, ladle out a little of the hot soup into the beaten egg yolks, whisk together, then whisk this mixture into the soup pot. The soup should thicken almost immediately. Remove the pot from the heat, and ladle the soup over the cheese-covered croûtes. Garnish each serving with a sprinkle of parsley and/or cilantro, and top with a few slices of ripe avocado. Enjoy!

Serves 8 as a substantial starter (with small croûtes) or 6 as an entrée

VARIATION:

Great Full-Meal Hangover Soup: For an even heartier entrée, place a poached egg on each croûte before ladling the soup over it. Wonderful! For a fine-but-not-fussy meal you'll be proud to set before anyone, try this

soup with The Salad (page 372) because one's cooked, the other raw. Besides, you can never have too much garlic.) Finish with a fruity dessert, like a really good baked apple made with brown sugar and served with gingerbread and a dollop of yogurt.

Aïgo Bouïdo

n Volume One of *Mastering the Art of French Cooking,* Julia Child, Simone Beck, and Louisette Bertholle say, "Along the Mediterranean, an *aïgo bouïdo* is considered to be very good indeed for the liver, blood circulation, general physical tone, and spiritual health. A head of garlic is not at all too much for 2 quarts of soup. For some addicts, it is not even enough." Ali-Bab, the nineteenth-century French author of *Gastronomie Pratique,* notes, "This soup is not suitable, of course, for a ceremonial banquet—in fact, I wouldn't even recommend it for a small dinner party! However, when all the guests are from the Midi, it proves to be an enormous success." And John Thorne, whose newsletter *Simple Cooking* and book of the same name are the height of clearsighted food writing, says, "Boiled water. . . . It doesn't sound very satisfying at all, and yet the Provençale also say of it, *aïgo bouïdo sauva la vido . . .* aïgo bouïdo, saver of lives."

Thorne describes the most basic version of "original, true 'stone soup'. . . made from nothing but the faith that we are not meant to starve. . . ."

It's garlic simmered in boiling water with a pinch of herb, maybe a chopped tomato, and a bit of olive oil ladled over dry bread. But, Thorne adds, "to serve it to others, the soup needs... not improvement exactly, but a little socialization."

Here is my slightly socialized version of this life-saver. Its starting place was my own love of garlic, and Thorne's Soupe à l'Ail Bonne Femme, in his newsletter.

Garlic is used here in three ways: sautéed and then simmered, simmered without sautéing, and mashed raw, then spread onto bread croûtes, crisp rounds of toasted bread.

5 tablespoons olive oil
2 large onions, chopped
8 cloves garlic, peeled
3 to 4 red, ripe tomatoes (peeled if you find tomato skin in the finished soup offensive), coarsely chopped
Pam cooking spray
5 cups Chicken Stock 1 (page 19) or Golden or Browned Vegetable Stock (pages 28 and 32) or any well-flavored chicken or vegetable stock or, if you like the simplicity of the flavor, spring water
2 pinches dried leaf sage
2 pinches dried rosemary
2 pinches dried thyme
Salt and freshly ground black pepper to taste
6 thick croûtes of French white or whole-wheat bread (page 96)
4 to 6 ounces Gruyère or Jarlsberg cheese, grated

1. In a 10-inch skillet, heat 4 tablespoons of the olive oil over medium heat. Add the onions and sauté until softened, about 4 minutes. Lower the heat slightly, put 2 cloves of garlic through a garlic press, and add them to the pan. Sauté 1 minute, stirring almost continually. Add the tomatoes and stir-fry for 1 minute.

2. Spray a large soup pot with the Pam, and pour the sautéed vegetables into it. Deglaze the skillet with a little of the stock or water and add the pan contents and remainder of the liquid to the soup pot. Add the herbs, salt, and freshly ground black pepper. Bring to a boil, then turn down the heat and cook at a low simmer, uncovered, for about 20 minutes.

3. Preheat the oven to 425°F.

4. Push 3 cloves of the remaining garlic through the press, add them to the remaining tablespoon of olive oil, and mix well. Brush the croûtes on one side with this oil. Divide the grated cheese among the croûtes, piling it onto the garlicked side of each, and pressing the cheese down slightly with your hand. Put the cheese-covered croûtes on a baking sheet, and bake in the oven until bubbly and golden, about 3 to 5 minutes.

5. While the croûtes brown, push the remaining 3 cloves of garlic through the press directly into the soup. Let the soup simmer another 5 to 10 minutes. To serve, place one hot, cheese-crusted croûte in each of 6 soup bowls, and ladle the hot garlic soup over it. And invite me, please!

Serves 6 as an entrée, with salad and dessert

VARIATIONS:

Rich Aïgo Bouïdo: Beat the yolks of 3 eggs with 1 cup of the hot soup, then whisk this mixture back into the pot. Barely simmer, stirring, for 3 to 5 minutes, or until the soup thickens slightly. This is a nice company starter, as long as you aren't serving any garlicphobes.

Extra-Garlicky Aïgo Bouïdo: Not for the faint of heart, but wonderful. If you have on hand any Garlic Oil (page 41)—and you should!—stir 2 tablespoons of it into the soup immediately before ladling over the croûtes. Yum!

Pesto Variation: If your garden's full of basil, or your fridge holds a jar of fresh pesto (page 41) or the commercially made kind, spread it on the croûtes before topping with the cheese.

GREENS

Now we come to a vegetable that couldn't have more of an Ozark pedigree—greens. Greens may be cultivated, like chard, collard, mustard, spinach, New Zealand spinach, cabbage, or kale. Greens may also be wild, like poke sallet, lamb's-quarter, sorrel, purslane, dandelion, dock, amaranth, and more. These are foraged from the woods and hedgerows, or even from the water: watercress. The leafy greens themselves may be the whole raison d'être of the plant, or the greens may have a tuberous root, with a life and purpose of its own as with the turnip and the beet. But however and wherever you find them, greens are delicious, versatile, and as much a part of the Ozarks as rocks in the garden.

Greens are incredibly plentiful in nutrients, and pop up continually in popular magazine lists of vitamin-rich, mineral-rich foods. When vitamin C was in, there were greens on such lists. When vitamin A was hip, greens made

the cut again. Ditto for iron, ditto calcium.... Greens will *always* be on these lists because they are good for you in ways science hasn't even discovered yet. Like Popeye, you can practically feel yourself growing muscles as you eat greens.

Besides, greens taste good. They are an acquired taste, but I have been their ardent devotee for so long, it's hard for me to remember a time when I didn't like them. Yet there *was* such a time, when I was first on my own in New York City. Already I was a lover of produce markets, and I used to go once a week to the enormous Essex Market (created when Mayor LaGuardia took all the pushcarts and vendors off the street and ensconced them in huge brick buildings around the city). There I discovered kohlrabi, fennel, and celeriac.

But I passed by the greens, other than salad greens and spinach. Although the other greens were bright and fresh, they also looked a little forbidding; the

large leaves looked tough, and some (like turnip) were a bit spiny. However, they were cheap, and I was both poor and adventurous. I decided to try them once, though I knew nothing about how to cook them.

And they were *awful.* I cooked them in *milk,* of all things, as someone (I might as well say it: some *Northerner*) had told me to do. They were bitter. They were sodden. They were tough. Well, they are still bitter, some a little, some a lot, but that's part of what I like about them now. I also know now how to cook them, and believe me, it's not in milk.

Not having grown up on long, long, long-cooked greens, with the bacon, ham, or salt pork so beloved by born-and-bred Southerners, the charm of this method of preparation eludes me. On the other hand, though I still prefer the quick stir-fry of greens, or their last-minute addition to a soup, I have to admit that slow-cooked greens—greens cooked until they lose their brightness and turn dark—taste a lot better to me now than they used to. Certainly they're quite wonderful this way in Gumbo Zeb (page 231). Perhaps, in time, as an adopted Arkansawyer, I will end up where my native friends began.

As people all over the world know, greens are natural with anything starchy: with corn bread or cornmeal dumplings (these are the tried-and-true, hands-down Ozark favorites); with potatoes (as in the famous Irish dish colcannon); with starchy beans and pasta (in minestrone and other European dishes); with sweet potatoes (in African, Southern, and hippie cuisines); and with rice (Indian-style curries of greens in number-less variations, and I've never had one that wasn't delicious). Many of our soups with greens play off this delicious natural affinity.

Can you feel your muscles growing already?

GREENS 101

First, you can't have a "green"; the word is always plural, "greens," like that other Southern favorite, "grits." You can't have a "grit," either. Another language note: however many greens you have, if you have enough, it's a "mess." A mess of greens generally weighs about 1 to 1½ pounds, but, of course, you might need a bigger mess if you're feeding a lot of people.

Second, though chard, turnip greens, kale, collard greens, et al. each have their distinctive flavors, they are used interchangeably in recipes in this and most other cookbooks. A combination of several greens are cooked together almost always, which balances and moderates their individual excesses—the heat of mustard greens, the faint bitterness of turnip, the sweetness of chard and beet.

Third, greens must *always* be washed well. I mean, yes, greens are supposed to be earthy food—but not in *that* sense.

Fourth, make sure the mess of greens you start with is really *large*. Greens cook down to almost nothing the minute they hit the heat.

CUTTING UP GREENS

Here's a relatively easy method for cutting up the intimidatingly huge mass of greens that you will generally start with in many recipes. This is the quickest way to get that mass into thin ribbons, the cut you will usually want for soup. Be sure to use a sharp knife, not (as some have tried) kitchen shears.

About the greens' ribs and stems—whether or not you remove them depends on how you'll be preparing the greens. If you're slow-cooking the greens for more than 40 minutes, as in Gumbo Zeb (page 231), just leave on the stems and ribs; they'll soften up during cooking. If, however, you plan a quick stir-fry or brief simmer, go ahead and remove any tough stems or center ribs.

To ribbon the leaves, stack a handful of the washed, possibly destemmed leaves on top of each other, facing in the same direction. First cut the leaves lengthwise 2 or 3 times, then crosswise in quick, attentive chops, cutting strips that are ⅛ inch or so wide. This will leave you with bright, quick-cooking ribbons about 1 to 2 inches long—perfect for minestrones, variations of The Soup (page 167), and many other recipes.

For the following Greens and Pot Likker Soup with Cornmeal Dumplings, however, a coarse chop with a knife or kitchen shears in irregular pieces is fine.

Greens and Pot Likker Soup with Cornmeal Dumplings

 kay, here's the traditional Ozark way with this, sworn to by generations, though in recent years all but retired in favor of greens and cornbread (see ours, page 352). This is home-stuff, designed to simmer on the back of the woodstove all day. Be sure to read About Dumplings (page 137) or they will come out like cannonballs.

SOUP:
1 large smoked ham hock, or 2 good-size
  chunks of smoked hog jowl (the average
  ham hock is slightly over ½ pound)
1 dried hot red chili pepper
4 quarts water
2½ pounds greens, approximately, any
  combination of turnip, mustard, kale,
  collard, spinach, beet, radish tops, poke
  sallet, dock, chard, watercress, or any
  other wild or cultivated greens, all
  washed very well and thinly sliced
Batter for Old South or New South
  Cornmeal Dumplings (page 136 or 138)

TABLE CONDIMENTS AND FIXINGS:
1 hard-cooked egg per diner
1 bunch scallions, trimmed whole
1 bunch radishes, washed and sliced
Cider vinegar
Tabasco or similar hot pepper sauce

1. In a large soup pot, preferably a heavy cast-iron dutch oven with a tightly fitting cover, combine the ham hock or hog jowl, chili pepper, 3 quarts of the water, and the greens, and simmer until the greens are tender and falling apart. At least 1 hour is traditional, 4 or 5 hours is not uncommon. Drain the greens, reserving both the greens and their liquid (the "pot likker"). Combine the meat picked from the hock or the jowl with the greens. At this point, you may continue with the recipe or proceed later. If you continue you'll be ready to eat in 30 minutes or so. Or allow the greens and pot likker to cool, refrigerate both, and complete the recipe later. If you wait, you'll be able to lift the congealed ham fat from the pot likker after it's gotten cold—not traditional, but in our fat-conscious world desirable to many.

2. Thirty minutes before serving time, add the last quart of water to the pot likker and bring it to a rolling boil. Make the batter for the dumplings as directed and cook them in the boiling pot likker. Meanwhile, in a separate pot, slowly heat the greens and meat over very low heat.

3. The minute the last dumpling is cooked, serve dinner, as follows: Spoon a portion of cooked greens and meat into each bowl—pottery bowls seem most appropriate here—add a couple of dumplings, and ladle a generous amount of the pot likker (which will have thickened a bit from some of the dumpling starch) over everything. Garnish each plate with a quartered hard-cooked egg, and pass the whole scallions, sliced radishes, and cruets of cider vinegar and hot sauce.

Serves 4 to 6 amply with all the fixings and dumplings

Note: These condiments are essential in making the greens come to life! Most people chunk their egg into the greens, sprinkle the soup liberally with the hot sauce, sparingly with vinegar, and nibble on the scallions and radishes as they eat, although some cut the scallions into the bowl. This cannot be called a pretty dish or an elegant one, it might not even be one you'll enjoy the first time you eat it. But to know it over time is to love it.

Greens and Pot Likker Soup Nouveau'Zarks-Style

 reens à la Southern hippie, more or less. It's akin to the previous recipe in taste, but more healthful. Now, you dyed-in-the-cotton Southerners laugh all you want, but I promise you this is incredibly good, soul-satisfying food. It remains faithful to the delicious spirit of the original while allowing the greens to contribute their vitality without being ambushed by all that deadening fat. It's home cooking rather than restaurant or company fare—but simply addictive.

SOUP:

2½ pounds greens, approximately, any combination of turnip, mustard, kale, collard, spinach, beet, radish tops, poke sallet, dock, chard, watercress, or any other wild or cultivated greens, all washed very well and thinly sliced (page 133)

4 quarts Golden or Browned Vegetable Stock (pages 28 and 32) or any well-flavored vegetable stock

1 dried hot red chili pepper

6 cloves garlic, peeled and put through a garlic press

1 tablespoon butter or olive oil (optional)

Batter for New South Cornmeal Dumplings (page 138)

2 to 3 tablespoons dark miso paste

2 tablespoons Garlic Oil (page 41; optional)

1 or 2 drops of liquid smoke or similar smoke flavoring (optional)

TABLE CONDIMENTS AND FIXINGS:

1 hard-cooked egg per diner

1 bunch scallions, trimmed and sliced

1 bunch radishes, washed and sliced

Cider vinegar

Tabasco or similar hot pepper sauce

1. In a large soup pot, preferably a heavy cast-iron dutch oven with a tightly fitting cover, combine the greens, stock, chili pepper, garlic, and optional butter or olive oil. Bring to a boil, then turn down the heat to medium-low and let simmer, partially covered, until the greens are wilted and tender, about 30 to 40 minutes. Drain the pot likker from the greens, reserving both. No need to chill and remove fat; there isn't any, except the optional 1 tablespoon, which you added by choice and so want it to be there. The chili pod is not removed; it cooks until it more or less dissolves, and if you get the hard stem

in your portion, you just put it on the side of your plate.

2. Thirty minutes before serving time, bring the pot likker to a rolling boil. Make the batter for New South Dumplings and cook them as directed in the boiling pot likker. Meanwhile, in a separate pot, over very low heat, slowly heat the greens.

3. The minute the last dumpling is cooked, season the pot likker as follows: Stir in the miso (it gives an essential, meaty taste) and garlic oil, if using (it's wonderful, though obviously not remotely traditional). Taste the pot likker. If you really pine for the smoky flavor ham gives, add a few drops of liquid smoke, but cautiously; it's strong.

4. Spoon a portion of the cooked greens into each bowl, add a couple of dumplings, and ladle a generous amount of the pot likker (which will have thickened a bit from some of the dumpling starch) over everything. Garnish each plate with a quartered hard-cooked egg, and pass at table the scallions, sliced radishes, and cruets of cider vinegar and hot sauce.

Serves 4 to 6 substantially with fixings and dumplings

VARIATION:

Chicken and Greens Soup with Cornmeal Dumplings: Substitute Chicken Stock 2 (page 20) or any well-flavored chicken stock for the vegetable stock; reserve the cooked chicken and omit the miso. Heap the bowls with not only cooked greens and dumplings, but with large pieces of the chicken as well. Ladle the pot likker on top. Not traditional, but awfully satisfying, and very, very good for you. Hard to believe something so simple can be as tasty as this soup. Garlic Oil (page 41) stirred in at the last is a winner here.

Old South Cornmeal Dumplings

These are heavier dumplings, "bready" as Ned likes to say. (He means it as a compliment, it is not so to me. But I do like these substantial dumplings once in a while, though I much prefer those made from the next recipe).

Here, a very thick cornbread batter is rolled into small balls, and cooked in pot likker (or stock). The dumplings double in size as they cook, so don't make them too big. Read About Dumplings, page 137, before making these or the following dumpling recipe.

4 quarts pot likker (see preceding recipe),
    any well-flavored chicken or vegetable
    stock, or water
¾ cup stone-ground yellow cornmeal
¾ cup unbleached all-purpose flour
2 teaspoons baking powder
1 teaspoon sugar
½ teaspoon salt
1 large egg
1 tablespoon butter, melted
½ cup milk, approximately, usually a
    little less (exact amount depends
    on the particular cornmeal's water
    content)
Unbleached all-purpose flour or
    cornmeal for coating the
    dumplings
Pam cooking spray

1. In a very large pot, bring the pot likker, stock, or water to a full boil (the bigger your pot, the better). Turn down the heat so that the liquid boils gently, just a tad more than a simmer.

2. Sift together the cornmeal, flour, baking powder, sugar, and salt. Separately, beat together the egg and melted butter. Pour this into the cornmeal mixture, and add just enough milk to make the batter hold together; usually a scant ½ cup. The mixture should be dry enough so that you can form it into balls, but not so dry that it falls apart. Roll the mixture into balls about the size of an unshelled pecan, drop each into the additional flour or cornmeal, and turn to coat. Set the floured balls out on a piece of waxed paper. Try to make the dumplings the same size so they'll cook in about the same length of time.

3. When all the batter is rolled, drop 6 of the dumplings into the gently boiling liquid of choice. Clamp a cover on the pot, glance at the clock, and don't lift the lid for 15 minutes. After the 15 minutes, remove the dumplings with a slotted spoon from the liquid to a warmed Pam-sprayed pot or casserole dish. Cover the dumplings to keep warm. Cook the next batch. Serve, with greens and pot likker and fixings, if using, as described in the preceding recipes.

Makes about 20 large dumplings

ABOUT DUMPLINGS

🐾 *Starchy, savory little somethings, cooked in hot stock—that's more or less what dumplings are. They can be light, delicate, and sophisticated, but generally we think of them as less ethereal, as plump, plain, grandma food. Plain or not, we love them so much that "dumpling" has long been an endearment, falling into disfavor only during the Age of Anorexia.*

Dumplings are not difficult to make, but do take a surprising amount of precision to be perfect. Perfect means moist but not leaden, neither wet outside nor undercooked inside. In case you don't have a grandma around to show you, here are eight tips for good dumpling cooking:

1. Use enough liquid for cooking the dumplings, at least 3 or 4 quarts.

2. Use a big enough pot, with a wide "surface." The pot should have a 4- or 5-quart capacity at least and be at least 8 inches in diameter. This is the largest size likely to be found in the average home kitchen; bigger's fine, but not smaller, unless you want to cook only 2 or 3 dumplings at a time.

3. Don't crowd the dumplings in the pot. They need room to expand, with enough hot liquid on all sides and with steam above. Don't try to fit in all the dumplings in one shot. Six to 8 marble- to pecan-size dumplings can be done in an 8-inch diameter, 4-quart-capacity pot (filled with 3 quarts of boiling liquid). If the dumplings

are very small, you may be able to cook a few more at a time.

4. Don't make the dumplings too large; smaller makes for a more delicate texture and insures that the insides will not be underdone, or the outsides overdone.

5. Form all of the batter into dumplings at once, setting them out on a piece of waxed paper so you can check for consistency of size and shape.

6. Roll the dumplings in flour or meal once they are made. This helps them hold together, and prevents a finished dumpling from having a ragged, uneven appearance. Drop in however many you plan on cooking in one pot's worth at the same time. Again, this permits even cooking.

7. Pot likker, water, or stock must be boiling when the dumplings are dropped in, but not boiling hard. If the water's too hot, the dumplings will disintegrate and/or stick to the bottom of the pot. Too cool and the whole thing'll turn into a pasty mass.

8. Dumplings are really cooked by steam as much as by hot stock. Put the cover on the pot once the dumplings are in, and don't lift *until the time specified by the recipe is up.* Use a kitchen timer—8 to 10 minutes can really get away from a person fast; if it does, there go your dumplings. 🐾

New South Cornmeal Dumplings

A far lighter and more delicate dumpling than the preceding, these are made with cooked cornmeal. Cooked cornmeal is polenta in Italian, mush in Southern; these dumplings have some kinship to certain Italian gnocchi. They are excellent.

I like to season these with a little of this and that in the herb line, but you could leave them plain. When these dumplings have been cooked in water, I enjoy them as I would pasta—with butter and Parmesan and freshly ground black pepper. Or maybe with a dab of pesto or some Garlic Oil (page 41).

Pam cooking spray
1½ cups water
1 cup stone-ground yellow cornmeal
½ teaspoon salt
½ teaspoon paprika
2 large eggs
1 tablespoon very finely minced onion
1 to 2 teaspoons finely chopped fresh herb,
*   such as sage or basil, or ½ to 1 teaspoon*
*   dried, crumbled (optional)*
Unbleached all-purpose flour for coating
*   the dumplings*
3 to 4 quarts pot likker, Chicken Stock 1
*   (page 19), Golden Vegetable Stock (page*
*   28), or any well-flavored chicken or*
*   vegetable stock or water*

1. Spray a small, very heavy pot with the Pam, and in it bring the 1½ cups water to a boil. Gradually whisk in the cornmeal, salt, and paprika, slowly stirring, then beating like crazy. Turn down the heat to very low and cook, stirring continuously with a wooden spoon, about 3½ minutes. By this time the cornmeal should be a very thick paste, so solid you'll have to scrape it from the pot. Remove the pot from the heat, beating the batter to cool it slightly. After about 1 minute, beat in 1 egg, then the other. Beat in the onion and chopped fresh or crumbled dried herb. Let the batter cool until lukewarm.

2. Fill a plate with flour. Roll the batter into small, marble-sized balls of equal size. As each ball is shaped, drop it onto the flour-filled plate and roll to coat it on all sides. Set the floured balls on a sheet of waxed paper until ready to cook.

3. Bring the stock or liquid of choice to a full boil in a large pot, then lower the heat so that the liquid boils gently. Drop 8 to 10 balls into the liquid, and cover the pot. Let the dumplings cook, undisturbed, for 9 minutes *exactly*. Scoop out the cooked dumplings with a slotted spoon, and transfer them to a warmed Pam-sprayed pot or casserole. Cover the casserole to keep the dumplings warm. Cook the next batch. Serve as soon as possible.

Makes about 30 small to medium dumplings

Colcannon Soup

his is homey and good, definitely not company stuff. Potatoes and kale (or other greens) come together in this soothing, delicious soup, inspired by what many consider Ireland's national dish—not corned beef and cabbage, but colcannon, potatoes mashed with cabbage. The cookbook *Laurel's Kitchen* offers a version of this done with kale which served as the mental starting point for devising my version.

I've used minimal fat in this recipe, which is why everything's sprayed with Pam.

Pam cooking spray
6 cups Chicken Stock 1 (page 19) or
*   Golden Vegetable Stock (page 28) or any*
*   well-flavored chicken or vegetable stock*
4 to 5 medium all-purpose potatoes,
*   scrubbed and diced*
1 tablespoon butter or mild vegetable oil
1 large onion, chopped
1 pound greens, any combination of
*   turnip, mustard, kale, collard, spinach,*
*   beet, radish tops, poke sallet, dock, chard,*
*   watercress, or any other wild or*
*   cultivated greens, all washed very well,*
*   thinly ribboned (page 133), and coarsely*
*   chopped*
1 cup milk
¼ to ½ cup heavy (whipping) cream or
*   evaporated skim milk*
Salt and freshly ground black pepper to
*   taste*

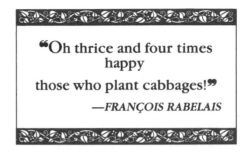

**"Oh thrice and four times happy
those who plant cabbages!"**
—*FRANÇOIS RABELAIS*

1. Spray a heavy soup pot with Pam, and in it bring the stock to a boil. Drop in the potatoes, turn down the heat, and let simmer 30 minutes.

2. Meanwhile, spray a 10-inch skillet with Pam and in it melt the butter or heat the oil over medium heat. Add the onion and sauté until softened, about 4 minutes. Lower the heat slightly, add the greens, and stir until they start to wilt, about 3 minutes. Cover the skillet and let the greens steam until fully wilted, 3 to 10 minutes.

3. When the potatoes are done, strain them from the stock, reserving both the stock and potatoes. Return the stock to the soup pot. Place the potatoes in a food processor with the milk and cream or evaporated milk and buzz until smooth. Combine this mixture with the stock in the pot, and stir in the sautéed greens and onion. Taste for seasoning. Reheat. Serve immediately.

Serves 4 as an entrée

Note: Instead of puréeing the potatoes in the processor (which does give them a thick, slightly gluey consistency), you may mash a few of them against the side of the pot, and add the cream directly to the soup.

GREEN BEANS

*I*n the old days, when I was a serious gardener, I used to grow green beans without fail each summer—after months of poring over the seed catalogs to choose the best varieties. Seed catalogs are always lovely fantasy reading, but bean names seem to me especially evocative: Kentucky Wonder, Blue Lake. . . . Then one year the woodchucks discovered the beans, then the deer; obviously the two- to three-inch-high bean plants were such an extraordinary delicacy to them they had to tell their friends. Then we started an inn, and I was no longer *just* a writer (a life that now seems to me almost monastically contemplative and very, very simple). And *then* we started a restaurant—whoa, Nellie! Now I'm lucky to jam a few tomatoes, some peppers, and a couple of basil plants in the ground, and I refuse to even consider planting anything I have to seriously fight the wildlife for. I buy my green beans at the farmer's market these days.

But I still make soups with green beans and I always will. Along with onions, potatoes, carrots, and cabbage, they are a vegetable I almost always use in mixed fresh vegetable soups, such as most versions of The Soup and in many (dry) bean-based soups. Thus my main appreciation of the green bean is as a team player, but I do have one soup in my repertoire in which they predominate. This is the Hungarian Green Bean and Potato Soup which follows.

Hungarian Green Bean and Potato Soup

*T*he inspiration and starting point here is a chilled Hungarian green bean soup called *habart bableves,* from Bernard Clayton's *Complete Book of Soups and Stews,* but the final result is quite different. I've substituted yogurt for the sour cream originally called for in this slightly sweet and sour soup, which was a big, four-star, let's-have-this-again-real-soon favorite with my dear and faithful recipe tasters. The humble ingredients meld synergistically. Caraway seeds are a flavoring you may be ambivalent about, but the amount required is tiny, not overwhelming. Though the soup has potatoes, it is light and piquant enough to serve as a starter.

The size of the green bean slices are all-important when used in soup. A bean cut lengthwise in thin diagonal slices allows it to cook quickly, and mysteriously releases lots of flavor, which adds much to the soup as a whole. These thin, barely recognizable slices are delicious, no tender-crispness here. You want the green beans meltingly soft. Also, your paprika must be good and fresh, not something that's sat in your cupboard for years. And the quality of the stock cannot be underestimated: It must be good and flavorful for this to work.

Don't add the cornstarch-yogurt mixture until immediately prior to serving time.

Pam cooking spray
12 ounces fresh green beans, trimmed and sliced into ¼-inch or shorter pieces (the easy way to slice: Stand beans upright in feed tube of food processor and cut using the slicing disc)
4 small all-purpose potatoes, scrubbed or peeled and cut into small, spoonable chunks
6 cups Chicken Stock 1 (page 19) or Golden or Browned Vegetable Stock (pages 28 and 32) or any well-flavored chicken or vegetable stock
3 tablespoons cider vinegar
3 tablespoons honey
2 to 3 cloves garlic, put through a garlic press
½ to 1 teaspoon caraway seeds
Salt and freshly ground black pepper to taste
2 tablespoons butter
1 large onion, diced
2 ribs celery with leaves, diced
2 tablespoons sweet Hungarian paprika
3 tablespoons cornstarch
3 tablespoons water
¾ cup plain yogurt

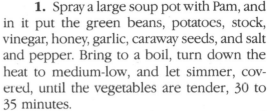

1. Spray a large soup pot with Pam, and in it put the green beans, potatoes, stock, vinegar, honey, garlic, caraway seeds, and salt and pepper. Bring to a boil, turn down the heat to medium-low, and let simmer, covered, until the vegetables are tender, 30 to 35 minutes.

2. Meanwhile, in a 10-inch skillet, melt the butter over medium heat. Add the onion and sauté until softened, about 4 minutes. Add the celery and sauté for another 2 or 3 minutes. Lower the heat slightly, and sprinkle the onion and celery with the paprika. Let the mixture cook another minute, stirring constantly. Scrape the sauté into the green-bean pot. Add a little liquid to the skillet and deglaze it, then scrape the pan contents into the pot. Take the soup off the heat.

3. When ready to serve, have the soup good and hot. Dissolve the cornstarch in the water, and smush with your fingers to make a smooth paste. Stir this paste into the yogurt. Whisk a ladleful of the hot bean stock into the yogurt-cornstarch mixture. Turn down the heat as low as possible, and stir the cornstarch-stabilized yogurt into the very hot soup. Using a wooden spoon, stir gently until the soup has thickened slightly, another 5 minutes. Taste it to make sure all of the raw cornstarch taste has cooked out, and also to check for seasonings. Besides salt and pepper, you may need to adjust the sweet-sour ratio with more cider or honey. Serve hot, accompanied by a good crisp-crusted, European-style bread (such as the French Country Bread, page 328).

Serves 6 to 8 as a starter

VARIATION:
The version above is the one I make at home, and very good it is for real-life, good-and-healthy cooking. But at the restaurant I do a

sinful calories-be-damned version, with a full cup of crème fraîche or sour cream substituted for the yogurt. In this case, cornstarch is not necessary, though it will stabilize the soup if you wish to use it. Also, if your stock was less full-bodied than it should have been and your paprika didn't come through for you with perfect freshness, this soup responds very well to the addition of 1 tablespoon or so of Garlic Oil (page 41) stirred in at the last, though dear knows it's not Hungarian. . . .

MUSHROOMS

*F*ortunate indeed are we mushroom lovers who've settled in the Ozarks. It's prime morel country, and most years we also have plenty of puffballs and chanterelles. And there are several farms nearby that grow shiitakes, those wonderful, rich Oriental mushrooms with a hearty taste somewhere between that of steak and lobster, yet with an earthy, vegetal succulence. Quite often in the restaurant we serve the local shiitakes as an hors d'oeuvre, simply roasted with garlic, olive oil, rosemary, other fresh herbs, and coarse salt—such a treat! But when the shiitakes are being harvested, odds are that if we don't use them as a first course, they'll appear in one of the entrées—or in a soup.

Mushrooms of any kind are naturals with cream and garlic; also with sherry, also nutmeg. A good cream of mushroom soup is always well received; in fact, I have never worked in a restaurant where, when it was the soup du jour, we failed to sell out. But non-creamy mushrooms can be just as scrumptious, and of course, considerably lower in fat and calories. Following are two good non-creamy ones, one quite soigné, one more peasanty.

Sherried Mushroom Broth with Varied Mushrooms

ou must be a lover of mushrooms, for there is little to this soup but them. If you are, you'll find the pure, essence-of-mushroom flavor here sublime. This is like the mushroom equivalent of French onion soup. It's sophisticatedly low calorie, and best served in tiny cups, for sipping rather than spooning.

6 cups Browned Vegetable Stock (page 32)
    or any well-flavored vegetable stock
1 ounce assorted dried mushrooms (see
    Note)
1 large onion, chopped
1 carrot, scrubbed or peeled and chopped
Salt and freshly ground black pepper to
    taste
1 pound fresh domestic white mushrooms
    (preferably a little older and slightly
    funky looking; these are very full-
    flavored and excellent in soup), wiped
    clean
1/3 cup dry sherry or to taste

1. In a small pot, bring 1 cup of the vegetable stock to a boil. Put the dried mushrooms in a bowl and pour the stock over them. Weight the mushrooms down with a plate, and let them soak, submerged, 45 minutes to several hours.

2. In a soup pot, combine the remaining stock, onion, carrot, and salt and pepper. Pulse-chop the fresh mushrooms in a food processor until they resemble a coarse paste and add to the soup pot. Bring this stock mixture to a boil, turn the heat down to low, and barely simmer over very low heat, partially covered, about 45 minutes.

3. Meanwhile, carefully strain the dried mushroom soaking stock through a fine-mesh strainer (dried mushrooms usually harbor a lot of grit and sand). Save this strained stock. Now take the mushrooms, and, one by one, rinse each carefully in very cold water, being alert to any grit. Slice the

---

SNOWED-IN SUPPER WITH NEDLEY AT HOME

*A Great Big The Salad
(made with romaine, fresh
spinach, and red leaf lettuce,
topped with grated carrots,
paper-thin purple onion slices,
crumbled blue cheese, diced
fresh tomato, grated fresh beets,
and alfalfa sprouts)

*Sherried Mushroom Broth with
Varied Mushrooms
(wild rice and sautéed
mushroom variation)

Whole-Wheat Bread and Butter

Dried Apricots / The Last of the
Christmas Chocolates

Brewed Columbian Decaf

---

soaked, cleaned mushrooms in thin ribbons and reserve.

4. Strain the stock mixture into a bowl, pressing hard on the solids to get out all the flavorful juice of the mushrooms. Or power-strain the soup (this will give you a slightly thicker, less brothy result). Combine the strained mushroom broth with the strained mushroom-soaking stock and the sliced soaked mushrooms. Reheat with the sherry. Season to taste. Serve hot in small cups.

Serves 6 as a small starter

Note: As for the dried mushrooms, I use a few of whatever's on hand: some dried porcini, dried shiitake, dried oyster mushrooms and/or morels, extended by a South American dried mushroom, a boletus, that is very tasty and less expensive than the European types. It is often found in natural foods stores, and is great in soup.

VARIATION:

Place 1 tablespoon of cooked wild rice in the bottom of each cup before adding the soup. Try sautéing a few young fresh domesticated mushrooms (or fresh shiitake, and/or morels, puffballs, or chanterelles—heaven!) in a bit of butter, and divide them among the cups.

Mushroom-Barley Soup

 Jewish soul-food classic. Everyone thinks their version is the best, and I'm no exception. Our Dairy Hollow Mushroom-Barley Soup uses white wine as well as stock, lots of herbs, and a dab of tomato paste. You can omit the dried mushrooms, but they do add a pleasant, aromatic depth to the soup. Once, cooking for a friend allergic to gluten, I made this with rice instead

of barley—it was just as good.

The soup thickens on sitting overnight, so if there are any leftovers, you'll need to dilute them with extra stock when you reheat. Anyway, it's a perfect potage for banishing the last long gray days of February.

7 cups Chicken Stock 1 (page 19) or Golden or Browned Vegetable Stock (pages 28 and 32) or any well-flavored chicken or vegetable stock
1 ounce dried porcini or morel mushrooms
½ cup pearl barley
2 tablespoons butter or mild vegetable oil, such as corn or peanut
1 large onion, chopped
2 ribs celery with leaves, chopped
2 carrots, scrubbed or peeled and sliced
1 parsnip, scrubbed or peeled and sliced
1 to 3 teaspoons tamari/shoyu soy sauce, or to taste
8 ounces fresh domestic white mushrooms, wiped clean and sliced
1½ cups medium-dry white wine
1 tablespoon tomato paste
3 to 4 tablespoons fresh dill or 1 to 2 tablespoons dried
2 bay leaves
½ teaspoon dried basil
½ teaspoon dried thyme
½ teaspoon dried oregano
Salt and freshly ground black pepper to taste

1. In a small pot, bring 1 cup of the stock to a boil. Put the dried mushrooms in a bowl and pour the hot stock over them. Weight them down with a plate so they stay submerged and let them soak for 1 hour or so. Meanwhile, precook the barley by bringing it to a boil with 1 more cup of the stock. Turn down the heat to medium-low, cover, and simmer slowly for 25 minutes or so, until the barley is somewhat tender and the liquid is absorbed.

2. Meanwhile, in a heavy 10-inch skillet, melt the butter or heat the oil over medium heat. Add the onion and sauté until softened, about 4 minutes. Add the celery, carrots, and parsnip, and cook another 3 minutes, stirring. Add the tamari/shoyu, lower the heat, and cook another 2 minutes, stirring frequently. Scrape the sauté into a large soup pot. Deglaze the skillet with a little of the remaining stock and add the pan contents to the soup pot.

3. Add the remaining stock, the partially cooked barley, the fresh mushrooms, wine, tomato paste, dill, bay leaves, basil, thyme, and oregano to the pot. Bring to a boil, then turn down the heat until the liquid just barely simmers. Cover, and let cook about 1 hour.

4. Towards the end of the hour, remove the dried mushrooms from their soaking liquid, reserving both the mushrooms and liquid. Rinse the mushrooms well to rid them of any lurking grit. Cut them into small dice, and add them to the simmering soup. Strain the mushroom soaking liquid through a fine-mesh strainer, and add it also to the soup. Season with salt and pepper to taste. The soup is now ready—but it's even better the next day.

Serves 4 to 6 as an entrée

ONONS

ONIONS

Cooking a dinner without onions is like playing Scrabble with only consonants on your tray.

Over the years, we've probably cooked for just about every kind of food allergy or special diet there is: low-cholesterol, sugar-free, vegetarian, vegan, diabetic, and gluten-free. We've fed— and fed well, I believe—guests who couldn't eat eggs, milk, seafood, mushrooms, green peppers, or strawberries. But the single biggest culinary challenge for me, and the one whose results I feel most iffy about, is when I'm asked to cook an entire meal without onions.

Although onions are rarely featured in the restaurant's dishes, they are almost always there, adapting, filling in the blanks, pointing up the flavors of every other ingredient. Just as a painter could not do without the color black because of the way it works with every other color, a cook is hard-pressed to do without onion. Soups, it seems to me, have a special need and affinity for onion.

Few people are unfamiliar with that delightful classic, French onion soup: slowly sautéed onions, drenched with good stock (usually beef or veal, but a good chicken or vegetarian stock is just fine), the onions simmered to a melting smoothness; the soup topped with a crisp croûte and gratinéed with melting Gruyère and/or Parmesan cheese. Not too much! Though this excess is common it makes the soup no less delicious if it's done from scratch.

Because recipes for the real thing are so widely available, here are two for unusual onion soups. They're a bit different from the classic, though they certainly owe an allegiance to it. Also, check out Cock-a-Leekie (page 73), a chicken-based onion soup made without the gratinée treatment, and Autumn Cream of Onion Soup with Brandy and Cider (page 261).

Onion-Wine Broth

 was astonished to learn that I could make a really lovely, slightly thick onion soup without all the tedious slicing and slow browning. This is *not* the same as the classic soup, yet it is as flavorful as any you could ask for. It's light and excellent on its own—use it as you would a consommé. Or embellish it with crisp, garlicky croutons or cooked noodles or crumbles of bacon, Tiny Meatballs (page 60) or New South Cornmeal Dumplings (page 138). I think it's best simple and straightforward, though, as the light note in a dressy dinner. Although dill is in it, it does not taste dilly.

If there is a trick here, it is to use a

stock of excellent flavor as the base. No canned broth, please. When made with the Golden Vegetable Stock or Dark Vegetable Stock, I consider this the vegetarian comfort-equivalent of chicken soup.

2 cups dry white wine
5 cups Chicken Stock 1 (page 19) or
  Golden or Browned Vegetable Stock
  (pages 28 and 32) or any well-flavored
  chicken or vegetable stock
2 teaspoons dried dill
1 teaspoon dried savory
2 small to medium carrots, scrubbed or
  peeled and coarsely diced
5 to 6 medium onions, peeled and
  quartered
Salt and freshly ground black pepper to
  taste

1. In a large soup pot, heat the wine, stock, and herbs, and bring to a boil. Add the carrots and onions. Return to the boil, turn down the heat, and let barely simmer until the onions are very, very soft, about 1½ hours.

2. Strain the stock, reserving the solids and liquids. Return the stock to the pot. Buzz the carrots and onions in a food processor until puréed. Return the purée to the stock. Heat through, and season to taste with the salt and pepper. Serve piping hot in cups. If this isn't delicious and curative, I don't know what is!

Serves 6 to 8 as a starter

Note: If your base stock lacked muscle, you may feel this soup should be enriched. This is easily done by swirling in, towards the end of the cooking, 1 tablespoon each of butter and olive oil, or better yet, some Garlic Oil (page 41).

CROÛTES

❧ *Croûtes are extra-crunchy oven-baked toasts of French or other rustic, crisp-crusted bread. Unlike breakfast toast made in the toaster, they are intended to be crisp all the way through, though only slightly colored on the outside. This is so that when hot soup is ladled over them (as it is in many different French, Italian, and Spanish soups) the bread will hold up, softening somewhat without disintegrating entirely.*

Croûtes are simply made. Just heat the oven to 300°F, lay bread slices directly on the rack, and toast for about 15 minutes, or until dry and crisp.

Let the croûtes cool to room temperature on a rack (if they're laid on a plate, steam condenses on the underneath side, inclining the croûtes to sogginess).

Croûtes can be made several hours in advance, or even the day before if, when fully cool, they are kept tightly wrapped. ❧

Oven-Baked Onion and Leek Soup Gateau

 his peasanty dish is just impossibly good. Though rustic, it is a little showy, predictably lovable. Bread, cheese, tomatoes, and sautéed onions are layered in a casserole, which is covered with hot stock and baked. Definitely kin to classic French onion soup.

An equipment note: You will need an oven-to-table casserole which can be placed directly on the heat; it need not have a tightly fitting lid. Your 5-quart enameled soup pot, if it is large enough and its handles flameproof, will do fine. You'll also need a funnel with as long a neck as possible, and two 10-inch skillets. (Two, because even though you could fit all those onions and leeks into one, the air circulation essential to good sautéing would be lost if you did and the onions would release their moisture instead of browning properly.)

1 long loaf French bread, preferably
    whole-wheat, cut into 1-inch slices and
    made into croûtes (page 147)
Pam cooking spray
4 tablespoons (½ stick) butter
4 large onions, very thinly sliced
2 leeks, white part only, split open
    lengthwise, very well rinsed, and sliced
    very thin
1 teaspoon sugar
2 teaspoons tamari/shoyu soy sauce
Additional butter, at room temperature
    (optional)
1 cup canned whole tomatoes, puréed in
    food processor and strained to remove
    seeds
1 tablespoon tomato paste
8 ounces Gruyère, Jarlsberg, or
    Emmenthaler cheese, grated
3 quarts Chicken Stock 1 (page 19) or
    Browned Vegetable Stock (page 32) or
    any well-flavored chicken or vegetable
    stock
Salt and freshly ground black pepper to
    taste

1. First, make croûtes and allow them
to cool.

2. Spray two 10-inch skillets with the
Pam. Divide the butter in half, adding 2 tablespoons to each skillet, and melt the butter
over medium heat. Add half of the onions
and half of the leeks to each skillet, and sauté
them, stirring often. Cook the vegetables
until they are limp and colored, without dark
edges, about 30 minutes. At about the 20-
minute point, sprinkle ½ teaspoon of sugar
into each skillet to facilitate browning, and
lower the heat. During the last 5 minutes of
cooking, add 1 teaspoon of the tamari/shoyu
soy sauce to each skillet, and stir attentively.
When the onions and leeks are done, remove
the skillets from the heat.

3. Spread the cooled croûtes sparingly
with the optional softened butter. Whisk together the strained puréed tomato and tomato paste until smooth, and spread it on
about one-third of the buttered croûtes (if
not buttered, spread the purée directly on
the bread). Gently pat a thin layer of grated
cheese about ¼ inch thick onto all the
croûtes. Reserve about 1 cup of cheese.

4. Pour the stock into a pot and bring
it to a boil. Generously spray a 5-quart dutch
oven with the Pam and assemble the gâteau:
Place a layer of cheese croûtes on the bottom
of the casserole and sprinkle the layer with
some of the remaining cheese. Cover the
bread and cheese with one-third of the sautéed onions. Add another layer of cheese
croûtes and cheese, and a good grinding of
black pepper. (Use salt, but only if your stock
is not salty; remember, the cheese is quite
salty, so go easy.) Repeat until all the cheese
croûtes and onions are used, adding pepper
to the layers as you go along. Top with a layer
of all the tomato and cheese croûtes. Gently
pat a blanket of the remaining cheese over
the top layer, covering it
completely. The casserole
must not be more than
two-thirds full, because
the bread will swell when
the stock is added.

5. Remove the hot
stock from the stove. Take
your funnel and poke it into the side of the
dish as far down as it will go. Gradually ladle
the hot stock through the funnel. Avoid dis-
turbing the top layer of cheese as much as
possible. Keep ladling until the liquid has
risen to about halfway up the top layer of
bread. Put the casserole on the stove over
low heat, and let barely simmer, uncovered,
for 30 minutes.

6. Fifteen minutes before the end of

that 30 minutes, preheat the oven to 300°F.

7. Transfer the casserole from stovetop to oven, and bake, uncovered, for about 1 hour. Every 20 minutes or so, re-insert the funnel into the casserole and ladle in a little more broth. The bread will absorb the liquid, but if your casserole has a 5-quart capacity and you are faithful about funneling in stock periodically, the finished dish will still be somewhat brothy—and oh, what a delicious broth!

8. When the uppermost cheese layer is a golden, crusted brown, with a somewhat cakelike appearance (hence the *gateau* in the title), it is done. Serve it, scooped from the casserole, immediately, and luxuriate.

Serves 10 to 12 as an entrée

VARIATIONS:
Garlicked Gateau: You know I think there can't be too much garlic. If you are of the same mind, spread the toasted croûtes generously with Garlic Oil (page 41) instead of softened butter. Mmmm!

Oven-Baked Onion and Leek Soup Gateau in a Pumpkin: Hard to believe it could be possible, but this is even more delicious, charming, and rustic than either of the above. Simply purchase a medium pumpkin, preferably one of the sweeter "pie pumpkins." Cut off its top, as for a jack-o'-lantern, and scoop out all seeds and fiber. Salt and pepper the inside of the pumpkin well.

Construct the gateau in the pumpkin instead of in the casserole. Bake for about 20 minutes longer (1¼ hours total) than instructed in the main recipe since this variation forgoes the stovetop simmer. Ladle out a scoop of pumpkin with each serving of soup.

PARSNIPS

❦ *Parsnips are unknown to many American cooks. These white, carrot-shaped roots with their earthy peel have a surprisingly delicate flavor, much like parsley, but sweet. I use them in many soups and stews, and have on occasion used parsnips in pie (cooked and mashed, as one would sweet potatoes in sweet potato pie) and cake (grated, as one would do carrots for carrot cake). They are a little too one-dimensional to stand on their own as a soup star, though I do make such a soup occasionally for really devoted parsnip aficionados. But I urge you to discover them as an addition to countless simmered dishes. They can sometimes be woody, which is why they're often either strained out of soup after lending their flavor, or else puréed and then put through a sieve or a power strainer.* ❦

GREEN PEAS

Green peas, like asparagus, say spring in every bite. Unlike asparagus, though, or virtually any other vegetable, they preserve this fresh springtime quality even through the freezing process (providing they're not then over-cooked). In fact, unless you can get your green peas almost straight from the garden, you may do better with the frozen kind. The natural sugars that give that essence-of-the-season sweetness to green peas quickly turn to starch if the peas sit around too long, and their charm is lost.

Since the commercial operations take the peas virtually from farm to freezer, the sweetness is intact. Snow peas, or edible pod peas, do not preserve their magic frozen; these must be used fresh.

> **"We** are still on the chapter of peas ... the impatience to eat them, the pleasures of having eaten them, the joy of having eaten them again, are the three questions which have occupied our princes for the last four days. There are ladies who, having supped with the King, go home and there eat a dish of green peas before going to bed. It is both a fashion and a madness.**"**
>
> —*MADAME DE MAINTENON (a lady to the court of Louis XIV),* LETTERS

Gingered Fresh Pea Soup with Snow Peas and Water Chestnuts

 make this soup once each spring. It's fussy in the making, but a revelation in the eating, with its voluptuous egg-thickening called *velouté* plus crisp Oriental textures and seasonings. This is Ozark-made, New American melting-pot cuisine. Delectable. The first time I cooked this, Ned said, "I want to write a haiku." Restaurant guests are equally poetic in their enthusiasm.

This soup requires fresh water chestnuts, which are sometimes difficult to find and always difficult to peel. If you can't get them or are unwilling to undertake the peeling, please fix something else. The fresh sweet, super-crisp crunch is essential here.

2 tablespoons butter or mild vegetable oil, such as corn or peanut
1 onion, chopped
Leaves from 2 ribs celery
2 teaspoons minced fresh gingerroot
2 teaspoons tamari/shoyu soy sauce
4 ounces fresh, small, tender snow peas, any tough strings or stems removed
10 fresh water chestnuts, peeled (do not substitute canned)
6 cups Chicken Stock 1 (page 19) or Golden Vegetable Stock (page 28) or any well-flavored chicken or vegetable stock
1 pound fresh just-shelled new peas, or frozen petit peas
1 teaspoon honey
¼ cup heavy (whipping) cream or evaporated skim milk
4 egg yolks, beaten
2 teaspoons toasted sesame oil
Salt and freshly ground black pepper to taste
Finely chopped scallions and toasted sesame seeds, for garnish

1. In a 10-inch skillet, melt the butter or heat the oil over medium heat. Add the onion and sauté over medium heat until it starts to soften, about 3 minutes. Add the celery leaves and gingerroot to the onion and sauté 1 minute more. Transfer the vegetables to a food processor and add the tamari/shoyu soy sauce. Buzz the mixture until smooth. Leave this purée in the food processor.

2. Steam the snow peas over boiling water briefly only until the peas sweat, 30 to 60 seconds at most. Immediately cool the snow peas by running cold water over them to stop cooking. Cut the snow peas crosswise into ¼-inch pieces. Dice the fresh water chestnuts into ¼-inch cubes. Combine the cut snow peas and diced water chestnuts, and set aside.

3. In a medium-size pot, bring 2 cups of the stock to a boil. Drop in the green peas, and let the stock return to a boil. Let the peas boil, uncovered, until barely tender, 5 to 10 minutes for fresh peas, 2 to 4 minutes for frozen. Drain the peas, reserving both the stock and the peas. Add the peas and the honey to the purée in the food processor and buzz again until smooth. For velvet smoothness (a must to me because I think the puréed pea skins have an objectionable texture) run the purée through a food mill, fine sieve, or power strainer.

4. In the soup pot, combine the pea-cooking stock with the remainder of the stock. Bring to a boil, then turn down the heat to low.

5. In a small, heavy pot, heat the cream or evaporated milk. Meanwhile, ladle a bit of hot stock into the beaten egg yolks, whisking well. Then gently whisk the yolks into the simmering stock. Stir gently with a wooden spoon until the soup thickens slightly. Add the hot cream or evaporated skim milk, then add the pea purée to the soup. Heat the soup until very hot, stirring; but do not allow it to boil. Add the sesame oil, and salt and pepper.

6. To serve, place a portion of snow peas and water chestnuts in each bowl. Ladle on the soup and garnish with the scallions and sesame seeds.

Serves 6 to 8 as a starter

SWEET PEPPERS

Green, red, yellow, and purple—peppers are a palette of beauty and deliciousness, bright, textural, healthy, and low-calorie. What more could you want of a vegetable? Oh, yes—they taste wonderful.

Red bell peppers are my favorite vegetable for eating out of hand—no contest. I'd rather eat a really good red bell pepper than a piece of fruit. They're sweet, lovely, and extraordinarily high in vitamin C. Unfortunately, they're expensive and spoil easily, so the only time I really get what I'd call enough of them is when they're ripe in our garden.

At the restaurant, we use them frequently for garnishes; nothing else gives that crunch, color, and sweetness. They are a must in Chilled Avocado Soup Mexique Bay (page 109). Then, there's Roasted Red Pepper Soup with Yellow Pepper Ribbons (page 262), an out-of-this-world special occasion soup we're really proud of.

Red bell peppers are nothing more than ripe green bell peppers. The green bells are good, and add distinctive freshness to many dishes, but they don't do it for me in the way the reds do. The purple peppers are nice for color contrast, but taste identical to the greens.

Yellow peppers, however, are as sweet as the reds, and are just as beautifully bright, though they may be even more perishable and expensive. They can be puréed by the same method as the reds.

POTATOES

Certainly America's best-loved tubers, lumpy, bumpy, homely potatoes are the ultimate curl-up-and-be-comforted food. And while baked, mashed, latke-d, and fried may all have their well-deserved fans, few would argue that potatoes as comfort food cure best served up as soup.

There are a couple of wonderful, rich potato soup recipes in the dairy chapter, and don't skip Colcannon Soup (page 139), in which potatoes and greens reveal their amazing affinity for one another. But here is the simplest of potato soups—nursery food, almost, nothing sautéed. Not for guests, it's a very plain soup, but good and comforting. Fix it for yourself on a blustery day when you're feeling sorry for yourself.

Leek and Potato Soup Simplicity

t will be a formidable temptation, but at least once, prepare this just as is: no dill, bay leaf, oregano or caraway, no milk or cream. Then feel free to start playing with it. I have to admit, I like bay leaf in here.

1 pound all-purpose potatoes, scrubbed and
    sliced
8 leeks, white part and 1 inch of green, split
    open lengthwise, very well washed, and
    sliced
4 cups Chicken Stock 1 (page 19) or
    Golden Vegetable Stock (page 28) or any
    well-flavored chicken or vegetable stock
4 cups spring water
1 to 3 tablespoons butter to taste (optional)
Salt and freshly ground black pepper to
    taste
Croûtes of whole-wheat French bread
    (page 147)
Grated Parmesan cheese, chopped fresh
    parsley, sour cream, kefir cheese, Crème
    Fraîche (page 50), or plain yogurt, for
    garnish

1. In a large, heavy soup pot, combine the potatoes, leeks, stock, water, and butter if using. Bring to a boil, turn down the heat to medium, and let simmer strongly, uncovered, until the liquid is reduced by about half, about 1 hour. Stir occasionally. Taste for seasoning and add salt and pepper if needed. Mash some of the potatoes into the soup to thicken it slightly.

2. Place a croûte in each soup bowl, and ladle in the soup. Top, if desired, with a bit of grated Parmesan, a sprinkle of parsley, or a dab of one of the dairy garnishes.

Serves 6 to 8 as an entrée

VARIATION:

Spread the croûtes with a little Garlic Oil (page 41) before ladling soup over them.

Also experiment with some or all of the following herbs, adding them to the stock and water: 2 bay leaves, 1 teaspoon dried oregano or basil, or ½ teaspoon dried rosemary.

Déjà Food: Combine the heated leftovers with the entire contents of a 16- to 28-ounce can of whole tomatoes, pulsed in a food processor just until chunky. Heat with any oddments of cooked vegetables you have lying around. Great vegetable soup fixings!

ON BEING NAMED "BEST" BY UNCLE BEN'S

❧*The first year we won it, the award came in two forms: a brass-on-wood plaque, which now hangs above our restaurant door, and a white-chocolate version, lettered in dark chocolate, which we promptly ate. Both versions named Dairy Hollow House "Best Inn of the Year," an honor shared with nine other inns in America.*

For three consecutive and wonderful years we won—and on the third year, instead of a chocolate plaque, we received a soigné crystal presentation piece, designed by Tiffany's, naming us an "Inn of Distinction." (The crystal piece, vaguely pyramidal, and about 10 inches tall, is a lovely thing. I asked Ned, "Do you think it would be vulgar if I wore it as a piece of jewelry?" He said, "Well . . . it did *come from Tiffany's.")*

Many people have asked us how Uncle Ben's "Bests" are selected: Did we enter a contest, did we have to use their rice? No. Here's the story: a few years after initiating their "Country Inn" rice mixes, Uncle Ben's began an "Inn of the Year" program, honoring America's small inns' contribution to high-quality service. Uncle Ben's brings together an independent panel of judges (at first ten, now expanded to fifteen) to pick out the ten inns they consider best in all America. (The panel rotates annually.) Only "full-service" inns, those serving dinner and breakfast, are eligible.

Judges might be magazine editors (like Cynthia LaFerle, of "Innsider"), authors of guidebooks (like Sara Pitzer, of Recommended Country Inns of the South*), or of newsletters (like Barry Gardner, of* Uncommon Lodgings*). Their identities are kept secret until after the judging. We were told by some of one year's judges at the Awards Dinner that they came up with a group list of eighty possible inns, and from there narrowed it down to ten. Uncle Ben's leaves the judges to make their decision as they wish. This is an award, not a contest; there are no strings attached, and no stuffable ballot box. An inn wins, simply, by being good, as that year's judges define it. Longevity's a factor, too, though no one said as much: an inn has to not just be good, but be good for long enough that enough people, judges included, have stayed there and had a good experience.*

We loved our three years of winning. Meeting our fellow innkeepers was perhaps the very best part of it. To network with such an intimate and select group of inns—from Vermont and Florida, Virginia and California, Washington and Maryland—was an energizing, delightful experience, one that left us psyched up and filled with good ideas.

Some excellent recipes from some of our co-winners are scattered throughout this book. ❧

PUMPKINS

*P*umpkins are abundant and lovable. Come fall, we heap them around our main entrance and by the Dairy Hollow sign at the Main House. And on the inner windowsill between the restaurant and the lobby, we sometimes march a line of baby fall pumpkins, sized in descending order. The arrangement on the front desk's always exceptional in the fall. One October favorite is a horn of plenty-shaped basket we picked up at a yard sale somewhere filled with potatoes, apples, sweet potatoes, squashes galore, and, of course, pumpkins.

Pumpkins come in all sizes, from teeny ones to huge. Only the small to medium eating pumpkins are sweet and truly suitable for cooking, though the big ones make a nice tureen, perfect for an autumn dinner party. (Cut off the lid, as for a jack-o'-lantern; scrape out the seeds and fiber; heat the inside by filling it with boiling water; pour out the water and fill with hot soup; bring it to the table. Ta-da!) Our Oven-Baked Onion and Leek Soup Gateau (page 147) can be made right in the pumpkin itself—dramatic and delectable.

If you can find them, there is a variety of pumpkin that has deeply cut ribs and a pale buff exterior instead of the bright orange we're all familiar with. (One guest, seeing such a specimen by the front door, remarked, "Did a vampire attack that pumpkin?") Its inner flesh is a vivid, vivid orange, however, and sweeter and more flavorful than any other pumpkin I have ever eaten. It is almost as sweet as that of the delectable butternut squash, whose meat can be used interchangeably with pumpkin in the following recipes. If you can find such a pumpkin, you're in business. (Or perhaps a friend will bring you one, as our former Dairymaid Gina Meadows did Ned and me several Octobers ago. What a nice pumpkin. What a nice friend.)

**"We ate our way from
A to Z
Enough for you?
Too much for me!**

**We ate so much
There are no scraps . . .
It's time for our
Thanksgiving naps!**

**Our sleep is deep,
and many snore . . .
When we wake up, we'll eat
some more!**

**O thanks for friends for food
for cheer
I'm glad Thanksgiving's once
a year!"**

—C.D.,
ALLIGATOR ARRIVED WITH APPLES

Pumpkin and Broccoli Chowder

his bright soup, really a variation of the preceding recipe but even fresher in taste and appearance, is a personal favorite. It's delicious as a starter, dimensional enough to be an entrée. The pumpkin or squash purée gives the soup a creamy texture; the bright green of the broccoli against the golden yellow soup is gorgeously festive.

3 to 4 tablespoons butter or mild vegetable
*   oil, such as corn or peanut*
1 large onion, chopped
1 tablespoon tamari/shoyu soy sauce
1 ripe tomato (peel it if you find tomato
*   skin in the finished soup offensive), diced*
4 cups Chicken Stock 1 (page 19) or
*   Golden Vegetable Stock (page 28) or any*
*   well-flavored chicken or vegetable stock*
4 cups freshly made pumpkin or butternut
*   squash purée (page 158) or canned*
*   pumpkin purée*
1 tablespoon maple syrup or honey
Salt and freshly ground black pepper to
*   taste*
1 bunch broccoli, tops cut into small
*   flowerets, stems julienned into strips*
*   roughly ¼ × 1 inch*
¼ to ½ cup heavy (whipping) cream

1. In a 10-inch skillet, melt the butter or heat the oil over medium-low heat. Add the onion and sauté slowly until almost limp but not brown, about 6 to 7 minutes. Add the tamari/shoyu soy sauce and the tomato. Cook, stirring often, until the tomato's juice has evaporated, about 5 minutes.

2. Transfer the sauté to a soup pot. Deglaze the sauté pan with a little of the stock, and add the pan contents, plus the remainder of the stock, to the soup pot. Add the pumpkin or squash purée, the maple syrup or honey, salt, and a touch of freshly ground black pepper. Heat, stirring often.

3. Separately, in a small pot with a tightly fitting lid, steam the broccoli flowerets and stems until tender-crisp (they should be a bright green), about 3 to 4 minutes.

4. Stir the steamed broccoli into the soup, then stir in the cream. Let the soup cook over low heat, stirring occasionally, until hot and the flavors have blended, 8 to 10 minutes. Do not let the soup boil. Serve hot.

Serves 8 as a starter

VARIATION:
Pumpkin and Broccoli Harvest Chowder: To make this into a full-fledged entrée soup, add some diced cooked potatoes with the broccoli. As an entrée it will serve 4.

Pumpkin and Tomato Bisque

Delicious, rich, elegant, and a majestic orange-red. Hard to believe it, but there's *no* cream in this wonder! We served this soup at the First Eureka Bank's Christmas party, and they were dubious when they read it on the menu—but loved it without exception. I mean those soup cups were scraped *clean!*

The soup freezes beautifully, in case you were thinking of preparing the soup ahead of time for the holidays.

3 to 4 tablespoons butter or mild vegetable
    oil, such as corn or peanut
1 large onion, chopped
3 to 4 cups Chicken Stock 1 (page 19) or
    Golden Vegetable Stock (page 28) or any
    well-flavored chicken or vegetable stock
1 can (28 ounces) whole tomatoes with
    their juices
1 tablespoon maple syrup or honey
4 cups freshly made pumpkin or butternut
    squash purée (page 158) or canned
    pumpkin purée
Salt to taste
Red Pepper Purée (page 46), for garnish
    (optional)

1. In a 10-inch skillet, melt the butter or heat the oil over medium-low heat. Add the onion and sauté slowly, stirring often, until limp but not brown, 6 to 7 minutes. Stir in 3 cups of the stock, and let simmer, partially covered, about 15 minutes.

2. Pour the tomatoes with their juice

OF PUMPKIN PURCHASE AND PURÉE PREPARATION

❦ *First off, be sure the pumpkin you're buying is a "pie pumpkin." These are smaller than the large jack-o'-lantern pumpkins, and the flesh is sweeter and less watery.*

If you need to know precisely the yield of purée you can expect from a given pumpkin, weigh it while it's whole. Figure 1 pound of raw, untrimmed pumpkin for each cup finished purée.

To fix the purée: Begin by slicing off the stem end of a pie pumpkin, then scooping out the seeds and strings. (If you like, you can rinse the goo off the seeds, dry them, and roast them on a baking sheet with a little oil and tamari/shoyu soy sauce; hull and eat them on a winter's night.) Cut the pumpkin in largish chunks and steam them over boiling water until they're tender when poked with a fork, about 10 to 12 minutes. Drain the cooked pumpkin in a colander, reserving the steam-ing liquid as a base for soup stock. When the pumpkin is cool enough to handle, remove the peel—a messy job, but it will more or less pull off with the judicious use of your fingers and a small, sharp knife. Put the peeled pumpkin in a food processor and buzz to a purée.

Butternut squash can be cooked and puréed in the same way. You get more meat and fewer seeds with butternut squash, certainly an advantage. Butternut squash is higher in sugar content and therefore sweeter than most pumpkins. Allow 1 pound uncut, whole, raw butternut squash for each 1½ to 1¾ cups finished purée.

Both pumpkin and butternut squash purées freeze very well. During the fall we always make up several pumpkins' worth of purée at one time and freeze it in quart containers. ❦

into a food processor. Add the maple syrup or honey, and purée. Add the pumpkin, and buzz again. Strain the stock, and add the strained-out onions to the processor. Buzz again, and, if an extra-smooth soup is desired, put through a power strainer.

3. Add the tomato-pumpkin purée to the stock. Season with the salt. Reheat, and serve very hot, garnished with the red pepper purée if using.

Serves 8 to 10 as a starter

> **"Of** the honesty and the sincerity of our sentimental fondness for the pumpkin there is no doubt. It is possible, indeed, that the aura of sanctity with which we have surrounded that gourd has limited our desire to find new culinary uses for it; for the French, who have no emotion one way or another about the pumpkin, which they call 'potiron,' have gone far beyond pumpkin pie. On a cold winter night, for instance, warmth and comfort that penetrate to the soul can be yours when a rich, creamy pumpkin soup is on the table."
>
> —LOUIS P. DE GOUY,
> THE GOLD COOKBOOK

Pumpkin-Apple Soup with Curry and Cream

ou can tell we really like pumpkin soup. This one, from the *Dairy Hollow House Cookbook*, we keep on the menu every October, all month long. Rarely does a night go by without a guest saying, "That soup alone was worth the price of dinner!"

There are five basic procedures involved in preparing this soup: making a special stock; steaming, peeling, and puréeing the pumpkin; preparing the apple-onion sauté; combining and assembling the soup; and garnishing it.

1 small to medium sweet-eating pumpkin, seeds and strings removed and reserved, cut into pieces roughly 4 inches square (see below)
3 crisp, well-flavored apples, such as Granny Smiths, Staymans, or Winesaps, unpeeled, cores with stems removed and reserved, fruit diced (see below)

PUMPKIN-APPLE STOCK:
Seeds and strings from the pumpkin
Cores with stems of the apples
2 heads garlic, papery skins left on, whole
1 large onion, unpeeled, quartered
1 large potato, unpeeled, quartered
Zest of ½ orange
1½ teaspoons salt
6 cups spring water

APPLE-ONION SAUTE:
Pam cooking spray
2 tablespoons butter
2 tablespoons mild vegetable oil, such as corn or peanut
1 large onion, diced
⅔ of the apple dice
1 tablespoon best-quality curry powder

ASSEMBLING AND GARNISHING THE SOUP:
½ cup apple juice concentrate, thawed
1 cup heavy (whipping) cream or evaporated skim milk
3¼ cups of the pumpkin-apple stock
⅓ of the apple dice
Crème Fraîche (page 50; optional)

1. Make the pumpkin-apple stock: In a large soup pot, combine all the stock ingredients and bring to a boil. Turn the heat down to low, and let simmer, covered, 45 minutes. Let cool. Strain and discard the solids.

2. Meanwhile, make the pumpkin purée, using the pumpkin pieces, as described on page 158.

3. Prepare the apple-onion sauté: Spray a 10-inch skillet with the Pam and in it heat the butter and oil over medium heat. Add the onion and sauté until somewhat softened, about 3 minutes. Add two-thirds of the diced apples, and sauté another 2 minutes, stirring often. Sprinkle the curry powder over the apples and onion, and continue to cook, stirring often, another 1 to 2 minutes. Remove from the heat, and scrape *half* of the mixture into a food processor.

4. Put the remaining onion-apple sauté in a large soup pot. Deglaze the skillet with ¼ cup of the stock, and scrape the pan contents into the pot. Add 3 cups of the pumpkin-apple stock and the pumpkin purée to the pot. (I have made this soup, deliciously, with anywhere from 2 to 4 cups pumpkin purée,

so just throw it in and don't fuss over the exact amount. After all, who wants a quarter cup pumpkin purée sitting in the fridge growing a beard?) Bring this mixture to a boil, turn down the heat, and simmer gently for about 10 minutes. Stir the soup occasionally.

5. Meanwhile, add the apple juice concentrate to the ingredients in the food processor. Buzz until smooth. Add this mixture to the soup pot with the heavy cream or evaporated milk. Continue cooking the soup over low heat until very hot. Do not permit it to boil.

6. Serve the soup garnished with the remaining diced apple and a dab of the optional crème fraîche. This is, as Jan Brown used to say, *too good.*

Serves 6 to 8 as a starter

VARIATION:

State Occasion Pumpkin and Apple Soup with Curry and Cream: Make Red Pepper Purée (page 46). Garnish each portion of the soup with a squiggle of purée.

RADISHES

Jan Brown, my collaborator on *Dairy Hollow House Cookbook,* and I were as a house divided on the subject of cooked radishes. She liked them; I couldn't stand them. However, she won me over on this very special mixed veg-

etable soup. It's a light, magical, quickly made soup that's contemporary and New Age in its flavors. There are lots of other things in the soup besides radishes. Mmmm . . . do you smell the aromas of the East drifting through your

kitchen? But wait—could it be . . . Italy? Sure thing. The imagination of my dear former collab knows no bounds, and the results are always delicious. No wonder the white rabbit comes to visit at Jan and Blake's. Hey, maybe she'll invite *us* over for lunch, too!

The White Rabbit's Favorite Spring Soup

should warn you—this is preferably served at the round oak table at Jan's. There, you can look out into the woods through the windows on either side of that faceted blue jewel of a window made by local glass artisan Jimmy Fliss.

Arame is seaweed, purchased from Oriental or natural foods stores. "I love the look of these dark slender strands floating in clear vegetable soups," says Jan. Arame comes out of the package dry, in small shards, and requires no preparation. It rehydrates in the soup.

Pam cooking spray
1 tablespoon olive oil
2 onions, finely diced
1 red bell pepper, stemmed, seeded, and diced
1 green bell pepper, stemmed, seeded, and diced
1 piece (2 inches) fresh gingerroot, halved
6 cups Golden Vegetable Stock (page 28) made with light miso
2 cups cauliflower flowerets
1 cup tiny radishes, washed and stemmed
1/4 cup dried arame (a variety of seaweed, available at natural foods stores)
1 cup coarsely grated carrots
1 cup thin ribbons of red cabbage
6 to 8 cloves garlic, peeled
1/2 cup loosely packed fresh parsley leaves
8 to 10 fresh basil leaves
4 leaves romaine lettuce, cut into tiny ribbons

1. Spray a heavy soup pot with Pam, and add the oil. Heat over medium heat, add the onions, and sauté until partially softened, about 3 minutes. Add the peppers and gingerroot, and sauté another 5 minutes. Add the stock and bring to a boil. Turn down the heat and let the mixture simmer, uncovered, 15 minutes. Remove the gingerroot.

2. Add the cauliflower, radishes, and arame to the pot. Let simmer another 10 minutes. Add the carrots and red cabbage, and simmer 5 minutes more.

3. In a food processor, combine the garlic, parsley, and basil. Pulse-chop a few times. Add a small ladleful of the soup, and buzz again until the garlic is finely chopped. Stir the garlic-herb mixture into the soup with the romaine. Turn off the heat, cover the pot, and let sit 5 minutes. Serve at once.

Serves 4 generously for lunch or 5 as a starter

SQUASH

🌱 *Every squash variety has its own character, but there are two basic types: summer (pale of flesh, soft of skin, not a good keeper) and winter (orange-yellow of flesh, hard of skin, and an excellent keeper). Any summer squash (golden crook-neck, pattypan, or zucchini) can be substituted for any other. Any of the winter squashes can be substituted for any other, as well as for pumpkins, with which they are kin.*

Here I must put in a word for the delectable butternut squash, pear-shaped, buff-colored on the exterior, a deep gold with in. This is by far the best tasting winter squash known to man or woman. Butternuts are sweet-sweet-sweet, but not at all starchy. They make the most unbelievably velvety, sweet purée for use as a side vegetable or in soup. Use butternut squash purée as a substitute for pumpkin purée in any of the pumpkin soups or diced, as a happy addition to any minestrone, to The Soup variation, or to chicken soups. 🌱

TOMATOES

A dream in pallid, icy, muddy February: tomatoes. Those big, heavy, irregular tomatoes, the kind you never get at a store—sustaining, meaty, dripping juice, and fitting the curve of your hand perfectly. The kind you don't even get at a farmer's market, but only out of your own garden. The kind you find only after you've parted that private, aromatic foliage, and reached up through the rustling hairy leaves. The kind of tomato there's only one of, and that one—just on the point of falling—is lush in your palm and still hot from the sun.

I say, praise February and praise sorrow; praise mud and ice; praise pallor. For how vivid, by contrast, they make summer, August, and tomatoes.

Tomato Soup with Cognac and Orange

 classic tomato soup, when made with the ripe, vibrantly garden-fresh tomatoes of summer and a little real cream, is a revelation. Our version has a hint of orange and clove, undetectable as such but wonderful. This is one soup you can be sure will please everyone. You could practically take before (soup) and after (soup) pictures of your diners, so great will the difference in their demeanor be.

Pam cooking spray
3 tablespoons butter
1 large onion, chopped
1 clove garlic, peeled and put through a garlic press
1½ teaspoons dried basil
2 tablespoons honey
3 to 4 whole cloves
4 pounds perfectly ripe tomatoes, cored and coarsely chopped
Grated zest and juice of 1 orange
Salt and freshly ground black pepper to taste
1 tablespoon tomato paste (if needed)
½ cup heavy (whipping) cream
3 tablespoons best cognac
Sour cream, kefir cheese, Crème Fraîche (page 50), or plain yogurt for garnish (optional)
Fresh basil leaves, for garnish (optional)

> **"**Tomatoes were heaped on the sink, so many, ripening in the garden too fast to get them all put up, ripening in a joyful explosion that had me picking twice a day. They were piled one atop the other, and they were squat and red and big like smiles and they reminded me of happy summer.**"**
>
> —*ANNIE GREENE,*
> *BRIGHT RIVER TRILOGY*

1. Spray a 5-quart, heavy, enameled soup pot with the Pam. In it, melt the butter over medium heat. Add the onion and sauté until it starts to soften, about 3 minutes. Turn the heat down slightly. Add the garlic, basil, honey, and cloves, and cook, stirring, for 2 minutes. Add the tomatoes, raise the heat to medium-high, and cook to evaporate the moisture, stirring constantly. When the tomatoes begin to turn into a bubbling, chunky liquid, 5 to 10 minutes, add the orange zest. Lower the heat and simmer until the tomatoes are very soft, about 20 minutes. Stir occasionally.

2. Remove the pot from the heat. Let the mixture cool slightly, pick out the cloves, and add the orange juice. Spoon the mixture into a food processor and purée (in batches, if necessary). Put the purée through a food mill, strainer, or, best yet, for absolute smoothness, a power strainer.

3. Return the purée to the soup pot. Reheat over medium-low heat, stirring often.

Taste; season with salt and pepper. Add tomato paste if the soup seems to need it. You might want to add a bit more honey. When the soup is very hot, just before serving, stir in the cream and cognac; do not permit the soup to boil after this point. Serve at once garnished, if desired, with a dab of sour cream or other dairy options and add a bright fresh basil leaf to each bowl.

Serves 4 to 6 as a starter

VARIATION:

This soup is pretty much perfection as is, but you can play with the garnish some. One of my faves: a few kernels of popcorn placed atop the soup *right* before serving, with (if you're feeling lavish calorically) a tiny nip of melting butter. This astonishes guests, and is delightful.

More formal, and just as beautiful, is a squeeze-bottled ribbon of any contrastingly colored or flavored purée: beet is a revelation, green pepper beautiful, dried green chili a whole new (Southwestern) take.

Déjà Food: If you're lucky enough to have some of this left over, you have lots of delicious options, even though reheating it is a delicate business (the cream and tomatoes have some tendency towards curdling). Sauté some vegetables (onions, broccoli, and carrots), cook some noodles, and toss a little of the soup with them for a nice vegetarian dish (no need to reheat the soup, the noodles and veggies will heat it through). Or buzz the soup with some hot cooked lentils or other legume and some hot pepper, reheating it over the lowest possible heat. Or stir the soup into anything curried. Or fry a few bread cubes in a bit of butter, moisten them with a few tablespoons of the soup, add a sautéed onion, and use as a fabulous omelet filling.

ZUCCHINI

*T*he thing about zucchini is, it's fecund. You may love or hate this quality; you may make zucchini soup, casserole, bread, muffins, and even chocolate cake (surprisingly moist and tasty, no kidding), or throw up your hands in despair. "You'd think more people would be suspicious of a vegetable whose only virtue is that any fool can grow one," harumphs John Thorne in his book, *Simple Cooking*. "Its much-touted versatility is just a polite way of saying that it constantly intrudes where it isn't wanted, a vegetable form of that

blandly grating familiarity, 'Have a nice day.'"

But I can't help but be impressed with all that generous summertime fertility. Generosity speaks to me. I like big portions. I like overflowing baskets of flowers, not minimalist ikeban (well, I *admire* it sometimes, but I don't really *like* it). I like giving guests more than what was promised at Dairy Hollow.

This is a trait we share with every really good innkeeper and inn in America. Innkeeper Mary Davies of Ten Inverness Way in Point Reyes, California, once told me, "Always err on the side of generosity." None of us knows what lies ahead for those we feed and care for.

Life is big, unknowable. It is best approached zucchini-like, all out.

Summertime Zucchini Soup

As anyone who has gardened can tell you, zucchini and their kindred summer squashes proliferate at a frightening rate. They invade the garden and summertime table with equal rapacity. Thin-sliced or grated and quickly sautéed in a little Garlic Oil (page 41), they are a wonderful side vegetable. They can also be stuffed with all manner of things and served as part of a vegetarian plate. But I especially like this very quick soup. It's low-calorie, low-cholesterol, and, served chilled, a midsummer staple for us at home. It is not one of those "Oh, I've-got-to-have-it" soups to swoon over, but it is still mighty good. Cooked rice, eventually puréed, serves as a substitute for heavier, more caloric butter and flour thickenings. I use this rice trick throughout the book; it's especially appropriate for summertime soups.

6 cups Chicken Stock 1 (page 19) or
    Golden or Browned Vegetable Stock
    (pages 28 and 32) or any well-flavored
    chicken or vegetable stock
3 tablespoons long-grain rice
3 small to medium zucchini, sliced
Pam cooking spray
1 tablespoon mild vegetable oil, such as
    corn or peanut
1 large onion, chopped
3 cloves garlic, peeled (optional)
Freshly grated nutmeg to taste
Salt and freshly ground black pepper to
    taste
Plain yogurt or sour cream or Crème
    Fraîche (page 50), if you're not watching
    fat grams, for garnish

1. In a large soup pot, bring the stock to a boil. Drop in the rice, turn down the heat to medium-low, and let simmer gently, covered, about 20 minutes. Drop in the zucchini, re-cover, and let cook until the zucchini is quite soft, 7 to 8 minutes.

2. Meanwhile, spray a 10-inch skillet with the Pam, and in it heat the oil over medium heat. Add the onion and sauté until limp but not browned, 5 to 6 minutes. Transfer the onion to a food processor.

3. Remove the stock from the heat and let it cool slightly. Strain, reserving both the liquid and the solids. Add the zucchini-rice mixture to the sautéed onion in the processor, along with the raw garlic, if using (the garlic gives the soup much more punch; sometimes I like this, sometimes I prefer the milder zucchini flavors to take center stage). Buzz the mixture until smooth. If you wish, for absolute smoothness, pass the purée through a power strainer.

4. Return the purée to the soup pot with the stock. Taste, and season well with nutmeg, salt, and pepper. Serve hot or cold, with or without a dab of yogurt, sour cream, or crème fraîche.

Serves 6 as a starter

VARIATION:
Substitute a thawed 11-ounce box of frozen spinach for the zucchini. Prep and cooking time is the same; garlic remains an option. I like this Spinach and Zucchini Soup very much chilled, with a little lemon juice added and a scored lemon slice floating atop it.

The Soup

THE SOLUTION TO DIETING

eet The Soup, that low-fat wonder which I have been bragging on since early in this book. After all that build-up, might you be disappointed? The Soup, after all, is just a good old vegetable soup. But at least three seasons of the year, it's Ned's and my at-home staple, and day in, day out, it pleases us. We don't serve it to inn guests in its more straightforward versions, but countless friends and co-workers who have lunched and dined on it over the years have been enthusiastic, usually to the tune of seconds or thirds. I think you'll like it as much as we do.

To understand why The Soup is a solution to dieting, it is necessary to understand the two weight loss approaches that have emerged over the years as the most healthful, effective, and sanest—and that also give those following them the least sense of deprivation. These two methods are exchange plans and low-fat/high carbohydrate diets. Most diet veterans will be familiar with at least the rudiments of both approaches, but for those of you who aren't, or who may need a refresher, here's a quick brush-up course.

Many people are used to the concept of "exchange plans"—the healthier weight loss plans of the last twenty years, including Weight Watchers, are based on some variation of the same. "Exchanges" are units of like nutritional foodstuffs within a similar calorie-range. For example, a typical weight-loss plan of this type would tell you to have one protein "exchange" at breakfast, two at lunch, and two at dinner. Such diets always include extensive exchange lists: a protein exchange might be 3 ounces of fish, 1 egg, 1 ounce of cheese, 4 ounces of

cooked dry beans, and so on. All choices on the lists (and any good food plan should give you a lot of choices) are nutritious and, again, within a certain calorie range. Weight loss plans of this type generally have exchange group lists for five food groups: protein, carbohydrate, fat, fruit, and dairy products. In addition, most have lists of "unlimited" foods, which are invariably vegetables. These foods are "unlimited," the plans explain, because they are extremely low-calorie, as well as healthful.

Exchange plans have a lot going for them. They're sane, for one thing, especially compared to the Grapefruit Diet, the Banana Diet, the Asian Stewardess Diet, the Marshmallow Diet, ad infinitum. They're fairly well balanced nutritionally. They're made up of real food, not instant mixes made from cow hide and egg white, and they do teach people who've been reared on fast foods the basics of eating right.

Problem is, they are a major hassle to follow. They are time-consuming beyond belief. They require lots of weighing and measuring and planning . . . *lots.* If you follow them to the letter (and you have to, for them to work) it can require strategic planning on the level of the invasion at Normandy. Also, many foods, even healthful ones, are restricted quan-

tity-wise. Some people feel hungry on exchange plans, and many feel, if not hungry, then somewhat deprived.

That's why the news from the diet front in the last five or six years has been so supremely heartening. The news is: no more dieting, at least dieting per se. The news is: limit fat grams, and you can eat pretty much what you want. Now, there is something of a catch 22 here, because many of the foods you and I love are pretty high in fat. But some are not. Some much-loved, satisfying foods that have previously been considered restricted on exchange plans and off-limits altogether on other types of diets are virtually fat-free—I'm talking . . . yes!— carbohydrates. Spaghetti. Potatoes. Most breads. Rice. No, this is not a hoax. According to current nutritional thinking, all those good old comforting starches (especially in their un- or less-refined forms) are absolutely okay. More than okay. Good for you. As long as you don't load them up with fats, you can actually have as much spaghetti as you like— with just a spare tomato sauce, instead of a fat-loaded Alfredo. One, even two, great big baked potatoes—with just yo-gurt and maybe a *touch* of butter and cheese—not with gobs of butter and cheese and sour cream.

This—the high-carb, low-fat, don't-think-much-about-calories-just-count-fat-grams way of eating—is mighty good news for people who love to eat, and it is becoming more and more popular. Why? Not only because, as mentioned, you get to eat more soul-satisfyingly, but because it is easy to live with. It is also probably even more healthful than the exchange plans: it appears to have many health benefits beyond the strictly weight-related. It is also extremely heart friendly and may even help prevent certain cancers, particularly those of the breast and colon.

How do you do it? Simple. The only thing you have to remember is fat grams: no more than 20 to 40 grams of fat a day for a woman; no more than 40 to 60 grams of fat daily for a man, or (for those of you still thinking calorically) roughly 20 to 30 percent of your total calorie intake. All the (fat free) carbohydrates, preferably whole grain, you can eat. Plus modest amounts of (low-fat) sources of protein, and, of course, lots and lots of those good old unlimited vegetables. More or less, this follows the updated suggested (but, at the eleventh hour, unapproved) USDA guidelines (they were pulled supposedly because of pressure

from the meat and dairy industries, but had already been sent to the press). This makes up the so-called pyramid of good eating which you have probably seen reproduced as often, of late, as I have. Basically, the way it works is, you get a fat gram counter, learn the fat gram contents of your favorites, count those grams daily until you've got it, and that's it. I mean—*really* simple.

Oh yes—and eat your The Soup on a regular basis.

High-carb/low-fat eating may actually, happily, spell the end to dieting

as we have known and suffered through it in the past. The Soup, and practical application of same, helps point the way to a delicious and satisfying future.

Because The Soup builds on the so-called "unlimited" vegetables and pushes them as far as possible toward maximum deliciousness and substance for minimum caloric count and fat-gram expenditure, it does work equally well whether you go the high-carb/low-fat route or follow an exchange plan.

See, even though most exchange plans *say* that some vegetables are "unlimited," when you look at some of the examples of specific menus they offer, what do you see? The vegetable choice is something like "½ cup zucchini" or "2 cups shredded lettuce." Well, if everything else you're eating is limited, a mere ½ cup of zucchini or 2 cups of shredded lettuce is not going to fill you up. If these vegetables are really unlimited, why not go to town with them in a big way? Find some way to cook them deliciously enough so that you won't feel deprived, then have, gosh, four helpings if that's what it takes to make you feel satisfied and non-deprived.

The Soup is that delicious way to cook them.

And if you're going to go the high-carb/low-fat route (as I do, pretty much, these days) you can add to The Soup all the pasta or rice or potatoes you want, which I promise you is going to *really* make you feel satisfied and non-deprived.

But, you say, let's face it, vegetable soup is vegetable soup, right? Won't it be dull after a while? No ma'am, no sir. I'm here to tell you, time cannot stale, nor custom fade, The Soup's infinite variety. Some of that variety comes from good seasonings and flair and international style in several different idioms. Then, there is a further range of options that can vary The Soup from day to day with delicious higher-fat add-ins like cheese or cooked chicken or fish that, whether you follow an exchange or the high-carb/low-fat approach, you can eat; just not in unlimited quantities.

So, here's what The Soup is. It's a strategy for having as much of many of the foods you like as it takes to fill you up without risking fat-gram or calorie-count overload. It's a bursting-with-flavor, continually variable vegetable soup, made with the kinds of vegetables the diets call "unlimited," and seasoned to a fare-thee-well. And this soup, in all its variations, serves as the base for further variations, based on selections from protein and/or carbohydrate exchange groups (if you still use them) and added directly to each portion of soup.

Why are these variable ingredients added to each portion, rather than to the whole pot? For two reasons: to keep The Soup interesting and to make it flexible in terms of satiety. Because The Soup is such a daily kind of thing, it's important that familiarity not breed contempt. It won't, if you make it one day with beans and one day with chicken, serve it one day over pasta with a little cheese on top, on another accompanied by toast or a tortilla or rice. Explaining the how-to's may seem time-consuming and a hassle, particularly if you choose to follow an exchange plan and all its attendant weighings-out-of-some-ingredients, but The Soup itself is easy.

Besides leaving you with an ever-changing soup that's incredibly much more interesting than the same-old same-old, doing it by the bowl allows you to have as many servings of the soup part as it takes to satisfy you. Say you have chosen to have grated cheese as your protein exchange or your high-fat choice. So you grate an ounce of Cheddar (one protein exchange; 10 fat grams), and you put it on a plate. Ladle a bowl of The Soup, and sprinkle some of the cheese on it. Have another bowl of The Soup, sprinkle some more cheese. Keep going until you are full, parceling your cheese out.

There. You've had a satisfying meal. Not only was it healthful, not only did you get to have a lot of it guilt-free, it was *good*.

> **"Pray for peace . . . But don't forget the potatoes."**
>
> —*JOHN TYLER PETEE,*

I am proud to say that The Soup is about as close to a diet as I get these days. At times when I'm not trying actively to lose weight, I don't bother being too precise with it. But post-Christmas, post-birthday, post-a-couple-of-months-of-recipe-testing, I go back to fat gram tallying. A nice low-fat breakfast, usually built around some kind of whole-grain cereal, hot or cold, and low-fat milk or yogurt, and fruit. For lunch, as much as I want of The Soup with another generous portion of the carb du jour plus maybe a third of my fat grams as whatever protein I'm in the mood for. For dinner, whatever I want—only perhaps slightly less of it than I want, and always with a big salad or heap of steamed vegetables spiked with lemon, and of course a nice big pile of pasta or whatever satisfying starch is on the menu. No dessert except maybe fresh fruit, or a baked apple, or something in that line.

And you know, if you eat this way most of the time, then you can also have your occasional creamy things and your chocolate things and your buttery things—and you can have them with as little guilt as you do your great big bowls of The Soup. Amazing but true. And *right*—because something so basic to life as food, something so celebratory as eating, that sings of our connection to each other and to the earth—well, it shouldn't be fraught with guilt and ambivalence. Let's hear it for joy—and The Soup.

THE SOUP

BASIC INGREDIENTS FOR ALL VERSIONS

Though the directions are lengthy, The Soup is the easiest thing in the world to make. The reason is you can do it a zillion different ways. Just remember, the very things that make The Soup so useful in real life make it nearly impossible to fix in regular recipe format; it's too, too flexible and variable. But read through the recipe a couple of times, and you'll get it. It's hard to put a yield on The Soup. Let's just say, serves 4 to 6.

LIQUIDS:
10 to 12 cups liquid of your choice, broken down roughly as follows:
8 to 10 cups brothy liquid of your choice, such as any fat-free vegetable stock, or water plus 2 or 3 cubes of Morga (vegetarian broth cubes, page 31), or defatted chicken stock, or leftover cooking liquid from beans or liquid drained from canned, cooked beans, or any combination of these
2 cups tomatoey liquid or purée of your choice, such as V8 or tomato juice, spicy tomato juice, diced fresh tomatoes, canned whole tomatoes in juice buzzed to a chunky purée in the food processor
1 to 2 cups red or white wine as called for under Basic Themes and Variations or Ethnic Themes and Variations

SEASONINGS AND AROMATICS (all optional):
Any of the herb or spice choices listed under Basic Themes and Variations or Ethnic Themes and Variations (these follow)
2 to 10 cloves garlic (I know this is an enormous range; I think one can hardly have too much garlic, but people are funny on the subject)
1 tablespoon to ½ cup dehydrated soup vegetables (optional; this is a preservative-free, salt-free soup mix from a natural foods store co-op; buy it in bulk; also, the exact amount you'll add for any 1 recipe's worth is dependent on how many fresh vegetables you'll be using, below)
1 to 3 large onions, diced (you may substitute 1 to 2 cups of diced shallots or sliced scallions, or 1 to 2 leeks, trimmed, split open lengthwise, and well washed)
1 tablespoon any favorite savory seasoning sauce, such as Worcestershire, Pickapeppa, or tamari/shoyu soy sauce (optional)
½ to 2 teaspoons of any favorite hot sauce, such as Tabasco, Frank's Louisiana, Crystal, or Cajun Sunshine
Salt and freshly ground black pepper to taste

VEGETABLES:
4 to 6 cups fresh and/or frozen vegetables, chosen from a combination of any of the following:
Fresh vegetables, such as green beans, stems and tails removed, sliced crosswise into slices about ⅛ to ¼ inch thick (sliced fresh green beans are simply magic in a vegetable soup); zucchini or yellow squash, split lengthwise into quarters, then into quarter-rounds about ⅛ inch thick; celery ribs, leaves included, diced; green or savoy cabbage, cored and shredded; greens, well washed, tough ribs removed (tougher greens, such as collard, turnip, chard, and beet tops should be sliced thin into thin ribbons); small tender spinach leaves may be left whole; carrots, split lengthwise into quarters, then into quarter-rounds about ¼ inch thick; butternut squash, peeled, seeded, and cut into dice about ¼ inch square
Frozen vegetables, such as 1 or 2 bags frozen mixed vegetables (16 ounces each; choose a mix free of added sauce or butter and without any added starchy vegetables, such as corn; my preferred choice is a supermarket brand called Mediterranean Vegetables, which includes cauliflower, zucchini, Italian green beans, and red bell pepper)

HOW TO MAKE THE SOUP:
BASIC THEMES AND VARIATIONS

Absolutely Quickest, Busy Day The Soup
(using frozen vegetables)

1. Working from the ingredients list above, in a large soup pot bring to a boil your brothy liquid of choice plus a choice of tomatoes or juice.

2. Make a choice or choices from the aromatics and seasonings at this point. Add to the boiling soup. If you've chosen dehydrated vegetables, let simmer over medium-low heat about 15 minutes. If not, proceed directly to the next step.

3. Drop in 1 or 2 bags of frozen vegetables. Bring the soup back to a boil. Turn down the heat to medium-low, and simmer, partially covered, until the vegetables are tender, about 30 minutes. Season to taste. Finis. If desired, add to individual portions a selection from the proteins or carbohydrates lists which follow (page 180). You're ready to eat. Good, eh?

Almost as Quick and Simple The Soup
(using fresh and frozen vegetables)

1. Working from the ingredients list on pages 172 and 173, in a large soup pot bring to a boil your brothy liquid of choice plus a choice of tomatoes or juice.

2. Make a choice or choices from the aromatics and seasonings list. Add to the boiling soup. If you've chosen dehydrated vegetables, let simmer over medium-low heat about 15 minutes. If not, proceed directly to the next step.

3. Assemble whatever fresh and frozen vegetables you will be using. (Remember, you'll need about 4 to 6 cups total.) If you're including the sliced green beans among your choices, give them a 5- to 10-minute head start, before adding the others. (If not using green beans proceed to the next step.)

4. Add any frozen vegetables you've selected and bring the soup back to a boil. Now add any remaining fresh vegetables, unless they are very, very tender, such as young fresh spinach leaves.

5. Bring the soup back to a boil again, then turn down the heat and simmer, partially covered, until the vegetables are tender, 20 to 30 minutes. If using fresh tender spinach, add in the last 3 minutes. Season to taste. If desired, add your selections from the protein or carbohydrate exchanges which follow.

Simple The Soup with Browned Onions

lightly more of a production. Although uncooked onions can be dropped directly into the simmering soup liquid, what browned onions do for a soup is magic. With a little care, onions can be browned with absolutely no fat.

1. Working from the ingredients list on pages 172 and 173, in a large soup pot bring to a boil your brothy liquid of choice plus a choice of tomatoes or juice.

2. Meanwhile, spray a medium-size cast-iron skillet very well with Pam. Put it over medium heat, and let it get fairly hot. Add the diced onion or onions (or shallots, leeks, or scallions) from the aromatics and seasonings list, and stir-fry. Raise the heat to medium-high for about 3 minutes, then turn it down to extremely low. For the next 20 to 30 minutes, let the onions cook, stirring them fairly often. (This slow cooking is the secret behind getting onions nice and brown and aromatic without added fat.)

3. Meanwhile, make another choice or choices from the aromatics and seasonings list. Add to the boiling soup. If you've chosen dehydrated vegetables, let simmer over medium-low heat about 15 minutes. If not, proceed directly to the next step.

4. Drop in any fresh or frozen vegetables you're using, proceeding as in steps 3 and 4 of the preceding recipe.

5. Once the vegetables are tender (after about 30 minutes), scrape the browned onions into the pot. Deglaze the skillet in which the onions were cooked with a ladleful of soup, being sure to scrape up any browned bits. Add this glaze to the soup pot.

6. Season to taste. If desired, add your selections from the protein or carbohydrate exchanges which follow. Mmm! Lunchtime!

VARIATION:

When the onions have cooked at medium-high about 2 minutes, add 1 to 2 finely diced carrots and 1 to 2 finely diced ribs of celery with leaves. Cook, stirring, another 2 to 3 minutes, then lower the heat and simmer. Follow the remaining directions as given.

Quick and Wonderful Garlicky The Soup

y favorite of all these quickie jazz-ups for The Soup; the garlic adds great vigor and freshness.

1. Follow any of the preceding variations, through adding the vegetables.

2. Then, as the soup simmers for its 20 to 30 minutes, drop into a food processor 6 cloves of garlic, the leaves from 1 small bunch of fresh parsley, the leaves from 1 small bunch of fresh basil, if available (or substitute 1 tablespoon of dried basil), and 1 rib of celery with leaves (optional). Buzz, pulsing on and off, until everything is chopped fine. Add this mix to the soup during the last 5 to 10 minutes of cooking.

3. Follow the remaining directions as given.

The Soup with Green Herbs

1. Follow all the steps as listed in any of the preceding variations, but add the following green herb aromatics to the boiling liquid right before the vegetables are added: 1 teaspoon dried thyme, 1 teaspoon dried savory, 1 teaspoon dried marjoram, 1 teaspoon dried sage, and 3 tablespoons minced fresh Italian (flat-leaf) parsley.

2. You may garnish, if you wish, with a little additional parsley, minced.

ADDING TEXTURE TO THE VARIATIONS

❦*Depending on how many vegetables you've added, The Soup may be thin and brothlike, or stewy. For a thicker soup, scoop out a ladle or two or three of the cooked vegetables, and buzz them in the food processor, then return them to the soup pot. For a thinner soup, add additional stock, V8 juice, or dry red or white wine.* ❦

IN GOOD COMPANY:
JAN BROWN

❧ *A huge chunk of Dairy Hollow House's style and general good vibes can be attributed to Jan Brown, my first co-chef and later my co-author on the first* Dairy Hollow House Cookbook. *Although Jan no longer works for us, we continue to feel her sweet influence in many areas.*

Jan, a Wichita native, started out a Kansas more-or-less farm girl but wound up influenced by many of the same culinary schools of thought as I did: French, Asian, natural foods; creativity born of a non-stingy economy. She brought her own interesting food sensibilities to the kitchen, and influenced mine. She and her husband, writer Blake Clark, acted as innkeepers when Ned and I were out of town during the inn's early days. Long before we had a restaurant, it was Jan who first prepared dinner for our guests—made in the tiny Innkeeper's House kitchen, carried across the street to the Farmhouse, and there served by Blake. Dinner in those days, and for a few years to follow, could hardly have been more personal.

In 1988, a serious fall broke both Jan's ankles and precluded her from the on-the-feet work of a full-time professional chef. She stepped out of the daily cycle of DHH kitchen life to return to quilting full time, and (with Blake) her earlier profession, taking care of kids in trouble, at a halfway house in Fayetteville, Arkansas. But

at regular intervals, we hear the wingbeats, and there is angel Jan, with that gentle but full-of-mischief smile and laugh like a dove-call, come to settle in comfortably for a few minutes or a few hours and catch up and have a cup of soup and a slice of bread and a cup of coffee and a cow cookie.

And her quilt, "Tea with Aunt Rose," hangs over the mantelpiece in our restaurant. It is a beaut—no question that it is "art," not "craft," finely crafted though it is. Its starting point, almost seven years ago, was six crocheted Oreo cookies Jan found in the bottom of a remnant box she bought at a local auction. Another such auction yielded several pieced fans from a partially completed Grandmother's Fan quilt, and from here, there, and everywhere, Jan compiled and composed other beloved found objects; antique buttons, four pairs of gloves, an embroidered sugar bowl, a silver spoon covered with roses, bits of chintzes, '30s rickrack, sprigged flour-sack fabric. It's a wonder.

Nearly every restaurant guest comments on it, many photograph it, and after all these years I smile as I go by—for the quilt itself, and for Jan. ❧

ETHNIC THEMES AND VARIATIONS

Around the world with The Soup. Classic recipes for minestrone, borscht, and other international vegetable soups appear elsewhere in this book; here are lightened-up, low-fat versions that remain true to the essence of the originals while opting for the simplicity and fat-sparing-ness we all strive for today, at least some of the time. If a jot less flavorful than the originals, these saner, quicker counterparts are delicious nonetheless.

French-Style The Soup

Enjoyable, elegant, and with fresh, clear flavors that are certifiably lightened-up French. Note that this is the only The Soup variation where certain liquids—chicken stock and white wine—are specified for the stock component. These liquids, plus the assortment of herbs, give this a distinctly French flavor. Follow the recipe for Simple The Soup with Browned Onions (page 174), using the ingredients below.

10 cups Chicken Stock 1 (page 19) or any well-flavored defatted chicken stock
1 cup canned tomatoes with juice, coarsely chopped
1½ cups dry white wine
2 ribs celery, finely chopped
2 medium carrots, scrubbed and finely diced
1 cup domestic white mushrooms, sliced
2 cloves garlic, peeled and put through a garlic press
1 teaspoon dried tarragon
1 teaspoon dried thyme
1 teaspoon dried savory
1 teaspoon dried marjoram
½ teaspoon dried sage
¼ teaspoon ground cloves
3 tablespoons minced fresh Italian (flat-leaf) parsley
2 to 3 cups sliced green beans
2 to 3 cups zucchini, sliced as described in the basic ingredient list
1 cup diced celery root (about ¼-inch dice)
1 parsnip, well washed, peeled if skin is very tough, and sliced into ¼-inch rounds (if the root is very thick, halve lengthwise before slicing)
1 cup sliced green or savoy cabbage, in thin ribbons
2 cups fresh spinach leaves, very well washed, hard stems removed
2 cups fresh or frozen peas

> **"**Tomatoes? Ask your nose! If they do not have the tempting odour of tomato, an aroma that should capture your attention even when the tomatoes are arm's-length away, then they were picked green and their flavor will make you think you are growing prematurely old and losing your sense of taste . . .**"**
>
> —HENRI CHARPENTIER,
> *THOSE RICH AND GREAT ONES, or LIFE*
> *À LA HENRI*

1. In a large soup pot, bring to a boil the chicken stock, canned tomatoes, and wine (step 1).

2. Sauté the celery and carrots with the onion (step 2). Add the mushrooms during the last 6 minutes of sautéing and the garlic during the last 3 minutes.

3. Meanwhile, add the tarragon, thyme, savory, marjoram, sage, cloves, and parsley (step 3). Turn down the heat to low and add the green beans (step 4). Simmer for 5 to 10 minutes, then add the zucchini, celery root, parsnip, and cabbage. Add the spinach and peas in the last 1 minute of cooking (after deglazing the skillet, step 5).

4. Follow the remaining directions as given.

To turn this soup into a full meal, add the following to each serving, checking the Exchange Plan and High-Carb/Low-Fat List (page 180) for quantities:

For carbohydrate: Toasted French bread (may be served with the soup, or placed in the bowl with soup ladled over it).

For protein: 3 ounces cooked chicken or 1 poached egg. Or go without added protein during the meal and have a 1-ounce wedge of cheese with fruit for dessert.

Russian-Style The Soup

ort of borscht, nyet? This is great winter fare. Follow the recipe for Simple The Soup with Browned Onions (page 174) adding the ingredients below.

2 ribs celery, finely chopped
2 cloves garlic, peeled and put through a
  press
2 bay leaves
1 teaspoon dried oregano
2 tablespoons chopped fresh dill, or more to
  taste
2 medium carrots, scrubbed and sliced
2 medium parsnips, scrubbed and sliced
3 to 4 cups sliced green or savoy cabbage,
  in thin ribbons
3 to 4 fresh beets, stem and root ends
  removed, scrubbed very well, and
  chopped into ½-inch dice

1. Follow step 1 of Simple The Soup with Browned Onions.

2. Sauté the celery with the onion (step 2). Add the garlic during the last 3 minutes of sautéing.

3. Meanwhile, to the boiling stock add the bay leaves, dried oregano, and fresh dill (step 3). Turn down the heat and add to the simmering stock the carrots, parsnips, cabbage, and beets (step 4).

4. Follow the remaining directions as given.

To turn this soup into a full meal, add the following to each serving, checking the Exchange Plan and High-Carb/Low-Fat List (page 180) for quantities:

For carbohydrate: Toasted dark rye bread or cooked kasha or boiled potato.

For protein: 1½ ounces kefir cheese or 3 ounces Cottage Cream (page 52).

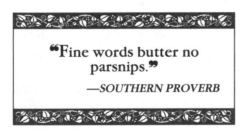

"Fine words butter no parsnips."

—*SOUTHERN PROVERB*

Mexican-Style The Soup

 ice and spicy. Good in either very hot or very cold weather. Follow the recipe and ingredients for Simple The Soup with Browned Onions (page 174), adding in the ingredients below.

1 to 2 fresh jalapeño peppers, finely diced
1 carrot, diced
1 rib celery, diced
3 cloves garlic, peeled and put through a
  garlic press
1 tablespoon ground cumin
2 teaspoons crushed coriander seeds
2 teaspoons chili powder
⅛ teaspoon cayenne pepper
2 to 3 cups sliced green beans
2 to 3 cups sliced yellow squash
1 cup sliced green cabbage in thin ribbons
3 tablespoons minced fresh cilantro
  (optional)

1. Follow step 1 for Simple The Soup with Browned Onions.

2. Sauté the jalapeños, carrot, and celery with the onion (step 2). Add the garlic during the last 3 minutes of sautéing.

3. Meanwhile, to the boiling stock (step 3), add the cumin, coriander seeds, chili powder, and cayenne pepper. Turn down the heat and add the sliced green beans to the simmering stock (step 4).

4. Simmer for 10 minutes, then add the squash and cabbage (step 4).

5. Follow the remaining directions as given. If desired, garnish the soup with the cilantro.

To turn this soup into a full meal, add the following to each serving, checking the Exchange Plan and High-Carb/Low-Fat List (page 180) for quantities:

For carbohydrate: Steamed or toasted corn tortillas or cooked rice or cooked corn.

For protein: Grated Monterey Jack cheese or a poached egg, plus canned pinto, kidney, or black beans, and a dab of Cottage Cream (page 52).

EXCHANGE PLAN AND HIGH-CARB/LOW-FAT LIST

FOOD	CARBOHYDRATES PORTION SIZE	EXCHANGES	FAT GRAMS
Loaf bread, any non-sweet, preferably whole-grain	1 slice	1	1.0
Pita bread, preferably whole-grain	½ round (6 inch)	1	1.0
Bagel, preferably whole-grain	½	1	1.0
English muffin, preferably whole-grain	½	1	2.0
Corn tortilla	1 (6 inch)	1	1.0
White rice	½ cup, cooked	1	1.0
Brown rice	½ cup, cooked	1	0.6
Grains, any, such as barley, couscous, kasha, or millet	½ cup, cooked	1	0.6 to 1.0
Pasta, any shape	⅔ cup, cooked	1	0.7
Potato	3 to 4 ounces, cooked	1	0.1
Corn, fresh	1 ear	1	0.9
Corn, frozen	½ cup kernels	1	0.2

Any low-fat rice cakes or crackers totaling between 70 and 100 calories and 2 fat grams or under per portion. (For example, Westbrae Sesame-Garlic Rice Cakes have about 30 calories and less and .1 fat gram apiece. So, exchange-plan portions would be three cakes at 90 calories and less than 1 fat gram.)

FOOD	PROTEINS PORTION SIZE	EXCHANGES	FAT GRAMS
Eggs	1 (hard-cooked or poached)	1	5.6
Chicken, all visible fat and skin removed	1½ to 3 ounces (cooked without added fat)	1	7.4*
Fish, most types	3½ ounces (cooked without added fat)	1	1.8 to 6
Meat, leanest cuts, all visible fat removed	2 to 3 ounces (cooked without added fat)	1	8 to 18
Grated hard or semi-soft cheese	1 ounce	1	6.1 to 9
Low-fat cottage cheese	4 ounces	1	2.0
Low-fat ricotta cheese	⅓ cup	1	6.0
Cottage Cream (page 52)	4 to 5 ounces	1	1.5
Dried legumes, any beans or peas, such as pintos, blacks, lentils, black-eyed	3 to 4 ounces (cooked; drained weight**)	1	0.5
Low-fat yogurt (plain, unsweetened)	½ cup	1	1.5
Nonfat yogurt (plain, unsweetened)	½ cup	1	0.0
Tofu, firm	4 ounces (well-drained)	1	5.0

🌰 *Most exchange plans tell you to choose 2 protein exchanges and 1 carbohydrate exchange for
lunch, and 2 protein exchanges and no carbohydrates for dinner (these break-outs can be re-
versed, too, depending on when you like your
larger meal). Men are usually permitted to add
an extra carb to both meals (lucky dogs . . . or so
I felt when I ate this way).*

*Most high-carb/low-fat plans tell you to limit
daily fat intake to 20 to 40 grams for women; 40
to 60 grams for men, but to eat pretty much as much
carbohydrate as it takes to satisfy you.*

*Here is a listing of standard protein and
carbohydrate exchanges, as well as fat-gram content. This will enable you to make calorie or fat-
sparing choices intelligently. But whatever you
choose—be sure to have lots of nice, filling, delicious, piping hot The Soup with it.*

*Be sure to remember, to not add these in-
gredients to the pot. Instead, after weighing and
measuring (sigh), place into each bowl and ladle
the soup over them, or eat on the side. I often use
leftover cooked grain or pasta straight from the
fridge—unless the ingredient is frozen, the steaming hot soup will warm it nicely.* 🌰

---

*Fat content varies with variety and cut; please check a
detailed fat-gram counter for further specific break-outs.

**Reserve liquid drained from beans for the soup pot.

Italian-Style
The Soup

 cousin to minestrone. Follow
the recipe for Quick and Wonderful Garlicky The Soup (page
175) adding the vegetables and aromatics suggested below.

FRESH VEGETABLES:
2 to 3 cups sliced green beans
2 to 3 cups sliced zucchini
*2 to 3 cups sliced green or savoy cabbage,
  in thin ribbons*

AROMATICS:
1 bay leaf
1½ teaspoons dried basil
1½ teaspoons dried oregano
½ teaspoon dried rosemary
½ teaspoon dried thyme

To turn this soup into a full meal, add
the following to each serving, checking the
Exchange Plan and High-Carb/Low-Fat List
(page 180) for quantitites:
   For carbohydrate: Toasted Italian
bread (it may be served with the soup, or
placed in the bottom of the bowl, with the
soup ladled over it).
   For protein: Grated Parmesan cheese
plus canned kidney or white beans.

VARIATION:
Use leftover cooked pasta instead of bread.
Or, instead of Parmesan sprinkled over the
soup, serve Gorgonzola in an accompanying
lemon-juice-dressed salad or with a crisp
apple for dessert. Sure beats dieting as we
have known it.

Greek/Middle-Eastern Style The Soup

 ice, fresh, faintly exotic flavors. Pleasant garnished with a thin slice of lemon. Follow the recipe for Simple The Soup with Browned Onions (page 174), using the ingredients below.

2 medium carrots, scrubbed and finely diced
2 ribs celery, finely diced
2 cloves garlic, peeled and put through a garlic press
2 teaspoons dried basil
1 teaspoon dried oregano
Tiny jot of cinnamon
Tiny jot of cloves
1 tablespoon chopped fresh dill
2 to 3 cups sliced green beans
1 to 3 cups sliced zucchini
2 to 3 cups sliced, well-washed greens, in thin ribbons

1. Follow step 1 for Simple The Soup with Browned Onions.

2. Sauté the carrots and celery with the onion (step 2). Add the garlic in the last 3 minutes of sautéing.

3. Meanwhile, add the basil, oregano, cinnamon, cloves, and dill to the boiling stock (step 4). Turn down the heat to low and add the green beans. Simmer for 5 to 10 minutes, then add the zucchini and greens.

4. Follow the remaining directions as given.

To turn this soup into a full meal, add the following to each serving, checking the Exchange Plan and High-Carb/Low-Fat List (page 180) for quantities:

For carbohydrate: Cooked brown rice or toasted whole-wheat pita breads.

For protein: Cooked chick-peas or lentils.

Hot, Hearty Bean Soups

LUSCIOUS, LUSTY LEGUMES

"If pale beans bubble for you in a red earthenware pot
You can oft decline
the dinners of sumptuous hosts."

—*MARCUS VALERIUS MARTIALIS*
MARTIAL EPIGRAMS, BOOK XIII, 85 A.D.

eans have been eaten by people who live close to the soil wherever and whenever they have inhabited our earth. In the Ozarks and the American South, throughout Mexico, Italy, India, Africa, and China, beans and legumes—slow cooked and succulent—have satisfied and sustained multitudes, from time out of mind.

Beans were one of the first crops domesticated and cultivated by prehistoric man. Bean remains dating back to 4,000 B.C. have been found in caves near Ocampo, Mexico; in Mesopotamia, remains date back to 2500 B.C. By comparison, the Chinese, whose soybeans date from about 2000 B.C., are practically Johnny-come-latelys in beandom. How many foods, when we are talking thousands of years, can be said to have been consistently part of the lives of humanity all over the world? How many of them are still eaten and still prepared more or less in the same way?

For, while you can eat meat, vegetables, and most other foodstuffs raw or cooked, basic bean preparation is universal. To be edible, dry beans must be slow-cooked in liquid for anywhere from 45 minutes (split peas) to four hours (chick-peas).

After the beans are cooked, and even during this basic cooking process, a person can go any which way with his or her beans, adding seasonings or vegetables, a joint of meat or a hunk of sausage; or a dribble of molasses or maple syrup. You can leave the mixture soupy or dry, distinct or puréed—the possibilities are without limit. The pot of beans native Ozarkians left to simmer on the back of a woodstove, the beans left to cook in an electric crockpot in a New York apartment, the "pale beans" bubbling in their "red earthenware pot" more than 1900 years ago in ancient Rome, the world's minestrones, frijoles, fejoidas, and cassoulets of past, present, and future; the new bean dishes finding their way onto chic restaurant menus today in our low-cholesterol/high-fiber/lots-of-complex-carbohydrate conscious world—all these have more in common than their different seasonings and national origins can disguise.

This is because they are all in the same botanical family, *Leguminosae*, commonly called pulses or legumes. The pulse family is an extended one; it includes fodder and forage plants (clo-

ver, alfalfa) grazed on by the world's better-off livestock; it even includes decorative trees and shrubs (like the beautiful and fragrant mimosa tree, whose fluffy pink blooms perfume the Ozark air each June). But generally when we speak of legumes or pulses, we mean the protein-rich mature seeds of certain members of the *Leguminosae* family: we mean beans, peas, lentils, soybeans.

The life cycle of these legumes is conducive to humanity's nourishment at every step. When a bean seed puts out a small rootlet, it may be eaten as a bean sprout. But if planted in the earth and left to grow, this sprout will eventually form quite pretty, vaguely butterfly-shaped blossoms. (In fact, according to Bert Greene in *Greene on Greens, Phasoleus vulgaris,* the plant that produces the succulent pod we know as a green bean, was originally brought from its native New World back to Spain as an ornamental. It remained strictly decorative for half a century until, says Greene, "a bunch of the pods fell into a pot of soup one day," when it was too close to dinner to start over, and was "served without amend and pronounced 'perfecto!' ")

For the green pods which neatly package the seed are, of course, edible. They're eaten fresh when the seeds are young and barely developed. These pods are our green beans and our snow-peas.

But leave this tender pod alone, and it will offer you three final gifts. Though the seed pod will grow tough and inedible, the seed inside—that is, the beans—will grow plump, swelling the pod pregnantly. When the pods are removed (the same way one shells green peas), the mature beans are revealed. Speckled or spotted or solid colored, starchy and high in protein, they are

A BEAN NOTE FOR GARDENERS

❧ *If you grow your own beans or ever plan to, know that even though any bean may be eaten immature (green) or mature (fresh shell or dried), some types which make a respectable dried bean are mighty stringy when young and immature, whereas others are succulent eating in their youth but disappointing when they mature. Read your seed catalogs closely. Some varieties are good all-purpose beans, and others are especially for picking green and immature or for shelling when they are mature.*

To my knowledge, the seed company with by far the greatest number of beans, as well as an assortment of obscure greens, is Vermont Bean Seed Company, Box 250, Fair Haven, VT 05743; (802) 273-3400. ❧

ready—if cooked attentively and seasoned with care—to become the basis of a hearty, delectable soup. The generic name for beans at this stage of their growth, regardless of the particular variety, is "fresh shell beans," and they are gift one. Fresh shell beans are commonly eaten all over the American South. ("We ate so many beans," a Berryville, Arkansas, native told me once, "it's a wonder we didn't have to shell our newborn babies.")

Here's gift two: If the freshly shelled bean is thoroughly dried, it becomes, well, a bean. Just a bean, plain and simple. Or, depending on its place in the pulse family, a pea or a lentil to sit in a glass jar with its kin in your kitchen and look attractive, biding its time and quietly holding its secret—its readiness at any time to be transformed by you into nourishing warming, delicious chili or soup; hearty, welcoming, and inexpensive.

Pea, bean, or lentil, if you don't eat it, if you save it to plant the following  spring, you permit it to offer its last gift, a seed, which may be used to start the whole cycle again. The bean is the seed, the alpha and the omega. And in planting this seed, as in eating, you have kinship with all humankind, throughout history.

BASIC DRIED BEAN COOKING

"Beans are a natural product," it says on the bag of dried beans the local market carries, putting a brave face on things, for the next line is "Despite the use of modern equipment, it is not always possible to remove all foreign material. Sort and rinse beans before cooking." By "foreign material," they mean tiny rocks or pebbles or pieces of straw as well as the odd moldy bean (unlikely) and, often, little bits of dried mud. Pick through the beans first, loosely sifting them with your fingers into a colander. Then rinse them well, running cold water over them. That should take care of the foreign material.

This done, presoak the beans—not absolutely necessary, but it does cut cooking time by as much as one-third. Just pour water or vegetable stock over the beans to barely cover and let soak overnight. *Never soak beans overnight in spoilage-prone chicken or beef stock except in the refrigerator.* In fact, in very hot weather even overnight presoakings in vegetable stock or water should be done refrigerated. To further abbreviate the cooking time, bring the vegetable stock or water to a boil before pouring it over the beans.

Next morning you're ready to cook the beans. Now, many people drain off the soaking water, rinse the beans well, and start with all fresh water or stock, for this does reduce beans' gas-making properties. But when you do so, there is loss of both flavor and vitamins, which have leached into the soaking liquid.

A STOCK NOTE

❧ *Bean soups are one of the few varieties of potage where full-flavored stock is not essential in most cases. This is because beans have so much flavor themselves and add body to the cooking liquid. Even water is okay for most bean soups (unless, as in a few selections here, the soup calls for canned or otherwise already-cooked beans, and thus you don't have that nice instead-of stock bean cooking liquid to work with). So, pretty much feel free to use water or any mild found or incidental stock in any bean soup recipe.* ❧

In any case, add enough additional liquid to cover the beans by about 1 to 2 inches. Transfer the beans to a heavy pot sprayed with Pam (a cast-iron dutch oven is the preferred bean-cooking pot around here, or a crockpot—ideal if you are not going to be in the kitchen to stir now and again) and bring to a boil ("high" on the crockpot). Turn down the heat to very low and let gently simmer ("low" on the crockpot), covered, until the beans are tender—tender enough so that you can mash them with your tongue against the roof of your mouth. Periodically check the beans as they simmer, adding additional water or stock to cover if necessary. Err on the side of cooking too long rather than too briefly.

Although various herbs and vegetables can simmer with the beans, don't add salt or anything acidic, such as tomatoes, lemon juice, or vinegar, until the beans are tender. Such additions toughen the bean if added too soon, greatly increasing the overall cooking time. Fat or oil also retards cooking time but not as badly.

For each bean type in this chapter, I give approximate liquid-to-bean proportions, cooking time, and yield for 1 cup of beans, although almost certainly you will want to cook more than 1 cup at a time! My proportions result in beans that are "soupy," rather than the slightly firmer consistency you'd want if they were to be used in a salad. But the proportions given are of necessity extremely flexible. Last year's crop of beans or lentils may take three times as long as this year's to cook or soak up the liquid more plenteously. After all, it's hard to be exact. Beans *are* a natural product.

A BEAN NOTE FOR THE TERMINALLY BUSY

How on earth can something that takes hours to cook possibly fit into the lifestyle and schedule of anyone you or I know, including ourselves?

In the case of beans, two ways:

1. Cook them in a crockpot. I have a friend, a New York editor, who cooks

beans this way about once a week. She places the soaked beans du jour (1 pound of beans is just about the perfect quantity for a crockpot) with the seasoning du jour in her electric crockpot first thing in the morning, pouring over them boiling water or stock to cover. She leaves the covered crockpot at high while she showers, gets dressed, makes the bed, feeds the cat, finds her keys, and so on. On her way out the door, she turns the heat down to low. When she gets home around six, not only are the beans done and ready to be turned into a delicious, nourishing meal but also her apartment is redolent with the smells of good home cooking. Smells that say, "This is home. Here you will be well cared for."

2. The other way for the terminally busy to incorporate beans into their diet is to rely on canned beans—jazzed up after the can is open, of course. They're expensive compared to dry beans but certainly economical compared to almost anything else precooked. They are also comparatively wasteful of our natural resources. Also, without cooking the beans with herbs, there's some diminution of flavor in many recipes. Still, why carp? Nothing could be easier, and

they're a good shortcut to resort to at least once in a while and not half bad. Be sure to buy plain beans, though —no tomato sauce, frankfurter slices, or salt pork.

To tell you the truth, I never use canned beans in a bean soup per se. If I'm having bean soup, I want it from scratch with all the seasonings. But I do use canned beans regularly as an addition to other soups, as in The Soup, where only a cup or two of cooked beans is needed. When you see a recipe that calls for 1 cup cooked chick-peas, who just happens to have a cup of chick-peas around? Whenever possible, the recipes that follow offer substitutions using canned beans.

A NOTE ON INDIVIDUAL VARIETIES OF BEANS
(AND THE BEAN RECIPES THAT FOLLOW)

Each variety of bean has its own character: in flavor, texture, color, length of cooking time, absorption of liquid, and compatibility with seasonings. For this reason, I've listed the beans alphabetically with a recipe or two for each. Nevertheless, beans are more alike than different and excellent combined intervarietally (so an excellent multibean soup kicks off the line up and a basic, very simple bean soup recipe follows).

In the recipes that follow these two basic soups, where it is essential that herbs and spices be cooked with the beans for the soup to have full flavor, I start with the beans uncooked and include their cooking in the recipe. In other cases, where seasonings can be added after cooking, I start with the already cooked bean. To cook the beans just follow the basic method preceding, or use canned.

If you soak the beans overnight, you will need less stock the next morning for cooking than you otherwise would have. In fact, the liquid amount is so mutable, I would much prefer to just stick with that old bean-cooking dictum: water (or stock) to cover the beans by 1 inch (or 2, or whatever). I've gone ahead and approximated liquid measurements in cups or quarts, but, if it looks like you're using too much or too little liquid, by all means adjust accordingly.

Bean Soup Mixes

Bean Mix: First, take a trip to your largest supermarket with an in-bulk section, or better yet, a good natural-foods co-op. Stroll the bean section. Then buy equal quantities of each and every dried bean you see: every bean listed here, plus any others. Don't forget lentils and split peas. A good natural foods store will have some obscure bean varieties: lovely calico beans, tiny round red aduki beans, tiny reddish-orange lentils from the Middle East. While you're there, go ahead and buy whatever you need for the herb mix, too. When you get home, mix all the beans together, fearlessly. Ten varieties is the minimum; sixteen or twenty is not uncommon (oh those *leguminosae!*). Just make sure you have a container with a tightly fitting lid that will hold them all—preferably one of glass, so you can admire the beans' pretty colors and shapes.

Herb Mix for Bean Soup: To make a not-quite-full quart of Herb Mix for Bean Soup, mix together the following:

½ cup dried parsley

¼ cup plus 2 tablespoons dried summer savory

¼ cup cumin seeds

2 tablespoons each fennel seeds, caraway seeds, dill seeds, cracked coriander seeds, sweet basil, and dried chervil (if available)

1 tablespoon each celery seeds, dried thyme (lemon thyme, if available), sage, oregano, rosemary, lavender, sweet marjoram

½ to 1 teaspoon cayenne pepper

Hillbilly Many-Bean Soup

The place may be called "Hillbilly Heaven," "Go-Hawgs Go-Ozark Bargain-Hunters Paradise," or "Paw's Possum Holler Old-Timey Hill'n'Dale Shoppe," and it may be anywhere in the Ozarks. But go in, and odds are excellent you will find a package or jar of colorful assorted beans, with a recipe attached, for what's usually called Ozark Bean Soup. There may be a packet of herbs attached, too, but most likely there'll just be a recipe card. In the jar—which may be a regular mason jar, but is probably one shaped like a razorback hog—are beans, brightly colored and varied. They're pretty enough so that you can understand how Jack might have sold his cow for a handful of them. Black-eyes, limas, split peas, lentils, calicos, pintos, ad infinitum—as many kinds of beans as the folks doing the packaging could lay their hands on. The accompanying recipe card, too, has an infinite number of permutations: maybe it calls for a ham bone, maybe herbs or tomatoes, maybe all three.

These bean soup mixes omnipresence indicates, for one thing, just how big a part of Ozark life bean soup was and is, and how it changes from kitchen to kitchen. The mixes also show just how canny local people have been in marketing the hillbilly image to the tourists—profiting from a not unkindly hick stereotype. For, of course, in the computer age, there are few hillbillies left.

Possum Holler can be as well accessed as Madison Avenue, and isolation is what the Ozark mountaineer depended on, to hone his and her independence and resourcefulness, qualities parodied in the hillbilly. (The fellow who fixes my computer grew up with seven kids in a one-room cabin in Metalton, Arkansas; and when computers first burst on the scene, there was a store selling them in Harrison called "Silicon Holler.") But the hillbilly image still sells, so, with alacrity, locals sell it.

> **"I** will arise and go now, and go to Innisfree,
>
> And a small cabin build there, of clay and wattles made;
>
> Nine bean-rows will I have there...."
>
> —*WILLIAM BUTLER YEATS*
> *"THE LAKE ISLE OF INNISFREE"*

While beans may be an essential and genuine part of old Ozark life, almost every bean in the mix can be found at a large supermarket almost anywhere in America, at considerably lower cost than when dressed up as Ozark Many-Bean Soup—although, naturally, the beans wouldn't come in a little glass moonshine jug.

Here is how to make your own Hillbilly Many-Bean Soup mix and herb mix, and then, how to turn it into soup—delicious, and at "resident"—not tourist—prices.

2 cups Bean Mix (page 189), washed and
    picked over
7 cups any well-flavored vegetable or
    chicken stock, or water if using a soup
    bone
1 soup bone, such as the bone from baked
    or smoked ham, cured pork shoulder, or
    a ham hock (optional)
1 bay leaf
1 fresh or dried chili
2 tablespoons Herb Mix (page 189)
1 large onion, chopped
1 to 3 cloves garlic, peeled and put through
    a garlic press or finely chopped
Salt and plenty of freshly ground black
    pepper to taste
1 can (16 ounces) whole tomatoes with
    their juice, coarsely puréed in a food
    processor
1 medium carrot, scrubbed or peeled and
    sliced
1 rib celery with leaves, sliced
2 medium potatoes, scrubbed and finely
    diced
4 ounces fresh green beans, trimmed and
    sliced
1 to 3 teaspoons Pickapeppa or
    Worcestershire sauce
1 or 2 drops honey
Minced fresh parsley or other mild fresh
    green herb, for garnish

1. In a large heavy soup pot, soak the beans in stock or water to cover overnight. (If using chicken stock, refrigerate.)

2. The next day add enough of the remaining stock or water to cover the beans by 1 to 2 inches. Add the soup bone if using, the bay leaf, and chili. Bring to a boil, then turn down the heat to very low and let simmer, covered, until the beans are tender, 1 to 3 hours depending on the type of bean.

3. Add the remaining ingredients ex-

cept the parsley. Simmer, covered, until the vegetables are tender, 20 to 25 minutes.

4. If using the soup bone, take it out, pick off any meat that clings to the bone, and return it to the soup. Take out the bay leaf and chili. Mash a couple cups of beans against the side of the pot with a wooden spoon to thicken the soup slightly. Serve hot, garnished with the parsley. This soup is even better the next day.

Serves 4 to 6 amply, as an entrée

Simple Pleasures Bean Soup

ariations on this straightforward preparation are numberless. *Specific suggestions as to herbs and other ingredients to cook with the beans are in the individual bean discussions that follow.* Remember, don't add salt or lemon or other acidic ingredients until the beans are tender. This recipe is very plain, monastic almost. I would certainly amend it in one of the ways described throughout this chapter.

Pam cooking spray

2 cups dried beans, any variety, washed
and picked over

6 to 8 cups any good vegetable or chicken
stock, or water if using a soup bone

1 soup bone, such as the bone from baked
or smoked ham, cured pork shoulder, or
a ham hock (optional)

1 bay leaf

1 fresh or dried chili

1 pinch each dried summer savory, basil,
marjoram, rosemary, thyme, and
oregano, or other herbs of choice, or 1
tablespoon Herb Mix (page 189)

1 large onion, chopped

1 to 3 cloves garlic, peeled and put through
a garlic press or finely chopped

Salt and plenty of freshly ground black
pepper to taste

Other vegetables or seasonings, see
suggestions for each bean entry,
following

Chopped fresh parsley or other green herb,
for garnish

Lemon wedges or cider, herb, balsamic, or
red wine vinegar (optional)

1. Spray a large heavy soup pot with the Pam and in it soak the beans in stock or water to cover overnight.

2. The next day add enough of the remaining stock or water to cover the beans by 1½ inches. Add the soup bone or ham hock if using, the bay leaf, and chili. Bring to a boil, then turn down the heat to very low and let simmer, covered, until the beans are tender, 1 to 3 hours depending on the type of bean (exact cooking times are given for specific beans in the following discussions of bean types).

3. Add the herbs, onion, garlic, salt, and pepper (beans need a lot of salt to come to life, especially if the ham bone wasn't used,

and respond well to plenty of black pepper, too). Add the other vegetables or seasonings now if called for in the individual bean entries that follow. Simmer, covered, until the onion and the other vegetables are softened and the flavors are blended, 20 minutes.

4. If using the soup bone, take it out, pick off any meat that clings to the bone, and return the meat to the soup. Also take out the bay leaf and chili. Mash a couple cups of beans against the side of the pot with a wooden spoon to thicken the soup slightly. Serve hot, garnished with the parsley. Pass the optional lemon wedges or the vinegar in a cruet at the table. With homemade bread, such a soup is fit for royalty.

Serves 4 to 6 as an ample entrée

VARIATIONS:

Almost-a-Dead-Ringer Vegetarian Bean Soup: The simplest way to make this soup vegetarian is to use a very flavorful vegetable stock and omit the ham bone. The vegetarian who wants that smoked ham taste, however, can add a few drops of smoke flavoring during the last 20 minutes of the cooking time. Proceed cautiously and flavor to your taste. Five minutes before serving, stir in 1 heaping tablespoon of miso into the beans. This is really good!

Garlicky Bean Soup: In a food processor, purée 1 cup of the beans with an additional 1 to 3 cloves of garlic (or much, much more), and as much cayenne pepper as you deem prudent. Stir this purée into the soup just before serving. Or you could purée the whole soup, with the additional garlic and the cayenne pepper until absolutely smooth. The garlic makes the very blandest bean soup sing with flavor, especially if you then squeeze some lemon juice over it.

SOUP WITH A SCOTSMAN

❦ *Those who love food and recipe culture form a curious net of connection, enhanced and untroubled by geography. So it is that I met, by mail, a native Scotsman, Mike McIlwraith. Chef, nutritionist, and cookbook author, living in the Inverness area, he is married to children's book novelist Mollie Hunter. Our lively on-and-off correspondence began five or six years ago.*

At that time, my mother, Charlotte Zolotow, was still at Harper & Row (now Harper-Collins), where she edited children's books for many years. She not only loved Mollie's writing, but Mollie herself, and, when she met him, Mike. I mean . . . a charming kilt-wearing chef would be hard for anyone to resist. Several years ago, she sent Mollie and Mike a copy of the first Dairy Hollow House Cookbook.

My correspondence with Mike began when he wrote to ask permission to use one of our recipes in a cookbook he was writing. And what recipe did he ask for? Of all things, fried chicken! It struck me at the time that often the most humble, simple food of a particular culture may seem most exotic outside that culture.

Naturally, a man like Mike would be the perfect person to give me the definite low-down on the two dishes I happened to know about, which handily enough were a bread and a soup. I wrote Mike that, of course, he could use the fried chicken recipe in his book, but would he

help me with mine? I was looking, I told him, for two "Scottish" dishes, Scotch broth and baps.

The first of these was a meaty barley-vege-table-bean soup I'd had exactly once when I had a very bad cold. It was fed to me by a feisty old Eureka Springs lady named Virginia Carey, who was then 76 or so. (This is the same lady who, when speaking of her own death, used to say "One of these days I'll just get on my broomstick and fly off." She died on Halloween.)

Baps were rolls I'd read about in Marion Cunningham's Breakfast Book. *"A friendlier roll you'll never meet," she says. That, and the very word "bap" was enough to raise my interest. Too, since most Ozark natives are of Scots-Irish descent, I was particularly eager, as I was curious to see if there were any existing connections at all between the two Scottish recipes and traditional Ozark cuisine.*

As it turned out, there was one: the "joint" of meat called for in Mike's Scotch Broth (page 219) is echoed in Cora Pinkley-Call's Ozark Heritage Soup, about which she says in her book, From My Ozark Cupboard: A Basic Ozark Cook Book, *'To make my heritage soup you must have a critter's shin bone with a joint—don't ask me why!' She hypothesized that the custom originated with her Native American ancestors; obviously it came from the other side of the family—and the Atlantic.* ❦

BLACK BEANS

*I*n an earlier cookbook, I called black beans the aristocrats of beans, and I was right, for they are among the most full flavored of beans as well as more expensive than most. They are my favorite beans.

Basics: 1 cup dried black beans, presoaked in water to cover overnight or softened with boiling water, will cook in 1 to 1½ quarts water in 1½ to 2 hours and yield about 2½ cups cooked beans. Black beans are sometimes hard to find canned, but Goya makes them. Look in the Mexican or Cuban food section of your grocery store. If making the Simple Pleasures Bean Soup (page 191), with black beans, follow the basic recipe through the soup thickening, step 4, and add a jigger of sherry at the end. Omit the lemon wedges.

> **"**Live in each season as it passes; breathe the air, drink the drink, taste the fruit, and resign yourself to the influence of each. Grow green with the spring, yellow and ripe with autumn.**"**
>
> —*HENRY DAVID THOREAU*,
> JOURNAL

Cuban Black Bean Soup

ed and I like black bean soup so much we served it at our wedding reception. This will make the third time I've repeated in print my recipe for this simple Cuban black bean soup—it's that fine. It's difficult to believe such ordinary ingredients could turn out so ambrosially. Enough olive oil to float an armada is one of its secrets, but it is good with less, too.

Pam cooking spray
2 cups dried black beans, washed and picked over
2½ quarts any well-flavored vegetable stock or water
2 bay leaves
1 fresh jalapeño pepper, chopped with seeds (if you want the soup just a little hot, remove the seeds and white pith from the pepper)
¼ to ¾ cup (if conscience allows) olive oil
3 large onions, chopped
2 green bell peppers, stemmed, seeded, and chopped
4 to 6 cloves garlic, peeled and put through a garlic press or finely chopped
Salt to taste
1½ to 2 cups cooked white rice, for serving
1 onion, chopped, for serving

1. Spray a large heavy soup pot with the Pam and in it soak the beans in stock or water to cover overnight.

2. The next day add enough of the remaining stock or water to cover the beans by 1 inch. Add the bay leaves and jalapeño, cover the pot, and bring to a boil. Turn down the heat to very low and let simmer, partially covered, until the beans are tender, about 1½ to 2 hours.

3. Meanwhile, in an 8- or 9-inch skillet, heat the oil over medium heat. Add the onions and sauté until softened, about 3 minutes. Stir in the garlic and cook a few seconds more.

4. When the beans are tender, add the onion mixture to them and season with salt. Let simmer another 20 minutes. Serve at once, or, even better, the next day. Pass the rice and chopped onion at the table.

Serves 6 to 8 as an entrée

VARIATIONS:

To make this soup with canned beans, pour 5 cans (15 ounces each) of black beans with their liquid into a heavy soup pot and add an equal amount of vegetable stock. Add the bay leaves, broken up a bit, and heat through. Then proceed as directed, adding diced jalapeño to the pepper-onion sauté.

Déjà Food: A little black bean soup, like any bean soup, is wonderful stirred into any vegetable soup. If you have a lot left over, you could make *Ned's Mother's Casserole,* a dish he loved as a child: ground beef browned with chopped onions and layered with mashed potatoes and black bean soup, then baked. He thinks maybe there was grated cheese on top. Nowadays, though, we are more likely to cook the soup down and use it to fill enchiladas. Every couple of years we do the calorically irresponsible but divine

Mock Turtle Soup with Black Beans. Measure leftover black bean soup into a food processor. Add 1½ teaspoons dry sherry and 2 to 4 tablespoons heavy (whipping) cream for every cup of soup. Purée, then heat through. When ready to serve, stir in half a hard-cooked egg white, diced, for each cup of soup, and garnish the soup with the crumbled yolk. This is so good it's almost overkill.

Black bean soup is delicious and attractive garnished with a few slices of ripe avocado, too.

Black Bean Soup Santa Fe

any people compare Eureka Springs to Santa Fe or Taos, New Mexico. They point out that both places have a strong concentration of artists and bohemians who've moved in from elsewhere; that the broader area itself has an indigenous folk culture (in New Mexico, that of the Indians; in Eureka, that of the Ozark mountaineers and farm families) which nourishes and interplays with the local fine arts communities. Both areas are somewhat isolated geographically, making the populations historically self-reliant and self-entertaining. Too, there's a magnetism, a feeling, about both places, indescribable yet palpable. Both were sacred ground to Native Americans, and visitors as well as residents of both places still feel that something.

Physically, the beauty of the moist, green, lush Ozarks, with its small steep mountains, is entirely different from the dramatic, arid desertscapes and arroyos of the San Cristobals. This may be why, when it comes to vacations, a number of Santa Fe-ans and Taos folks come here, and a number of Eurekans go there: if you respond to one, you'll respond to the other, yet their characters are entirely different.

Several summers back, Ned and I visited New Mexico for the first time, for a week. We rafted the Rio Grande and bought turquoise trinkets for the folks at home. We browsed some incredible art galleries, and toured the fabulous Museum of American Folk Art in Santa Fe (see if you can get Mary Noel as a guide). We had massages. We stayed at a lovely bed-and-breakfast inn in Santa Fe (Grant Corner Inn), and checked out of a horrible one in Taos which shall remain nameless. Ned bought me a denim jumper and a copy of *Death Comes for the Archbishop*. I bought him two wooden folk-art cats. In short, we were tourists and had a blast.

We also ate very well. New Mexican cooking is a feast, unlike Mexican, unlike Tex-Mex, unlike anything except its own full-flavored self. It's a cuisine of green chili, fiery and vibrant; red chili, also fiery but with a completely different character; rice cooked with dried safflower blossoms, not saffron, as the seasoning; and, everywhere, beautiful, mysterious-looking tortillas made of dusky blue cornmeal.

At one restaurant, whose name I've regrettably forgotten, my old favorite, black bean soup, was on the menu. It differed from mine only slightly in the seasonings, but had an imaginative presentation that we liked.

1 recipe Cuban Black Bean Soup (page 194)
2 tablespoons cumin seeds
6 to 8 sturdy, hard-type crusty rolls, round, about the size of a fist
6 ounces Monterey Jack cheese, grated
¼ cup or so finely chopped fresh cilantro, for garnish

1. Prepare the Cuban Black Bean Soup, adding the additional cumin seeds with the beans. When the beans are tender, purée half of them in a food processor and return them to the pot, then add the sautéed vegetables. Continue simmering.

2. Slice off the tops of the rolls in which the soup will be served and set them aside. Dig out the soft crumb from the rolls with a sharp knife. Excavate further with a serrated grapefruit spoon. You want a good sturdy shell which the soup can fill; at the same time, you don't want too much bread in proportion to the soup.

3. Preheat the oven to 400° F. Raise the heat under the soup.

4. Place the hollowed-out rolls on a baking sheet. Using a small ladle, scoop as

much soup as possible into the rolls. Cover the soup with the grated cheese until it is invisible, and slide into the oven. Bake until the exterior of the rolls are slightly crustier and the cheese has melted, 5 to 7 minutes.

5. Meanwhile, toast the reserved roll tops.

6. Set each roll in a soup bowl, sprinkle each with a little cilantro, and serve immediately, with the toasted roll top on the side. You'll need a spoon, knife, and fork to eat this. Pass additional cilantro at the table.

Serves 6 to 8 as an entrée

VARIATION: Can't get the right kind of rolls? Okay, just toast pieces of French bread, slice them onto the top of the soup, sprinkle liberally with grated cheese, run under the broiler or melt in a hot oven, and you've got it. Either way, this is a *serious* full meal!

BLACK-EYED PEAS

Starchier and a little blander than some of the other beans, black-eyed peas are eaten all over the South. When I grew my first vegetable garden with my Texan ex-husband, he introduced me to that plain, satisfying dish familiar to Southerners—freshly shelled black-eyed peas mixed with black-eyes in their early, green bean stage, and bacon or salt pork, a chili, and quite a bit of water. All are cooked together a long time and served with cornbread, of course. Today, though, my favorite way with black-eyes is the Black-Eyed Pea Soup with Arkansalsa and Crème Fraîche.

Basics: 1 cup dried black-eyed peas, presoaked in water to cover overnight or softened with boiling water, will cook in 3 cups water in 1 to 1½ hours and yield about 2¼ cups cooked peas. Black-eyed peas are widely available canned. If making the Simple Pleasures Bean Soup (page 191) with black-eyed peas, sauté the onion with 1 or 2 diced green bell peppers in 2 to 3 tablespoons mild vegetable oil, such as corn or peanut, before adding to the soup (see step 3). Add 1 to 3 teaspoons Pickapeppa or Worcestershire sauce and 1 tablespoon tomato paste, and proceed as directed.

Black-Eyed Pea Soup with Arkansalsa and Crème Fraîche

ll over the South, people eat black-eyed peas on New Year's day to ensure good luck in the coming year. Ever since the January 1st when some guests brought a can of black-eyes with them and gagged down spoonfuls cold and plain right out of the can with breakfast, I tell all our guests who book a reservation at that time of year not to worry, that we will include black-eyes in their New Year's Day meal.

This delicious, hearty soup, faintly spicy in itself and topped with the addition of a dab of fresh hot salsa, is more interesting by far than the traditional combination of black-eyes, ham hocks, salt, pepper, and maybe a shot of Tabasco. This way is also healthier—no saturated fats except in the dab of crème fraîche, or sour cream. The salsa adds a nice jazzy Southwestern note of freshness, just what a black-eyed pea needs. You'll find yourself eating this more often than once a year, sighing with satisfaction every time.

Don't be fazed by the long ingredient list; it's got mostly seasonings, and preparation goes quickly.

Pam cooking spray
1 pound black-eyed peas, washed and
 picked over
Any well-flavored vegetable stock or water
 to cover (about 1½ to 2 quarts)
2 bay leaves
½ teaspoon dried oregano
½ teaspoon dried basil
1 tablespoon cumin seeds
1 teaspoon dried summer savory
1 teaspoon cracked coriander seeds
Freshly ground black pepper to taste
2 tablespoons tomato paste
1 cup additional vegetable stock or water
1 cup Spicy Hot V8 vegetable juice
1 tablespoon Pickapeppa or Worcestershire
 sauce
1 teaspoon tamari/shoyu soy sauce
1 teaspoon Tabasco or similar hot pepper
 sauce
2 salt-free Morga vegetarian bouillon cubes
 (page 31)
3 cloves garlic, peeled and put through a
 garlic press
1 to 2 tablespoons mild vegetable oil, such
 as corn or peanut
1 large onion, chopped
2 medium carrots, scrubbed or peeled, and
 finely diced
1 large green pepper, stemmed, seeded,
 and diced
2 ribs celery with leaves, finely diced
Salt and freshly ground black pepper to
 taste
Garlic Oil (page 41; optional)
Arkansalsa (recipe follows)
Crème Fraîche (page 50), sour cream, kefir
 cheese, or plain yogurt, for garnish
Fresh cilantro sprigs, for garnish

1. Spray a large heavy pot with the Pam, and in it soak the beans in the stock or water to cover overnight.

2. The next day, add enough of the remaining stock or water to cover the beans by 2 inches. Bring to a boil, then turn down the heat to very low, and add the bay leaves, oregano, basil, cumin seeds, savory, coriander seeds, and several generous grinds of black pepper. Cover the beans and let them simmer, stirring occasionally, until thoroughly soft and cooked—until you can easily squash a bean against the side of the pot with a wooden spoon. Taste one—it will be extremely, creamily soft, though very bland at this point. Don't worry, things are about to get much more interesting in Black-Eyed Pea-land. Keep the soup over low heat.

3. Dissolve the tomato paste in the additional cup of stock or water, and add it to the simmering black-eyes with the V8, Pickapeppa or Worcestershire sauce, soy sauce, Tabasco sauce, Morga cubes, and garlic. Give the mixture a good stir to combine.

4. Spray a 10-inch skillet with Pam, and in it heat the oil over medium heat. Add the onion and sauté until transparent, about 4 minutes. Add the carrots, green pepper, and celery, and continue sautéing until they soften a bit, another 2 minutes. Stir these vegetables into the simmering soup, scraping the skillet to get out any little flavorful bits. At this point the soup will be on the thick and stewlike side; if you want it soupier, add additional stock. Now taste. Turn up the volume by adding salt and pepper and maybe a little good old garlic oil. Its flavor will really come alive at this point, but only begin to dance truly after another 15 minutes or so of uncovered simmering.

5. Ladle the hot soup into bowls, and top each serving with Arkansalsa, a dab of crème fraîche or any of the other dairy choices, and a sprig of cilantro. Pass additional salsa and crème fraîche, or other dairy dabs, at table.

Serves 8 to 10 as an entrée

VARIATION:

To make this soup with canned black-eyes, use 5 to 6 cans (15 ounces each) of plain black-eyes. Combine one can of black-eyes in a food processor with the oregano, basil, cumin seeds, summer savory, coriander seeds, and pepper and buzz until smooth. Spray a soup pot with Pam, and in it combine the purée with the canned beans, their liquid, and a slightly less than equal amount of good chicken or vegetable stock. Add the bay leaves, broken up a bit, and heat, stirring often. This operation takes you to the point in the recipe where the Pickapeppa and further ingredients are added. Proceed as directed.

Déjà Food: See Cornbread Pie à la Hippie (page 355), an excellent use for leftovers. Also, like many bean soups, Black-Eyed Pea Soup was made for reheating with tomato juice or V8.

Arkansalsa

 here are dozens of varieties of hot peppers which could be used to make this salsa. Choose whatever's available and fresh, and use a lot or just a smidgen according to how incendiary they are—and how fiery you like your food. "To taste" in my case would mean 1 or 2 jalapeños, or 1 scotch bonnet, or 1 red Thai chili—but I like things hot.

1 large onion, peeled
½ green bell pepper, stemmed and seeded
Fresh red and green chili peppers to taste
1 tomato, peeled and seeded
Juice of ¼ lemon
1 tablespoon finely minced fresh parsley
2 tablespoons finely minced fresh
   cilantro
¼ teaspoon salt

►Dice all the ingredients through the tomato into pieces a bit bigger than the head of a wooden kitchen match; the smallness and uniformity of the pieces are important here. Toss all together with the lemon, herbs, and salt—the consistency should be more relishy than saucelike.

Makes about 1½ cups

CHICK-PEAS (GARBANZOS)

*C*hick-peas are the little, round, clefted beans of pale gold, sometimes sold as garbanzo beans or ceci beans. They get tender but never meltingly soft like other beans.

Basics: 1 cup dried chick-peas, presoaked in water to cover overnight or softened with boiling water, will cook in 5 to 5½ cups of water in 3 to 4 hours and yield 2 to 2½ cups cooked peas. Chick-peas are available canned; you can usually find them in the Mexican food section of the supermarket—look for "garbanzos." If making the Simple Pleasures Bean Soup (page 191) with chick-peas, follow the basic recipe, adding 1 tablespoon Worcestershire or Pickapeppa Sauce, and 1 teaspoon each of dried mustard, honey, curry powder, and ground ginger when seasonings are called for in step 3. Or forgo all these, and add a bunch of assorted fresh greens, thinly sliced, in the last 15 minutes of cooking. Then squirt in the juice of 2 lemons, and add a tablespoon or so of tamari/shoyu soy sauce.

Chick-Pea Soup Mamusia

he two soup recipes in which, to me, chick-peas really come into their own are the Wintery Chicken and Pasta Soup with Chick-Peas (page 63) and Mollie Katzen's Gypsy Soup in her *Moosewood Cookbook*. To my taste Gypsy Soup is among her most inspired: sweet potatoes, chick-peas, and tomatoes are a magic combination. My soup differs from hers only slightly, and I have named it after my favorite gypsy in literature, Mamusia (or Madame Laoutaro) in Robertson Davies' *What's Bred in the Bone*.

2 tablespoons olive oil
1 large onion, chopped
2 or 3 bell peppers (preferably 1 each green, red, and yellow), stemmed, seeded, and chopped
1 rib celery with leaves, chopped
1 teaspoon finely chopped fresh gingerroot
2 cloves garlic, peeled and put through a garlic press or finely chopped
1 bay leaf
1 tablespoon sweet Hungarian paprika
1/8 teaspoon ground cinnamon
Tiny pinch of saffron threads
Pinch of cayenne pepper
One or two gratings of nutmeg
6 cups Golden or Browned Vegetable Stock (pages 28 and 32) or Chicken Stock 1 (page 19) or any well-flavored vegetable or chicken stock
3 medium or 4 small sweet potatoes or yams (12 to 16 ounces), peeled and diced
1½ teaspoons dried basil
1½ teaspoons dried summer savory
1 can (15 ounces) whole tomatoes with their juice, coarsely puréed in a food processor
2 teaspoons honey
2 cups cooked chick-peas
8 ounces greens, such as turnip greens and spinach, washed very well and thinly sliced (page 133)
1 tablespoon tamari/shoyu soy sauce, or to taste
Salt and freshly ground black pepper to taste

1. In a 10-inch skillet, heat the oil over medium heat. Add the onion and sauté until softened, about 3 minutes. Stir in the bell peppers and celery and sauté 2 minutes more. Add the ginger, garlic, bay leaf, paprika, cinnamon, saffron (crushing the threads between your fingers), cayenne, and nutmeg. Sauté 1 minute more and transfer to a large heavy soup pot. Deglaze the skillet with a little of the stock and add the deglaze to the pot.

2. Add the remaining stock, the sweet potatoes, basil, and savory to the pot. Bring to a boil, then turn down the heat to medium-low, and add the tomatoes and honey. Let simmer, covered, about 10 minutes. Stir in the chick-peas and heat through, then add the greens (you may have to mash the lid down on them but they will cook down). Cook, covered, 5 to 10 minutes longer. Season with the soy sauce, salt, and pepper. Serve hot. Sometimes I add sliced fat black olives to the soup just before serving, which makes it even more wonderful, if possible.

Serves 4 to 6 as an entrée

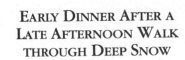

EARLY DINNER AFTER A LATE AFTERNOON WALK THROUGH DEEP SNOW

❧

*Chick-Pea Soup Mamusia

*Thick Slices of French Country Bread and Butter

Garlic Slaw (from Dairy Hollow House Cookbook)

Apple Crisp with Cream or Yogurt

CRANBERRY BEANS

Also called *borlotti*, cranberry beans are *fagioli romani*, which translates "Roman beans." These are the classic beans for minestrone, which is truly incredible when made with fresh shell cranberry beans—often available in large farmer's markets in metropolitan areas or small rural roadside stands, but rarely the suburban supermarket in between.

Basics: 1 cup dried cranberry beans, presoaked overnight in water to cover or softened with boiling water, will cook in 3½ cups water in about 2 hours and yield 2 to 2¼ cups cooked beans. If making the Simple Pleasures Bean Soup (page 191) with cranberry beans, do the Garlicky Bean Soup variation, adding 1 cup tomato juice and a handful of fresh parsley to the beans in the food processor. Then proceed as directed. Cranberry beans are not available canned as far as I know, although you could probably find imported canned beans in a larger city. If you can't get cranberry beans, use navy, pinto, or kidney beans, even limas, instead.

Minestrone

 t is almost insulting to give a recipe for this luscious Italian soup, which is by nature improvisational, taking advantage of what is in season. Any single component could change and it would still be minestrone: a classic bean and vegetable soup, usually entirely vegetarian, amply seasoned with herbs (fresh are much preferred), and usually including tomato, some starch, and a cooked green or cabbage. About the only vegetables that won't turn up in minestrone are mushrooms, artichokes, or a yellow vegetable like winter squash or sweet potatoes. Which is not to say you couldn't put them in if you wanted to.

Angelo Pellegrini, that Italian-American food writer of great heart, soul, and humor, says of minestrone, "The best time to go in for minestrone with a vengeance is in the fall, for then one may not only procure all the necessary vegetables and herbs, but also (perhaps) fresh, ripe *romani* beans in the shell. . . . In a sense, minestrone is a seasonal as well as regional dish. By using the dry beans and whatever vegetables are available, one may prepare it at any time during the year; but if one wants the best, it must be made in the early fall months, especially since fresh basil is the real secret of the extraordinary soup." He's right, as usual.

Pam cooking spray
1 pound dried cranberry beans, washed and picked over, or 4 cups fresh shell beans
4 quarts any well-flavored vegetable stock or water
6 to 8 cloves
3 or 4 large onions, unpeeled, halved
12 garlic cloves, peeled, 3 put through a garlic press
2 bay leaves
½ to 1 teaspoon dried red pepper flakes
¼ cup olive oil
1 large onion, chopped
4 to 6 ripe tomatoes, diced, or 1 can (20 ounces) whole tomatoes, drained and coarsely puréed in a food processor
1 teaspoon honey
⅛ teaspoon ground allspice
1 teaspoon dried summer savory
1 teaspoon dried oregano
½ teaspoon dried rosemary
½ teaspoon dried thyme
½ teaspoon dried savory
Salt and freshly ground black pepper to taste
¼ savoy cabbage, thinly sliced; and/or 2 to 3 cups greens, such as turnip greens and chard, washed very well and thinly sliced; and/or 3 to 4 cups cut green beans (1-inch pieces); and/or 3 medium carrots, scrubbed and sliced
5 tablespoons chopped fresh parsley
1 cup lightly packed fresh basil leaves, chopped
3 to 4 cups cooked pasta or 2 to 3 cups cooked white rice or 8 to 10 Garlic Bread Croûtes (page 96) or 2 cups cooked diced scrubbed potatoes
Chopped fresh parsley, for garnish
Freshly grated Parmesan cheese, for serving

1. If using dried beans, soak them, in the refrigerator, in a bowl in enough stock to cover overnight.

2. The next day, spray a large heavy soup pot with the Pam, and in it bring the remaining stock to a boil. Add the soaked or fresh beans to the pot with the soaking stock. Stick a clove in each onion half and add to the pot along with 3 whole cloves garlic, the bay leaves, and the red pepper flakes. Bring to a simmer, cover the pot, turn down the heat, and let simmer, stirring occasionally, until the beans are tender, about 2 hours for dry beans, 1¼ hours for fresh beans. Drain the beans, and return the stock to the pot. Remove the onion halves, bay leaves, and cloves from the beans, and in a food processor purée the beans with the cooked garlic. Stir this purée into the stock.

3. In a large skillet heat the oil over medium heat. Add the chopped onion and sauté until it starts to soften, about 3 minutes. Add the tomatoes, increase the heat, and cook, stirring frequently, about 5 minutes. Stir in the 3 pressed garlic cloves, the honey, allspice, and herbs; continue to cook until much of the tomato liquid has evaporated. Add the tomato mixture to the bean soup and season with salt and pepper.

4. Bring the soup to a boil, then turn down the heat to very low and simmer, covered, 15 minutes. Then add the vegetables and the 5 tablespoons parsley and simmer, covered, until tender, about 15 minutes.

5. Meanwhile, purée the remaining 6 cloves garlic and the basil in a food processor. Stir this basil mixture into the soup and simmer 3 minutes more.

6. Place a little pasta, rice, potato, or a croûte in each serving bowl, and ladle the steaming hot soup on top. Garnish with the fresh parsley and serve with Parmesan cheese.

Serves 8 to 10 as an entrée

VARIATIONS:

Tuscan Minestrone: Use navy beans, red onions, and croûtes for the starch; add 2 teaspoons fresh thyme leaves to the tomato sauté. Pass bowls of chopped red onion, parsley, grated Parmesan, and a cruet of olive oil at the table.

Déjà Food: A little leftover minestrone finds new life when heated with tomato juice and/or good stock, and served with a poached egg placed in the bottom of each bowl.

BEAN LORE

Beans have been associated throughout history with luck, good and bad. The ancient Romans thought the little black spots on their beans symbolized death, and were holy but unlucky. Consecrated to the souls of the deceased, these beans were offered as a sacrifice to Apollo. Later, in Greece, beans were used in voting: white beans "for" and black "against." When the Greek mathematician Pythagoras warned, "Abstain from beans," he really meant "Stay out of politics."

In Shakespearean England, a single bean was baked into the Twelfth Night cake, part of the Christian celebration of Epiphany. Whoever found the bean was King or Queen of the Bean, becoming master of ceremonies for the evening and ensuring his or her good luck throughout the year. Baking a bean into a Christmas cake or bread is still common in many European countries.

Closer to our own Southern tradition of having black-eyed peas on New Year's Day is the Italian custom of eating lentils on that day. Each lentil is said to represent a coin, ensuring prosperity for the coming year.

GREAT NORTHERN BEANS

*T*hese somewhat bland but agreeably flavored pale beans may be used interchangeably with navy beans, which they resemble closely. Great Northerns are slightly larger than navys, and buff-colored rather than white.

Basics: 1 cup dried Great Northern beans, presoaked overnight in water to cover or softened with boiling water, will cook in about 1½ to 2 hours in 2¾ cups water and yield 2 ample cups cooked beans. If making Simple Pleasures Bean Soup (page 191) with Great Northern beans, follow the basic recipe, adding the grated zest of 1 orange with the green herbs and 2 teaspoons hot pepper sauce and a pinch of cumin seed when called for in step 3. Just before serving, stir in a few tablespoons of tomato paste and the juice of the orange.

Jerry Stamps's Great Bean and Corn Chowder

*J*erry Stamps is a pharmacist, friend, and superlative cook. In fact, one of his recipes, Chicken Breasts Eldred, appeared in *Dairy Hollow House Cookbook* and has been cited several times in letters from grateful readers. This is his way with bean soup. It's very, very good and quite simple because the onions are not sautéed separately.

Pam cooking spray
2 cups dried Great Northern beans, washed and picked over
2 quarts any well-flavored vegetable or chicken stock, or water
1 heaping teaspoon dried basil
1 heaping teaspoon dried oregano
1 heaping teaspoon dried rosemary
1 heaping teaspoon dried thyme
1 heaping teaspoon dried summer savory
1 bay leaf
1 can (16 ounces) whole tomatoes with their juice, coarsely puréed in a food processor
1 large onion, chopped
3 to 4 tablespoons olive oil
Large pinch of cayenne pepper
½ pound summer sausage, thinly sliced (optional)
7 or 8 domestic white mushrooms, trimmed and sliced
1 can (16 ounces) whole kernel corn, including liquid, or 1 to 2 cups leftover cooked corn kernels
Salt and freshly ground black pepper to taste

1. Spray a large heavy soup pot with

Pam, and in it soak the beans in the stock or water to cover overnight. (If using chicken stock, refrigerate.)

2. The next day add enough of the remaining stock to cover the beans by 1 to 2 inches. Bring to a boil, then turn down the heat to very low and add the herbs and bay leaf. Simmer, covered, until the beans are tender, about 1½ to 2 hours. Add the toma-toes, onion, olive oil, and cayenne; continue to cook another 20 minutes. Stir in the sausage, if using, and mushrooms; cook another 10 minutes. If you want the texture more souplike, thin the chowder with additional stock. Just before serving, add the corn, salt, and pepper, and heat through.

Serves 6 to 8 as an entrée

KIDNEY BEANS

Kidney beans are good, well-flavored beans, which get pleasantly tender when cooked. They are pretty in the mixed-bean jar, too. When making chili, I sometimes replace the pintos with kidney beans; and, of course, they are wonderful and classic in minestrone as made in America (in Italy, you would use cranberry beans or *fagioli romani*).

Basics: 1 cup dried kidney beans, presoaked in water to cover or softened with boiling water, will cook in 1½ to 2 hours in 3½ cups water and yield 2 heaping cups cooked beans. Kidney beans are easily available canned, although the canned beans taste a little sweet because a bit of sugar is unaccountably added to them. Kidney beans make a particularly delicious Simple Pleasures Bean Soup (page 191). Follow the basic recipe, adding a few tablespoons salsa, 1 to 3 teaspoons Pickapeppa or Worcestershire sauce, ¼ teaspoon dried mustard, and a pinch of ground cloves when called for in step 3. Proceed as directed.

Kidney Bean Soup Bercy

nspired by a casserole in *The Gold Cookbook* by Louis P. De Gouy, this soup makes excellent use of kidney beans. Canned beans are fine here or, even better, use already cooked beans if you have them on hand. Like Bean and Barley Soup Bourguignon (page 215), this soup relies on red wine to boost the flavor. It is also good with pintos, calico beans, or red beans.

2 tablespoons butter

1 large onion, chopped

2 green bell peppers, stemmed, seeded, and
   diced

1 yellow bell pepper, stemmed, seeded, and
   diced

1 red bell pepper, stemmed, seeded, and
   diced (optional)

1 rib celery with leaves, diced

3 cloves garlic, peeled and put through a
   garlic press or finely chopped

3½ cups cooked kidney beans

1 tablespoon honey

2 teaspoons Pickapeppa or Worcestershire
   sauce

1 bay leaf

1 teaspoon dried summer savory

1 teaspoon dried basil

¼ teaspoon ground cloves

Pinch of cayenne pepper

Salt and freshly ground black pepper to taste

1 to 1½ quarts any well-flavored vegetable
   or chicken stock, or water

2 cups hearty red wine

¼ cup tomato paste

Sour cream or plain yogurt, for garnish

Finely chopped fresh
   parsley, for garnish

1. In a 10-inch skillet, melt the butter over medium heat. Add the onion and sauté until softened, about 3 minutes. Add the bell peppers and celery; sauté another 3 minutes. Stir in the garlic and sauté another half min-ute. Remove from the heat and stir in the beans, honey, Pickapeppa or Worcestershire sauce, the bay leaf, summer savory, basil, cloves, cayenne, and salt and pepper.

2. In a large heavy pot, bring the stock, wine, and tomato paste to a boil. Stir in the bean mixture, turn down the heat to very low, and let simmer, partially covered, until the flavors are blended, about 30 minutes. Taste and adjust the seasoning. Serve very hot, garnishing each bowl with a dollop of sour cream or yogurt and a sprinkle of parsley.

Serves 4 to 6 as an entrée

VARIATION:

Leftovers make an excellent Mock Turtle Soup with Black Beans. See the Déjà Food variation of Cuban Black Bean Soup (page 195).

THE INFAMOUS KIDNEY BEAN JOKE

🍎*A man walks into a store and says to the clerk, "Say, y'all have any kidley beans?"*

The clerk says, "I'm sorry sir, we don't. Perhaps you mean kidney beans?"

The man replies irritably, "I said kidley, diddle I?"🍎

LENTILS

I am very fond of these flavorful flat brown beans, which cook quickly, take happily to a variety of seasonings, and are widely available. I probably fix one or another sort of lentil potage more often than any other legume soup at home, and lentil soups often appear on the menu at the restaurant.

Basics: 1 cup dried lentils in 3½ to 4 cups water will cook in 30 to 50 minutes without presoaking and yield 2½ to 3 cups cooked lentils. Lentils are not usually available canned, but they cook so rapidly that this is not a problem. Simple Pleasures Bean Soup (page 191) with lentils is a particular favorite of mine. Follow the basic recipe, adding 1 to 3 teaspoons Pickapeppa or Worcestershire sauce, lots of freshly ground black pepper, and 2 or 3 diced potatoes after the lentils have cooked for about 15 to 25 minutes, and 2 sliced carrots and 2 sliced celery ribs when called for in step 3. Simmer the vegetables until tender. Add some minced garlic, say 2 or 3 cloves, and a touch of cayenne during the last 20 minutes of cooking. Don't forget the lemon-wedge garnish.

Greek Lentil and Spinach Soup with Lemon

I mentioned earlier that lentil soup is my favorite at-home legume soup. After years of making lentil soups of every description, I've finally settled on this as my number one choice. It's brightly sparked with plenty of lemon and the spicy crunch of coriander and cumin seeds. The greens (prevalent in Mediterranean bean soups of all kinds) add both healthfulness and flavor, and the minimum amount of oil makes it a boon to fat-gram counters. I've been playing with this one for some time; I knew it had reached perfection with the addition of the faintly sweet butternut squash. The green of the spinach and the bright orange of the squash floating in the rich brown soup make it most pleasing to the eye, too.

This is perfect at any vaguely Greek- or Middle Eastern-style dinner. I served it recently to friends, with a couscous salad, a plate of sliced feta and olives, some baba ganoush with whole-wheat pita, and fresh pineapple and Medjool dates for dessert. It was wonderful, and completely dispelled the damp and dark of a drizzly Ozark January night.

Pam cooking spray
1 pound lentils, washed and picked over
2¼ quarts plus 1 cup any well-flavored
   vegetable stock or water
1 dried poblano chili or 1 fresh
   jalapeño
2 teaspoons whole coriander seeds
1½ teaspoons whole cumin seeds
1 teaspoon dried oregano
1 teaspoon dried basil
½ teaspoon dried thyme
2 bay leaves
2 small potatoes, scrubbed and diced
1 box (10 ounces) frozen chopped
   spinach or 1 bag (10 ounces) fresh
   spinach, well washed, stems removed,
   and chopped
2½ cups peeled and diced butternut
   squash
1 tablespoon olive oil
1 large onion, chopped
2 ribs celery with leaves, sliced
3 large cloves garlic, peeled and finely
   chopped
Salt to taste
⅓ cup freshly squeezed lemon juice
Paper-thin slices of lemon, for garnish

1. Spray a large heavy soup pot with Pam, and in it combine the lentils, stock or water, chili, coriander seeds, cumin seeds, oregano, basil, thyme, and bay leaves. Bring to a boil, then turn down the heat to very low and let simmer, partially covered, about 30 minutes.

2. Add the potatoes and spinach, cover again, and let simmer another 15 minutes. Add the butternut squash. Cover again and

let simmer while you do the next step.

3. Spray a 10-inch skillet with Pam, and in it heat the olive oil over medium heat. Add the onion and sauté until it starts to soften, about 3 minutes. Add the celery and garlic, and sauté another 3 minutes, stirring often. Add this mixture to the soup; deglaze the skillet with a little soup and add the pan contents to the pot. Add salt, and taste for seasoning.

4. Just before serving, add the lemon juice. Stir well, and taste again. Serve hot with a lemon slice floating on top of each bowl of soup.

Serves 4 to 6 as an entrée, with a hearty salad (like a Greek) and bread

> **❝One** morning in November I awoke at 6:30 A.M. and looked out on a grey landscape that would have dispirited Gustave Doré: palpably damp, lunar in its deleafed desolation, it made my bone marrow feel as though I had somehow extracted it and left it in a dish on the back step all night. It was one of those mornings when a man could face the day only after warming himself with a mug of thick coffee beaded with steam, a good thick crust of bread, and bowl of bean soup.❞
>
> —*RICHARD GEHMAN*

INN GOOD COMPANY :
SANDY AND THE ALLISON-APARICIO-HABER CLAN

I have the pleasure of cooking, on a daily basis, with Sandy Allison, a tough Texas cookie who is a complete pushover. This dear person with bright blue eyes can raise hell with the laundry service for delivering us the wrong color napkins . . . but she tears up at the right song or poem or story. A fine cook, she teaches and learns in equal measure, and keeps the kitchen together body and soul, working with dozens of suppliers: small local growers, like the Millers who bring us rabbits, as well as the big purveyors whose trucks cause traffic jams on Spring Street. Balancing creativity with business, Sandy experiments and evaluates: Not only will she try three batches to discover the definitively best mixed-grain ice box roll, but she will, say, take the temperature of the water in four different coffee machines and a warmer to answer, conclusively, the question of which is best for tea or to keep cider at a constant temp. She also works hard, and beautifully, at the catering-and-group-bookings side of our operation.

A Eureka transplant who at one time owned a local deli, Sandy is a gifted folk artist and seamstress. Each Christmas she manages to find time to make, on a commission basis, a few extraordinary Santa Clauses and tree-top angels.

Sandy has lived here for the past fifteen years with her extended family (most of whom have, at one time or another, worked for us) on 40 acres or so of beautiful Ozark hilltop known to the Allison clan as "the Hill." It's sort of a commune, except everyone has separate houses, and all the members are related. I keep threatening to write a TV series about life on the Hill.

There's Sandy, her handsome husband Jim (who occasionally gets pressed into service as a maître d' here), and her two kids, both in their twenties. Sandy and Jim's son Corey sometimes works for us as a bus-boy. Their daughter, Robbie, is the mother of adorable T. J., Sandy's beloved grandson, and one of Dairy Hollow House's unofficial Best Baby Boys.

Sandy's sister, Rose Aparicio, is also a Diary Hollow mainstay. Rose lives on the Hill in a separate house, with her four children. She was our main breakfast and "prep" cook for a year or so, took another year or so off to have a baby

(Ethan—our other Best Baby Boy), and returns to us again this spring. Hooray, Rose! Which have we missed more—Rose's sweet smile, or her meticulous attention to her sister's detailed "prep list"? One of Rose's children, gorgeous, willowy Walana, with the sleepy eyes and the deadly sense of humor, has also been part of Dairy Hollow— a dishwasher and on-and-off evening assistant to me on busy nights. I will miss her when she goes off to college.

Sandy and Rose's mom, Edna, is another Hill resident. Edna, feisty and unflappable, makes our jams and jellies. And then there's their father (Edna's ex), Leo, an affable builder/inventor artist. Leo now lives with Leta, who for years ran the Craft Attic, a shop I sorely miss when it comes time to chase down art supplies or stencil brushes.

How on earth do they all manage to get along?

I put this question to Sandy once. She did not seem to see anything extraordinary in what her family was doing. She pointed out that of course they fight like cats and dogs from time to time, and then they just make up and go on. "Just like any family," she said. I pushed her a little more. "Well," she said, "we decided, when we began to seriously talk about moving out of Dallas and coming on up here, that we would all just look after each other, no matter what." She paused. "And," she said, "we have." 🍎

Sandy's Great Lentil Soup with Greens and Garlic

Sometimes simplest is best. This great, easy, healthy, homey lentil soup, developed by our kitchen manager, Sandy Allison, can't be beat. You wouldn't think that this would be so different from the previous soup, but it is, and the few ingredients belie its deliciousness. The garlic and olive oil give a rich, almost meaty taste, yet it is vegetarian, and tastes even better the next day. It is based on a recipe given Sandy by Marquita Sorce, another local cook. Ned and I thought we knew everything there was to know about lentil soup but we just flipped the first time we had this, and it's been a periodic winter craving of ours.

Sandy prefers using green lentils for this, as opposed to the more widely available brown lentils. The green variety, usually available at natural foods stores, is quite flavorful, and being smaller, much quicker cooking and very tender.

Pam cooking spray

3 tablespoons olive oil

2 large onions, chopped

2½ cups lentils, preferably green,
washed and picked over

2 quarts, approximately, Browned Vegetable
Stock (page 32) or any well-flavored
vegetable stock or spring water

2 teaspoons cumin seeds

Salt and freshly ground black pepper to
taste

1 head fresh garlic, separated into cloves
and peeled

1 to 1½ pounds assorted fresh greens, such
as spinach, collards, and turnip greens; a
combination is best, washed very well
and chopped

⅓ cup plain yogurt or sour cream, for
garnish

⅓ cup good homemade salsa (see
Arkansalsa, page 199), for garnish

Finely chopped fresh cilantro, for garnish

1. Spray a large iron skillet with Pam, and in it heat the oil over medium-low heat. Add the onions and sauté until the onions are very soft but not burned, about 10 minutes. If you wish, you may use extra olive oil (tastiest) or cut it back (saner in terms of fat grams).

2. Meanwhile spray a large heavy pot with Pam and transfer the sautéed onions to it. Add the lentils and stock or water. Deglaze the skillet with a little of the water, and add the deglaze to the soup pot. Bring to a boil, then turn down the heat and simmer gently till the lentils are extra-soft, 45 to 60 minutes. Add the cumin seeds, salt, and pepper.

3. Scoop out a ladleful of soup, and purée it in a food processor with that wonderful head of garlic. Add the garlic-lentil purée to the soup and return the soup to a boil. Drop in the greens, partially cover, and

let simmer another 10 to 15 minutes. Correct the seasonings and serve. It's delectable as is, but you may gild the lily by garnishing with a dab of yogurt or sour cream, some good homemade salsa, and some finely chopped cilantro.

Serves 4 to 6 as a starter

Lentil Dal

f you love real Indian food—the kind you get at Indian restaurants—and wonder why your curries at home don't taste the same, it's because the curry recipes in most non-Indian cookbooks are Anglo-Indian, less dimensional and less spicy. This, however, is the real thing—high in protein and incredibly good. It's exotic, so we don't usually serve it at the inn (except during one of our mystery weekends which involves a colonel who served Her Majesty under the raj, and maintained a fondness for the cuisine). The Déjà Food suggestion at the end domesticates the dish enough to make it acceptable to the general non-mystery public. We probably make dal at home once a month, since it's easy to do in a crockpot. With rice and plain yogurt or, better yet, chopped fresh tomatoes, onions,

and cukes tossed with a little yogurt, it is dinner.

Pam cooking spray
2 cups lentils, washed and picked over
5 to 6 cups water
1 bay leaf
3 tablespoons butter
1 large onion, chopped
1 tablespoon minced fresh gingerroot
1 tablespoon cumin seeds
1 tablespoon black mustard seeds (do not substitute yellow)
1½ teaspoons ground coriander
1½ teaspoons turmeric
Pinch of ground cloves
Pinch of cayenne pepper (or to taste)
Salt and freshly ground black pepper to taste
2 to 3 cups hot cooked rice, for serving

1. Spray a large heavy soup pot with the Pam, and in it place the lentils, water, and bay leaf. Bring to a boil, then turn down the heat to very low and let simmer, covered, until the lentils are very soft, about 1 hour.

2. Meanwhile, in a large skillet melt the butter over medium heat. Add the onion and sauté until softened, about 3 minutes. Add the gingerroot and all the spices, turn down the heat slightly, and cook, stirring constantly, 3 minutes. Stir this spice mixture into the lentils and continue to cook until the lentils are very soft and the soup is thick and sauce-like. Season with salt and pepper. Serve hot over the cooked rice. It is even better the next day.

Serves 4 to 6 as an entrée, with the rice

VARIATIONS:
In India this is most usually made with yellow split peas called *moong dal*, which can be found in some specialty shops. Regular green split peas will work, too, but I think the lentils are tastiest.

Déjà Food: I can't tell you how wonderful this soup is blended with an equal amount of almost any creamy soup you may have on hand; Deep-December Cream of Root Soup (page 266), and pumpkin and tomato soups all meld with extraordinary grace with Lentil Dal.

> **"T**ake long walks in stormy weather or through deep snow in the field or woods, if you would keep your spirits up. Bear with brute nature. Be cold and hungry and weary . . . Ah, but is this not a glorious time of year for your deep inward fires?**"**
>
> —*HENRY DAVID THOREAU,*
> *JOURNALS*

Harira

 n a rural town the size of Eureka if you get a craving for exotic ethnic food, you cook it yourself. This is my vegetarian version of harira, the glorious spicy soup eaten all over Morocco in a thousand variations. I took as inspiration the harira recipes in Paula Wolfert's *Good Food from Morocco*, the definitive, sensual book on the subject. The soup's flavors are fantastic—sweet, hot, spicy, somehow floral—warming and great. This was the featured player at the 1987 Dairy Hollow staff party, the theme of which was "Morocc'n'roll."

½ cup dried chick-peas
2 to 2½ quarts any well-flavored vegetable or chicken stock or water
Pam cooking spray
1 cup lentils, washed and picked over
4 tablespoons (½ stick) butter
1 large onion, chopped
3 ribs celery with leaves, chopped
¾ cup chopped fresh parsley
1½ teaspoons turmeric
1 teaspoon ground cinnamon
2 pounds fresh tomatoes, puréed in a food processor and strained
Small pinch of saffron threads
Small pinch of ground ginger
1 teaspoon freshly ground black pepper, or more to taste
4 ounces very fine noodles, such as vermicelli
Optional thickener: 3 tablespoons unbleached all-purpose flour whisked into ½ cup stock, or 3 or 4 large egg yolks, lightly beaten
Salt to taste

1. In a bowl, soak the chick-peas in water or some of the stock to cover overnight. (If using chicken stock, refrigerate.)
2. The next day, drain the chick-peas. Spray a large heavy pot with Pam, and in it place the chick-peas. Add the stock (including the soaking stock) and bring to a boil.

Turn down the heat to very low and let simmer, covered, until the chick-peas start to soften, about 2 hours. Add the lentils and continue to simmer for 1 hour.
3. Meanwhile, in a 10-inch Pam-sprayed skillet melt the butter over medium heat. Add the onion and sauté until it starts to soften, about 3 minutes. Add the celery, parsley, and turmeric; continue to sauté for 3 minutes. Stir in the cinnamon, turn down the heat to very low, and cook, stirring often, for 10 minutes. Remove the skillet from the heat and stir in the tomato purée, saffron, ginger, and pepper.
4. When the lentils and chick-peas are tender, stir in the tomato mixture. Gently simmer, partially covered, about 15 minutes.
5. Meanwhile, cook the pasta in a large pot of salted boiling water until barely tender. Drain.
6. Five minutes before serving, thicken the soup if you want: Either stir in the flour paste, or whisk a little of the hot stock into the egg yolks, then whisk this mixture back into the soup; simmer, stirring often, until slightly thickened. Season with the salt.
7. If you plan to serve all the soup, stir in the noodles. Otherwise, put a scoop of noodles in each bowl and ladle the hot soup over the top.

Serves 6 to 8 as a starter or 4 to 6 as an entrée, with couscous (of course)

LIMA BEANS

According to Irma Mazza, author of the 1947 *Herbs for the Kitchen*, "that creamy goodness which is limas stands far up in front when the rating of beans begins." Creamy, yes, but frankly not my favorite bean. The lima needs attention to be good. Be sure to use plenty of seasoning when cooking limas, and, if at the end the soup is still bland, give it life with a dash of hot pepper sauce and a squeeze of lemon or shot of vinegar. Garlic Oil (page 41) wouldn't hurt, either.

I use dried limas most often as one of the bean crowd in Hillbilly Many-Bean Soup (page 190). I also occasionally make a chowder with them or treat them Mexican-style as in Chili Dairy Hollow (page 221) or Southwestern-style as in Black-Eyed Pea Soup with Arkansalsa and Crème Fraîche (page 198). Lastly, I combine them in the soup that follows with more flavorful red beans, red wine, red wine vinegar, tomatoes, barley, and herbs in a lusty, loosely French manner—an idea which had its roots in the excellent book *Laurel's Kitchen*.

Basics: 1 cup dried limas or baby limas, presoaked overnight in water to cover or softened with boiling water, will cook in about 1¾ hours in 3½ to 4 cups water and yield 2 cups cooked beans. Lima beans are sometimes available canned (these are dry, not green limas). To make Simple Pleasures Bean Soup (page 191) with limas, sauté the onion until softened in about 2 tablespoons butter with 2 diced ribs celery, 2 sliced carrots, and 1 diced bell and/or hot pepper before adding to the soup (see step 3). Towards the end of the cooking, purée a 15-ounce can of whole tomatoes, with their juice, in a food processor and add it to the soup with a pinch or two of ground cloves and a bit of freshly grated nutmeg. Heat through and serve as directed.

Lima beans are also great in the Garlicky Bean Soup variation of this simple soup. Limas are one of the better beans to cook with a ham bone, since they tend toward blandness.

Bean and Barley Soup Bourguignon

What, you may wonder, is peanut butter doing in this soup? Well it melts into the soup in an indefinable way, adding a rich smoothness and a hint of sweet—quite wonderful. This is a hearty soup and just the thing to have simmering on the stove on a gray, rainy day.

Pam cooking spray
½ cup dried baby lima beans
½ cup dried regular lima beans
1 cup dried red beans
2 quarts Browned or Golden Vegetable
    Stock (pages 32 and 28) or Chicken
    Stock 1 (page 19) or any well-flavored
    vegetable or chicken stock
1 bay leaf
1 teaspoon dried basil
1 teaspoon dried sage
1 teaspoon dried oregano
¼ cup pearl barley
2 cloves garlic, peeled and finely chopped
Salt and freshly ground black pepper to
    taste
1 large onion, chopped
2 medium carrots, scrubbed or peeled and
    diced
2 ribs celery, diced
½ pound green beans, trimmed and sliced
    ½-inch thick
1 can (15 ounces) whole tomatoes with
    their juice
1½ cups hearty red wine
¼ cup tomato paste
2 tablespoons peanut butter (creamy or
    chunky)
1 tablespoon honey
1 tablespoon Pickapeppa or Worcestershire
    sauce
2 to 4 tablespoons red wine vinegar

1. Spray a large heavy pot with Pam, and in it soak the limas and red beans in enough stock to cover overnight. (If using chicken stock, refrigerate.)

2. The next day add enough of the remaining stock to cover the beans by 2 inches, then drop in the bay leaf and herbs. Bring to a boil, then turn down the heat to very low and let simmer, covered, until the beans are nearly done, about 1 hour. Add more stock

if necessary to keep the beans covered.

3. Stir in the barley and garlic; continue to simmer until the beans are very tender and the barley is almost done, about 30 minutes. Season with salt and pepper. Add the onion, carrots, celery, and green beans; simmer, covered, until the vegetables are nearly done, about 15 minutes.

4. Place the tomatoes, with their juice, in a food processor, and coarsely purée. Add the red wine, tomato paste, peanut butter, honey, and Pickapeppa or Worcestershire sauce. Buzz until blended. Stir this mixture into the soup and simmer over very low heat 15 minutes longer. Stir in the vinegar to taste and serve hot.

Serves 6 to 8 as an entrée

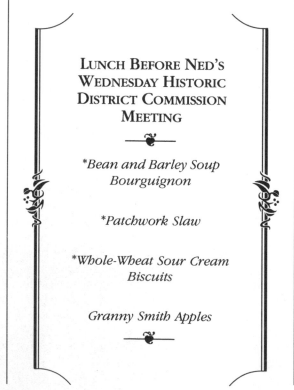

LUNCH BEFORE NED'S WEDNESDAY HISTORIC DISTRICT COMMISSION MEETING

❧

*Bean and Barley Soup
Bourguignon*

Patchwork Slaw

*Whole-Wheat Sour Cream
Biscuits*

Granny Smith Apples

❧

NAVY BEANS

Navy beans—small white beans—are one of the more commonly eaten beans in the Ozarks. They are delicious and succulent, cook to a melting softness, and take well to a variety of seasonings, particularly herbal. These are the beans most often used for Boston baked beans and the famous Senate bean soup, but I prefer them in Italian or Greek dress.

Basics: 1 cup dried navy beans, presoaked in water to cover or softened with boiling water, will cook in about 1½ to 2 hours in 3½ cups water and yield 2¼ cups cooked beans. To make Simple Pleasures Bean Soup (page 191) with navy beans, do the Garlicky Bean Soup variation, adding cayenne and, at the very end, the juice of 1 fresh lemon. Dill is also pleasant in this soup: Add 1 teaspoon of dill seeds when the beans are cooking and 2 tablespoons dried dillweed during the last 20 minutes of cooking. Place sprigs of fresh dill on top of lemon slices for the garnish.

Greek Navy Bean Soup

Pam cooking spray
2 cups dried navy beans, washed and picked over
1½ to 2 quarts Golden Vegetable Stock (page 28) or Chicken Stock 1 (page 19) or any well-flavored vegetable or chicken stock
2 large onions, chopped
1 bay leaf
1 scant tablespoon dried oregano
1 scant tablespoon dried basil
1 teaspoon dried thyme
1 teaspoon dried dill
1 teaspoon dried rosemary
Pinch of cayenne pepper
2 medium carrots, peeled and sliced
3 medium potatoes, peeled and diced
2 ribs celery with leaves, diced
2 fresh or 2 drained whole canned tomatoes, finely chopped
Salt and freshly ground black pepper to taste
4 tablespoons olive oil
½ cup coarsely chopped fresh parsley
2 cloves garlic, peeled
Juice of 1 lemon
Additional chopped fresh parsley, for garnish
Paprika, for garnish
Paper-thin lemon slices, for garnish

1. Spray a large heavy pot with the Pam, and in it soak the beans in enough stock to cover overnight. (If soaking in chicken stock, refrigerate.)

2. The next day add enough of the remaining stock to cover the beans by 1½ inches. Bring to a boil, then turn down the heat to very low. Add 1 of the onions, the bay leaf, herbs, and cayenne. Gently simmer, covered, 1 hour. Add the carrots, potatoes, celery, and tomato. Let simmer, covered, until the beans and vegetables are meltingly tender, about 30 minutes. Season with salt and pepper.

3. In a large Pam-sprayed skillet, heat the oil over medium heat. Add the remaining onion and sauté until softened, about 3 minutes. Scrape the onion into a food processor, add the parsley, garlic, and lemon juice, and purée until smooth. Stir the purée into the soup. Taste and adjust the seasoning, adding more lemon juice and cayenne if needed. Cook about 5 minutes more. Serve hot, garnishing each bowl of soup with parsley, paprika, and a lemon slice.

Serves 4 to 6 as an entrée

DINNER FROM SALONIKA

*Greek Navy Bean Soup

Greek Salad (from Dairy Hollow House Cookbook *)*

*French Country Bread

Greek Walnut Cake

Fresh Fruit

PEAS

The split pea entry comes later in this chapter, and fresh green peas are in the vegetable chapter. The peas under discussion here are the whole dried round peas, sometimes called "marrowfat peas."

Basics: 1 cup dried whole peas, presoaked in water to cover or softened with boiling water, will cook in about 1½ hours in 2½ cups water and yield over 2 cups cooked peas. To make the Simple Pleasures Bean Soup (page 191) with dried peas, do the Garlicky Bean Soup variation and add a healthy pinch of curry powder. Proceed as directed.

Scotch Broth

cotch broth, good from bite one, improves by being cooled and reheated the next day. It is a nourishing, wonderful soup; great when you have a cold, or on a freezing or drizzly day. Please note that the real thing is considerably thicker than the Scotch broth you may be familiar with. Mike McIlwraith (see box, page 193) says, "It should almost be thick enough to allow a spoon to stand up in it." If you want yours more brothy than porridgelike, double the amount of water or stock you use. As to the choice of meat, lamb shanks are the "joint" American-style Scotch broth is most often made with.

Mike notes that Scotch broth "is a peasant dish that used anything to hand. When times were hard the soup was made almost exclusively of kale and to this day it is called 'kale' in some households. However it is usually based on a mutton or beef broth. When beef, it was always the cheapest cut. Skirt or shin or marrow bone. Mutton was used more widely. It was never lamb but now it is

difficult to get anything else. A sheep's head was very popular. The head was singed of its wool and split open, usually by the butcher, but the housewife was expected to be capable of it. My grandmother was. . . . The trotters also were often cooked in the broth, to add strength to the stock. It was a favorite Sunday dinner in Scots Presbyterian households, because it could be cooked on Saturday and leave the Sunday free for church.

"With a hunk of bread it is a meal in itself."

½ cup dried whole peas, such as marrowfat, washed and picked over
Joint of beef, mutton, or lamb (1¼ to 1½ pounds)
6 cups spring water or any well-flavored vegetable stock
Salt and freshly ground black pepper to taste
½ cup pearl barley
2 carrots, scrubbed or peeled and sliced
2 large onions, chopped
4 leeks, white part and 1 inch of green, split open lengthwise, well washed, and sliced
3 small turnips, rinsed and diced
⅓ pound cabbage or kale, or a combination, washed well and chopped (page 133)
Finely chopped fresh parsley to taste (about ¼ cup)

1. In a bowl, soak the peas in tap-water to cover overnight.

2. The next day, put the joint in a sufficiently large heavy pot and add the spring water or stock. Season with the salt and pepper, and bring to a boil. Skim off any foam that rises to the surface. Add the barley and peas, turn down the heat to low, and let simmer slowly for 2 hours. "Cooking time will be variable according to the kind of meat, but when tender, remove it and set aside and leave the peas and barley to simmer on until they are done," says Mike.

3. Skim off surplus fat from the soup, leaving just enough "to make the surface look like shot silk." Add all the vegetables, and adjust the seasoning. Add the parsley. Let simmer over low heat, covered, until the vegetables, peas, and barley are all done, at least 45 minutes to 1 hour. They should be quite soft.

4. Meanwhile, pick the meat from bone. You may then either dice it and stir it back into the soup, or serve it with potatoes as a second course. "Sometimes," Mike says, "there might be oatmeal dumplings—*hodgills*—cooked in the soup, or a coarse brown bread of whole wheat served with it, or a leftover bap" (see Scotch Baps, page 344).

Serves 8 as an entrée, with bread and a salad

VARIATIONS:

American-Style Scotch Broth: Double the amount of water or stock called for, and use lamb shanks for the meat. Add 2 bay leaves.

Vegetarian Scotch Broth: Use a good, strong vegetable stock such as Browned or Golden (pages 32 and 28) for the liquid. Brown the vegetables in butter or oil before adding to the barley-pea mixture, and throw in a bay leaf or two and a few of your favorite herbs, as well as a hit of Garlic Oil (page 41). Well . . . it's not exactly Scotch broth but it is soothing, nourishing, and good.

PINTO BEANS

*T*he pinto, spotted like the pony, is a wonderful bean, cooking up to tender creaminess and quite delectable when well-seasoned. It's a favorite of mine, and also the first bean I really got to know and love.

Born and (mostly) bred in New York City, I was unfamiliar with beans until 1969, when I met my ex-husband, the proverbial long, tall Texan. He introduced me to radical politics, Eastern philosophy, environmentalism, natural foods, seriously hot food, and beans—

pinto beans in particular. One of these I've dropped completely, another was the starting point for some thinking which turned out very differently but happily from where it had begun, and the other four remain ongoing, enthusiastic parts of my life. (You guess which is which.) Well, four out of six isn't bad.

Basics: 1 cup dried pinto beans, presoaked in water to cover or softened with boiling water, will cook in about 3 hours in 4 cups of water and yield 2¼

> **❝If you want to know the people of a nation, I am sure you can judge a great deal more about them from their cooking and eating traditions than you can from the words and actions of their public officials.❞**
>
> —*PYOTR KROPOTKIN,*
> *MUTUAL AID*

cups cooked beans. To make the Simple Pleasures Bean Soup (page 191) with pinto beans, follow the basic recipe, adding extra garlic, tamari/shoyu soy sauce, and 2 teaspoons Pickapeppa or Worcestershire sauce when called for in step 3. A dash of cinnamon is a refreshing surprise, too. A 15-ounce can of whole tomatoes, puréed with their juice, would not be amiss here, added to the soup in its last 20 minutes of cooking, nor would using the pinto beans in the Garlicky Bean Soup variation.

Chili Dairy Hollow

o me, pinto beans are the beans for a chili pot, although my friend Kachina has converted me to the pleasures of black bean chili. Now one of my occasional culinary pen pals, John (*Simple Cooking*) Thorne, makes a convincing case that traditional chili, that half-breed of Mexican and chuck-wagon cookery, did not include onions, tomatoes, or beans. He goes so far as to assert that the chilis that have them, and especially the meatless chilis that have recently become popular, are nothing less than a feminist plot! What can I say? I love good vegetarian chili— guilty as charged.

This recipe makes an ample amount, and chili freezes so beautifully it's silly to make any less. It should be said it is really more a stew than a soup, but it's too good to quibble over the point.

Chili is best made the day before. Serve it over rice, topped with cheese and other fixings like chopped onions, jalapeños, sprouts, diced fresh tomatoes, sliced avocados, and sour cream or yogurt. Or serve it over tortilla chips or with steamed tortillas; as a sauce over cheese enchiladas; or with cornbread (page 354). Or mix the chili with tomato juice and bake it with cornbread on top—a fine way to serve it the next day. It also goes well with New South Cornmeal Dumplings (page 138) or with cooked macaroni.

Pam cooking spray

1 pound dried pinto beans, washed and
   picked over

2½ to 3 quarts any well-flavored vegetable
   stock or water

2 bay leaves

2 Morga vegetarian bouillon cubes

1 ancho chili (dried, very dark, triangular
   chili)

1 fresh jalapeño or dried pequin chili

Freshly ground black pepper to taste

¼ cup mild vegetable oil or olive oil

2 large onions, chopped

3 green bell peppers, stemmed, seeded,
   and chopped

1 tablespoon cumin seeds

2 teaspoons ground cumin

2 teaspoons ground coriander

2 teaspoons sweet Hungarian paprika

¼ teaspoon cayenne pepper, or to taste

1 tablespoon hot chili powder

½ teaspoon dried oregano

4 or 5 cloves garlic, peeled and put
   through a garlic press or finely
   chopped

1 can (16 ounces) whole tomatoes with
   their juice, coarsely puréed in a food
   processor

¼ cup tomato paste

2 to 3 teaspoons Pickapeppa or
   Worcestershire sauce

1½ teaspoons tamari/shoyu soy sauce, or to
   taste

Salt to taste

1 tablespoon honey (optional)

2 tablespoons masa harina (tortilla corn
   flour) stirred into 3 tablespoons cold
   water (optional thickener)

1. Spray a large heavy pot with Pam,
and in it soak the pinto beans in water to
cover overnight.

2. The next day add enough stock to
cover the beans by 1½ inches. Bring to a boil,
turn down the heat, and add the bay leaves,
Morga cubes, ancho chili, jalapeño, and lots
of black pepper. Simmer over low heat, covered, until the beans are nearly tender, about
2 hours.

3. Meanwhile, in a 10-inch skillet, heat
the oil over medium heat. Add the onions
and sauté until they start to soften, about 3
minutes. Stir in the bell peppers and sauté
about 2 minutes more. Add all the remaining
herbs and spices; cook, stirring constantly, 1
to 2 minutes. Add the garlic, cook 30 seconds
more, and scrape this mixture into the beans.
Deglaze the skillet with a bit of the bean
cooking liquid, and add the deglaze to the
pan.

4. Add the tomato purée, tomato paste,
and Pickapeppa or Worcestershire sauce to
the chili. Season with the soy sauce, then with
salt (be sure to use enough). Adjust the hot-
ness with the cayenne. Stir in the honey, if
using (it cuts the acidity of the tomatoes).
Simmer, partially covered, until all is tender
and the seasonings are well blended, about
45 minutes. If you want the chili very thick,
add the optional thickener of masa harina
and cook, stirring frequently, over low heat
for a few minutes. Watch the chili closely and
stir often, if you thicken it; it has a much
greater tendency to stick to the pot.

5. Just before serving, pick out the bay
leaves and stems from the ancho chili and
jalapeño and mash a couple of cups of the
beans against the side of the pot to further
thicken it. Mash any visible pieces of the
ancho and jalapeño into the pot as well.

6. Serve the chili with any of the fixings
mentioned in the headnote. It will taste even
better the next day. Refrigerate, covered, for
short-term storage, or freeze for longer term.

Serves 8 to 10 as a generous entrée

RED BEANS

*R*ed beans are flavorsome and pretty—part of the New Orleans classic red beans and rice. They are delicious cooked with limas or in Kidney Bean Soup Bercy (page 206) and a must in Hillbilly Many-Bean Soup (page 190), and they make a toothsome Mock Turtle Soup Louisianne (page 225).

Basics: 1 cup dried red beans, presoaked in water to cover or softened with boiling water, will cook in 3½ cups of water in about 3¼ hours and yield 2¼ cups cooked beans. Red beans are available canned. To make Simple Pleasures Bean Soup (page 191) with red beans, add the seasonings suggested in the entries for kidney or pinto beans (pages 206 and 220) when called for in step 3 of the basic recipe. Proceed as directed.

Creole Red Bean Soup-Stew

ith Texas to the west, heartland Missouri to the north, deep-South Tennessee and Alabama to the east, and Louisiana due south, Arkansas has elements of all these regions in its cuisine. Southern or farmland

cooking is probably the most widely enjoyed, but Tex-Mex and Cajun-Creole foods are always appreciated, although it is more usually eaten out—the notable exception being chili, which everyone makes at home.

Eureka Springs has an affinity for Louisiana in general and New Orleans in particular. Dozens of former New Orleans residents live here, and even greater numbers commute there from here, or spend part of the year here and part

there. As with Santa Fe, there is something about New Orleans that is similar to Eureka—an archaic architectural style, an artistic population, a willingness to lay business aside and go fishing.

There is a definite New Orleans seasoning, both literal and metaphorical, in Eureka, and nowhere more so than at the beloved Center Street Bar and Grill. There, chef-owner Vernon LeBlanc, born and bred in New Orleans, turns out such specialties as gumbo with chicken and andouille, and red beans and rice. This is not his recipe, but ours, although they are kin. Mine is a variation of the red beans and rice in Leon Soniat's cookbook *La Bouche Creole*. It is more a stew than a soup, and divine. The vegetarian version is, too, although Leon might have problems with that on principle.

Pam cooking spray
1 pound dried red or kidney beans, washed
*   and picked over*
3 quarts water or any well-flavored
*   vegetable stock*
1 thick slice (2 to 4 ounces) smoked ham
1 thick slice (2 to 4 ounces) pickled pork
*   (optional)*
2 large onions, chopped
2 large green bell peppers, stemmed, seeded,
*   and chopped*
1 rib celery with leaves, chopped
1 large carrot, scrubbed or peeled and
*   sliced*
4 or 5 cloves garlic, peeled and put through
*   a garlic press or finely chopped*
2 bay leaves
1 dried whole chili pepper
2 teaspoons sugar
1 to 2 tablespoons white or cider vinegar
Tiny pinch of ground allspice
Tiny pinch of cayenne pepper
Tiny pinch of ground cloves
Tiny pinch of good-quality chili powder
Freshly ground black pepper to taste
Salt to taste

ONION SALAD GARNISH:
2 onions, sliced paper thin
3 tablespoons olive oil
1 tablespoon white or cider vinegar
Salt and freshly ground black pepper to
*   taste*

3 to 4 cups hot cooked rice, for serving
Finely chopped fresh parsley, for garnish

1. Spray a large heavy soup pot with Pam. Add the beans and enough water or stock to cover and soak overnight.

2. The next day, add enough of the remaining water or stock to cover the beans by 1½ inches. Add the ham and pork, if using, and bring to a boil. Turn down the heat and add all the vegetables and seasonings except the salt. Cover the pot and let simmer over very low heat, stirring occasionally, until the beans soften, about 2½ hours.

3. Remove the meat from the soup and dice it, discarding the gristle. Mash about one-third of the beans against the side of the pot to thicken the soup; remove any remnants of the dried chili. Season the beans with salt and return the meat to the pot.

4. In a pretty bowl, combine all the ingredients for the onion salad garnish. Heat the soup until good and hot. To serve, spoon the rice into bowls, ladle the soup over it, top each serving with a few tablespoons of the onion salad, and garnish with the parsley.

Serves 6 to 8 as an entrée

VARIATION:

For the vegetarian version, omit the ham and pork and use a hearty vegetable stock (pages 27 to 34) for both soaking and cooking the beans. Use double the amount of onions, carrots, and celery. Add a little liquid smoke, about ⅛ teaspoon, along with the vegetables and seasonings.  At the last, stir in 1 to 2 heaping teaspoons each light and dark miso dissolved in a bit of the bean stock.

Mock Turtle Soup Louisianne

n spring, a young turtle's fancy turns. Suddenly, for about three weeks starting in late March, the eastern box turtles that live more or less unseen all year round are highly visible, all over the Ozarks. They've left their (to them) cozy beds of leaf mold, and are on the march in search of romance. And if you happen to be going to the airport in Fayetteville to pick someone up round about the first part of April, add an extra 15 minutes to the trip. No doubt you'll see several turtles crossing Highway 23, and you'll want to, quick, pull over, jump out of the car, and carry them across to the other side of the road. Saving turtles is a springtime rite, and a deeply satisfying one.

Having looked directly into the ancient, otherworldly faces of so many of these reptilian kin, I could never bring myself to eat turtle soup in the unlikely event it were offered to me. So I have no idea if the rich, dark beany soups that are called "mock turtle" are at all close to the real thing. I do know that, often laced with sherry and speckled with bits of hard-cooked egg, they are delicious. A variation appears for a creamy one under Black Beans. Here is one without cream, made from puréed red beans and seasoned with a browned roux. It's quite elegant, contains a large amount of sherry, and, the *coup de grâce*, actual mock-turtle *eggs*! You can use plain old hard-cooked eggs if you don't want to mess with making these little dumplings of seasoned hard-cooked eggs, but somehow this bit of folly is so appealing. This recipe was developed from a description given me by some Baton Rouge restaurant guests, which was followed by a sojourn in several of my good old Junior League cookbooks.

2½ cups dried red beans, washed and picked over
Pam cooking spray
About 6 cups Browned Vegetable Stock (page 32) or any well-flavored vegetable stock
¼ cup mild vegetable oil, such as corn or peanut
¼ cup unbleached all-purpose flour
2 cloves garlic
4 tablespoons (½ stick) butter
2 large onions, diced
2 ribs celery, diced
1 green bell pepper, stemmed, seeded, and diced
1 red bell pepper, stemmed, seeded, and diced
Juice of 1 lemon (about 2 tablespoons)
1 teaspoon Tabasco or similar hot pepper sauce
½ teaspoon dried thyme
Salt to taste
1½ cups best dry Amontillado sherry
3 hard-cooked eggs, chopped, or Mock Turtle Eggs (recipe follows)
Lemon slices, for garnish
3 to 4 tablespoons finely minced fresh parsley, for garnish

1. In a bowl, soak the red beans overnight in water to cover. The next day, spray a large, heavy pot with Pam, add the beans, and cover with the vegetable stock to a depth of 1½ inches. Bring to a boil, turn down the heat to very low, and let simmer, covered, until the beans are very tender, about 2½ hours. Drain the beans, reserving the liquid. Allow the beans and cooking liquid to cool slightly.

2. Prepare a brown roux (page 242) using the oil and flour. It should take 45 minutes to 1 hour to make.

3. Between stirs of the roux, begin to purée the cooked beans with the garlic and a little bean cooking liquid in a food processor. Purée in batches. Return all the batches but the last to the soup pot. When the roux is done, buzz it in the processor with the remaining batch of beans. Return the puréed beans with the browned roux to the soup pot. Stir very well to combine everything. Bring to a boil, turn down the heat to low, and simmer, covered, for 15 minutes.

4. Spray a 10-inch skillet with Pam, and in it melt the butter over medium heat. Add the onions and sauté until quite limp but not brown, about 6 minutes. Add the celery and peppers and cook, stirring often, another 5 minutes. Scrape the sautéed vegetables into the soup, along with the lemon juice, Tabasco, thyme, and salt. Stir well. Cover the soup pot, and continue to simmer over the lowest possible heat for 1½ hours. This can be done in advance.

5. Thirty minutes before serving, add the sherry, and reheat over low heat. Make the Mock Turtle Eggs, if using. Dip one side of each lemon slice in the parsley. Serve the soup very hot, with a little hard-cooked egg or 2 Mock Turtle Eggs in each bowl or cup, and a parslied lemon slice afloat on top.

Serves 6 to 8 as a starter

Mock Turtle Eggs

3 hard-cooked eggs
1 raw egg
1½ teaspoons unbleached all-purpose flour,
*   plus additional*
A few dashes of salt, pepper, and cayenne
*   pepper*

1. Bring a saucepan of water to a boil. Meanwhile, in a food processor, combine the hard-cooked eggs, the raw egg, 1½ teaspoons flour, and seasoning. Buzz to an almost-smooth consistency.

2. Put a little additional flour on a plate. With your palms, roll the egg mixture into small, egg-shaped balls, a little smaller than an egg yolk. Roll each of these "turtle eggs" in the flour on the plate.

3. Drop the "eggs" into the boiling water and let them cook for about 3 minutes. Lift out with a slotted spoon and serve in Mock Turtle Soup. These can be made up to 1 hour in advance.

Makes about 12 "mocks"

SPLIT PEAS

With lentils, split peas are the quickest cooking of all dried legumes, and mighty comforting—a wintertime staple. The Spanish-Style Split-Pea Soup, which has puréed spinach, continues to be an ongoing cold-weather fave at the restaurant.

Basics: 1 cup dried split peas in 3 to 3½ cups of water will cook in about 1 hour without presoaking and yield 2½ cups cooked peas. The peas are not available canned, but they cook quickly. To make Simple Pleasures Bean Soup (page 191) with split peas, follow the basic recipe, adding an extra bay leaf and garlic clove, and 2 teaspoons Pickapeppa or Worcestershire sauce when called for in step 3. Stir in a diced potato and cook until nearly tender; add a sliced carrot and a sliced rib of celery and cook until all the vegetables are tender. Proceed as directed.

The herb mix for Hillbilly Many-Bean Soup (page 189) is excellent with split peas. Split peas are also good done spicily in place of the lentils in Lentil Dal (page 212) or, more simply, with cayenne and tamari/shoyu.

Pea Soup with Caraway Adelle

I first read Adelle Davis's *Let's Cook It Right* more than twenty years ago. From her I learned how to steam vegetables and make an exquisite salad (see The Salad, page 372). "For me," she noted, "caraway seed added to split-pea soup makes the difference between mediocrity and sheer delight." She was right, too. Here's my recipe for this simple, straightforward, wonderful home soup.

2 cups dried split peas
7 cups any well-flavored vegetable or
  chicken stock or water
1 bay leaf
2 to 3 teaspoons caraway seeds
1 jalapeño pepper, seeded for a less hot
  soup, and diced
1 large onion, chopped
2 ribs celery, diced
2 carrots, scrubbed or peeled and sliced
  2 or 3 small potatoes, scrubbed and diced
2 to 3 cloves garlic, peeled and put
  through a garlic press or finely chopped
2 teaspoons Pickapeppa or Worcestershire
  sauce
Freshly ground black pepper to taste
Salt to taste

► In a large heavy soup pot, combine the split peas, stock or water, bay leaf, caraway seeds, and jalapeño. Bring to a boil, then turn down the heat to low, and let simmer, covered, 30 minutes. Add the remaining ingredients except the salt and continue to simmer until the peas and vegetables are tender, about 30 minutes more. Season with salt and serve hot.

Serves 4 to 6 as an entrée

Déjà Food: Measure the leftover pea soup (or Simple Pleasures Bean Soup variation, page 191) and place it in a food processor. Add an equal amount of V8 juice, 1 tablespoon evaporated skim milk or heavy whipping cream per cup of soup, a pinch of curry powder, and another of sugar. Purée, and heat through. You can add a bit of chicken stock, too, if you have it, and want the soup a little thinner. This is *potage mongole—* quite elegant.

Split-Pea and Herbed Greens Soup

his is another homey split-pea delight, but with some Greek flavor-notes. It is both healthful and easily made.

Pam cooking spray
1 cup dried split peas
7 cups any well-flavored vegetable or chicken stock
2 tablespoons long-grain white rice
1 bay leaf
3 small zucchini, quartered lengthwise and sliced
2 tablespoons olive oil
1 large onion, chopped
2 ribs celery with leaves, diced
2 carrots, scrubbed or peeled and sliced
1 pound assorted fresh greens, such as chard, turnip greens, spinach, collard greens, and kale, rinsed very well and ribboned
2 cloves garlic, peeled and put through a garlic press or finely chopped
¼ cup chopped fresh basil leaves or pinch of dried
Pinch of dried oregano
¼ cup chopped fresh Italian (flat-leaf) parsley
Salt and freshly ground black pepper to taste
Juice of 1 lemon
Paper-thin lemon slices, for garnish
Finely minced fresh parsley, for garnish

1. Spray a large soup pot with the Pam, and in it combine the split peas, 4 cups of the stock, the rice, and the bay leaf. Bring to a boil, then turn down the heat to low, and let simmer, covered, until the peas are done, about 45 minutes to 1 hour. Add the remaining stock and the zucchini and continue to simmer until the zucchini are not quite tender, about 10 minutes.

2. Meanwhile, in a 10-inch skillet, heat the oil over medium heat. Add the onion and sauté until softened, about 3 minutes. Add the celery and carrots; sauté another 2 or 3 minutes. Add the greens, pop the cover on, and lower the heat slightly. Steam the greens until wilted, about 4 minutes. Stir in the garlic, steam 3 seconds more, and remove the pot from the heat. Transfer the greens mixture to a food processor with the herbs and a scoop of the split pea soup. Buzz smooth.

3. Return the purée to the soup in the pot and season with the salt and pepper. Heat through, then stir in the lemon juice just before serving. Ladle the hot soup into bowls and garnish with the lemon slices and minced parsley.

Serves 4 to 6 as an entrée

Potage de Guisantes Barcelona
Spanish-Style Split Pea Soup

 his recipe is from our 1989 staff holiday party, which was Spanish. We made enough for our party guests and the restaurant as well.

It was extremely popular: two cooks, four inn guests, and most of the party attendees requested the recipe. *Muy bueno.* Its starting point was a recipe in the *International Encyclopedia of Cooking* by Myra Waldo to which my soup remains pretty faithful, but it was influenced by techniques described by Colman Andrews in his *Catalan Cuisine* as well as by my personal taste.

Pam cooking spray
2 cups dried split peas
2 quarts any well-flavored vegetable stock
1 large onion, sliced
2 carrots, scrubbed or peeled and sliced
5 cloves garlic, peeled
2 bay leaves
1 box (10 ounces) frozen chopped spinach, thawed
Salt to taste
¼ cup olive oil
3 onions, chopped
6 fresh tomatoes, chopped
2 tablespoons chopped fresh basil leaves or 2 teaspoons dried
2 tablespoons minced fresh parsley
Freshly ground black pepper to taste
Additional minced fresh parsley, for garnish

1. Spray a large soup pot with Pam, and in it combine the split peas, stock, sliced onion, carrots, 2 cloves of the garlic, and the bay leaves. Bring to a boil, then turn down the heat to low, and simmer, partially covered, 1 hour. Add the spinach and season with the salt (at least 1 teaspoon). Continue to simmer another 30 minutes. Let cool slightly and remove the bay leaves, then purée the soup in a food processor.

INNECDOTE

 *In the first* Dairy Hollow House Cookbook *I mentioned that we had never had a bounced check or an item stolen. Some readers have asked me if that is still the case. By now, we have had a bounced check: one. Nothing stolen—although once we did get a towel back in the mail with a note saying "R. and I seem to have left with this. We were reading the cookbook on the way home, found this when we unpacked, and didn't want to be your first thieves."*

2. Meanwhile in a 10-inch skillet heat the oil over medium heat. Add the chopped onions and sauté until they start to soften, 3 minutes. Turn down the heat to medium-low and continue to sauté until the onions are wilted, another 6 to 8 minutes. Turn down the heat further to very low and cook, stirring often, until the onions are meltingly soft and caramelized, about 10 minutes more. (Watch so that they don't burn.)

3. Add the tomatoes to the onions, increase the heat to medium-low, and cook down until very thick, reducing the heat as the liquid evaporates. Remove from the heat. Put the remaining 3 cloves garlic through a garlic press and add to the tomato mixture. Stir in the fresh herbs and plenty of freshly ground pepper.

4. Stir the tomato-onion mixture (called *sofregit* and a seasoning staple of Spanish cuisine) into the pea purée, and heat through. Serve at once, garnished with additional parsley, or let stand overnight and reheat the next day.

Serves 6 to 8 as an entrée

Gumbo Zeb

HISTORY IN A BOWL
AND MORE

umbo is more than soup. It is legendary, as full of history as it is ingredients, and capable of infinite variation. Fragrant, spicy but subtle, with elusive colorations and undertones, gumbo is warming in winter, yet even when steaming hot, refreshing in summer. It takes happily to what is freshest and best, yet accepts with good grace the addition, if need be, of frozen items. It can be the best hearty vegetarian fare known to man or woman; it can also feature anything that swims, walks, flies, jumps, or crawls. My particular version (she says immodestly) was once dubbed gratefully by a reviewer "killer gumbo."

Now, something this good doesn't come easily. You might groan when you first read the recipe, especially if you've never had a good gumbo in a restaurant that really understands gumbo-making, and so have no earthly idea why a person would want to go to this much trouble for a soup. Almost certainly you'll have to read the recipe more than once. There are lots of steps, and they are time consuming, and fairly labor-intensive. Besides being exacting, Gumbo Zeb is rich with oil and butter. It is, however, worth every minute, and every calorie. Once you've tasted it, well, gumbo will make you a believer. It's a soup about which people become evangelical.

GUMBO 101

Gumbo could have been concocted only in this peculiar soup kettle, the American melting pot; and only in one part of that melting pot, Louisiana, Ar-

kansas's due South neighbor; and only at one time in that place, 1790–1800. That's when and where five distinct cultures met, merged, and melded, creating Creole cuisine.

This distinctive cooking style began with the Choctaw Indians and their knowledge of herbs and spices. One herb in common usage was sassafras. The young, tender, mitten-shaped leaves of this tree (which grows all over the Ozarks, where its root is commonly used to make tea) were dried and ground to a powder, as a seasoning. The powdered leaves added a pleasant astringency, and were also a mild diaphoretic, that is, they made you sweat more freely, a salutary effect in hot climates as sweating cools the body. (Witness the hot cuisines of Mexico, Thailand, and India, to name a few).

When French settlers arrived on the scene in the early eighteenth century, they were introduced to sassafras and many other herbs by the Choctaw. The French called the herb "filé," pronounced *fee-lay,* from *filer,* to make threads. "Anyone who has misused this seasoning knows very well how appropriately it was named," remarks Leon Soniat in his book *La Bouche Creole.* "Filé has to be added at the very end of the cooking process—not boiled—because it gets thready or gummy. When [a dish] has had filé added to it [and is reheated], the results are usually disastrous."

French culture was the dominant influence in what became Creole cooking. The French brought a centuries-long tradition of cuisine in which economy married flavor, an attitude that turned out elegant, carefully prepared food, and wasted absolutely nothing. French sauces, the roux (a flour-shortening mixture used to thicken sauces), and techniques like sautéing also added much to what would become Creole cuisine.

For the French as for the Choctaws, the economy of Louisiana was primarily agricultural. Given French upper-class tradition, it was probably inevitable that the owners of large landholdings outside New Orleans would leave their plantations to become absentee landlords, living off the staggering profits. These were used, in part, to create an elegant life in the new city, which was built in the finest European style. One reason the profits were so great was that enormous bloodstain on America's history, slavery.

If our starting point for gumbo had been etymological rather than chronological, we would have begun with the slaves. They were brought primarily from Central Africa to work the plantations, and they carried okra seeds with them. The Bantu-Congolese word for okra is *kingumbo,* later bastardized to *gumbo* (though many gumbo soups do not contain okra). Okra, of course, is a vegetable to which few Southerners require introduction. These tender, succulent pods are mucillagenous (non-

okra lovers say slimy) when cooked in liquid. Along with okra seed, the slaves brought two African cooking techniques: long, slow cooking in heavy iron pots, and the combining of herbs and vegetables with a stock base, a method at that time almost never used in France. Outnumbering whites by some five to one outside the city of New Orleans, the Africans were the third greatest formative influence on Creole cooking.

In 1762, France ceded New Orleans and the French Caribbean islands to Spain, and so the Spaniards arrived in Louisiana. They intermarried with the Louisiana French, and the resultant ethnically-mixed children were called "Creole" (from the Spanish verb *crear,* to create, to be born). So strictly interpreted was the definition of Creole (white-skinned persons born in the New World, whose ancestors came from Spain, France, and/or Portugal) that when the French who had settled in Canada were ousted by the English in 1755 and came to live in Louisiana, neither they nor their children were permitted to use the designation "Creole." Instead, looked down on by "real" Creoles, they were called "Acadians," after the region from which they began their exodus; in the vernacular, they were "Cajuns."

The Spanish brought a fourth influence to this cuisine: a love of

highly seasoned foods, a penchant for combining meat and poultry in the same dish, and the use of rice in or with these spicy, savory concoctions.

But the fifth and final wave that created Creole cuisine did not break on New Orleans until thirty years or so after the Spaniards arrived. This fifth group was also of mixed Spanish-French descent, but with a difference. They were refugee Creoles, from the Caribbean; about eight thousand of them, fleeing from the violent slave revolts on the islands of Haiti and Martinique. They flooded New Orleans between 1790 and 1800. (This was about thirteen years prior to the Louisiana Purchase, of which Arkansas was also a part.)

The cuisine of the island Creoles was essentially the same as that of the Louisiana Creoles, but with one small, red-hot difference: the cayenne pepper. Cayenne, indigenous to the islands, came to Louisiana with the refugees. And this was the final foundation stone of what we know today as Creole cooking, hence, to the quintessential Creole dish, gumbo. Native American and African ingredients, cooked with French technique, Spanish flair, and Caribbean heat—that is Creole cuisine, and that, most emphatically, is gumbo.

GUMBO COMES TO THE INN (AND NOTES OF A COOKBOOK READER)

Cut now from New Orleans two centuries ago to the Ozarks, on a winter's day in 1986. Things slow down around Eureka Springs in January; the tourist season is over, and professional and home cooks start experimenting. Cold weather always brings soup to the minds of cooks.

A bit restive, I meandered into an area I hadn't much explored as a cook, that of the then-trendy Cajun cuisine. I had an idea of what I thought gumbo was—a spicy soup with tomatoes, rice, okra, and some form of chicken or seafood. This is indeed what the good old *Joy of Cooking* (wrongly, it turns out) calls gumbo. I made a couple of tasty soups along this line; tasty, but not ambrosial, and not what I had in mind and memory from forays to New Orleans. I hit the books.

Like many people who read cookbooks, I do so not only for the recipes and imaginings of new combinations of flavors, but for the unfailing sense of connection that really understanding a dish brings. Food gets at the universal questions through the small, particular, and personal. Ideally a recipe, if written wisely, tells its reader not only how to fix a dish, but about nature, culture, attitude. It shows how people care for themselves and one another through the most basic and yet often most elevated and ritualized of human occupations, feeding. It explains succinctly the forces of history, geography, and environment. Food is about life itself.

The first six recipes in Leon Soniat's warm, informal *La Bouche Creole* are for various gumbos. From Soniat I learned the details of the all-important roux, and that with a "nut-brown" roux (page 242), the holy triumvirate of green peppers, celery, and onion, and a well-seasoned cast-iron pot, "you could branch out into a thousand different directions and still wind up with a Creole masterpiece."

Soniat delineates three types of gumbo: the third, which he describes as the king of gumbos, was called Gumbo Z'Herbes, "gumbo of herbs" or "green gumbo." Soniat explains that although Gumbo Z'Herbes was made throughout the year, it was traditional, in Creole-Catholic New Orleans, to serve it on Holy Thursday in commemoration of the Last Supper because it included thirteen greens, one for Jesus and one for each disciple. He recalls going to market with his mother, hearing the vendors cry, "Get your greens, lady, your twelve greens, your fifteen greens, your seven greens," the number changing with what each produce stall had to offer.

I began my experiments with a vegetarian version of Soniat's Gumbo Z'Herbes, omitting the ham and beef by preference and the oysters by necessity (not many fresh-shucked oysters up here in the Ozarks, though good greens straight from the garden there are in abundance). The seasonings—there were nine, in addition to eight vegetables—were excellent to my taste, but the gumbo was rouxless and tomato-less, and not quite what I'd had in mind. I'd decided that *my* gumbo should have Choctaw filé; French panache and a brown roux; Spanish spiciness and verve; African slow-simmered soup-stewiness; and island cayenne. Along with that I would add as many authentic seasonings and greens as I could pack in. I could almost taste it in my mind. If I could make a gumbo that had this meatless, spicy, wonderful, very substantial base, I thought I might have the best of all gumbo worlds.

I went from *La Bouche Creole* to a very American source of recipes: Junior League cookbooks. I started reading the Southern ones even more compulsively than usual in my search for the ultimate gumbo. The pick of the lot proved to be *Cotton Country Collection,* from the Junior League of Monroe, Louisiana. It had eight gumbos—some with tomatoes, with roux, with turkey or chicken carcasses, with okra and/or filé. One recipe included a can of shoe-peg corn, another of butter beans and a package of noodles (even I, new to gumbo though I was, thought, "Oh, come on!"). I learned more about roux-making, and found another Gumbo Z'Herbes, titled Green Gumbo. Its directions began, "First, 'you wash your hands'. This is a spin-off of the famous Gumbo Zeb of south Louisiana." Gumbo Zeb—I liked the name a lot. Nor can I deny a fondness for the seventeen-ingredient seafood gumbo that began with the proviso, "First of all, Gumbo should be a two-day affair. Peel your shrimp... chop your vegetables... cover and put in the refrigerator. The next day, making the gumbo will be a happy thing." This same recipe concludes with a cheery "Good luck!"

HOW A YANKEE LEARNED TO MAKE A WICKED GUMBO THAT WAS TRULY HER OWN

I wound up, over a period of a few months, taking what I liked best out of, in all, twenty-one different gumbo recipes, and adding a few zips and zaps of my own. I call my gumbo Gumbo Zeb, though it is not the traditional soup by that name. But it is bursting with greens and flavors, and I like the story the name tells: that the French Gumbo des Herbes evolved into the Creole Gumbo Z'Herbes and from there to Gumbo Zeb. It also sounded like it could have been a recipe from someone's uncle Zebulon. Good old Uncle Zeb, famed for his gumbo.

Between the time I developed this patchwork quilt of a recipe and the present, we opened the Restaurant at Dairy Hollow. Of course, we'd been feeding inn guests for years, and their word-of-mouth on our gumbo had been great.

Too, I'd gotten intrigued enough by gumbo lore and mythology to have written a story on it for our state's magazine, *Arkansas Times*. The story included the recipe I'm about to give you. And, in the credit-where-credit-is-due department, editor/writer Mike Trimble came up with the single best line in the *Arkansas Times* piece, which I have helped myself to in this cookbook: "Youx, Toux, Can Doux a Roux." And then Trimble did himself one better. The following letter to the editor was published in the magazine a few months later, in response to my story and recipe.

"Being from Louisiana and having eaten gumbo all over the state and in fine restaurants, I decided to make this recipe. It is by far the best we have ever eaten. So from a Louisianan who can doux a roux, thanks a million for the new recipe."

Trimble titled the letter in the column, "Houxray."

Between article and rep, we were getting requests for gumbo from the moment we started taking reservations, before the restaurant doors were even open. Although we don't keep it on the menu all the time, a lot of our guests wish we did, and have been known to sulk when we don't. Though we can usually beguile them with something else, in a way, I don't blame them: Although we are known for our soups, our Gumbo Zeb is one of the very best. To say it's good is understatement, but to say how good it is, is bragging.

Over time, I began picturing Uncle Zeb clearly. He had become, in my mind,

my great-great-grandfather's Confederate brother, Zeb the Reb, black sheep of my Yankee family.

Whenever I make Gumbo Zeb, the ghost of Uncle Zeb is, I imagine, proud of me.

PRELIMINARY UNDERSTANDING OF GUMBO-MAKING

Gumbo-making, Dairy Hollow House-style, is a matter of first making a rather large batch of what we call Gumbo Base. This is a highly seasoned, very thick, vegetarian concentrate, which serves as the stepping-off point for an infinite variety of gumbos.

The base consists of four separate components which are eventually combined. The first is browned roux (see sidebar on Roux, page 242). The second is a vegetable sauté, a sort of mirepoix, really. The third is a very, very highly seasoned paste of tomatoes, herbs, spices, buzzed in the food processor. And the fourth is greens, cooked in stock and tomato juice, in an enormous soup pot. It is to this pot that you will, when directed in the recipe, add the other three components. And what you have in the pot, after all the components have been added, is nothing more and nothing less that that magic Gumbo Base.

This base will be diluted later with stock of one kind or another, and finished with additions compatible with that stock. But the dilution and finishing is fairly simple; it's making the base that's the big deal.

I suggest reading the recipe over carefully, maybe a couple of times, especially the part about the roux. Then go shopping, wash and prep the vegetables, and make the roux. Finish putting the Gumbo Zeb Base together the next day so the gumbo-making can be, as the *Cotton Country* contributor noted, "a happy thing." Once you have the base on hand, turning it into completed gumbo can be done any time. The base freezes very well, so a morning of gumbo-making can keep you supplied for weeks or even months (if you choose to save the soup for special occasions).

My Uncle Zeb says to tell y'all *bonne chance* and *bon appétit.*

Gumbo Zeb Base

Any recipe is most expeditiously made if all the ingredients are laid out before one begins the actual preparing. In gumbo making, assembling your readied ingredients beforehand is a *must*. Measure out your spices, wash and chop your vegetables and greens, lay out the ingredients for each mixture on its own tray before you begin any actual recipe directions. There'll be a lot going on, you'll have your hands full; you cannot possibly assemble the ingredients as you go. If in the ingredients list I miss any greens you have frozen from last year's garden, or if you chance to find some green exotics at the local supermarket, by all means add them. Also, if you can find only fresh cabbage, go ahead and drop in the boiling stock mixture 10-ounce boxes of frozen greens, as many of the varieties mentioned as you can find.

ROUX:
1 cup mild vegetable oil, such as corn, peanut, or soy
1 cup unbleached all-purpose flour

VEGETABLE SAUTÉ:
8 tablespoons (1 stick) butter
2 large onions, chopped
2 green bell peppers, stemmed, seeded, and chopped
1 bunch celery with leaves, chopped
1 large bunch (8 to 10 large) scallions, chopped

SEASONING PUREE:
8 cloves garlic, peeled
1/4 cup Pickapeppa or Worcestershire sauce
1/4 cup tomato paste
1 tablespoon Tabasco sauce
2 teaspoons dried basil
2 teaspoons dried oregano
2 teaspoons dried thyme
1 teaspoon paprika
1/4 to 1/2 teaspoon cayenne pepper
1/4 to 1/2 teaspoon ground allspice
1/4 to 1/2 teaspoon ground cloves
6 to 8 good grinds of fresh black peppercorns
1 can (16 ounces) whole tomatoes, drained, coarsely chopped, the juice and tomatoes reserved separately
1 bunch fresh Italian (flat-leaf) parsley, leaves and stems, rinsed and coarsely chopped

STOCK AND GREENS:
Pam cooking spray
6 cups any well-flavored chicken or vegetable stock, or bottled clam juice
2 cups tomato juice or V8 vegetable juice
1 teaspoon salt
4 bay leaves
6 bunches greens, ideally 1 bunch each mustard greens, spinach, turnip greens, beet tops, collard greens, arugula, and watercress, very well washed and finely ribboned (page 133; also see Note below)

1 1/2 cups tomato or V8 vegetable juice

1. Make the roux with the oil and flour (see Youx, Toux, Can Doux a Roux, page 242). While the roux cooks, proceed with the other steps, but be *sure* to keep an eye on it, stirring very frequently. (I'm going to keep reminding you to stir; don't be aggravated at me for nagging, it's just easy to forget to stir it, and if it burns even a little it's ruined and you have to start again. Big drag.)

2. Prepare the vegetable sauté: In a heavy cast-iron skillet, melt the butter over medium heat. Add the onions, and sauté until softened, 5 to 6 minutes. Add the bell peppers and celery; lower the heat slightly and continue sautéing another 10 minutes. (Don't forget that roux—keep stirring it while the vegetables sauté.) Add the scallions, and sauté until limp, about 5 minutes more.

3. Meanwhile, between the sautéing and the roux-stirring, you will have time to prepare the seasoning purée (trust me, you will). Place all the ingredients for the seasoning purée except the tomatoes and parsley in a food processor. (Pause to stir the roux and the vegetable sauté.) Buzz the purée ingredients until the garlic is chopped fine.

4. Check the roux again (has it started to brown?), then add the tomatoes and fresh parsley to the food processor. Chop coarsely.

5. Pause to take note of where you are, and to go stir the roux and vegetable sauté. (By now you have three mixtures: the roux, the sautéed vegetables, and the spicy, chunky paste in the food processor.) So far, so good. When the vegetables have softened, remove from the heat and set them aside. Keep working on the roux until it has reached a nice toasty brown. It may be ready now, or it may take a little longer.

6. Now prepare the stock and greens into which the other three mixtures will eventually go. Spray a large soup pot with Pam. In it, bring to a boil the stock and tomato or V8 juice. Add the salt and bay leaves. Drop in the fresh greens. Bring back to a boil, then turn down the heat to medium-low and simmer, covered, about 30 minutes.

7. Stir the roux. By now, it should be properly browned, but if it isn't, continue to cook it, stirring. When the roux has browned, remove it from the heat and let it cool for a few minutes. Drain off any excess oil that has separated out, but be sure to leave every bit of the browned flour. Vigorously whisk in the 1½ cups tomato or V8 juice. It will be smooth and thick, a pale orange paste.

8. When the greens have finished their 30-minute simmer, remove them from the heat. Add to the stock pot the roux mixture, the vegetable sauté, and the seasoning purée. Give a taste and adjust the seasoning, set the pot back on the stove, and let simmer over the lowest possible heat, covered, another 15 minutes. Stir often.

9. Remove from the heat and let cool to room temperature. That's it—you've got your concentrated Gumbo Base, enough when made into soup to feed 10 to 15 hearty eaters. It freezes well, so for smaller batches of Gumbo Zeb, use part now, and freeze the rest in small portions.

Makes 5 to 6 quarts

Note: Bunch size, like the greens used, may vary widely and unproblematically. Supermarket bunches typically weigh about 1 pound, but if you have a smidgen of one green and a lot of another, don't worry; it will balance out by the end. Too, smaller-leaved greens (such as arugula and watercress) come in smaller bunches than giant-leaved greens (collard, turnips). Just use your discrimination.

COMPLETING THE GUMBO ZEB BASE

Now we get to what you went through all that for—the steaming hot, completed Gumbo Zeb, deliciously finished with additional stock and substance, and varied as you please. The following recipes all make 4 to 6 entrée servings, leaving you plenty of base to freeze for another day and another variation.

The basic rule is that the base is diluted with any savory liquid or stock to taste. Equal parts base and stock make a delicious soup, but if you like a particularly fragrant, spicy gumbo, you might use 60 percent base to 40 percent savory liquid.

Please note that gumbo is improvisational, so feel free to experiment, combining freely the ingredients listed in any of these variations. For instance, although I've included ham in only one version, and okra in only one, both of these are commonly added to gumbos of every other kind, seafood, chicken, turkey, duck, and so on.

LAGNIAPPE

❧ *Lagniappe means a little something extra, something good and unexpected. Here are some non-soup uses for the Gumbo Zeb Base:*

❖ *Use as an omelet filling; the resulting Omelette Creole is delicious, a very popular dish at brunch.*

❖ *Dilute the base slightly (3 parts base to 1 part stock), and serve hot over poached eggs resting on a bed of rice. Too good, as my collaborator Jan Brown used to say.* ❧

Chicken Gumbo Zeb

6 cups Gumbo Zeb Base (page 237)
4 to 6 cups any well-flavored chicken stock
3 to 4 cups coarsely diced cooked chicken
1 cup cooked white rice
Filé powder
Finely chopped fresh parsley, for garnish

1. In a large soup pot, combine the base and stock. Bring to a boil, turn down the heat to medium-low, and let simmer gently, stirring occasionally, for 30 minutes.

2. Stir in the chicken pieces and let simmer until the chicken is heated through.

3. In each serving bowl, place a mound of rice, and ladle the hot gumbo over it. Sprinkle about ¼ teaspoon filé powder on each portion, and garnish with the parsley. Pass additional filé at table.

Serves 4 to 6 as an entrée

VARIATION:

Turkey Gumbo Zeb, Duck Gumbo Zeb, and Goose Gumbo Zeb are all memorable, and a great change of pace from a holiday bird. Simply pick the meat from the bones and carcass of leftover fowl. Make a stock from the carcass (page 22) and proceed as above, adding the reserved poultry meat in place of the chicken.

Andouille Gumbo Zeb

1 to 1½ pounds andouille or other smoked sausage, sliced
6 cups Gumbo Zeb Base (page 237)
4 to 6 cups any well-flavored chicken stock
1 cup cooked white rice
Filé powder
Finely chopped fresh parsley, for garnish

1. In a skillet, fry the andouille or other sausage over medium heat until slightly browned, 4 or 5 minutes. Cook out as much fat from the sausage as possible, and discard.

2. In a large soup pot, combine the base, stock, and andouille. Bring to a boil, turn down the heat to medium-low, and let simmer gently, stirring occasionally, for 30 minutes.

3. In each serving bowl, place a mound of rice, and ladle the hot gumbo over it. Sprinkle about ¼ teaspoon filé powder over each portion, and garnish with the parsley. Pass additional filé at table.

Serves 4 to 6 as an entrée

Chicken and Andouille Gumbo

¾ to 1 pound andouille or other smoked sausage, sliced
6 cups Gumbo Zeb Base (page 237)
4 to 6 cups any well-flavored chicken stock
1 to 2 cups coarsely diced cooked chicken
1 cup cooked white rice
Filé powder
Finely chopped fresh parsley, for garnish

1. In a skillet, fry the andouille or other sausage over medium heat until slightly browned, 4 to 5 minutes. Cook out as much fat from the sausage as possible, and discard.

2. In a large soup pot, combine the base, stock, and andouille. Bring to a boil, turn down the heat to medium-low, and let simmer gently, stirring occasionally, for 30 minutes.

3. Stir in the chicken pieces and let simmer until the chicken is heated through.

4. In each serving bowl, place a mound of rice, and ladle the hot gumbo over it. Sprinkle about ¼ teaspoon filé powder on each portion, and garnish with the parsley. Pass additional filé at table.

Serves 4 to 6 as an entrée

YOUX, TOUX, CAN DOUX A ROUX

❦*What turns good soup into a glorious gumbo? Simple: roux. There's nothing much to roux (pronounced like the last syllable of "kangaroo") on the face of it—mere flour and oil, cooked and stirred together until brown. Roux serves to thicken the gumbo slightly (less so than you would think, since the long cooking decreases the flour's thickening power) and, more importantly, flavors it.*

It's hard to believe, until you've tried it yourself, just how big a difference roux makes to the flavor. What could be plainer than flour and oil? But the browned roux, when part of an already wonderful soup, creates a flavor that is extraordinarily good: aromatic, nutty, hearty, distinctive. It's roux, not okra or filé powder, that makes gumbo gumbo.

1. Start with a well-seasoned heavy cast-iron pot or skillet. Into the skillet, pour 1 part oil—not olive oil, but any mild oil such as peanut or corn. Turn the heat to medium and using

a wire whisk immediately beat in 1 (equivalent) part unbleached all-purpose flour. (In the recipe for Gumbo Zeb Base, the "part" is a cup, but it can easily be scaled up or down, as long as quantities of oil and flour remain equal.)

Note the color—a pale parchment-cream with a barely yellow tinge. Keep stirring. Many recipes direct you to stir constantly, but I think "very frequently" is more apt. You can, for instance, leave the roux while you pull ingredients out of the fridge. Come back to the stove and whisk the roux. Peel an onion; whisk the roux. Chop the onion; whisk the roux. You get the idea. But you do, definitely, need to be in the kitchen as the roux cooks, keeping a close eye on it the entire time, and stirring often.

2. The roux will gradually begin to color and to scent the room. Its aroma is peculiar; not bad but not tantalizing; strangely unfoodlike. As it colors, keep whisking. It will become a light brown first, then the brown of a camel's hair coat, then peanut-butter colored, then the brown of a caramel, then the brown of a chocolate caramel. My own preferred roux coloration is deep brown, just a shade or so past caramel, but not quite the chocolate caramel stage. Preparing your roux ought to take at least 45 minutes; 1¼ hours is preferable. It cannot be hurried.

3. When the roux starts to become fairly brown, the oil will separate out partially from

the flour. Don't take a roux off the fire before this point. After this point, it's a matter of taste. The darker the roux, the stronger the nutty, rich flavor—there's no way to know how brown to make a roux so it will be just right to your taste until you've made a few gumbos. If you go off to answer the phone, and come back to a roux with little black specks, it is ruined and you will have to start over. Period.

A roux can be made ahead of time and refrigerated. The advantage to this (besides convenience) is that you can then easily pour off all the excess oil that has separated out. (You can drain off some, though, after the roux has cooled for about 15 minutes.) I have never kept a browned roux longer than two or three days before using it, but since there's nothing in it that would spoil, I imagine it would keep well for a couple of weeks. But why would you want to wait that long for gumbo?

If you doux the roux ahead of time, reheat it gently before using. 🌿

Crab Gumbo Zeb

e don't get seafood like fresh crab up here in the Ozarks, but for those of you who have access to it, this is a real treat. It's messy to eat, since some of the crab meat is served in the shell.

6 to 8 hardshell crabs
4 to 6 cups any well-flavored chicken or
   fish stock
6 cups Gumbo Zeb Base (page 237)
1 cup cooked white rice
Filé powder
Finely chopped fresh parsley,
   for garnish

1. In a large pot, bring the stock to a boil. Drop in the crabs and boil for about 20 minutes. Remove the crabs and reserve both crabs and stock.

2. In a large soup pot, combine the base and the stock. Bring to a boil, turn down the heat to medium-low, and let simmer gently, stirring occasionally, for 30 minutes.

3. When the crab is cool enough to handle, remove the shells and clean the crab bodies (page 245). Crack the crab claws. Add the crab meat and cracked claws to the gumbo and let simmer another 10 minutes.

4. In each serving bowl, place a mound of rice, and ladle the hot gumbo over it. Sprinkle about ¼ teaspoon filé powder on each portion, and garnish with the parsley. Pass additional filé at table.

Serves 4 to 6 as an entrée

Seafood Gumbo

The only time we really envy people who live anywhere else in America is when we read a recipe like this. Crabs, shrimp, oysters—bounty from the sea—makes an already great gumbo ascend to a culinary Olympus. This recipe is ideal party fare, but warn everyone about the crab claws; they're usually highly visible, but you can never tell what people'll notice.

4 to 6 cups any well-flavored chicken or
  fish stock
4 to 6 hardshell crabs
1 to 1½ pounds raw shrimp in the shell,
  peeled (save heads—if you can get
  them—and shells) and deveined
6 cups Gumbo Zeb Base (page 237)
24 oysters, shucked but liquid reserved
1 cup cooked white rice
Filé powder
Finely chopped fresh parsley, for garnish

1. In a large pot, bring the stock to a boil. Drop in the crabs, and shrimp shells and heads, and boil for about 20 minutes. Remove the crabs from the stock, and reserve both crabs and stock. Strain the stock, discarding the shrimp heads and shells.
2. In a large soup pot, combine the base and stock. Bring to a boil, turn down the heat to medium-low, and let simmer gently, stirring occasionally, for 10 minutes.
3. Add the shrimp to the gumbo, bring to a boil, then lower the heat and let simmer. Continue simmering, stirring occasionally, for 5 minutes.
4. When the crab is cool enough to

handle, remove the shells and clean the crab bodies (page 245). Crack the crab claws. Add the crab meat and cracked claws to the gumbo and let simmer another 10 minutes.
5. Add the oysters and their liquid, and let simmer until the oysters' edges just begin to curl, about 5 minutes. Remove the gumbo from the heat.
6. In each serving bowl, place a mound of rice, and ladle the hot gumbo over it. Sprinkle about ¼ teaspoon filé powder on each portion, and garnish with the parsley. Pass additional filé at table.

Serves 6 to 8 as an entrée

Gumbo Zeb with Ham and Poached Trout

When this soup appears on our menu, whatever other soups we offer come in a distant second place. It's truly wonderful—a very inland Ozarks gumbo, full of flavor.

4 to 6 cups any well-flavored chicken or
  fish stock or leftover court bouillon (page
  25)
2 or 3 whole trout, 10 ounces each,
  preferably bone in, cleaned
6 cups Gumbo Zeb Base (page 237)
2 cups diced smoked ham
1 cup cooked white rice
Filé powder
Finely chopped fresh parsley, for garnish

CRAB CLEANING

There's something very Tom Jones *about cleaning a cooked crab. Here's how.*

1. Hold the crab top-side up. Starting at the front, pull the shell up and away from the body. Scrape out any of the yellow-green viscera that may be in the corners of the shell. This is called "crab butter" thanks to its buttery taste, and can be added with the crab meat proper to any soup calling for crab. You can discard the top shell unless you plan to use it as a serving dish for deviled crab or the like.

2. Turn the crab over, and lift both the narrow triangular underside shell parts and the soft spines below it.

3. Turn the crab right side up again, and remove the white spongy tissue (gills that because of their shape are somewhat creepily called "dead-man's fingers"). Also remove and discard the intestine (which is firm and white). You'll see some more crab butter; scrape it out and use it as described above.

4. Grasp the crab legs and claws close to the body firmly and twist them off. Crack the shells using a nutcracker, and pick out the meat using a small fork or a nut-pick.

5. Hold the crab body and snap it in half; for some varieties of crab, you may need to use more force, chopping it in half with a cleaver or knife. The flesh of the body is segmented by thin, hard, sharp shells, not unlike a grapefruit is segmented by membrane. Pick the meat out from between these small bits of shell very carefully; it is disconcerting to bite into one.

---

1. In your largest skillet, sauté pan, fish poacher, or whatever will accommodate the trout, heat the stock. When the stock comes to the boil, put in the trout and immediately turn down the heat so the liquid simmers. Cover the vessel, and let the trout poach until done—the fish will be firm, and their eyes white—about 6 to 8 minutes. Gently lift the trout from the poaching liquid and let cool to room temperature. Reserve the stock.

2. In a large soup pot, combine the base and fish-enriched stock. Add the smoked ham. Bring to a boil, turn down the heat to medium-low, and let simmer gently, stirring occasionally, for 30 minutes.

3. When the trout is cool enough to handle, remove all the skin (it will peel right off). Cut off the heads, reach into the trout cavity, and pull out the backbones (they will come right out, ribs attached, all in one piece). Gently pull the trout flesh apart into good-sized pieces, keeping an eye out for the few "floating ribs," loose bones here and there in the fish. Set the trout meat aside.

4. Just before serving, add the cooked trout pieces to the gumbo, and heat through.

Remove from the heat as soon as the trout is hot (see Note).

5. In each serving bowl, place a mound of rice, and ladle the hot gumbo over it. Sprinkle about ¼ teaspoon filé powder on each portion, and garnish with the parsley. Pass additional filé at table.

Serves 4 to 6 as an entrée

Note: If you're not sure if everyone will be ready to eat at the same time, don't put the cooked trout in the gumbo. Instead, put some trout meat in each serving bowl on top of the rice, then ladle on the soup.

Okra Gumbo Zeb

his is a simply delicious vegetarian gumbo. Just amazingly good and rich. It is somehow very right on a hot summer's night, packed as it is with the bounty of the garden.

2 tablespoons mild vegetable oil, such as
    corn or peanut
1 tablespoon butter
2 pounds fresh okra, rinsed, stemmed, and
    sliced into ⅛-inch rounds
6 cups Gumbo Zeb Base (page 237)
4 to 6 cups Browned Vegetable Stock (page
    32) or any well-flavored stock
1 cup cooked white rice
Filé powder
Finely chopped fresh parsley, for garnish

1. In a large skillet (preferably one made of something other than iron, which discolors okra) combine the oil and butter over medium heat. When hot, add the okra, and stir-fry until every bit of stringy mucilaginousness is gone, 6 to 8 minutes.

2. In a large soup pot, combine the sautéed okra, base, and stock. Bring to a boil, then turn down the heat to medium low, and let simmer gently, stirring occasionally, for 30 minutes.

3. In each serving bowl, place a mound of rice, and ladle the hot gumbo over it. Sprinkle about ¼ teaspoon filé powder on each portion, and garnish with the parsley. Pass additional filé at table.

Serves 4 to 6 as an entrée

VARIATION:
Gumbo Zeb with Okra and "Soysage":
Soysage is a tasty, spicy vegetarian "sausage" made by many different companies. It is dark brown and firm, sturdy in both flavor and texture. Soysage generally comes in squares, which you slice, not links. You'll find a local brand in the refrigerated case at most natural foods stores. Of course it is free of saturated fats, and low in fat of any kind compared to regular sausage.

Take a 6- to 8-ounce package and slice the soysage into rectangles about ¼ inch thick. In a skillet, brown the slices in a few tablespoons of vegetable oil over medium heat, turning once (3 to 4 minutes per side). When cool enough to handle, dice the browned pieces into bite-size pieces.

Sprinkle several pieces of browned soysage over the rice before ladling on the hot gumbo. I guarantee you, any vegetarians who eat this will, one, fall on the floor with delight and, two, love you forever.

Delectable
Dairy
Soups

FROM DAIRY HOLLOW

airy Hollow takes its name from the numerous dairies that dotted this particular Eureka Springs valley in the days when milk was locally produced and delivered. The last of the original dairies that gave our wooded hollow its name was still in existence when I first came to Eureka Springs in 1972. That was the Rhiel Dairy, run single-handedly by Ethel Rhiel.

I was single and nineteen when I met Mrs. Rhiel. She was a widow in her seventies then, with long hair in a bun, from which a few tendrils escaped; they curled around a still-lovely face—high, fine cheekbones, bright blue eyes. Mrs. Rhiel milked eight Jersey cows by hand twice a day. (Jerseys are buff-colored, smallish cows with great big dark brown eyes and long, long lashes; you often see them in photographs of Switzerland. Their milk has a high percentage of butterfat and is, I think, the best in the world. I know all this because I once had, for a year, a close relationship with a Jersey cow named Jerz. But that is another story.)

If you were lucky, you got on Mrs. Rhiel's milk list. Once a week at a designated time, you'd go up the hill to her house and pick up your milk, where it would be waiting in a refrigerator in the immaculate milk house. The milk, easily a third cream (the top cream so thick you could lift it and spread it with a knife), would be in a glass gallon jar with a piece of waxed paper twisted in under the lid. Since time began, no milk ever tasted so good. If spring, new life, and the yellow of the year's first daffodils were to combine in a single taste, it would be like that milk.

I liked Mrs. Rhiel being up the road from me. Since I lived only a tenth of a mile down, I'd walk up each Thursday, my milk day, to her farm. Throughout the week, I'd see the pick-up trucks and late-model cars bump slowly up and down the road, knowing the people in those cars and trucks were taking home with them something even better than that milk—contact with Mrs. Rhiel. She was warm, determined, and enthusiastic. Her interest in everyone she met was equal to her independence. Like many people who care about others, she was kind, not to earn moral brownie points, but because it was a natural outgrowth of a satisfying life. To this day, whenever I hear that odd old-fashioned phrase "the milk of human kindness," I think of her.

I did not then think of Mrs. Rhiel as what is now called a role model; I just liked her. But in doing something archaic, and doing it well in her own way in the place she loved, she substantiated my decisions about the character I wanted for myself, much as the milk from her Jerseys substantiated my custards, the yogurt and crème fraîche I made from scratch, my cream of celery and potato soups.

Mrs. Rhiel is dead now, and I am in my late 30s, married to a tall, blue-eyed historic preservationist I met at a potluck dinner in Little Rock. Eventually (I'm condensing a lot here) I talked that man into leaving a well-paying job at an architectural firm so that we could have a noncommuter marriage in the town we loved, adding on to, and making a full-time business of, the tiny inn we had started years earlier. And that, in a nutshell, is how Dairy Hollow House came to be. Our logo has always been a cow, and over the years guests have sent us cows—pottery cows, plastic cows, cow bells and cow mugs, cow potholders, cow prints, cow postcards, and cow doorstops; cow jewelry, cow buttons, funky cows and fine arts cows—literal-looking and more imaginative ones. We now have quite a herd, and every room or suite in the inn boasts at least a couple of cows.

This story comes full circle: Ned and I purchased the small farmhouse, the first component of Dairy Hollow House, from Mrs. Rhiel's daughters. It was built by her ancestors, the McIntyre family, over a hundred years ago.

With such impeccable connections, it's natural that we love dairy products. As you may remember from the section Delicious Dabs (page 47), my belief in the odd dollop of crème fraîche or yogurt to enhance a multitude of soups is unlimited, and my restraint, for reasons of calorie and fat gram awareness, is somewhat reluctant. Although I know that these delectable products are high in cholesterol and supposed to be dreadful for the arteries and good health in general, I don't quite believe it—at least

not as simplistically as it is stated in the mass media. And I have to confess—brag is probably more like it—that for the past twelve years my doctor has congratulated me on my exemplary rock-bottom cholesterol count. To what can I attribute this, given my consumption of these products plus eggs plus cheese? Well, I don't eat red meat, don't drink, am overall calorie and fat gram aware (which does somewhat limit my intake of these luscious foods), eat lots and lots of fresh vegetables, and probably have a good gene pool (at least, as far as heart-health goes; given my family's tendency towards eccentricity, I probably ought not just use "good" without qualification). I have a positive attitude, a life I like, and I walk a lot. And I eat an abnormally large amount of garlic, which some people think is incredibly salutary, although I eat it just because I love it.

There are milk-, cream-, or cheese-enriched soups throughout this book, but those in this chapter are the ones in which these ingredients dominate; the ones that come to mind when, in planning a menu, I need something distinctly creamy, milky, or cheese-based to round out a particular meal. Here you'll find various vegetable cream soups, herb cream soups, and so on (not all made with cream as such, some with fat-gram-sparing evaporated skim milk or yogurt), each dimensional enough so that the cream or milk doesn't overwhelm everything else. But there's definitely enough "dairy" in each of the recipes in this chapter so that you wouldn't plan a custard for dessert or a cream-sauced entrée to follow any one of these soups.

As with nut soups and many of the specialty soups throughout these pages, these cream soups tend to be once-in-awhile, special-occasion soups. The daily soups remain for me chicken, bean, and, most especially, vegetable and mixed vegetable soups. But there is nothing like these voluptuous, decorative creams for festive times.

Cream-, milk-, or evaporated-skim-milk-based soups begin this chapter, then there are a few yogurt-based soups, and lastly some favorites enriched with cheese.

CREAM-AND MILK-BASED SOUPS

Betty Rosbottom's Cream of Artichoke Soup

From Betty Rosbottom's wonderful *Cooking School Cookbook*. Ned and I tried Betty's soup at home and found it perfectly, swooningly marvelous. We now serve it at the restaurant on Valentine's Day, when hearts of all types are de rigeur. So what if artichokes aren't Ozarky? Sometimes you've just got to expand your horizons a little.

As Rosbottom notes, "This is one of those dishes that would appear to be far more sophisticated than their simple preparations would imply."

6 tablespoons (¾ stick) butter (see Variation for reduced fat version)
2 cups coarsely chopped leeks, white part only, first split open lengthwise and well washed
2 boxes (10 ounces each) frozen artichoke hearts, thawed and coarsely chopped
5 cups Chicken Stock 1 (page 19) or Golden Vegetable Stock (page 28) or any well-flavored chicken or vegetable broth
⅓ cup julienned leek greens
1 cup heavy (whipping) cream
¼ cup freshly grated Parmesan cheese
Salt and freshly ground white pepper to taste
Finely minced fresh parsley, for garnish

1. In a heavy soup pot, melt the butter over medium heat. Add the chopped leeks and sauté until softened, 3 to 4 minutes. Add

the artichoke hearts and cook another 2 minutes. Stir in the stock and let simmer, uncovered, until the leeks and artichokes are tender, about 25 minutes.

2. Meanwhile, place the leek greens in a fine-mesh sieve and, dipping the sieve into the stock, blanch the leeks until bright green, about 1 minute. Drain and set aside.

3. In a food processor, purée the soup in batches, then press the purée through a large-mesh sieve to remove any fibers.

4. Return the soup to the pot, stir in the cream, and reheat. Stir in the cheese, a bit at a time, over medium-low heat, then season with the salt and pepper. (The soup and leek greens can be made up to this point 1 day in advance. Refrigerate the soup, and the leek greens wrapped in a moistened paper towel, then in plastic wrap.) Ladle the hot soup into bowls and garnish each serving with the leek greens and a sprinkle of the parsley.

Serves 6 to 8 as a starter

VARIATION:

To make a slightly saner version calorically, first spray the skillet well with Pam cooking spray, and reduce the butter to 2 tablespoons, even to 1. Substitute evaporated skim milk for the cream.

Asparagus and White Wine Soup

nother too-good-to-leave-it-out recipe from *Dairy Hollow House Cookbook*. I would feel cheated if spring went by without a couple of batches of this soup. It says spring to me as clearly as the first daffodil.

½ cup water
½ cup dry white wine
2 dozen asparagus spears, tough ends removed
2 tablespoons butter
1 tablespoon unbleached all-purpose flour
1 cup milk
⅔ cup finely grated extra-sharp Cheddar cheese
Pam cooking spray
Salt and freshly ground white pepper to taste
1 cup heavy (whipping) cream (see Note)

1. In a small pot, bring the water and wine to a boil. Add the asparagus and simmer, covered, just until tender, about 5 minutes. Quickly drain the asparagus, reserving both asparagus and liquid, and cool both.

2. In a 10-inch skillet, melt the butter over medium heat. Add the flour and cook, stirring constantly, about half a minute. Add the milk, stirring to smooth any lumps. Cook, stirring constantly, until the mixture is thick and smooth, 2 to 4 minutes. Don't let it boil. Add the cheese and heat until the cheese is completely melted. Remove from the heat.

3. Place the asparagus on a cutting board, cut off the pointy tips, and set aside. Put the stalks in a food processor, add the asparagus cooking liquid, and purée. For absolute smoothness, press the purée through a food mill, fine sieve, or power strainer.

4. Spray a medium-size soup pot with Pam, and in it combine the asparagus purée with the cheese sauce. Heat through but do not allow it to boil. Season with salt and pepper. Stir in the cream and heat through again. Slice the asparagus tips ½-inch thick and stir them into the soup. Serve the soup very hot. I have never found a garnish for this soup that wasn't distracting, so I serve it as is, pristine and delectable.

Serves 4 as a small starter

Note: In my more fat-aware moments, I have substituted 1 cup milk mixed with 2 tablespoons cornstarch as well as 1 cup evaporated skim milk for the cream. With either substitution, the soup is still superb.

Blushing Cream of Cauliflower Soup

auliflower makes a surprisingly delicious cream soup, but it's awfully white. To make it even more delicious and less white, I have added red peppers and a faint hint of tomato. Because I like real cream in this soup, the amount of butter is cut way back and the thickener is potato rather than a roux.

1 large head cauliflower, broken into flowerets
Pam cooking spray
1 tablespoon butter
1 tablespoon mild vegetable oil, such as corn or peanut
1 large onion, chopped
1 carrot, scrubbed or peeled and finely diced
1 rib celery with leaves, finely diced
3 red bell peppers, stemmed, seeded, and diced
6 cups Chicken Stock 1 (page 19) or Golden Vegetable Stock (page 28) or any well-flavored chicken or vegetable stock
1 cup dry white wine
4 fist-sized all-purpose potatoes, peeled and diced
1 tablespoon tomato paste
1 teaspoon dried basil
½ teaspoon dried thyme
1 cup milk
1 cup heavy (whipping) cream
Salt and freshly ground black pepper to taste
½ yellow bell pepper, stemmed, seeded, and diced, for garnish
Minced fresh parsley, for garnish

1. Steam the cauliflower over boiling water until barely tender, about 5 to 7 minutes.

2. Spray a large skillet with Pam. Add the butter and oil and heat over medium heat. Add the onion and sauté until wilted, about 2 minutes. Add the carrot and celery

and sauté 2 minutes more. Add 2 of the bell peppers and sauté another 2 minutes. Scrape half the sautéed vegetables into a heavy soup pot and set the other half aside. (If you want a smooth soup, add all the sautéed vegetables to the soup pot.)

3. Add the stock, wine, potatoes, tomato paste, basil, and thyme to the soup pot. Bring to a boil, then turn down the heat to medium-low and let simmer, uncovered, 10 minutes. Add the cauliflower and continue to simmer until the potato is done and the cauliflower is quite tender, about 20 minutes. Let cool slightly.

4. In a food processor, purée the soup in batches and return it to the soup pot. Reheat, then stir in the remaining sautéed vegetables, the milk, cream, and about three-quarters of the remaining bell pepper. Season with salt and pepper. Heat the soup through, being careful not to let it boil. Serve hot, garnished with the remaining red pepper, the yellow pepper, and a bit of minced parsley.

Serves 6 to 8 as an entrée

Déjà Food: For a really luscious cauliflower casserole, combine leftover soup with freshly steamed cauliflower flowerets in a buttered baking dish. Top with grated cheese and herbed, dried bread crumbs. Bake in a 350° F oven until bubbly.

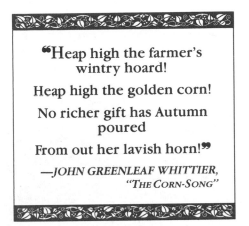

> **"Heap high the farmer's wintry hoard!**
>
> **Heap high the golden corn!**
>
> **No richer gift has Autumn poured**
>
> **From out her lavish horn!"**
>
> —*JOHN GREENLEAF WHITTIER,*
> *"THE CORN-SONG"*

New World Corn Chowder

This chowder was invented one January night in our pre-restaurant days in honor of our old friend Bob Joblin of Little Rock, who was staying at the inn. The dominant influence is New Southwestern. The idea: Start with a corn chowder, feature half a dozen vegetables native to the New World, season boldly with chili powder, cumin, and chilies, then go for something with both texture and smoothness—soothing comfort and conflagration. Optional but glorious is a garnish of ribbons of bright red bell pepper and dark, earthy green chili purées. In its simpler form, without this garnish, this is a soup you will make again and again. It gets better with each reheating—it's substantial, satisfying, and just so good.

2 quarts Chicken Stock 1 (page 19) or
Golden Vegetable Stock (page 28) or any
well-flavored chicken or vegetable stock

4 fist-sized all-purpose potatoes, scrubbed
and cut into ¾-inch dice

2 medium butternut squash,
peeled, seeded, and
cut into ¾-inch dice

1 bag (16 ounces)
frozen corn kernels

1 tablespoon honey

2 teaspoons Pickapeppa
or Worcestershire
sauce, or to taste

2 tablespoons butter

2 tablespoons mild
vegetable oil, such
as corn or peanut

1 large onion, chopped

1 green bell pepper, stemmed, seeded, and
diced

3 ribs celery with leaves, finely diced

1 tablespoon good-quality chili powder (or
to taste)

2 teaspoons ground cumin

2 cloves garlic, peeled and put through a
garlic press or finely chopped

3 tablespoons unbleached all-purpose flour

1 cup milk

1 cup heavy (whipping) cream

1 Morga vegetarian bouillon cube

Salt and freshly ground black pepper to
taste

1 jalapeño pepper, seeded and sliced
(optional)

2 tablespoons juice from pickled jalapeños
(optional)

Crumbled corn tortilla chips, sour cream or
plain yogurt; Arkansalsa (page 199) or
prepared salsa; and/or fresh cilantro
sprigs; or green chili and red pepper
purées (page 46), for garnish

1. In a large heavy soup pot, bring the stock to a boil. Lower the heat slightly and add the potatoes. Let simmer, covered, about 10 minutes. Add the squash and continue to simmer until both the squash and potatoes are barely tender, about 8 minutes more. Stir in the corn, honey, and Pickapeppa or Worcestershire sauce. Turn down the heat to very low and simmer, covered, about 20 minutes.

2. Meanwhile, in a 10-inch skillet, heat the butter and oil over medium heat. Add the onion and sauté until starting to soften, about 3 minutes. Add the bell pepper and celery with leaves and sauté 5 minutes more. Sprinkle the chili powder, cumin, and garlic over the vegetables. Turn down the heat to medium-low and cook, stirring constantly, about 1 minute. Sprinkle the flour over the vegetables and cook, stirring, another minute. Gradually add the milk, stirring to smooth any lumps, and cook until thickened, about 1 minute. Transfer about one-third of this mixture to a food processor and set the remaining mixture aside.

3. Transfer about half the potatoes and squash from the soup pot to the food processor. Add the cream and purée. Stir the purée back into the soup in the pot and add the remaining sautéed vegetables. Add the Morga, salt, plenty of black pepper, the jalapeño, and the jalapeño juice.

4. Heat the soup over medium-low heat until very hot, stirring frequently. Do not allow it to boil. Taste and adjust the seasoning. Ladle into soup bowls and add your choice of garnish.

Serves 6 to 8 as a generous entrée

VARIATIONS:

Summer Corn Chowder: Substitute fresh jalapeño pepper, seeded and diced, for the canned jalapeño, and replace the jalapeño

juice with 1 tablespoon cider vinegar. Use fresh corn cut from the cob and steamed for about 30 seconds instead of the frozen. Four cups of corn is plenty.

Calorie-Aware Corn Chowder: Spray the sautéing skillet generously with the Pam and reduce the butter and oil to 1 teaspoon each. Substitute 1 cup thickened evaporated skim milk for the whole milk and flour. Pour ¾ cup of the skim milk into the skillet with the sautéed vegetables and spices and heat until hot; dissolve 2 tablespoons of cornstarch in the remaining ¼ cup skim milk and whisk it into the hot milk and vegetable mixture. Cook until smooth and thick. Use another cup of evaporated skim milk to replace the cream. Garnish the soup with a spoonful of yogurt instead of sour cream. You have just saved yourself about 1,000 calories, virtually all from fat. The flavors are intense enough so that the loss is hardly noticed.

Chicken Corn Chowder: Make Chicken Stock 2 (page 20) using apple cider as part of the liquid. Cut the cooked chicken into large cubes. Use this stock in the basic recipe, as directed, and add the cooked chicken during the final reheating.

Corn and Squash Blossom Chowder: In the summer, when the squash plants are taking over the garden, gather the yellow-or-

CHOWDER: FROM THE FRENCH CHAUDIÈRE, OR "STEW POT"

❦ *What is a chowder? We'll take some liberties and define it capriciously: a thick soup or stew, sometimes containing fish, shellfish, or chicken; often containing potatoes or other hearty vegetables; always containing milk or cream. After all, Eureka is hundreds of miles from serious chowder-disagreement country—New England, where they like it creamy, and Manhattan, where they hold firm for a tomato base. Even so, their arguments apply only to clam chowder, and we never even see saltwater clams here.*

So in time-honored Ozark tradition, we make do. And we have plenty to make do with: garden vegetables, the area's legendary poultry and dairy products, fish from our countless lakes and rivers, and especially the several culinary influences I have already alluded to: Cajun-Creole, drifting up from South Louisiana, down-home Southern cooking from Tennessee to the east, hearty farm cooking from Kansas, Missouri, and Oklahoma. And southwest of Arkansas is the state that has yielded the greatest culinary influence in recent years—Texas. ❧

ange squash blossoms—those still closed, just starting to open—as many as you have, up to 1 pound. Rinse them, slit them open and remove any bugs that may be lurking inside, then slice crosswise—stamens, stems, and all. Add the blossoms to the skillet with the bell pepper and celery. Proceed as directed in the basic recipe.

Ancho Chili Corn Chowder: Soak a dried ancho chili in sufficient hot stock to cover until softened, about 1 hour. Add both the chili and the soaking liquid to the remaining stock, and proceed to cook the potatoes and squash as directed in the basic recipe. Pick out and discard the chili's woody stem, but purée the chili itself with the potatoes and squash.

Déjà Food: Reheat any leftover soup with tomato soup or a can of whole tomatoes puréed in the food processor. Or thin it down with more milk and stock. Or serve it with grated sharp Cheddar or jack cheese over the top.

Curried Cream of Eggplant Soup-Stew

oluptuous and with a kick, this curried cream soup is built around eggplant, a vegetable rarely found in soup. (Give eggplant the treatment described in the Note if it is at all bitter.) The apple and tomato are not distinguishable as such, but add, respectively, sweetness and acidity that balance the whole nicely. Note that the eggplant is baked, not sautéed, since this vegetable is notorious for sopping up oil if given the chance. When puréed, baked eggplant has a dreamy, silken texture.

This is a five-star favorite with both restaurant diners and my official recipe testers. There is something very special about the soup.

1 large eggplant, peeled and sliced in ¼-inch rounds (see Note)
6 cups Chicken Stock 1 (page 19) or Golden Vegetable Stock (page 28) or any well-flavored chicken or vegetable stock
¼ cup long-grain white rice
2 tablespoons butter, or mild vegetable oil, such as corn or peanut, if you are serving the soup chilled
1 large onion, chopped
1 Granny Smith apple, peeled, cored, and finely chopped
1 ripe tomato, chopped
1 to 1½ tablespoons best-quality curry powder
Pinch of cayenne pepper
1 tablespoon tamari/shoyu soy sauce, or to taste
2 teaspoons honey or sugar, or to taste
Salt and freshly ground black pepper to taste
1½ cups half-and-half or evaporated skim milk
Diced red bell pepper, for garnish
Finely chopped fresh parsley, for garnish

1. Preheat the oven to 400° F.
2. Oil a baking sheet and spread the

eggplant slices on it. Cover with aluminum foil and bake until very tender, about 30 minutes. Remove the foil and let cool.

3. Meanwhile, in a large, heavy soup pot combine 5 cups of the stock with the rice. Bring to a boil, then turn down the heat to medium-low and let simmer, covered, until the rice is tender. Strain the stock. Transfer the rice to a food processor and return the stock to the soup pot.

4. In a 10-inch skillet, melt the butter over medium heat. Add the onion and sauté until it starts to soften, about 3 minutes. Add the apple and sauté 1 minute. Stir in the tomato, curry powder, cayenne, soy sauce, and honey. Increase the heat to medium-high and cook, stirring constantly, until most of the liquid is evaporated. Stir in the remaining 1 cup stock and cook, stirring frequently, 1 minute more. Scrape this mixture into the food processor with the rice.

5. Add half the eggplant to the food processor and purée. Stir the purée into the stock. Coarsely chop the remaining eggplant and add it, too, to the stock. Season with salt and pepper, then stir in the half-and-half. Barely simmer the soup, uncovered, for 15 minutes. Serve hot, or chill deeply, and garnish with the red pepper and parsley. This soup reheats beautifully as long as you do it gently over low heat. It's even better on the second day.

Serves 6 to 7 as a starter

> **❝I** read the autobiography of an eggplant where the stem joins the purple satin skin. If each member of that junction is firmly attached, if the union between the big vegetable and the segment of vine on which it developed is still firm then the eggplant is fresh; if they have begun to detach themselves the eggplant has begun to spoil.**❞**
>
> —*HENRI CHARPENTIER,*
> *THOSE RICH & GREAT ONES, OR A LIFE*
> *À LA HENRI*

Note: Cookbooks frequently recommend soaking eggplant slices in salted water before cooking to remove any bitterness. But not all eggplants are bitter, in which case it's a waste of time and nutrients. So cut the eggplant open and take a nibble. If the flavor isn't bitter, don't soak it. If it is, cut the eggplant into thick slices and combine with 1 tablespoon salt and 1 quart of water in a bowl. Keep the eggplant submerged with a plate and can or large jar on top. Let soak for 30 minutes, then drain and pat dry.

Déjà Food: Reheat any leftover soup with a can of any kind of beans and 2 puréed tomatoes. Serve as a vegetarian curry over cooked rice. Top it with chopped roasted peanuts, if you like.

Creamy Garlic Soup with White Wine

his divine soup is loaded with butter and cream. No substitutions work. Make it just once in your life if you must, but make it right or don't make it at all. It's a rich glory of smooth garlic, white wine, and cream topped with tiny, very crisp, garlicky croutons. Garlic lovers, you'll regret it forever if you pass this by!

½ cup (1 stick) butter
4 whole heads garlic, cloves separated and peeled
Tiny Garlic Croutons (recipe follows)
3½ cups Chicken Stock 1 (page 19) or Golden Vegetable Stock (page 28) or any well-flavored chicken or vegetable stock
¼ cup dry, fruity white wine, such as Moselle
3 tablespoons unbleached all-purpose flour
1½ cups heavy (whipping) cream
2 large egg yolks
Salt and freshly ground black pepper to taste
Finely minced fresh parsley, for garnish

1. In a heavy 10-inch skillet, melt the butter over medium heat. Set aside 5 cloves of garlic for the croutons and add the remaining garlic to the skillet. Turn down the heat to very low and gently cook, stirring often, until the garlic is quite soft and only slightly colored, 10 to 15 minutes.

2. Meanwhile, make the Tiny Garlic Croutons.

3. Using a slotted spoon, transfer the garlic to a food processor, leaving as much butter as possible in the skillet. Add ½ cup of the stock and the wine, and purée until absolutely smooth.

4. In a medium-size saucepan, heat the remaining 3 cups of stock until hot. Heat the butter in the skillet over very low heat. Whisk in the flour and cook, stirring constantly, for 1 or 2 minutes. Gradually add the hot stock, stirring to smooth any lumps; cook, stirring frequently, until the mixture is smooth and thick, 2 or 3 minutes. Return to the saucepan, adding the garlic purée, then 1 cup of the cream. Simmer gently over very low heat until the soup no longer has a raw flour taste, about 3 minutes.

5. In a small bowl, lightly beat the egg yolks and the remaining ½ cup cream. Whisk in 3 tablespoons of the soup, then pour this mixture into the remaining soup. Heat, stirring constantly, until hot and thick. Do not let it boil. Season with salt and pepper. Serve immediately in small cups, topped with the croutons and the minced parsley.

Serves 6 as a starter

"The ambrosia, which the Greeks and Romans insisted was the food of their gods, was probably only a clever way with garlic...

—*LOUIS P. DE GOUY,*
THE GOLD COOKBOOK

Tiny Garlic Croutons

*3 very thin slices homemade or Pepperidge
   Farm whole-wheat bread*
3 tablespoons butter
*5 cloves garlic, peeled and put through a
   garlic press*

▶ Remove the crusts from the bread
and cut the bread into tiny squares, no bigger
than ¼ inch. In a small skillet, melt the butter
over medium heat. Add the bread cubes and
cook, stirring frequently, until browned and
crisp, 2 to 3 minutes. Transfer the croutons
to a small bowl. Add the garlic and toss to
combine.

Makes 1 cup

Cream of Leek, Herb, and Garden Lettuce Soup

his is the perfect answer for
what to do with thinnings of garden lettuce. No garden? Raid the
market for any salad greens with person-
ality: chicory, oak leaf lettuce, red leaf,
watercress, or a combination of these. A
rice thickening and a less-than-usual
amount of cream (you can substitute
evaporated skim milk) makes this soup
less fat-laden than most cream soups but
still quite delicious. The flavor will vary
according to the herbs used. Go easy on
stronger herbs, like rosemary or sage.

*6 cups Chicken Stock 1 (page 19) or
   Golden Vegetable Stock (page 28) or any
   well-flavored chicken or vegetable
   stock*
¼ cup long-grain white rice
Pam cooking spray
*2 tablespoons butter or mild vegetable oil,
   such as corn or peanut*
*3 leeks, white part and 3 inches green, split
   open lengthwise, well washed, and
   chopped*
1 rib celery with leaves, sliced
*1 medium carrot, peeled, halved
   lengthwise, then thinly sliced
   crosswise*
*2 to 3 cups lightly packed assorted
   lettuces or other salad greens, sliced
   into ribbons*
*½ cup lightly packed fresh Italian (flat-leaf)
   parsley leaves, finely chopped*
*½ cup lightly packed mixture of fresh
   herb leaves, such as sorrel, tarragon,
   thyme, oregano, rosemary, and sage
   (anything but dill), finely
   chopped*
*¼ cup lightly packed fresh basil leaves,
   finely chopped*
*1 cup heavy (whipping) cream or
   evaporated skim milk*
1 tablespoon all-purpose flour
1 teaspoon honey or sugar, or to taste
Freshly grated nutmeg to taste
Salt and freshly ground pepper to taste

1. In a heavy soup pot, bring the stock to a boil. Add the rice, turn down the heat to medium-low, and let simmer, covered, until quite soft, about 30 minutes.

2. Meanwhile, spray a 10-inch skillet with Pam. Add the butter to the skillet and melt over medium heat. Add the leeks and sauté until softened, about 3½ minutes. Add the celery and carrot and sauté 3 minutes more. Add the salad greens and herbs, cover the skillet, and let them sweat until wilted, 1 to 2 minutes. Lift the cover and remove from the heat.

3. Strain the stock, reserving both the rice and the stock. Transfer the rice to a food processor and return the stock to the pot. Add half the cooked vegetables and herbs, the cream, flour, and honey to the food processor; purée until smooth. Stir the purée and the whole vegetables into the stock. Simmer, stirring frequently, until slightly thickened and free of any raw flour taste, about 10 minutes. Season with nutmeg, salt, and pepper. Serve hot.

Serves 5 to 6 as a starter

VARIATIONS:
Spinach Cream Soup: Substitute 2 pounds rinsed fresh spinach leaves or 2 boxes (10 ounces each) frozen chopped spinach for the salad greens and herbs. I like a bit of garlic sautéed with the leek for this, and a dab of crème fraîche or yogurt on top of the finished soup, along with a sprinkle of diced red bell pepper. If you run the soup through a power

strainer, thicken it with 2 tablespoons cornstarch, and squiggle red pepper purée over the top (page 46). This way the soup is dressy enough for a formal dinner, as delectable as it is pretty.

Calorie-Aware Chilled Cream Soup: Use oil for sautéing instead of butter. Let the vegetables cool a bit before puréeing, then substitute plain yogurt, buttermilk, or Cottage Cream (page 52) for the cream. Chill deeply. This makes for a fascinating soup, highly refreshing.

Cream of Leek and Chervil Soup Rabbit Hill

n June of 1988 circumstances conspired to create a magic evening for me: two or three hours over dinner in one of Vermont's most beautifully sited inns with a pair of America's warmest innkeepers. The inn was Rabbit Hill Inn in Lower Waterford, Vermont; the innkeepers, John and Maureen Magee, a couple in love with their calling. I was delighted when I met them again a year and a half later when they, like us, were selected for the first time by Uncle Ben's as a "Best Inn of the Year" in 1989. It would be the first of three times (the maximum number of years an inn is permitted to win) that

Dairy Hollow and Rabbit Hill would share this honor.

At Rabbit Hill, you can walk or picnic around tiny, lovely Lower Waterford; you can swim, float, or fish the nearby Connecticut River; or you can curl up in a corner of one of the inn's rambling old buildings and read, nap, or dream. And then you can go to dinner, and, if you are lucky, have a bowl of this wonderful rich-rich-rich soup. This is so good I haven't brought myself to try any of my calorie-sparing tricks, but you could. (For another recipe from John and Maureen, see Rabbit Hill Inn Oatmeal-Molasses Bread, page 338.)

½ cup (1 stick) butter
12 leeks, white part only, split open
    lengthwise, well washed, and cut into ¼-
    inch-thick slices
1 tablespoon finely minced garlic
4 large all-purpose potatoes, peeled and
    diced
1¼ cups Chicken Stock 1 (page 19) or
    Golden Vegetable Stock (page 28) or any
    well-flavored chicken or vegetable stock
4 cups heavy (whipping) cream
1 cup very finely chopped fresh chervil
    leaves
Salt and freshly ground white pepper to
    taste
Juice of ½ lemon
Additional chopped fresh chervil, for
    garnish

1. In a 10-inch skillet, melt the butter over medium heat. Add the leeks and garlic; sauté until softened, about 5 minutes. Add the potatoes, turn down the heat to low, and cook, stirring often, until the potatoes start to soften, about 15 minutes. Scrape the vegetables into a heavy soup pot.

2. Deglaze the skillet with the stock, add the pan contents to the pot, and bring to a boil. Turn down the heat to medium-low and let simmer, covered, 30 minutes. Stir in the cream and barely simmer 15 minutes. Add the chervil, salt, and pepper; simmer, covered, another 15 minutes. Let cool slightly.

3. In a food processor, purée the soup in batches, then put the purée through a food mill, fine sieve, or power strainer. Return the soup to the pot and add the lemon juice. Taste and adjust the seasoning, then reheat gently. Serve hot, garnished with fresh chervil.

Serves 6 to 8 as a small, very rich starter

Autumn Cream of Onion Soup with Brandy and Cider

his soup is creamy but not overwhelmingly so; plenty of wine gives a pleasant astringency and cuts the cream—actually crème fraîche. This is one of my favorite fall soups. It is a good starter for a wide variety of autumnal dinners—roast beef or venison, rabbit, or game hen. Every time we serve it, at least one or two people request the recipe.

2 tablespoons butter
2 tablespoons mild vegetable oil, such as corn or peanut
4 large onions, preferably 2 each red and yellow, very thinly sliced
2 leeks, white part and 1 inch green, split open lengthwise, well washed, and thinly sliced
4 cups Chicken Stock 1 (page 19) or Browned Vegetable Stock (page 32) or any well-flavored chicken or vegetable stock
¼ cup thawed frozen apple juice concentrate or 1 cup fresh cider cooked down to ¼ cup
¼ cup cognac
2 medium all-purpose potatoes, peeled and diced
1 whole head garlic, cloves separated and peeled
2 bay leaves
2 teaspoons fresh thyme leaves or 1 teaspoon dried
1 tablespoon light miso
1½ cups Crème Fraîche (page 50)
Freshly ground nutmeg to taste
Salt and freshly ground black pepper to taste
2 tablespoons cornstarch
⅓ cup heavy (whipping) cream
Finely chopped fresh parsley or scallions, for garnish

1. In a large skillet, heat the butter and oil over medium-low heat. Add the onions and leeks and sauté slowly until quite limp, about 30 minutes.

2. Meanwhile, in a heavy soup pot bring the stock, apple juice concentrate or cider, cognac, potatoes, garlic, bay leaves, and thyme to a boil. Turn down the heat to medium-low and let simmer, covered, until the potatoes are quite soft, about 30 minutes. Drain well, returning the stock to the pot. Remove the bay leaves from the solids and discard. Transfer the solids to a food processor. Add the miso and crème fraîche and purée.

3. Stir the sautéed onions and the purée into the stock. Season with nutmeg, salt, and plenty of pepper. (The soup can be made ahead of time up to this point. Refrigerate, then reheat before proceeding.)

4. To finish the soup, heat it almost to a boil. Dissolve the cornstarch in the cream and stir it into the soup. The soup will thicken almost immediately and have a clear, glossy finish. Serve very hot in small cups, garnished with the parsley.

Serves 8 as a starter

Roasted Red Pepper Soup with Yellow Pepper Ribbons

 n enchanting transmutation of flavor and texture happen to peppers when they are roasted. They go from deliciously crunchy to deliciously melting, from crisp, garden-sweet to dusky, smoky-sweet, and mys-

terious. Unfortunately, roasting and peeling peppers takes a bit of work.

This soup makes use of this pepper alchemy and has the sprightly colors of a Mexican street fair. If making two purées seems too fussy, just make the red pepper purée for the soup, and garnish with diced yellow bell peppers.

Pam cooking spray
8 red bell peppers
6 yellow bell peppers
Salt to taste
Few drops of fresh lemon juice
2 tablespoons butter or mild vegetable oil,
*   such as corn or peanut*
1 large onion, chopped
1 medium carrot, scrubbed or peeled and
*   sliced*
1 tablespoon tamari/shoyu soy sauce, or to
*   taste*
2 ripe tomatoes, peeled, seeded, and finely
*   chopped*
3 cloves garlic, peeled and put through a
*   garlic press or finely chopped*
1 teaspoon honey or sugar, or to taste
4 to 5 cups Chicken Stock 1 (page 19) or
*   Golden Vegetable Stock (page 28) or any*
*   well-flavored chicken or vegetable*
*   stock*
1 cup heavy (whipping) cream
Freshly ground black pepper to taste
2 tablespoons cornstarch
Finely chopped fresh basil leaves or parsley,
*   for garnish*
Toasted slivered almonds, for garnish

1. Preheat the oven to 425°F.

2. Spray 2 baking sheets well with Pam. Place the peppers on the baking sheets and poke each one once with a fork. Bake until most of the skin is charred and the peppers are slightly collapsed, about 30 to 40 minutes.

Cover the peppers with clean kitchen towels and let cool to room temperature.

3. Make 2 pepper purées, one red and one yellow: Core, seed, and peel the roasted peppers. Cut the flesh into large pieces, then purée each pepper color separately in a food processor, making sure to wash the food processor bowl and blade between each batch. (If you have a power strainer, remove the stems and seeds from the peppers, purée, then put the purée through the strainer, which will separate the skins from the flesh.)

4. In a heavy saucepan, quickly boil the yellow purée until reduced by half. Season with salt and the lemon juice. Set aside for garnish.

5. In a 10-inch skillet, melt the butter over medium heat. Add the onion and sauté until it starts to soften, about 3 minutes. Add the carrot and sauté another minute or so. Stir in the soy sauce and cook until the soy sauce evaporates. Add the tomatoes, garlic, and honey. Turn up the heat to medium-high and cook, stirring often, until most of the liquid has evaporated. Scrape this mixture into a heavy soup pot.

6. Add 4 cups of the stock and the red pepper purée to the pot. Bring to a boil, then turn down the heat and cook at just under a boil, uncovered, for 20 minutes. Measure 3 tablespoons of the cream into a small bowl, reserve, and stir the remaining cream into the soup. Turn down the heat to low. Season with salt and pepper. Taste and add more soy sauce or honey if needed. Heat through until very hot.

7. Dissolve the cornstarch in the 3 tablespoons cream and stir it into the soup. It will thicken the soup slightly almost immediately. Cook, stirring, until there is no raw cornstarch taste, 2 to 3 minutes.

8. Transfer the yellow pepper purée to a small squeeze bottle, the kind sold in supermarkets for ketchup or mustard. Ladle the soup into warmed bowls and squiggle the yellow purée across the top of each bowl. Sprinkle with basil or parsley and a few almond slivers. Serve at once.

Serves 8 to 10 as a starter

VARIATIONS:

You could use 8 yellow bell peppers and 6 red, and make a yellow pepper soup garnished with red pepper purée. Or, just as delicious, omit the garnishing purée and top with a dab of olive paste—puréed pitted Greek or Italian black olives. Use olive oil instead of the butter if you go this route.

The Governor's Inn Cream of Spinach Soup

 can't wait to visit Deedy and Charlie Marble's late-Victorian inn, built around 1890 in Ludlow, Vermont, as a home for Governor William Wallace Stickney. Everything I have read about the inn and every picture of it I have seen has me convinced that this is my kind of place. Impeccably restored and full of touches like flannel sheets for cold nights and ample picnics in flower-bedecked baskets year-round,

The Governor's Inn sounds irresistible. Meeting the Marbles—they were two-time "Best Inn of the Year" winners—was one of the highlights of the Chicago awards dinner in 1989. Since our off-season is their on-season, we may yet get to be guests at each others' inns. I'm looking forward to it, but until then I can taste Deedy's cooking in this delectable soup, as well as in her Graham Muffins (page 368).

Make this soup the night before you want to serve it to allow the flavors to blend.

4 chicken or salt-free Morga vegetarian
   bouillon cubes
4 cups light cream or half-and-half
1 package (10 ounces) frozen chopped
   spinach, cooked according to package
   directions, drained, and puréed
½ cup dry vermouth
1 teaspoon grated lemon zest
½ teaspoon ground mace
Salt to taste
2 hard-cooked eggs, finely chopped, for
   garnish

1. The night before serving the soup, crumble the bouillon cubes into the cream in a small saucepan, and heat until scalded. Pour the cream into the top of a double boiler and stir in the spinach and remaining ingredients except the eggs. Refrigerate overnight.

2. Just before serving, reheat the soup over simmering water. Season it with salt if you used the Morga. Then, says Deedy, "Serve from a wonderful soup tureen into warmed soup bowls." Garnish each serving with the chopped egg.

Serves 4 to 6 as a starter

Augusta's Chilled Tomato Soup with Basil Cream

ere is one of two creamy tomato soups. This one is luscious, elegant, and perfect for indolent dog days. The recipe was given to us by Augusta Prince, who, as Augusta Dabney, has appeared on and off Broadway, in soaps, commercials, and movies. As Augusta Prince, however, she is the ultimate gracious hostess and a lifelong friend of the family.

½ cup lightly packed fresh basil leaves, coarsely chopped
¾ cup heavy (whipping) cream
2 cups seeded, peeled, coarsely chopped dead-ripe tomatoes
2 cups Chicken Stock 1 (page 19) or Golden Vegetable Stock (page 28) or any well-flavored chicken or vegetable stock
2 cups milk
1 teaspoon honey or sugar
Salt and freshly ground black pepper to taste
Fresh whole basil leaves, for garnish

1. Early in the day, put the chopped basil leaves in a small bowl. Scald the cream in a small saucepan and pour it over the basil. Let steep 1 hour, then strain the cream and chill deeply.

2. In a food processor, purée the

INN GOOD COMPANY: CHARLISA CATO

❦ *Charlisa Cato and I—we're two young women in Eureka Springs—and have been for such an amazingly long time.*

I have a vivid picture of her in her early 20s, a little tiny thing, a one-time dancer (she studied with the Joffrey), and long-haired, holding center stage at the long-since-defunct Quiet Night nightclub, singing "Honky-Tonk Woman"—and the whole place (me included) joining in, a cappella, for the last verse. Like the subject of "Honky-Tonk

Woman," she is from Memphis. In those days, she ran the Coffee Store in downtown Eureka.

These days Charlisa, an active environmentalist and a board member of the National Water Center, works for us part-time at our front desk, happily conversing with guests, solving problems, and meeting guests' special requests (like arranging day-long hikes through the Ozark National Forest). And she's developed the most amazing laugh—effervescently bubbly—I am so glad she is part of DHH. ❦

chopped tomato, stock, milk, and honey until very smooth. Transfer the purée to a bowl, and season with the salt and pepper. Chill deeply.

3. When ready to serve, whip the basil cream. Ladle the chilled soup into chilled glass cups or stemmed glasses. Dollop each serving with the whipped cream and top with a fresh basil leaf.

Serves 4 to 6 as a starter

Tomato Bisque

 omey, warming, wonderful, this soup is a favorite with children, and could not be more different from the preceding one. It is fine and low-fat, and made with cupboard staples—evaporated skim milk and canned tomatoes—so remember it next time you are snowed in.

1 tablespoon butter or mild vegetable oil,
*   such as corn or peanut*
1 large onion, chopped
1 can (28 ounces) whole tomatoes, coarsely
*   chopped, with their juice*
1 tablespoon light brown sugar or honey
1 bay leaf
2 whole cloves
1 teaspoon dried basil
Salt and freshly ground black pepper to
*   taste*
1 cup plus 3 tablespoons evaporated skim
*   milk, or more as needed*
2 tablespoons cornstarch

1. In a 10-inch skillet, melt the butter over medium heat. Add the onion and sauté until it starts to soften, about 3 minutes. Add the tomatoes with their juice, the brown sugar, bay leaf, cloves, basil, and salt and pepper. Simmer, stirring occasionally, until all is hot through, about 5 minutes.

2. Meanwhile, in a medium-size heavy saucepan, heat 1 cup of the evaporated milk to just under a boil. Dissolve the cornstarch in the remaining 3 tablespoons evaporated milk and whisk it into the hot milk. Cook, stirring constantly, until thick, smooth, and free of any raw starchy taste, about 1 minute.

3. Remove the cloves and bay leaf from the tomato mixture. Very slowly add the tomato mixture to the hot thickened milk (if you add it all at once, the milk may curdle). Heat through, but do not boil. If you wish, thin the soup with extra milk. Serve very hot, immediately.

Serves 2 to 4 as a lunch entrée, accompanied by bread

Deep December Cream of Root Soup

 he turnip? No! There is no poetry in a turnip," wrote Louis P. DeGouy, author of *The Gold Cookbook*. Well, I am no turnip fan; in fact the subject is one of the few my dear

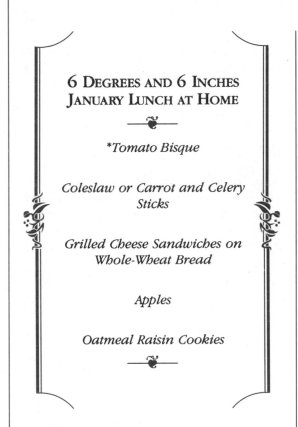

6 DEGREES AND 6 INCHES JANUARY LUNCH AT HOME

❧

*Tomato Bisque

Coleslaw or Carrot and Celery
Sticks

Grilled Cheese Sandwiches on
Whole-Wheat Bread

Apples

Oatmeal Raisin Cookies

❧

one-time collaborator Jan Brown and I have had words over. But despite them, this soup is pretty poetic. We've served it regularly at our New Year's Eve dinners; it's that festive, and always tremendously popular.

As you might guess from its name, this is a celebration of roots—sweet potatoes, white potatoes, onions, carrots, beets, turnips, even rutabagas. The preparation makes these humble vegetables taste positively transcendent, and the garnish—a squiggle of bright beet purée—makes it as elegant as it is delicious. Certainly I'd rank this high in my personal cream-soup hall of fame, and other tuber devotees will feel the same.

If you don't have a power strainer of some sort, you will need to peel the vegetables.

4 or 5 small beets
Mild vegetable oil, such as corn or peanut
4 cups Golden Vegetable Stock (page 28) or
    Chicken Stock 1 (page 19) or any well-
    flavored chicken or vegetable stock
Salt to taste
1 small sweet potato or yam, scrubbed and
    chopped
1 fist-sized all-purpose potato, scrubbed and
    chopped
2 turnips, scrubbed and chopped
1 rutabaga, scrubbed and chopped
2 tablespoons butter
1 large onion, chopped
1 or 2 cloves garlic, peeled and put through
    a garlic press or finely chopped
2 parsnips, scrubbed and chopped
2 carrots, scrubbed and chopped
1 cup milk
Freshly grated nutmeg to taste
Freshly ground black pepper to taste
½ cup heavy (whipping) cream

1. Preheat the oven to 350°F.
2. Rinse the beets, dry, then rub lightly with vegetable oil. Wrap them in aluminum foil, and bake until tender, about 45 to 60 minutes depending on the size. Unwrap and let stand until cool enough to handle. Slip the skins from the beets. In a food processor, purée the beets with any of the juice left in the aluminum foil until smooth and thick. Thin by adding 1 to 4 tablespoons of the stock to make the beets a purée rather than a thick paste. Put the purée through a food mill, fine sieve, or power strainer. Salt it lightly, then pour it through a funnel into a squeeze bottle, the kind sold in supermarkets for table

dispensers of ketchup or mustard. This is your garnish; set it aside.

3. In a heavy soup pot, bring the stock to a boil. Add the potatoes, turn down the heat to medium-low, and let simmer, covered, until half done, about 15 minutes. Add the turnips and rutabaga; simmer another 15 minutes.

4. In a 10-inch skillet, melt the butter over medium heat. Add the onion and sauté until it starts to soften, about 3 minutes. Add the garlic, parsnips, and carrots and sauté another 3 to 4 minutes. Scrape this mixture into the soup pot and simmer the soup another 15 minutes.

5. Strain the stock, returning the stock to the soup pot. Transfer the vegetables to the food processor and purée until smooth. For an absolutely smooth soup, put the purée through a food mill, fine sieve, or power strainer.

6. Stir the vegetable purée and the milk into the stock. Season with nutmeg, salt, and pepper to taste. Stir in the cream and

reheat very gently (or refrigerate and reheat the next day). Ladle the piping-hot soup into warmed teacups. Shake the squeeze bottle of beet purée a couple of times, then use it to draw an irregular line of beet purée over each serving.

Serves 8 as a starter

Déjà Food: Root soup is a great leftover and even tastier the second night. If there's not enough to go around, reheat what you have, then add a few chopped canned tomatoes with a bit of their juice and a bit of stock or cream. Make a full meal out of it by topping with some grated sharp Cheddar cheese.

The beet purée freezes well. Save it for your next foray into soup making. Or combine it with an equal amount of plain yogurt or buttermilk and add a few sliced scallions and a grated hard-cooked egg—a wildly improbable but delectably tonic soup.

YOGURT-AND BUTTERMILK-BASED SOUPS

*T*art, tangy, incredibly refreshing, yogurt and buttermilk are exquisite cultured-milk products, especially suited for uncooked summertime soups. Each has its own individual characteristics, but in uncooked dishes, they can often substitute for each other.

In the Ozark hills, buttermilk is

drunk at the table to this day, a taste acquired in the time before refrigerators. Many an Arkansawyer, great and small, sups happily on a big wedge of homemade cornbread crumbled into a glass or bowl of ice-cold buttermilk. Before you sneer, you'd better try it.

Yogurt is the thicker of the two, and

is famous for its healthfulness. Its benign bacteria create B-vitamins in the gastrointestinal tract. But more to the point, yogurt is delicious. Full-fat yogurt is creamy and rich; Brown Cow brand yogurt even has a layer of "yogurt cream" on the top—the stuff is out of this world. However, low-fat yogurt has a lightness that is most pleasant, and even some completely fat-free yogurts, such as Stonyfield, have a delicious flavor and lightness. In any case, tartness is a big part of yogurt appeal, as is its silken smoothness. Dannon, available all over America, is quite acceptable. Although yogurt can be cooked without curdling if a little care is exercised, heat will destroy those friendly bacteria.

To get good buttermilk, it is necessary to be an informed consumer. Read the label on the carton. If it has a long list of chemicals, additives, thickeners, butterflakes, and gums, pass it by. It should list just one ingredient—cultured buttermilk. This is often called "Bulgarian-style." If you have only had "chemicalized" buttermilk, you have a treat in store when you taste the real thing—it's tart, tangy, flavorful where the other is—well, once you've tasted the real thing, you'll know—fakey. By the way, buttermilk when heated curdles far more easily than yogurt.

Yogurt Cream of Jerusalem Artichoke Soup

ears and years ago I got a yogurt maker as a gift. I never did keep up with making yogurt on a regular basis, but I loved the soup recipe that came with the machine, an early version of the following. My version is a little homey—I've never served it in the restaurant, for instance—but I remain abidingly loyal to its sweet-tangy flavors.

5 cups Chicken Stock 1 (page 19) or Basic
*   Golden Vegetable Stock (page 28) or any*
*   well-flavored chicken or vegetable*
*   stock*
1 pound fresh Jerusalem artichokes,
*   scrubbed and sliced about ¼ inch thick*
2 tablespoons butter or mild vegetable oil,
*   such as corn or peanut*
1 large onion, chopped
2 teaspoons tamari/shoyu soy sauce, or to
*   taste*
3 tablespoons unbleached all-purpose flour
2 cups plain yogurt
1 teaspoon honey or sugar, or to taste
Salt and freshly ground black pepper to
*   taste*
Tiny Garlic Croutons (page 259), for
*   garnish*
Finely chopped fresh parsley, for garnish
Paprika, for garnish

1. In a large soup pot, bring the stock to a boil. Drop in the Jerusalem artichokes, turn down the heat to medium-low, and let simmer, covered, until tender, 20 minutes.

2. Meanwhile, in a 10-inch skillet melt the butter over medium heat. Add the onion and sauté until it starts to soften, about 3 minutes. Add the soy sauce and cook until the liquid evaporates. Sprinkle the flour on and cook, stirring constantly, about 3 minutes. Add about 1 cup of the

hot stock, stirring to smooth any lumps and cook, stirring often, until smooth and thickened, and there's no raw-flour taste, about 5 minutes. Add the yogurt and remove from the heat.

3. Whisk the yogurt mixture into the stock and artichokes. Cook over very low heat until hot through; do not boil. Sweeten with the honey and season with salt and pepper. Serve immediately, garnished with the croutons and a sprinkle of parsley and paprika.

Serves 6 to 7 as a starter

OH, JERUSALEM

Jerusalem artichokes have less than nothing to do with real artichokes. They are in fact knotty, potatolike tubers—the delicious edible root of the common sunflower. They are quite sweet in flavor. When raw, they are crunchy and very much like water chestnuts or jicama. When cooked, their taste is something between that of sweet corn and sweet potatoes. Oddly, belying their taste and texture, they are not starchy, which makes them a sterling potato substitute for diabetics. A very good high protein pasta made from Jerusalem artichoke flour is available at natural foods stores.

Scrub Jerusalem artichokes extremely well, for dirt hides in their knottier portions. Some people peel them before cooking and some after (the peel comes off much more easily after cooking but you have to remove the peel while the artichokes are still fairly hot), and some, like myself, don't peel them at all.

The common explanation for the Jerusalem of the name is that it is a corruption of girasole, Italian for sunflower. But that still leaves "artichoke" unexplained, and, besides, why should a native American plant bear an Italian misnomer? Puzzle it all you like, but do get to know this underappreciated vegetable.

Turkish Noodle Soup with Mint and Yogurt

ave faith in me on this one, gang. If I'd first seen it in a cookbook, I'd be skeptical, too; the ingredients couldn't be more improbable. Fortunately, I had it in a Turkish restaurant in New York many years ago before I knew what was in it. I loved it so much I tried hard to get the recipe, even stooping to flirtation. I was only twenty-two or so and could still get away with stuff like that, but perhaps not with the proficiency I would have wished, for the chef would only part with the ingredients (though he did send over an anisette).

From his list, I played with the ingredients, until reaching this approximation. The result is just *delicious*—too good to believe, and quite healthful. I crave it regularly. The soup's starch is up to you: very thin pasta, barley, rice, or, as I first had it, oatmeal. I like pasta the best.

This soup's quite tangy; I like it that way. If you are a major yogurt lover like me, go for fifty-fifty yogurt and stock on the liquid; but if you are less fond of yogurt, try 1 part yogurt to 4 parts stock or water.

Pam cooking spray
1 teaspoon unbleached all-purpose flour
3 cups plain yogurt
1 large egg, lightly beaten
4 cups any well-flavored vegetable or chicken stock
4 ounces vermicelli or angel hair pasta, or ⅓ cup old-fashioned rolled oats
2 tablespoons butter
1 large onion, chopped
5 cloves garlic, peeled and put through a garlic press or finely chopped
½ cup lightly packed fresh mint leaves, chopped, or 2 tablespoons dried
Salt and freshly ground black pepper to taste
Freshly grated Parmesan cheese, for serving (optional)

1. Spray a heavy soup pot with the Pam, and in it mix the flour and ½ cup of the yogurt. Add the egg and whisk until smooth. Add the remaining yogurt and the stock; stir until blended. Bring to a boil, stirring frequently, then turn down the heat to medium-low, add the pasta or oatmeal, and simmer, uncovered, about 10 minutes.

2. Meanwhile, in a 10-inch skillet, melt the butter over medium heat. Add the onion and sauté until it starts to soften, about 3 minutes. Add the garlic and mint; sauté 1 minute more, stirring constantly. Remove from the heat and add to the yogurt mixture.

3. Simmer the soup another 5 minutes. Season with salt and pepper and serve hot, passing the Parmesan cheese at the table. The soup will keep in the refrigerator for a day. If refrigerated, reheat gently and thin it with additional stock since the soup thickens on standing.

Serves 4 as an entrée when accompanied by salad and bread

VARIATIONS:

Turkish Rice Soup: Cook ½ cup converted long-grain rice in 1 cup water for 10 minutes. Meanwhile, begin the soup in a separate pot. Add the partially cooked rice and any un-absorbed rice cooking water to the soup after all the yogurt has been added in step 1. Proceed with the recipe.

Turkish Barley Soup: Follow the same method above, using ¼ cup barley to 1 cup water.

> **"**He handed me a big tomato, scarlet, fragrant, less than twelve hours from its vine. 'That colour is the sunlight,' he told me, 'The skins of fruits and vegetables are subtly charged with the properties of the life-giving sun. Eat it and you will understand magic.'**"**
>
> —HENRI CHARPENTIER,
> *THOSE RICH & GREAT ONES, OR LIFE
> À LA HENRI*

Chilled Tomato Soup with Basil and Buttermilk

his is as close as I get to regular tomato gazpacho, a soup I ought to like but don't. This is, to me,

far more interesting and refreshing. The buttermilk must be best-quality Bulgarian-style; if you can't get it, substitute plain yogurt or plain, yogurtlike kefir, not kefir cheese. And don't even consider making this soup with winter tomatoes; you need the garden-red, heavy globes, and that's it.

6 ripe garden tomatoes, coarsely chopped
¼ cup lightly packed fresh basil leaves
1 clove garlic, peeled and coarsely chopped
Salt and freshly ground black pepper to taste
1 cup Bulgarian-style buttermilk, plain yogurt, Cottage Cream (page 52), or plain kefir
Sugar or lemon juice if needed
Sliced scallions, for garnish

▶ In a food processor, purée the tomatoes, basil, garlic, salt, and pepper until smooth. For absolute smoothness, put the purée through a food mill, fine sieve, or power strainer. Stir in the buttermilk and taste for seasoning. You may wish to add a touch of sugar or a few drops of lemon juice. Chill deeply and serve in iced cups, garnished with the scallions.

Serves 4 as a starter

VARIATION:
You can pass minced onion, minced green and red bell peppers, chopped tomatoes, and diced cucumber at the table to let guests amend their soup if they like.

Marge Parkhurst's Yogurt Cream of Celery Soup

arge and her husband, John, are both fine Eureka cooks and the guiding spirits behind Ozark Creative Writers, a group that has its annual conference here in October. Lifelong food people, they put out a newsletter called "The Peppermill." It's always a cheery day when one arrives in my mailbox.

Marge says she suffers from "depression mentality, though I'm never depressed. My motto in cooking is using whatever is in the refrigerator, whatever I have, whatever is on sale. Waste bothers me." This tangy, simple, delicious celery soup accommodates itself to whatever is on hand.

½ cup (1 stick) butter or margarine
2 to 3 bunches celery, sliced crosswise into ½-inch-thick pieces
4 cups (or as needed) spring water or Golden Vegetable Stock (page 28) or Chicken Stock 1 (page 19) or any well-flavored vegetable or chicken stock
Grated zest and juice of 1 lemon or lime
Salt and freshly ground black pepper to taste
1 cup plain yogurt, heavy (whipping) cream, or milk

1. In a 10-inch skillet, melt half the butter over medium-low heat. Add half the celery and sauté until slightly softened, about 5 minutes. Scrape the celery into a heavy soup pot. Repeat this step with the remaining butter and celery.

2. Add enough spring water or stock to cover the celery. Bring to a boil, then turn down the heat to medium-low and let simmer, covered, until the celery is tender, about 10 minutes.

3. Drain the celery, returning the stock to the pot. Set aside about half the celery, and purée the rest in a food processor. Add the whole celery and celery purée, lemon zest and juice, salt, and pepper to the stock and heat through. Stir in the yogurt and heat through again. Serve immediately.

Serves 4 to 6 as a starter

Chilled Corn Chowder with Dill and Scallions

here is no earthly reason why something so simple should be so good. Much depends on the sweetness of the corn, so make sure it is fresh and good. Restorative, refreshing, and easy for summer.

2 cups cooked corn kernels
1 bunch scallions, white and 2 inches of
    green, sliced
Juice of ½ lime or lemon
2 teaspoons fresh dill leaves
Salt and freshly ground black pepper to
    taste
1 quart Bulgarian-style buttermilk or plain
    yogurt
Small fresh dill sprigs for garnish

▶ In a food processor, purée the corn, scallions, lime juice, dill, salt, and pepper until smooth. Add 1 cup of the buttermilk and process until blended. Transfer the mixture to a bowl and whisk in the remaining buttermilk. Chill deeply. Serve in frosted glasses or chilled cups, garnished with dill sprigs.

Serves 4 to 5 as a starter

"Good Foods" Cucumber Yogurt Soup

Everybody has a cucumber yogurt soup, which they will tell you is refreshing and easy. I couldn't resist adding my couldn't-be-simpler version to those of the throng. It originated with a recipe card promoting Good Foods yogurt I found in a health food store more than a decade ago. This soup is a summertime staple.

It has a thin consistency, which makes it perfect for sipping.

4 cups peeled, sliced, seeded cucumbers (see
    Note)
2 cups spring water
2 cups plain yogurt
2 or 3 cloves garlic, peeled and put through
    a garlic press or finely chopped
1 tablespoon walnuts, lightly toasted (page
    316)
¼ cup lightly packed fresh mint leaves
1 tablespoon finely chopped fresh dill
1 teaspoon honey
Salt and freshly ground black pepper to
    taste

▶ Put half of the cucumber slices in a food processor with the remaining ingredients and purée. Transfer the purée to a bowl. Stir in the remaining cucumbers and chill at least 4 hours before serving.

Serves 6 to 8 as a starter

Note: To seed the cucumbers, slice them in half lengthwise and scrape out the seeds with the tip of a spoon.

Yogurt Soup with Fresh Dill

Another fresh-flavored, quick summer soup, good hot or cold, with a texture that is smooth and custardlike.

5 cups Chicken Stock 1 (page 19) or
    Golden Vegetable Stock (page 28) or any
    well-flavored chicken or vegetable
    stock
1 fist-sized all-purpose potato, scrubbed or
    peeled and chopped
1 medium carrot, scrubbed or peeled and
    sliced
2 tablespoons mild vegetable oil, such as
    corn or peanut
1 large onion, chopped
1 rib celery with leaves, chopped
1 cup plain yogurt
2 large egg yolks
¼ to ⅓ cup lightly packed chopped fresh
    dill, or to taste
Salt and freshly ground black
    pepper to taste
Sour cream or plain
    yogurt, for garnish
Finely chopped fresh
    parsley, or small
    dill sprigs, for garnish

1. In a heavy soup pot, bring the stock
to a boil. Add the potato, turn down the heat
to medium-low, and let simmer, covered, for
10 minutes. Add the carrot and continue to
simmer until the carrot starts to soften, about
5 minutes.

2. In a 10-inch skillet, heat the oil over
medium heat. Add the onion and sauté until
it starts to soften, about 3 minutes. Add the
celery and continue to sauté 2 to 3 minutes.
Scrape the vegetables into the soup pot.
Cover and simmer 30 minutes.

3. Drain the vegetables, returning the
stock to the pot. Purée the vegetables in a
food processor, then stir the purée into the
stock. Heat to a near boil.

4. Whisk the yogurt and egg yolks to-

gether in a small bowl, then whisk in a ladleful of the hot soup. Turn down the heat
under the stock until the liquid barely simmers. Stir the yogurt mixture into the stock
and cook over medium-low heat, stirring
gently but frequently, until slightly thickened.
Remove from the heat. Stir in the dill and
add the salt and pepper to taste. Serve at
once, or chill deeply and serve cold. Either
way, garnish each serving with a dab of sour
cream or yogurt and a sprinkle of parsley or
dill sprigs.

Serves 6 as a starter

MID-JULY DINNER TO
CELEBRATE THE BLOOMING
OF THE GRAND
COMMANDER LILLIES

Yogurt Soup with Fresh Dill

*Curried Lentil Salad with
Vegetables*

Oven-Poached Rainbow
Trout with Tomatoes
Provençale

Zucchini Stuffed with Herbed
Rice

Lemon Meringue Pie

ON DIETARY SENSITIVITIES: NOTES FOR HOST AND GUEST

❦ *Perhaps I'm just sensitive to this because a member of my family and several close friends belong to Alcoholics Anonymous, but there are many people who cannot touch even a small amount of alcohol. Any good host should be aware of this. Even wine cooked in soup for a lengthy amount of time can trigger reactions in people who can't tolerate it and a host would do best considering a substitute dish, if unsure of a guest's preferences.*

Certain alcoholic additions to soups are put in at the last minute. These include liqueurs and cordials and the occasional last-minute shot of vermouth or cognac or sherry. In such cases, one can simply pass the liquor in a small pitcher at table, so that diners may amend their potage individually.

This brings up the whole question of special diets, allergies, dislikes of a specific food, and preferences on principle, such as vegetarianism. It's my feeling that any good host, innkeeper, or restaurateur should absolutely and graciously accommodate any diner who cannot, should not, or doesn't want to eat a particular food. A big deal should not be made of it; it's not like the person chose to break out in a rash at the sight of strawberries, or became a vegetarian to irritate the kitchen staff. If a low-cholesterol diet will help keep my friend or guest around this mortal coil for an extra decade or two, believe me, I want to do everything in my power to make it

possible for him or her to stay on the diet easily. When questioned as to whether working with the given dietary restriction would be possible, the attitude of the server, host, or chef must and should be a heartfelt, "Of course, it's no problem at all." And if the guest has met his or her responsibility, it won't be.

For the guest has a responsibility here, too. And that is, let a host know in advance about particular food sensitivities. Whether a "host" is the one who invited you to dinner, the innkeeper who wants to make your stay perfect down to the last detail, or a Swiss-trained maître d', each wants to meet your needs, and have you delighted with the whole experience. For goodness sake, don't avoid telling because you feel it will call attention to yourself or make trouble. It causes much more trouble to quietly pick around and hope no one will notice; someone will. You'll be unhappy because you can't eat the entrée with the green peppers; your hosts will wonder what was wrong with the eggplant Provençale.

I still sigh over the gentleman in the Peach Blossom Suite who said, as Ned was delivering his breakfast basket with its piping hot orange muffins, its shirred eggs Mornay in their cunning ramekins, its cinnamon sugar-glazed baked apple, "Oh, hi, Ned. Listen, I forgot to tell you I'm allergic to wheat, eggs, milk, and milk products—and I don't eat sugar." ❦

CHEESE SOUPS

Blue Satin Broccoli Soup

his is my variation of one of Maytag's (see page 278) own recipes—delicate and truly delicious. Of course, first make sure those you are serving it to are blue cheese lovers.

1 bunch broccoli
3½ cups Chicken Stock 1 (page 19) or Golden Vegetable Stock (page 28) or any well-flavored chicken or vegetable stock
4 tablespoons (½ stick) butter
1 large onion, chopped
1 rib celery with leaves, chopped
1 carrot, scrubbed or peeled and sliced
1 green bell pepper, cored, seeded, and diced
⅓ cup unbleached all-purpose flour
4 ounces Maytag Blue cheese or any good-quality blue cheese, crumbled
1 cup half-and-half
1 cup milk
¼ cup dry sherry
Small pinch of cayenne pepper, or dash of Tabasco or similar hot pepper sauce
Freshly grated nutmeg to taste
Salt and freshly ground black pepper to taste
Toasted slivered almonds or Tiny Garlic Croutons (page 259), for garnish

1. Trim the tough ends from the broccoli stems. Cut off and separate the flowerets. Peel the stems and cut into strips, about ½ inch long and ¼ inch wide. In a heavy soup pot, bring the stock to a boil. Add the broccoli flowerets and boil 5 minutes. Drain the flowerets, returning the stock to the pot, and quickly cool the broccoli under cold running water.

2. In a 10-inch skillet, melt the butter over medium heat. Add the onion and sauté until it starts to soften, about 3 minutes. Add the broccoli stems, celery, carrot, and bell pepper. Cover the skillet and let the vegetables steam for 2 minutes. Remove the lid, sprinkle the flour over the vegetables, and cook, stirring constantly, about 3 minutes.

3. Gradually add the warm stock, stirring to smooth any lumps. Simmer, stirring often, for several minutes. In a food processor, purée this mixture in batches, and transfer to the soup pot.

4. Heat the purée over medium heat until hot. Add the blue cheese and cook, stirring constantly, until smooth. Stir in the half-and-half and milk; heat until very hot but not boiling. Stir in the sherry, cayenne, nutmeg, salt, pepper, and the broccoli flowerets. Taste for seasoning. Heat through and serve immediately, garnished with the toasted almonds or garlic croutons.

Serves 6 to 8 as a starter

SINGING THE MAYTAG BLUES

You know the TV ad about the lonely Maytag repairman? It may have had its start because of one of the original Maytags—Elmer, to be precise. He was, if not lonely, at least bored with washing machines as his sole occupation. His pride and joy was dairy farming, and his herd of prize-winning Holstein-Frisians.

Two sons inherited Elmer's model dairy farms. Though less fascinated with things bovine than their father, they kept the operation. Then, "happily," according to the Maytag account, "about that time, Iowa State University had patented a process for making blue cheese. A marriage was arranged—the Maytag family would build the plant and caves, the university would train the cheesemakers.

The marriage worked, and in 1941 the first wheels of Maytag Blue rolled off. Little has changed in the production method since then. The cheese is still entirely made by hand and is fully aged. Virtually all of the cheese is sold by mail order, and it's still a very small, friendly family operation."

The cheese is made in Newton, Iowa, where Ned's sister lived with her husband and three children for several years. Their annual Christmas present to us was often a wheel of delicious, rich, and creamy Maytag Blue. We rationed our Christmas Maytag very carefully!

To get your own Maytag catalog, write Maytag Dairy Farms, Route 1, Box 806, Newton, Iowa 50208; or call (800) 247-2458. In Iowa call (800) 258-2437.

Cream of Pear and Spinach Soup Miss Kay

In every cookbook I do, I dedicate at least one recipe to Miss Kay, my first cooking mentor.

Miss Kay initiated me into much kitchen arcana, including the combination of blue cheese and pears, a collaboration that still wins me decades later. In 1990 I headed to Florida for Miss Kay's 100th birthday. This is for you, Miss Kay. Happy Birthday!

Additional yogurt, or crème fraîche, may be substituted for the heavy cream called for here.

2 tablespoons butter or mild vegetable oil,
    such as corn or peanut
3 large leeks, white part and 2 inches
    green, split open lengthwise, well washed,
    and thinly sliced
1 bunch celery with leaves, chopped
1½ pounds fresh spinach, stems included,
    well rinsed
5 cups Chicken Stock 1 (page 19) or
    Golden Vegetable Stock (page 28) or any
    well-flavored chicken or vegetable
    stock
1 pound ripe pears (2 or 3 depending on
    the size), peeled, cored, quartered, and
    coarsely chopped
4 ounces Maytag Blue cheese, crumbled
½ cup heavy (whipping) cream
¼ cup plain yogurt, Crème Fraîche (page
    50), sour cream, or kefir cheese
Salt and freshly ground black pepper to
    taste
Sour cream or plain yogurt, for garnish
Small spinach leaves, for garnish

1. In a 10-inch skillet, melt the butter over medium heat. Add the leeks and sauté until they start to soften, about 3 minutes. Add the celery and sauté 5 minutes more. Pile the spinach in the skillet and cover with a heavy lid. Turn down the heat slightly and steam until the spinach wilts, about 5 minutes.

2. Meanwhile, in a heavy soup pot bring 1 cup of the stock to a boil. Add the pears and simmer, covered, over medium heat until quite tender, about 15 minutes.

3. Transfer the pears with their cooking liquid and the spinach mixture to a food processor and purée. For absolute smoothness, put the purée through a food mill, sieve, or power strainer. Pour the purée into the soup pot.

4. Add the remaining 4 cups of stock

to the soup pot and heat until hot. Whisk in the blue cheese and cook, stirring frequently, until smooth. Add the cream and yogurt, or other dairy choice, and season with salt and pepper. Heat through but do not let the soup boil after the cheese has been added. Serve very hot, garnished with a dab of sour cream or yogurt and a small spinach leaf.

Serves 4 to 6 as a starter

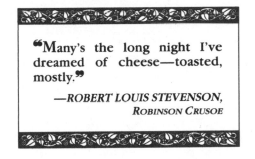

"Many's the long night I've dreamed of cheese—toasted, mostly."

—ROBERT LOUIS STEVENSON,
        ROBINSON CRUSOE

Tomato and Potato Cheddar Soup with Beer

his is a variation on our beloved pear and potato soup in *Dairy Hollow House Cookbook*. Rich, hearty, and warming—like its straight-potato cousin, this is a soup I always think of when the weather first gets cold. This is exceptional made with Vermont Cheddar, a white, sharp, supremely tasty cheese that melts wonderfully well.

Pam cooking spray

2 cups beer or ale

5 or 6 large all-purpose potatoes, scrubbed,
sliced ¼ inch thick

4 cups, approximately, Chicken Stock 1
(page 19) or Golden Vegetable Stock
(page 28) or any well-flavored chicken
or vegetable stock, or spring water

3 bay leaves

½ teaspoon dried basil

½ teaspoon dried oregano

4 tablespoons (½ stick) butter or mild
vegetable oil

1 large onion, chopped

1 rib celery with leaves, chopped

1 medium carrot, scrubbed or peeled and
sliced

5 cloves garlic, peeled and put through a
garlic press or finely chopped

5 ripe tomatoes, coarsely chopped, or 1 can
(15 ounces) whole tomatoes with their
juice, coarsely chopped

1 tablespoon tamari/shoyu soy sauce, or to
taste

2 teaspoons Pickapeppa or Worcestershire
sauce

2 tablespoons all-purpose flour

1 cup heavy (whipping) cream or
evaporated skim milk

Tabasco or similar hot pepper sauce to taste

½ teaspoon dry mustard

12 ounces extra-sharp Cheddar cheese,
shredded

Salt and freshly ground black pepper to
taste

Finely chopped fresh parsley, for garnish

1. Spray a large heavy pot with Pam, and in it pour the beer. Add the potatoes and enough stock or spring water to cover. Add the bay leaves, basil, and oregano. Bring to a boil, then turn down the heat to medium-low and let simmer, covered, until the potatoes are tender, about 30 minutes.

2. Meanwhile, in a 10-inch skillet melt the butter over medium heat. Add the onion and sauté until it starts to soften, about 3 minutes. Add the celery, carrot, and garlic; sauté 5 minutes more. Stir in the tomatoes, and soy and Pickapeppa or Worcestershire sauces. Increase the heat to medium-high and cook, stirring frequently, until the liquid evaporates and the mixture is a thick paste, 10 to 20 minutes. Sprinkle the flour over the mixture; cook, stirring constantly, 1 to 2 minutes. Gradually add the cream, stirring constantly. Continue to cook until smooth and thick. Season with the hot pepper sauce and dry mustard.

3. Stir the cream mixture into the soup pot. Turn down the heat so that the liquid barely simmers and stir in the cheese. Cook, stirring often, until the cheese is melted and the potatoes are falling-apart tender, about 20 minutes. Keep the heat very, very low and stir often, for the soup will want to stick. If possible, let the soup sit a couple hours before reheating and serving. Season with salt and pepper. Serve hot, garnished with the parsley.

Serves 6 to 8 as an entrée

Sweet Harvest

FRUIT SOUPS

n northwest Arkansas in early February, spring seems distant some days. But all at once, no matter if it's gray and chill, a blaze of yellow lights up the still-wintry garden, vivid against the gray limestone wall. And in front of it, there's a wash of intense violet-blue. The King Alfred daffodils and iris *reticulata* are in bloom once more; the old creaking world has renewed itself again.

Soon after this, I might find asparagus and strawberries at the produce section at Hart's, and after that our own asparagus, and sugar snaps (from our garden some years, or, in busier years, from the folks at Dripping Springs Garden or elsewhere). After that, it's only a few more busy, flying-by weeks as visitors begin returning to town, tulips, lilacs, redbuds, and dogwoods bud, in their turn, then blossom, and go until our own, infinitely more flavorful Arkansas strawberries are in season. We use them for shortcakes, on top of cereal or pancakes, in sweet breads, and, of course, in soup.

July brings local blueberries, acid and flavorful, with a sour-sweet tang more wild-tasting than cultivated and peculiar to the Ozarks. There's about a ten-day period in early July, when King's Berry Farm has raspberries, red and black. We call there daily to see how the harvest is looking (raspberries are very rain-sensitive, so the time of the yield, or even if there'll be one, is unsure and changing). Blackberries are another July crop with all-or-nothing dependency on rainfall; 1988 was a bountiful blackberry sum-

mer, and brought about my very favorite fruit soup of all, Blackberry Burgundy Soup, and shelves overflowing with jars of blackberry jam. The local summer apples also begin arriving in the too-hot July days. These are relatively undistinguished apples, it's true, but when we can't wait until October for fresh homemade apple pie, we zap the apples we have with a little lemon juice and come up with something mighty passable, especially when covered with thick, summer-yellow cream. By August, we're all groaning in anticipation of fall, living for the moments we can steal to get away to Beaver Lake to cool off. But even the dog days have their reward: incredibly juicy, full-flavored local peaches, and melons galore—honeydews, cantaloupes, and watermelons literally by the truckload.

The best of all this bounty is on display at the county fairs in early September (ours is the Carroll County Fair, held in nearby Berryville). By then, the first really good Arkansas apples have become available, and in a month or so there'll be the very best varieties: Arkansas Blacks, Black Twiggs, Stayman Winesaps. The pears have also arrived: exquisite, meltingly sweet pears for eating out of hand from Lisa and David Reeves over in Berryville, as well as firmer, tarter cooking pears, given to us each year by Ruth Eichor, sackfuls of them, from the hundred-year-old pear trees on her farm. Yo-anka offers still another variety of pear—ugly, bumpy things, but with a distinctive, utterly addictive

sweetness with the decided taste of burnt sugar.

FALL FLAVORS

October and November bring more tourists to our area than any other time of year. The trees blaze wondrously, the huge, dignified sycamores that line Spring Street are a vision as they canopy overhead in bright reds and golds—and, oh, those spectacular maples in front of the Eureka Inn, and that heartstopping one by Heart of the Hills Inn, and everywhere the vivid, vivid dogwoods, red leaved and hung with tiny red berries. Those of us who serve the public are frantically busy now, tired all the time, in high gear; our lives balanced only by the sweetness of stolen, here-and-there moments of seeing the beauty around us. I take a lot of late-night or early-morning walks this time of year, sometimes alone and sometimes with friends; we commiserate on how much too busy we are, we top each other's stories of outrageous overwork, as we inhale the loveliness around us. In late October and early November, we might pick some dead-ripe persimmons from a wild persimmon tree—sweet as a Medjool date, sensual, plump, and wrinkled. Ned and I married well over a decade ago in October in the Ozarks. When I see the year's first ripe persimmons, I remember picking a handful for Ned on one of our first walks together as husband and wife. He looked doubtful, astonished, and slightly impressed. But he bit into a persimmon and his eyes

widened with pleasure—game for anything, and full of trust.

I've already mentioned the serious apple contenders of the season: Winesaps, Arkansas Blacks, Black Twiggs. The Blacks are so fine an apple that my Uncle Joe, who was raised on a rice farm near McCrory, Arkansas, but later moved to New York, remembered them to his dying day. Knowing that I now lived in the state he'd called home, he mentioned those apples each time I saw him in his last years. The last two autumns of his life, there was no Black apple harvest at all due to hail, so I was unable to send him any. The October following his death, though, there was a fine crop: I sent three perfect Arkansas Blacks to my aunt. I thought, as I drove to Banta's Orchard that year, on a heartstopping beautiful late fall day, the sky a bright cloudless pure flag-blue, the trees ablaze, of something a friend of mine once said: that death interrupts an experience of life, but never life itself.

In the long days of December and January, we make do well enough with dried, frozen, and (occasionally) some home-canned fruit Yo-anka brings; and we rely on the bounty of other climes. Fresh cranberries are a bright note now in flavor and color; we use them a lot during their brief tenure for cranberry breads and muffins, cranberry pies and upside-down cakes, cranberry sorbet, and two perfect, festively bright cranberry soups. One is our own invention, one borrowed from The Inn at Long Last, in Vermont—both are fine holiday starters, chilled soups that really work in cold weather. For suddenly it's the holidays again—and it's time to embroider the names of last year's Christmas Eve party staff on the runner Jan Brown made for me years ago (see page 290).

When the holidays are over, all the tourists home, and most of the shops like our restaurant closed until spring, when the only outside colors beside the evergreens are the browns of the leafless trees and the blue and gray shadows they cast, it is comforting to come home from marketing and remove from the grocery bags those gleaming yellow and orange planets of citrus. The citruses add intriguing notes to many soups, but they star in our luscious soup, Orange Blossom Special. How much they add to winter life! Long before they're eaten, the eye consumes them. The oranges, grapefruits, limes, and lemons heaped in a crockery bowl on the pine table give a golden cast to the winter light, softened as it comes through the mist we have up here often in winter.

INN GOOD COMPANY: BECKY SISCO

❧ *It was a long haul to get Rebecca Sisco to come to work for us. From the minute I met her and saw that sweet smile and obliging but feisty, slightly sassy manner, I knew she was meant to be part of DHH.*

I first saw this essential "Beckyness" maybe a decade ago, when Ned and I rented a canoe from Trigger Gap, the float service she and her husband David run on the banks of the King's River (David is also produce manager at Hart's Family Center; almost everyone in Eureka has at least two jobs). I was pretty sure we had Becky intrigued for the long haul when, after badgering her for years to come and try working for us, she put in a stint as a Saturday morning breakfast chef.

Over the years, Becky (a blue-eyed blonde mother of three) experimented with just about every job we have to offer: not only part-time breakfast cook but bookkeeper (for one year), dinner server (pre-restaurant), and for two summers, Dairymaid. But when she discovered the front desk, the fit was perfect. She mixes easygoing warmth, fanatic attention to detail (essential for taking reservations) and a willingness to do whatever it takes to make a guest happy.

We got a fringe benefit in Becky, too. When guests ask, "Where on earth did you get these gorgeous artichokes?," it's fun to be able to reply with a shrug, "Oh, our front desk head's sleeping with the produce manager." ❧

On winter days I sometimes take a lemon and rub it between my palms. Its flowery smell belies its tartness; it evokes the languid lemonade-and-iced-tea days that have been and will come again. Days that are, as a person ages, closer and closer to each other, each season rejoiced in more for its brevity, days moving up and down like the horses on the carousel at the Carroll County Fair. On that carousel last year, I saw Peggy, our very first Dairymaid a decade ago—now married, with a child of her own. We waved gaily to each other, she and her child and husband all wearing glow-in-the-dark neon necklaces.

And so we circle. Our tenancy on this wondrous earth is brief, and fruit, each in its season, reminds us of that, making each bite even sweeter.

ABOUT FRUIT SOUPS

Fruit soups are still odd to many, making them all the more pleasant a surprise on a menu. If not too sweet, a good, clear-flavored fruit soup is a perfect and balancing addition to many different menus. Think of fruit's role as a starter: a really attentively done fresh fruit coupe, a wedge of melon or a perfect fig (maybe prosciutto-wrapped, maybe not) or, in a more formal meal, as a fruit in the form of sorbet, later in the meal. As starter or intermezzo, fruit's simplicity, clarity, and naturalness set off more complex, rich dishes. A fruit soup refreshes in this way.

Fruit soup is usually unsuitable as a main dish (though I have been known

> **"Let my beloved come to . . . his garden, and eat his choicest fruits."**
>
> —*Song of Solomon 4:16*

to make an at-home, nibbling-around-the-edges breakfast or lunch out of leftover fruit soup, maybe with yogurt and a piece of cinnamon toast). These soups are rarely hearty, nor are they dimensional—the best tend to be built around one or two ingredients. Too many flavors tend to compete, not coalesce, in a fruit soup, which can muddy the taste. Although there are some exceptions, a main ingredient or two predominates in most of the following recipes.

Most of the following soups are simple to make, sophisticated, versatile, and relatively low in calories. Yet they are *soups*—not juice, fruit yogurt, dessert, or that delicious but unsouplike concoction natural foods delis call a "smoothie." This is achieved by keeping the soups from being too sweet, and making sure they have a subtly "cooked" quality, whether chilled or hot.

Here are some tricks that allow single flavors to predominate, supply an unsweet note, and provide a cooked quality to fruit soups.

Use wine. The liquid best used in fruit soups, as stock is in other soups, is most often wine—sometimes red, sometimes white, sometimes a rosé. Even the driest wine has some fruity notes; its origins are after all in the

arbor. Wine's use frequently marries and matures the flavors of the fruit it is combined with, and it also cuts sweetness.

Use some thickening. To create a finished, non-dessert quality, I usually thicken the wine (or the stock I may be using) very slightly at some point. This necessitates a brief period of cooking. Most often this thickening is done before adding the wine or stock to the fruit preparation. Since many fruit soups are served cold, and since their whole reason for being is lightness and refreshment, I pass up heavier thickenings like butter and flour roux. Instead, I use a bit of cornstarch. This, in small amounts, is the perfect fruit soup thickener; it's fat-free and gives a lovely, jewellike high-gloss sheen. Do read, however, all the pointers and cautions on thickening with cornstarch below.

Sweeten minimally, but "fruitily." Although fruit soups should not be overly sweet, some sweetener is often necessary either because a fruit is particularly tart (like cranberries or blackberries), or to intensify flavor. Although I use sugar occasionally in the recipes that follow, more often I find the taste of honey, maple syrup, or, especially, undiluted frozen apple juice concentrate most compatible with fruit preparations. These do the trick, turning up the volume of the main ingredients without overpowering them, adding more than just sweetness. The same is true for the shots of liqueur, such as the Grand Marnier used in Orange Blossom Special, that, here and there, also find their way into the recipes.

For ultimate results, go for ultimate smoothness. Several of the recipes herein call for puréeing ingredients, then putting them through a strainer or food mill too. This is a bother; sometimes, however, as with Blackberry Burgundy Soup (page 290), it is vital, otherwise the miniscule hard seeds would mar a smooth, soulful texture. At other times, as with the divine Rosé and Apple Velvet Soup (page 288), straining is optional, but recommended; it takes out every bit of fibrous pulp and gives a texture of dreamy smoothness. The difference straining makes is between very good and superlative.

In this context I must tell you that power strainers take the tedium out of this activity. Cuisinart makes a good one, generally fine for home use. It is not, however, the sturdiest piece of equipment in the world. If you'll be doing lots of straining, a Champion juicer works even better, and holds up flawlessly. Serious cooks should investigate both.

THICKENING WITH CORNSTARCH

Thin broths and other liquidy soups may be rich and flavorful, but they lack body. In the case of a nonsweet soup, making a thin soup thicker is optional, depending on the use you plan to make of it in a given meal. But in the case of a fruit soup, where you definitely want to get across *soup,* not *juice,* the addition of a little—not too much—body is called for. Enter thickening.

Thickening, in one way or another, generally involves cooking a carbohydrate in the liquid to be thickened. Depending on the particular carbohydrate

a recipe calls for, the starch used "gives itself up" as a distinct entity, thereby thickening the liquid it's cooked in. In various recipes throughout this book, you'll find potato, rice, barley, and other grains, even bread, cooked in soups to thicken them. These sorts of thickenings result in substantial, stewlike soups, with chunks of potato, grain, or bread floating in them (unless, of course, you purée such soups in a food processor).

Cornstarch or flour produces a smoother texture than other kinds of thickening. Of the two, I prefer cornstarch in fruit soups, because it is easier to work with, and does not require a preliminary dispersal into fat as with a roux. A fat-free thickener gives a cleaner taste to the finished recipe, and a texture that has a natural affinity for fruit preparations. Of course, not having to use fat also saves calories and fat grams.

Don't confuse cornstarch and cornmeal; they are very different. Cornmeal is whole or degerminated grains of corn, ground. The starchy endosperm, the fiber, and (in whole-grain meals), the protein- and vitamin-rich germ, are included. Run a bit of cornmeal through

your fingers; the texture is granular.

Cornstarch, on the other hand, is pure carbohydrate. Pinch a bit of it and it feels powdery, not grainy; it has a "squeaky" texture.

Cornstarch is simple to work with. First of all, you'll want to combine it with a small part of the liquid called for in the recipe—wine, juice, broth, whatever. Mush the starch into the liquid with your fingers until no lumps are discernible either to the eye or the fingertips. (I usually do the mushing in a glass measuring cup into which I've measured the requisite amount of liquid.) The cornstarch will tend to settle, pastelike, to the bottom of the liquid, which will turn cloudy.

Meanwhile, as directed in specific recipes, you will have heated the remaining liquid, bringing it to a boil, then turning the heat down to get a very active simmer. Into this, you pour the dissolved cornstarch mixture, whisking a few times to incorporate it quickly, then stirring with a spoon. Soon—perhaps almost immediately, perhaps in a few minutes, depending on the specific recipe, the proportion of starch to liquid, and whether the liquid was hot enough when you added the paste—soon, the liquid will thicken. It will become smooth, visibly glossy, and thicker, with a pretty sheen. (We don't much use cornstarch as a thickener in America, but you'll recognize the characteristic sheen it produces from the look of Chinese restaurant sauces.) Taste the liquid—until you're used to working with thickeners you always should as a final precaution. When such a thickening is completed by cooking, the liquid will have no tinge of raw-floury taste or tex-

ture. At this point, remove the thickened liquid from the stove, and proceed with the recipe.

This is all a very simple, 1-2-3 process that, as in making an omelet or with most basic kitchen *modi operandi,* takes longer to explain than do. However, there are a few tricks to cornstarchery.

Cornstarch—now don't get alarmed —can unthicken after thickening, but not if you follow the rules I just set down. Remember to have the greater amount of liquid hot but not boiling when you stir in the cornstarch-liquid paste; it can be nerve wracking waiting for the liquid to thicken if it wasn't hot enough and can result in the two usual causes of failure, overcooking and overbeating. You want to stir often, but, other than that quick, immediate whisking, you want to stir gently; overbeating will break down the thickening. And so will overcooking; once the starch has done its work and the liquid is clear, free from cloudiness or a floury taste, remove it promptly from the heat, and continue with the next step.

I dedicate these directions to my mother, with whom, in my early cooking days, I have stood over many a pot, both of us wondering aloud, "Is it thick yet?"

Rosé and Apple Velvet Soup

f Eve had cooked the apple before offering it to Adam, this soup might have been how she'd have done it. Certain spices—ginger, nutmeg, clove, and most especially cinnamon—are so delicious with apples their use together has become a cliché. It is a formidable temptation for a cook not to reach for them automatically when doing an apple recipe. But unadulterated apple, if it's well flavored and cooked to intensify its appleness, is exquisite and surprises the palate, which subconsciously expects the spicy notes. This chilled soup has the charm of pure apple butter: no cinnamon or sugar, nothing but apples cooked to the point of essential, ambrosial taste. Rosé wine (red is too assertive, and white too wimpy) cuts the sweetness and colors the soup a lovely rusty rose.

This soup would be a good start for almost any dinner of simply roasted poultry or pork. It's one chilled soup that does as well in the winter as the summer, for it's also exquisite hot. Try it hot at a New Year's Eve supper, at any especially festive brunch, or, cold as a first course at Thanksgiving. One guest described it, saying, "Mmmm, applesauce for adults!" I know this doesn't sound appetizing, but he was most enthusiastic.

Pam cooking spray
4 cups plus 2 tablespoons rosé sec
1 cup firmly packed dried apple
    slices
2 tablespoons thawed frozen apple juice
    concentrate
2 tablespoons maple syrup
1 tablespoon cornstarch
Crème Fraîche (page 50) or plain yogurt,
    for garnish
Rose petals or toasted walnuts, for
    garnish (optional)

1. The day before cooking the soup, spray an enamel soup pot with the Pam. In it bring the 4 cups of rosé to a boil. Drop in the apple slices, turn down the heat to very low, and simmer, covered, 30 minutes. Remove from the heat and let the apples sit, covered, overnight.

2. The next day strain the apples from the rosé, returning the wine to the pot. Purée the apples in a food processor, then put the purée through a food mill, fine sieve, or power strainer, if you want an absolutely smooth soup.

3. Meanwhile, add the apple juice concentrate and maple syrup to the wine and bring to a boil. Turn down the heat and let simmer. Dissolve the cornstarch in the additional 2 tablespoons rosé or water and whisk this mixture into the hot liquid. Cook, stirring gently, until clear, smooth, and slightly thickened, and there is no uncooked starchy taste, which should be almost immediately. Remove from the heat and whisk in the apple purée.

4. Serve immediately or chill deeply. Garnish each bowl with a dab of crème fraîche or yogurt and, if you wish, a rose petal or a few toasted walnuts.

Serves 4 to 6 as a starter

VARIATION:
Okay, if you must, add 1 cinnamon stick and/ or a slice of fresh gingerroot, and a clove with the dried apples to the boiling wine; remove and discard these aromatics when you strain the apples. Top each bowlful of soup with unsweetened whipped cream, a slice of red apple, and a sprinkle of freshly grated nutmeg. This is great, all right, but try it first with just apples.

> **"We** would be pressing cider in a week, and our friends, acquaintances, and neighbors had begun bringing apples.... The fragrance of apples was strong. Blades of sunlight gleamed in the cracks between the boards, and the whole of the dusky, lofty space was striped with molten lines, vertical in the sides and horizontal in the gables.... (Soon) perhaps twenty people, adults and children, would be working and chattering here, some feeding apples to the motor-driven grinder in the loft, others pushing the pulp down a wooden chute, still others leveling it in layers on the platform of the huge old press. The fragrant, many colored apples, in the meantime, were waiting in boxes and feedbags by the grinder."
>
> —*GEORGE DENNISON,*
> *LUISA DOMIC*

CHRISTMAS AT THE INN: THE DAIRY HOLLOW TABLE-RUNNER

The pleasures of the kitchen and table are only one phase of the sensual, tangible joys of inn-keeping. When I work in the farmhouse garden at the time the ancient peony—the one that was here long before we came—is blooming; when I make flower arrangements with the spring dogwood and the bright red tulips, or hold up paint sample chips against tiles for the redo of the Iris Room bath; when I scrunch six calicos together in my hand for curtains, to see how the colors and patterns work together; when I do these things, I know how fortunate I am to have this diverse, sense-filling life of connection and sweetness.

And then there is the Christmas table-runner.

Even before I met Ned, my friend Bill Haymes and I had been having Christmas Eves together for years. By 1984, the year the table-runner debuted, Ned and I had been married six years, Haymes had bought the inn with us two years earlier, we were all three good friends. Christmas Eve dinner had become a Dairy Hollow tradition. It was the annual staff party—staff then meaning us, Jan Brown and her husband Blake, and friends of the inn (like Louis and Elsie, see page 309).

Another tradition had also developed. Because there was at that time no place to get ethnic food in Eureka Springs, each year we'd pick a different nationality and (after some serious hitting the cookbooks) do a whole dinner of its food. Recipes would be distributed, and each person would bring a dish or two. We did French, Russian, Mexican, Polish, and Greek dinners this way; we did what we wound up calling Morrocc'n'Roll (cous-cous—plus-plus). Eventually this evolved to regions of foreign countries as well as the U.S.; we did Tuscany and Provence; we did New Mexico Mexican. When we did France we discovered the charming custom of the Revillion, or Christmas Eve dinner, which traditionally has 13 desserts, one representing each apostle, and one for Christ. Well, hey, we thought, anything for dessert. The 13 desserts, regardless of nationality, joined us the year of France and has remained part of the cheerful and caloric madness ever since.

And there was another change. Dairy Hollow House kept growing. Pretty soon we had more and more staff and more and more "friends of," and it got difficult to schedule Christmas Eve, since many people had other commitments. So the party got moved to December 23, a day we took to calling "Christmas

Adam." We also started opening up the dessert part to any guests who were staying at the inn at this time.

And through it all was the runner.

Now, I forget where we got the idea from, but sometime in 1984, Jan Brown and I talked over this concept: a festive, decorative table-runner; a panel of cloth to be used on the Christmas table, and which could be signed by guests at the annual party. After the party, I'd embroider in the year, then the nationality we had celebrated and where we had done our celebrating—perhaps the restaurant, perhaps its kitchen, and so on. Last, I'd embroider in the signatures—all in one specific chosen color for each year, so a glance could tell us, in years to come, who had been there when.

Jan came up with the actual runner, and it's a beautiful, quirky piece of work, a panel of white cloth, edged in pieced patchwork patterns, mostly in Christmas colors, but with a few recycled old pieces, sweetly faded and breathing history, thrown in. And I, by God, have stuck with it all these years, embroidering those names, year after year. I usually wind up finishing the cloth at the last minute—a week before the party of 1996, count on it, I'll be doing '95's names. I have done this last-minute embroidery on a plane, at home, at other people's homes; I have sometimes completed it the day of the party. Occasionally Ned takes pity on me and picks up

thread and needle, and actually embroiders in a name or two himself. Really, it's pleasant, restful work—you wind up sort of meditating on the person whose name you're embroidering, and thinking over the previous year and all its changes and demands—it's nice, thoughtful.

All those years, all those nationalities, all those friends. And did I mention that in 1990 the table-runner grew? Yes, Jan Brown turned it into a table-cloth; she had to, we were running out of space for the names, and she did this border of trees. . . . And I see I haven't said a word about some other DHH holiday traditions, like the Sugardumb Fairy, who dons a white tutu and attempts to distribute the gifts (only she is not very bright, and the kids have to help her) and the annual appearance of the Farquardt Family, the imaginary hillbilly family to which we all belong, Ferral Farquardt and Hazel Nutt Farquardt, April May (affectionately known to us as "Apey") Farquardt and Foggy Farquardt, Velveeta Farquardt and Sammy Farquardt, and Zebulon and Magnolia and Bucky and all the rest; and the Farquardt family song and the official Farquardt family joke. . . .

No. There's no time to go into all that. But I'll tell you this much: I can look at Morocc'n'roll (1987; orangey-yellow) and tell you exactly who was there that year. And many of them still come. And I'll tell you this: it makes a person feel good.

Apey May, I know she'd agree with me. ❧

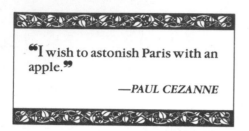

Curried Apple and Sweet Potato Soup

T his sweet-hot soup, heartier and less single-minded of flavor than most fruit soups, took inspiration from a bowl of organic apples brought to me by farmer David Reeves and my daydreaming of a return to India.

In India they have no curry powder as such but combine different spices for each dish. Usually the spices are first cooked in oil or ghee (clarified butter), which makes all the difference in the world. I've used curry powder here rather than specify individual spices, but I did stick with that vital, taming precooking. Beer in the stock adds a pleasant dusky, unsweet note, playing off the sweetness of the apples, the sweet potatoes, and the heat of the curry.

Soaking is involved, so start a few hours ahead of time. In fact, it's best to put this together a day or two before you plan to serve it so the flavors have a chance to meld nicely.

¼ cup dark raisins
1 bottle (12 ounces) light pilsner beer, such as Labatt's Blue
4 tablespoons (½ stick) butter
1 onion, diced
2 tart apples, unpeeled, cored and diced
1 tablespoon best-quality curry powder
2 teaspoons finely minced fresh gingerroot
2 tablespoons unbleached all-purpose flour
Pam cooking spray
3 to 4 cups any well-flavored chicken or vegetable stock
¼ cup thawed frozen apple juice concentrate, or more to taste
1 piece (1 inch) cinnamon stick
1 teaspoon tamari/shoyu soy sauce, or more to taste
2 medium sweet potatoes, peeled and finely diced
Salt and freshly ground white pepper to taste
Cayenne pepper to taste (optional)
1 red-skinned apple, cored and cut into large julienne, for garnish
Crème Fraîche (page 50), sour cream, or plain yogurt, for garnish
Thin lemon wedges, for serving

1. In a bowl, soak the raisins in the beer for at least 30 minutes or as long as overnight.

2. When you are ready to start making the soup, melt the butter in a 10-inch skillet over medium heat. Add the onion and sauté until it starts to soften, about 3 minutes. Add the diced apples and sauté again until somewhat softened, 3 to 4 minutes. Sprinkle with the curry powder, turn down the heat to medium-low, and cook, stirring often, about 8 minutes. Stir in the ginger and cook 2 minutes longer.

3. Meanwhile, drain the raisins, reserving both the beer and the raisins. Sprinkle

the flour over the apple mixture and cook over low heat 1 minute. Gradually add the beer, stirring to smooth any lumps, and cook until hot, smooth, and free of a floury taste, 5 to 7 minutes. Transfer this mixture to a food processor. Add the raisins and buzz until smooth.

4. Spray a heavy enameled soup pot with the Pam, and in it combine the stock, apple juice concentrate, cinnamon stick, and soy sauce. Bring to a boil, add the sweet potatoes, and turn down the heat. Simmer, partially covered, until the potatoes are tender, about 30 minutes.

5. Remove the cinnamon stick from the hot stock and stir in the apple purée. Season with salt and white pepper. You may wish to add a bit more apple juice concentrate to sweeten it, a pinch of cayenne if you want it spicier, and/or a little more soy sauce. Simmer over low heat for several minutes more to meld the flavors.

6. Ladle the hot soup into bowls, sprinkle each bowl with the julienned apple, and top with a generous dollop of crème fraîche, sour cream, or yogurt. Pass the lemon wedges at the table; a squeeze sets this soup off nicely, but it's also good without.

Serves 6 to 8

VARIATION:

For a more peasanty main dish, add 1 or 2 chopped tomatoes to the apple sauté before adding the flour and cook until most of the tomato juice evaporates. Add 1 can (15 ounces) chick-peas to the soup with the apple purée and thin the soup with a little stock. This combination sounds improbable, but it's surprisingly good and satisfying. No apple or crème fraîche garnish, though.

Déjà Food: Measure leftover soup and pour it into a food processor. Add half as much heavy or light cream, or milk thickened with cornstarch (page 286), and purée. Heat through. This makes a more elegant soup, suitable as a starter for a sophisticated dinner.

BANANAS

When Ned and I first lived together, he was working on a how-to book about renovation in Little Rock's 1880 Governor's Mansion Historic District called "Fixing Up Your Old House." He had illustrated it liberally with many drawings of gutters, drains, window sashes, and so on, and how one might best repair them. In most cases several examples of good, mediocre, and poor repairs were shown, each labeled Yes, No, or Maybe.

One day Ned was going marketing and I had written "bananas" on the list. "Now, listen, I need them for tonight," I told him, ever the cheerfully bossy wife.

"Please be sure and get some with dark spots on them. A lot of spots is best, though a few will do, but definitely not greenish yellow." Even as I spoke, Ned had quickly sketched three bananas on the market pad—Yes, No, and Maybe bananas.

When he came back from shopping, he said, "You'll be happy to know they had bananas that were spotted just right." I began to sing—and Ned joined in almost immediately — "No, we have Yes bananas, we have Yes bananas today!"

Sally's Chilled Banana Almond Soup

My friend Sally Williams Gorrell, whose general idea of supper runs to deciding to pop popcorn around about nine in the evening, will probably be astonished to learn she has a recipe in this book. When Sally and I get together these busy days we have

so many things to catch up on that we never even get to food, so I have no idea if she still makes this, but I do, regularly.

During those long-ago days when Sally and I were both single and in our twenties, we each had boyfriends who lived in Little Rock (four hours drive from here). Often I caught a ride down with her, and if it was late when we arrived, I'd spend the night at the apartment she kept. One morning, she fixed me a blender creation I've been making ever since. Banana, orange, and almond, smoothed out by the unifying, assertive tang of yogurt. Great!

My only revision is freezing the bananas (see facing page) before blending them, which adds an easy, voluptuous thickness to the whole thing. You could call this a smoothie or a shake, except that, especially with the frozen bananas, it is best eaten with a spoon out of a cup. Have it for breakfast or with brunch; as the starter to a light, summery meal, or a spicy one like an Indian curry dinner. It might sound uninspired on a read-through, but you will be amazed at the synergy of these ingredients.

It makes up quickly, but once you've made it, serve and eat it immediately.

2 cups plain yogurt
2 tablespoons thawed frozen orange juice
  concentrate
½ teaspoon vanilla extract
3 bananas, peeled, frozen, and cut into
  chunks
1 tablespoon raw almonds or cashews
Sugar or honey or sugar substitute to taste
  (optional)
Coarsely crumbled crisp banana chips, for
  garnish (optional)

1. In a food processor place all the ingredients except the almonds, honey (if using), and banana chips. Process with several pulses to get the banana chopped, then buzz until smooth, adding the honey (if using) and nuts while the machine is running. (The honey won't blend properly unless the machine is on when it's added.) The texture should be icy smooth, except for a few pieces of almond here and there.

2. Serve the soup in chilled tea cups with the banana chips atop each cup for the garnish. I have also garnished this with crisp cinnamon croutons, which definitely makes it more souplike.

Serves 2 to 4 as a starter or makes 1 or 2 breakfast-in-a-glass servings

ON FREEZING BANANAS

❦*Banana cognoscenti know that this fruit, always picked green and ripened off the tree, is at peak flavor and sweetness only when the yellow peel is deeply speckled with brown. This moment of perfection, though, is only a day or two away from overripe, so if you find bananas at the market at such a point, they are sure to be a bargain. Buy them up. You can always make banana bread or muffins. For myself, though, I usually just peel them, cut them in half, and freeze them solid. Peeling before freezing is essential.*

Even frozen, bananas will be soft enough to slice coarsely and toss in the blender or food processor. Puréed, they are the basis for any number of wonderful concoctions: smoothies, soups, sherbetlike desserts, shakes. The reason they are so perfect for this is that frozen they add a creamy thickness that is both low calorie and delicious; you have to try it to believe how good it is. Frozen bananas also make a great blender base for sweet alcoholic concoctions if your taste runs in that direction. Or try frozen bananas blended virtuously with cold apple juice, or with milk, peanut butter, a little honey, and maybe a few sweet, soft dates. Try them puréed with milk and cocoa powder and a little honey; with pineapple juice and cream of coconut (to which you may add rum); or with cream and crème de cacao. You can sweeten and flavor any of these with honey or sugar or a sugar substitute, and add a drop of vanilla.

A thawed frozen banana, however, is a sodden, near-liquid mess, although it can still be used in those good old banana breads or muffins.❦

BLACKBERRIES

*T*he when, if, and how of Arkansas blackberries, tame and wild, are rain-dependent. Some years the crop is so abundant that in addition to eating our fill, in every conceivable way, we still have enough left over to put up dozens and dozens of jars of jam for use at the inn. Most years, they're a rare, brief treat. And occasionally, a season goes by without a single blackberry reaching maturity. This uncertainty adds to blackberry's allure.

Blackberries possess not only the sweet-acid balance which most much-loved fruits have, but a unique flavor undernote. This is a faint, pleasant bitterness, intriguing and deliciously perverse, which makes these berries as inspiring to cook with as to eat out of hand. (The only other food I can think of that has this captivating bitter note is chocolate.)

exquisite soup. I loved it so much I couldn't bear to drop it until the next blackberry season, so I tried it, with some trepidation, with frozen blackberries. To my delight, it was very nearly as wonderful. The frozen berry advantage: the soup's deep color and dusky flavor make it most suitable for an early fall dinner, by which time the fresh berries are gone. This is the perfect starter for a meal of game or duck.

2 quarts fresh blackberries or 2 bags (16 ounces each) frozen unsweetened blackberries, thawed
2 cups plus 2 tablespoons good hearty Burgundy
½ cup sugar, or to taste
1 piece (1 inch) cinnamon stick
2 tablespoons cornstarch

2 tablespoons wildflower honey, or to taste
Unsweetened whipped cream or Crème Fraîche (page 50), for garnish
4 fresh mint leaves, for garnish
4 fresh blackberries or strawberry slices, for garnish

Blackberry Burgundy Soup

*H*ands down, my favorite fruit soup. Several years ago, a good blackberry season inspired this

1. In a food processor, purée the berries, then put through a food mill, fine sieve, or power strainer to remove all seeds. Set aside.

2. In a medium-size, heavy enameled pot, bring 2 cups of the Burgundy, the sugar, and cinnamon stick to a boil. Let cook at a low boil 5 minutes. Then lower the heat and let simmer. Dissolve the cornstarch in the remaining 2 tablespoons of Burgundy and whisk this mixture into the simmering wine. Cook, whisking gently until clear, smooth, and thick and there is no uncooked starchy taste, which should be almost immediately. Remove from the heat.

3. Stir the blackberry purée and honey into the soup. Taste and add more honey or sugar if needed. Chill overnight in the refrigerator.

4. Just before serving, remove the cinnamon stick. Serve the soup in small cups, garnished with a dollop of cream, a mint leaf, and a fresh blackberry or strawberry slice.

Serves 4 as a small starter

Déjà Food: If you have any soup left over, stir in sliced strawberries, whole blueberries, and maybe a touch of blackberry cordial, and there you are.

RASPBERRIES

❧*My absolutely favorite berry, and so rare and spectacular when fresh that I can't bring myself to make soup out of them. But I do cook with the frozen kind, and, oh my. Raspberry Rosé Soup is a wonderful thing, with the most gorgeous jewellike color and ambrosial, very fresh flavor. Simply follow the directions for Blackberry Burgundy Soup (page 296), substituting rosé wine for the burgundy and frozen raspberries for the blackberries. Serve it in tiny cups, garnished with pale pink geranium blossoms, if available (yes, they are edible).*❧

BLUEBERRIES

*B*lueberries are slightly tricky to work with. Puréed and then chilled, they sometimes set up or jell (at least our tart Ozark blueberries do), because of their natural pectin. But you can still make great blueberry soups if you use whole berries, as in the two recipes that follow. You can also make an excellent Blue-

berry and Blackberry Burgundy Soup by stirring a handful or two of blueberries into the prepared Blackberry Burgundy Soup (page 296).

Blueberry Sauternes Soup

Plump blueberries float suspended in a sweet, but not too sweet, liquid the color of pale honey. This soup is perfect for a sweltering summer day.

3 cups Sauternes or late-harvest Riesling
1 cup apple juice
¼ to ½ cup mild clover honey
2 tablespoons packed light brown sugar
1 tablespoon blueberry vinegar, or to taste
1 thick slice orange, seeded
1 stick (about 2 inches) cinnamon
Several gratings of nutmeg
3 tablespoons cornstarch
2 cups fresh blueberries
Unsweetened whipped cream or Crème Fraîche (page 50), for garnish
Fresh mint leaves, for garnish

"When the hills are green with spring, we think nothing can be more pleasant and satisfying, but now comes the time of ripening. The hills are brooding beneath the summer sun; most of the wild blossoms have come and gone. The wild fruit are in many stages of ripening. . . .**"**

—ROY WEBSTER,
UNDER A BUTTERMILK MOON:
A COUNTRY MEMOIR

1. In a medium-size, heavy enameled pot, combine the Sauternes or Riesling, ¾ cup of the apple juice, ¼ cup honey, the brown sugar, vinegar, orange slice, cinnamon, and nutmeg. Bring to a boil, then turn down the heat and let simmer. Taste for sweetness and add more honey or a few drops more of vinegar if necessary.

2. Dissolve the cornstarch in the remaining ¼ cup apple juice and whisk this mixture into the simmering liquid. Cook, whisking gently, until clear, smooth, and thick, which should be almost immediately. Remove from the heat and pick out the cinnamon stick. Chill deeply.

3. Just before serving, remove the orange slice and stir in the blueberries. Ladle the soup into bowls and garnish each serving with a dollop of whipped cream or crème fraîche and a mint leaf.

Serves 4 to 6 as a starter

Blueberry Orange Brunch Soup

 ne step up from a compote, this sunny concoction is a fresh, light addition to any festive brunch. Cook it quickly so the freshness of the orange juice isn't lost.

5 cups fresh orange juice
2 to 4 tablespoons honey
5 tablespoons cornstarch
¼ cup fresh lemon juice
2 cups fresh blueberries
2 oranges, peeled, seeded, and cut into
*   segments*
Freshly toasted cashews, for garnish
Toasted flaked coconut, for garnish
Grated lime zest, for garnish
Plain yogurt, for serving
Honey, for serving

1. In a medium-size, heavy enameled pot, quickly bring the orange juice and 2 tablespoons of the honey to a boil. Turn down the heat and let simmer. Dissolve the cornstarch in the lemon juice and whisk into the hot orange juice mixture. Cook, whisking gently, until clear, smooth, and thick, which should be almost immediately. Remove instantly from heat. Taste for sweetness and add more honey if needed. Chill deeply.

2. Just before serving, stir the blueberries and orange segments into the soup. Ladle into bowls and garnish with the cashews, coconut, and lime zest. Pass the yogurt and honey at the table.

Serves 6 to 8 as a breakfast fruit course

VARIATION:
Add 1 or 2 more cups of other fresh fruit to the soup—strawberries, green grapes, melon balls, sliced banana, or pineapple chunks, but no more than two kinds.

BLUEBERRY SEASON SUNDAY BRUNCH

*Blueberry Orange Brunch Soup

Croissants, Blueberry Muffins, and Cinnamon Raisin Bread

Butter, Blueberry Jam, Yogurt, and Honey

Shirred Eggs Mornay in Ramekins

Very Thinly Sliced Petit Jean Mountain Ham

Chocolate-Dipped Oatmeal Walnut Drop Cookies (from Dairy Hollow House Cookbook)

Café au Lait

CHERRIES

No fruit is so sensual as perfectly ripe cherries: dark glossy and alluringly cleavaged. Throw your head back, and dangle one by its stem into your mouth. Better yet—have someone else do it for you. And, oh, that sweet, juicy explosion of flavor!

Montmorency cherries, yellow fruit blushed with pink, are an exceptional treat.

Chilled Cherry Soup Hungarian-Style

Russia and many eastern European countries are noted for their cherries, as well as the use of sour cream in many dishes. This soup includes both. Unlike most of the other fruit soups in this chapter, sour cream or yogurt is mixed into the soup instead of garnishing the top. Remember this pretty, daintily pink soup next Valentine's Day, or if there is a wedding reception in your future. It's nice at brunch, too.

2¾ cups dry red wine
2 cups apple-cherry or apple juice
½ cup packed light brown sugar or honey, or to taste
2 bags (16 ounces each) frozen pitted tart cherries or 1 bag each dark sweet and tart red cherries
1 piece (about 2 inches) cinnamon stick
¼ cup cornstarch
¼ cup Peter Heering, Cherry Kijafa, kirsch, or additional dry red wine
1 drop (no more) almond extract
1 cup heavy (whipping) cream, sour cream, Crème Fraîche (page 50), or plain yogurt, or a combination (I prefer 2 tablespoons each heavy cream and crème fraîche, the rest yogurt; sour cream is traditional)
Sour cream or Crème Fraîche, for garnish
Fresh mint leaves, for garnish
Fresh unstemmed cherries, for garnish

1. In a large, heavy enameled pot, combine the wine, juice, sugar, frozen cherries, and cinnamon stick. Bring to a boil, then turn down the heat and let simmer, uncovered, 10 minutes. Taste for sweetness and add more sugar if needed.

2. Dissolve the cornstarch in the cherry liqueur and whisk the cornstarch mixture into the simmering liquid. Cook, stirring gently, until clear, smooth, and thick, which should be almost immediately. Remove from the heat and stir in the almond extract. Chill deeply.

3. Just before serving, remove the cinnamon stick and stir in the heavy cream or other dairy choice. Pureé in a food processor if you want the soup smooth and sippable. Ladle the soup into chilled cups and garnish each serving with a dab of sour cream, a mint leaf, and a cherry.

Serves 8 as a starter

INNECDOTE

🍎*Dairy Hollow House may have the only restaurant on the face of the earth where, at least once, the desserts were garnished* after *they had been set before the guests.*

In any restaurant, some behind-the-scenes friction between "front of the house" (waitstaff) and "heart of the house" (kitchen staff) is considered inevitable. Ours is pretty mild, but occasionally there are flares of definite love-hate, especially between John Mitchell, our headwaiter, and everybody else. (It should be said that John is a bona fide Eureka original. In addition to waiting tables at Dairy Hollow, he owns an antique shop, has a small pickled garlic business, has a tiny vineyard, and restores old Jaguars. John is great with the guests, but has these moments when he saves all his charm for the dining room.)

One night I had these gorgeous, gorgeous Montmorency cherries: almost as big as small plums. I planned to garnish my desserts with them.

John was having one of those nights—he was driving the kitchen people, including me, to distraction. He'd race in: "That was two—no, one—no, three pork loins . . ." and race out, only to race back in: "Where are my four pork loins? I need them now!"

"Oh, what is his problem?" I muttered to the dishwasher. The final straw came when he snatched the desserts and scurried out to the dining room with them when I had turned away for a moment—meaning I couldn't put those succulent cherries on the plates.

Well! Dessert is when I make the rounds, anyway, chatting with guests. So I put on a clean chef's jacket, put my beautiful cherries in a bowl, got out our best pair of sugar tongs, and marched out into the dining room.

"Hello! How was everything? Good, I'm glad you're enjoying it . . . Listen, my waiter stole the desserts before I'd had a chance to garnish them—would you mind if I put one of these cherries on your plate?"

And I did—with the elegant silver tongs.🍎

CRANBERRIES

*T*art bursts of color and flavor to light up the holidays. What cranberry relish does for a plate, cranberry soup does for a menu.

Cranberry Apple Soup with Burgundy

lush with late autumn flavors and colors, this is an excellent variation on the theme that runs through so many of the fruit soups in this chapter—fruit, juice, and wine, sweetened and seasoned just a bit, then slightly thickened. Cold or hot, chunky or smooth, it's very good.

3 cups apple juice
½ cup packed dried apple slices
Pam cooking spray
2 cups cranberries
4 cups good hearty Burgundy or Beaujolais
½ cup packed dark brown sugar (or more to taste)
1 cinnamon stick (about 2 inches; optional)
5 tablespoons cornstarch
Crème Fraîche (page 50), for garnish
1 apple, Arkansas Black or Granny Smith, cored and julienned, for garnish

1. The night before making the soup, in an enameled saucepan bring 1 cup of the apple juice to a boil and pour it over the apple slices in a bowl. Let soak overnight.

2. The next day, spray a large heavy pot with the Pam. Coarsely chop the rehydrated apples and combine with the soaking liquid, the remaining 2 cups juice, the cranberries, 3⅔ cups of the wine, the sugar, and cinnamon stick in the pot. Cook over medium heat until the cranberries pop, about 7 minutes. Taste the soup and add more sugar if it needs it. Turn down the heat and let simmer.

3. Dissolve the cornstarch in the remaining ⅓ cup wine and whisk this mixture into the simmering soup. Cook, whisking gently, until clear, smooth, and thick, which should be almost immediately. Remove the soup from the heat and remove the cinnamon stick.

4. Serve this soup hot in mugs, or chill deeply and serve it cold. The hot soup is good left chunky, but the chilled is best puréed in a food processor and then strained. Garnish each serving with a dollop of crème fraîche and a thatch of the julienned apple.

Serves 8 as a starter

The Inn at Long Last's Chilled Cranberry Cream Soup

Pam cooking spray
2 cups spring water
1 cup sugar
3 cups cranberries
¼ teaspoon freshly grated nutmeg
⅛ teaspoon ground cinnamon
⅛ teaspoon ground cloves
1 cup chopped, cored, peeled apple,
  preferably McIntosh, Granny Smith, or
  Arkansas Black
Grated zest and juice of 2 oranges
1 teaspoon vanilla extract
1 cup buttermilk, preferably Bulgarian-style
¼ cup Grand Marnier or other orange
  liqueur
Sweetened whipped cream, for garnish
Fresh mint leaves, for garnish
Whole cranberries, for garnish

My mother spends part of each summer in Vermont with her sister, my Aunt Dot, at Dot's beautiful restored farmhouse near Saxton's River. She often sends me a New England food gift or two—a pound of sharp Vermont Cheddar, some maple syrup, a cookbook. Knowing my soupy predilection, she once sent me a charming book titled *Soups... At Long Last,* which features 26 original soup recipes from The Inn at Long Last in Chester, Vermont. The recipes, by former chef Michael Brown, are introduced by innkeeper Jack Coleman, a self-described soupaholic. Unabashed. Unrepentant. With soups as good as his, he shouldn't even think of repenting.

This soup is festive, beautifully colored, and most refreshing. It's not too sweet but sweet enough, with the delicious zing of buttermilk (try to get the cultured Bulgarian-style buttermilk).

1. Spray an enameled heavy pot with the Pam, and in it cook the water and sugar over low heat, stirring frequently, until the sugar dissolves. Stir in the cranberries and spices; simmer over low heat, uncovered, 15 minutes.

2. Add the apple, orange zest and juice, and vanilla. Bring to a boil, then turn down the heat to medium-low and let simmer, uncovered, 15 minutes more.

3. Let the soup cool to room temperature. Transfer to a food processor and coarsely purée. Chill deeply.

4. Just before serving stir in the buttermilk and Grand Marnier. Ladle the soup into chilled bowls and garnish each serving with a dollop of whipped cream, a mint leaf, and whole cranberry.

Serves 8 to 10 as a starter

Note: At Dairy Hollow we usually make this by replacing the water with apple juice and cutting back on the sugar.

MELON

*I*f you don't mind looking silly at the market, you can find the ripest, most flavorful melon of the lot by simply pressing the stem end. It should feel very slightly spongy and give a little. If it does, lift the melon and sniff. Buy only those with a sweet, melony fragrance.

Orange Cantaloupe Soup

reshly squeezed orange juice and a really fragrant ripe cantaloupe make all the difference in the world in this summery, bright-flavored soup.

3 cups fresh orange juice
½ cup dry white wine
½ cup honey
1 teaspoon grated orange zest
1 piece (1 inch) cinnamon stick
¼ cup cornstarch
¼ cup fresh lemon juice
4 to 5 very ripe flavorful cantaloupes,
  seeded, peeled, and cut into large chunks
¾ cup heavy (whipping) cream, thick plain
  yogurt, or Bulgarian-style buttermilk
Fresh mint leaves, for garnish

1. In a medium-size, heavy enameled pot, bring the orange juice, wine, honey, orange zest, and cinnamon stick to a boil. Turn down the heat and let simmer. Quickly dissolve the cornstarch in the lemon juice and whisk this mixture into the simmering liquid. Cook, whisking gently, until clear, smooth, and thick, which should be almost immediately. Remove from the heat and take out the cinnamon stick. Chill deeply.

2. In a food processor, purée the cantaloupes with the cream in batches and stir this purée into the chilled juice mixture. Chill again. Serve in chilled cups with a mint sprig garnish. Wouldn't this be nice served in cantaloupe halves? Yes indeedy!

Serves 4 to 6 as a starter

Watermelon Soup

atermelon juice is probably what the gods drank on Olympus. It's reason enough to own a Champion juicer, which takes chunks of this fruit, seeds and all, and turns them into a heavenly juice that bursts of summertime. If you don't have a Champion but do have a food processor, you can still make this soup, but you'll have to seed the watermelon first. It's important to chill the melon first before you juice or purée it.

This soup is not thickened or cooked—you couldn't do that to watermelon juice. Rose water gives a flowery bouquet and taste, and gin a tiny zing, but the soup's good without them, too. Add a few tablespoons of chopped fresh mint instead.

6 cups very cold watermelon juice made from ripe, chilled, seeded watermelon (see above)
1¾ cups buttermilk, preferably Bulgarian-style, or plain yogurt
1 tablespoon gin (optional)
½ teaspoon rose water (optional)
Small pinch of salt
Chilled watermelon balls, for garnish
Finely chopped fresh mint, for garnish

▶ Combine all the ingredients except the garnish and chill deeply. Serve in large chilled goblets and garnish with the watermelon balls and fresh mint.

Serves 6 to 8 as a starter

Déjà Food: Use any leftovers to make Three-Melon Soup, adding cut up cantaloupe, honeydew melon, and more watermelon.

ORANGES

*D*oes the eye crave the color, the mouth the taste, the body the vitamin C? No matter. In the dark January days, the citruses are at their best and we hunger for them. I go through spells of two or three grapefruits or oranges a day and each one feels essential. But citrus soup? Ah, yes. Lucious Orange Blossom Special is perfection at any holiday brunch, unequaled for a winter wedding breakfast, a pleasure that sparkles both eye and mouth.

Orange Blossom Special

his glorious chilled citrus soup, enlivened with Grand Marnier, orange and grapefruit sections, and fresh orange juice is a show-stopper, perfect for a first course at brunch, an

excellent starter for any spicy meal. It's wonderful without the heavy cream called for, but the tiny bit of cream really does perfect it. The cream exerts a subtle but decisive gentling influence. Don't even think about making this from frozen orange juice concentrate—fundamental freshness is all. With or without the cream, the color of the soup is that of a New Mexico sunrise.

4 cups fresh orange juice
1¼ cups rosé wine
¼ cup orange blossom or clover honey
¼ cup cornstarch
3 grapefruits, peeled, seeded, and cut into
  segments
3 navel oranges, peeled, seeded, and cut
  into segments
1 lemon, peeled, seeded, and cut into
  segments
1 lime, peeled, seeded, and cut into
  segments (you won't get much fruit once
  all the white pith and membranes have
  been removed, but you just need a little)
¼ cup Grand Marnier or other orange
  liqueur (optional)
¼ to ½ cup heavy (whipping) cream
  (optional)
Grated lime zest, for garnish

1. Into a large heatproof pitcher or bowl, pour 3 cups of the orange juice, and chill.

2. In an enameled small saucepan, bring the remaining 1 cup orange juice, 1 cup of the wine, and the honey to a boil. Turn down the heat and let simmer. Quickly dissolve the cornstarch in the remaining ¼ cup wine and whisk this mixture into the simmering liquid. Cook, whisking gently, until clear, smooth, and thick, which should be almost immediately. Remove from the heat and let cool to room temperature. Stir in all the citrus sections and the Grand Marnier, if using. Add this mixture to the chilled juice, whisk to combine, and chill deeply.

3. Just before serving, stir in the optional cream. Ladle the soup into stemmed glasses and garnish with lime zest.

Serves 6 to 8 as a starter

PEACHES AND NECTARINES

One of my earliest childhood memories is of accompanying my mother to her best friend's house, and

being given a huge peach. Vividly I remember biting into the yellow flesh, which was so explosively juicy I had to

lean over to keep the juice from dribbling all over me.

If you want peaches like this, try for locally grown fruit in the summertime only. Sniff the fruit before you buy it; it should be decidedly fragrant. Never buy a peach in winter, and smell carefully before you buy any large peaches; they're often flavorless. The flesh should yield easily to the gentle pressure of a thumb.

Often the smaller junkier-looking peaches with questionable spots here and there are the tastiest.

Nectarines are essentially peaches without fuzz. The two fruits may be used interchangeably.

Nectarine Soup Ellen

his soup is as fast as can be and so refreshing on a hot night—just the thing to perk an August appetite. It's named for Ellen Fly, for whom I first made it. Good thing Ellen asked for a copy of the recipe, since I subsequently lost it and had to call her for it. Ellen is the food editor at the *Tulsa Tribune* and has been an ardent supporter of Dairy Hollow House since its pre-restaurant days. And would you believe—given her last name—she was a flight instructor for years?

8 dead-ripe nectarines
1 cup dry white wine
Grated zest of 1 orange
Juice of 2 oranges
¼ cup honey, slightly warmed
Fresh mint leaves, for garnish
Nectarine slices, for garnish

▶ Pit all the nectarines and drop them into a food processor. Crack open one of the pits, fish out the almondlike kernel inside, and drop it into the food processor as well. Add the wine, orange zest, and juice. With the machine running, drizzle in the honey. Purée the whole until smooth, then chill deeply. Just before serving, whisk the soup well or shake it in a covered container. Pour the soup into chilled stemmed glasses, garnish with mint leaves, and arrange a nectarine slice on the edge of each glass. This one's for sipping.

Serves 4 to 6 as a starter

❝ 'So,' he said, 'you can eat with enthusiasm still? I think, now it is time you learned to cook the same way. Anything you do must be accomplished with enthusiasm else it is worthless...' ❞

—HENRI CHARPENTIER,
THOSE RICH & GREAT ONES, or LIFE
À LA HENRI

Peach Soup with Almonds

Peaches, cherries, and almonds are botanical kin, and their flavors enhance each other beautifully, as this soup proves. There's something romantic and summery about it. Wouldn't you enjoy sipping it from a stemmed glass, barely swinging in a porch glider, on a darkened front porch as the moon rose, and . . . why, who is that with you?

*2 cups unsweetened organic peach nectar
   (available at natural foods stores)*
1¼ cups dry white wine
*2 tablespoons thawed frozen apple juice
   concentrate*
*2 tablespoons sugar or honey,
   or to taste*
4 tablespoons cornstarch
10 to 12 perfectly ripe peaches, peeled
*¼ cup blanched almonds, lightly
   toasted*
¼ cup amaretto liqueur, or to taste
*1 cup plain whole-milk yogurt or crème
   fraîche*
*Crème Fraîche (page 50) or unsweetened
   whipped cream, for garnish*
Fresh peach slices, for garnish
Fresh unstemmed cherries, for garnish

1. In a medium-size, heavy enameled pot, bring the nectar, 1 cup of the wine, the apple juice concentrate, and the sugar to a boil, then turn down the heat and let simmer. Dissolve the cornstarch in the remaining ¼ cup wine and whisk this mixture into the simmering liquid. Cook, whisking gently, until clear, smooth, and thick, which should be almost immediately. Remove from the heat and taste for sweetness, adding more sugar if needed. Let cool to room temperature.

2. Halve and pit the peaches; drop the fruit into a food processor. Crack open 3 of the peach pits, remove the small almondlike kernels inside, and add them to the peaches. Add the almonds and purée. For an absolutely smooth soup, press the purée through a food mill, fine sieve, or power strainer.

3. Stir the peach purée into the thickened wine mixture. Drizzle in amaretto to taste, then whisk in the 1 cup yogurt or crème fraîche. Chill deeply.

4. Ladle the soup into chilled cups. Dollop crème fraîche or heavy cream on each serving and arrange a peach slice and cherry on top.

Serves 6 to 8 as a starter

VARIATION:
Don't purée the peaches; rather cut them into chunks and stir into the thickened, chilled soup. The texture is pleasing.

OH, WHAT A NIGHT

🌿 *Eureka Springs has been a colony of artists for over a hundred years. Louis and Elsie Freund are the links in that chain that precede me and my generation. He's a one-time WPA artist and muralist; she's a watercolorist who for many years made the most extraordinary clean-lined jewelry. But their best work of art may be their marriage and the life they have created with each other: a life of home and roots in Eureka, travel all over the world, "following their bliss" in the arts, reading aloud and discussing what they read, true companionship and mutual devotion—but plenty of feistiness to keep it lively. At every phase, they have always made room for comrades of all ages—artists, idealists, philosophers, plain folks, fanatics. I am one Louis and Elsie made room for, and what they embody— art, love, community—keeps me jazzed not only about Eureka, but about the reality of custom building an artistic, one-of-a-kind existence that works for life.*

Their fiftieth anniversary was our restaurant's first big do, and brought together friends and artists from all over the country. Louis and Elsie insisted that we could cater their anniversary only if we could join them at the table (we did; the "way" was Rebecca Sisco, with whom I worked beforehand and between courses). Big bowls of Queen Anne's lace and sweet peas filled the room; these had been the Freunds' wedding flowers. Their old friend Carmen Pappas, a concert harpist from Chicago, drove down with an enormous, splendid, golden harp, and played a medley which included compositions ranging from "Afternoon of a Faun" to "As Time Goes By."

Listening to those notes, golden as the harp itself, which followed a dinner that had been delicious, interesting, and celebratory I glanced over the lovely room. It was replete with full and happy people, most of whom had known each other for years, and who were bound by friendship. Louis and Elsie, handsome, funny, loving, crowned the picture. That night I felt angels had come to live in the restaurant, approving and entirely benign, showering invisible gold dust from somewhere in the corners of the ceiling. It was the first moment for me of complete perfection in the restaurant; a moment when our dreams and vision meshed perfectly with the reality. Peak moments like that night are precious and fleeting; but every so often I look up, and I just know the angels that came with Louis and Elsie are in permanent residence. 🌿

STRATWBERRIES

*T*he charm of their plump, seed-dotted valentine shape and their glowing red color alone would be enough to entice most of us. But when you've inhaled the scent of a perfectly ripe strawberry, tasted its juicy flesh with its distinct sweetness and hint of acidity, the strawberry becomes a small ecstasy of spring.

Our best strawberries are the ones grown about six miles east of the inn. Your best strawberries are the ones grown closest to you.

Chilled Strawberry Soup with Crème Fraîche

*P*erfect for spring, for romance, and just on its own account. This soup is the prettiest pink; it's a little sweet, a little on the tea-roomish, prissy side—but no less delicious for that.

1½ cups rosé wine
¼ cup thawed frozen apple juice
concentrate
1 to 2 tablespoons honey, or to taste
2 tablespoons cornstarch
2 tablespoons raspberry or strawberry
vinegar, or to taste
1 tablespoon grenadine syrup
2 tablespoons kirsch
4 cups fresh strawberries
1 cup Crème Fraîche (page 50) or plain
yogurt
½ cup half-and-half or evaporated skim
milk
Unsweetened whipped cream or additional
Crème Fraîche, for garnish
Fresh mint leaves, for garnish

1. In a large enameled saucepan heat the wine, apple juice concentrate, and honey to a boil. Turn down the heat and let simmer. Mix the cornstarch, vinegar, and grenadine together until smooth, then whisk into the simmering liquid. Cook, whisking gently, until clear, smooth, and thick, which should be almost immediately. Stir in the kirsch and remove from the heat. Taste; there should be a sweet-tart balance. Add more honey or vinegar if necessary. Let the soup cool to room temperature.

2. Set aside 4 to 6 perfect strawberries for the garnish. Hull all the remaining berries, slice half of them, and in a food processor purée the remaining half. Whisk the strawberry purée, crème fraîche or yogurt, and the half-and-half into the thickened wine; stir in the sliced berries. Chill deeply. Serve

🍎 *Grenadine is a sweet, bright red syrup made from pomegranate juice and sugar. It adds a bit of sweet-tart flavor compatible with any berry or cherry soup, but is mostly used for its intense red hue. Grenadine gives a blush to Chilled Strawberry Soup with Crème Fraîche, nonalcoholic drinks (like a Shirley Temple), and otherwise (Tequila Sunrise).* 🍎

the soup in glass cups and garnish each cup with a dab of whipped cream, or additional crème fraîche, a mint leaf, and a strawberry.

Serves 4 to 6 as a starter

VARIATION:
To spare the calories and cholesterol, thicken the wine with an additional tablespoon of cornstarch and substitute 1½ cups good-quality low-fat buttermilk, or half buttermilk and half plain yogurt, for the crème fraîche and the half-and-half. You may omit the honey and sweeten the soup with a sugar substitute.

Déjà Food: Use any leftover soup as a pretty background sauce for a fresh fruit plate. Swirl a spoonful of the soup on a white plate and on it carefully arrange sliced fresh strawberries, green grapes, a few raspberries or blackberries, a wedge of fresh pineapple, slices of banana, and melon balls. Garnish with a sprig of fresh mint. A lovely early summer breakfast or light dessert.

Fruited Oatmeal Soup, The Inn at Brandywine Falls

his will make you rethink oatmeal. Of course, it's *not* oatmeal, it's Fruited Oatmeal Soup, beautifully served in a silver chafing dish by Katie and George Hoy, and accompanied by various toppings. "If we called it oatmeal, many people wouldn't try it," says the indefatigable George. I am probably one of those people, but I did try their Oatmeal Soup—it was so good I went back for seconds (and would have gone back for thirds if there hadn't been so many other glorious things for breakfast that morning).

The Hoys prepare the soup in a microwave, and suggest you do the same, for superior results. But they also offer a stove-top version for (a) times when the microwave is broken; (b) stone-age cooks like me who do not have a microwave.

The fruit in the soup varies from day to day, depending on availability and

innkeeper's whim. Katie used pear when we were there. What the Hoys call the "condiments"—that is, an array of delicious optional help-yourself toppings for the soup—also vary.

Like I say—this is *really* good; much better than you'd think from the simplicity of the ingredients. Do try it.

Pam cooking spray, if using stove-top
   cooking method
4½ cups milk, preferably 2 percent
⅔ cup rolled oats (not the instant oatmeal
   kind)
⅔ cup oat bran
Either a hard fruit choice (such as 2 pears,
   peeled, cored, and diced; or 2 apples,
   peeled, cored, and diced; or 1 cup dried
   apricots, diced; or 1 cup raisins) or a soft
   fruit choice (such as 2 peaches, diced;
   1½ cups grapes, halved and seeded if
   necessary)
"Condiments" for serving (see Note)

Microwave directions

1. Mix the milk, oats, and oat bran in a large Pyrex bowl. If the fruit you've selected is on the hard list, add it, too.

2. Microwave this mixture, covered, on High (100 percent power) for 10 minutes. Remove and stir.

3. If using one of the soft fruits, add it now.

4. Microwave, covered, on Medium (50 percent power) for 10 minutes more. Remove and stir.

5. Serve, hot, preferably from a silver chafing dish, on a sideboard, accompanied by accompaniments, to which breakfasters may help themselves.

Stove-top directions:

1. Spray a large heavy pot with the Pam, and in it mix the milk, oats, and oat bran. If the fruit you've selected is on the hard list, add it, too.

2. Slowly bring the mixture to a boil, stirring often, then *immediately* turn down the heat as low as it will go. Cover, and let cook 20 minutes, stirring once in a while.

3. If using one of the soft fruits, add it now.

4. Continue cooking, covered, for another 20 minutes. Stir once in a while.

5. Serve, hot, preferably from a silver chafing dish, on a sideboard, accompanied by condiments, to which breakfasters may help themselves.

Serves 4 to 6

Note: Condiments include the following, set out separately: a pitcher of milk, bowls of brown sugar, sour cream (unbelievably good on this), yogurt, homemade granola, and toasted nuts. The Hoys serve fruit as a separate course, but if you aren't doing so, a bowl of sliced berries and another of sliced bananas would also be delicious condiments.

Nut Soups

FROM SOUP TO . . .

uts, of any type, are not the stuff of everyday soups. They are caloric and expensive, and their flavor is rich as all get out. But when puréed, nuts add a creaminess beyond duplication. Well-prepared soups in which nuts dominate are delicious in the same way soups featuring pure cream are; they are divine, elegant indulgences. Save them, like cream-enriched soups, for special occasions—starters for dressier meals in which the entrée will be simple. I have never served a nut soup that was not enormously popular with guests.

If you aren't inclined to use nuts as soup stars, think of them instead as character actors. Few are the soups that are not improved by a sprinkle of toasted slivered almonds, a few toasted regular or black walnuts, pecans, or pistachios chopped into tiny crumbs. Shelling pistachios is a labor of love, but their taste, texture, and seductive fresh green color make it worthwhile. Hazelnuts top the list for labor-intensive preparation, since they must be freshly shelled, then roasted, then skinned; still, their exquisite essence-of-the-harvest flavor is worth the work once in a while.

Broccoli and Almond Soup with Sesame

 pen sesame. These clean, fresh-tasting flavors are springlike and pleasing, though rich. They have an Oriental note, and combine ever-agreeable, ever-available broccoli with toasted almonds and sesame.

1 large or 2 small heads (bunches) broccoli
Pam cooking spray
5 to 6 cups Chicken Stock 1 (page 19), Basic Golden Vegetable Stock (page 28), or any well-flavored chicken or vegetable stock
2 tablespoons butter or mild vegetable oil, such as corn or peanut
1 large onion, chopped
1 clove garlic, peeled and put through a garlic press
½ cup almonds, blanched, skinned, and toasted (page 316)
3 tablespoons sesame seeds
Salt and freshly ground black pepper, to taste
2 teaspoons toasted Oriental sesame oil
Sour cream, yogurt, or red bell pepper purée (page 46), for garnish
Coarsely chopped roasted, salted almonds, not blanched, for garnish

1. Separate the stems and flower heads of the broccoli. Trim the tough ends from the stems, then peel the tender parts. Coarsely chop both flowerets and peeled stems.

2. Spray a heavy soup pot with Pam. In it, bring the stock to a boil over high heat. Add all the chopped broccoli, turn down the heat to medium, and let simmer, partially covered, until the broccoli is tender (a bit more tender than you would want it as a side vegetable) but not mushy, about 10 minutes. Drain, reserving both stock and broccoli. Let cool slightly. Return the stock to the soup pot, and transfer the broccoli to a food processor.

3. Melt the butter in a medium-size skillet over medium heat. Add the onion and sauté until it starts to soften, about 3 minutes. Stir in the garlic, and stir-fry for another 30 seconds. Add the onion mixture to the broccoli in the processor. Deglaze the skillet with a few tablespoons of the stock and add this deglaze to the processor, along with the toasted almonds.

4. Toast the sesame seeds: Heat a small cast-iron skillet over medium heat, then add the seeds. Stir constantly until they begin to pop and start to become golden brown and fragrant, 2 minutes. Add 2 tablespoons of the seeds to the food processor. Reserve the remaining seeds for garnish.

5. Process the broccoli mixture to a thick, smooth purée. Stir this purée into the reserved cooking stock, and season to taste with salt and pepper. Then stir in the sesame oil and reheat the soup over medium heat until piping hot.

6. Ladle the soup into bowls and garnish with dabs of sour cream or yogurt, or a squiggle of red pepper purée (or both, or neither). In any case, finish with a sprinkle of the remaining toasted almonds and sesame seeds.

Serves 6 as a starter

VARIATION:

To add texture and a bright green note: separately steam or stir-fry some small broccoli flowerets just until tender crisp, and add them to the finished soup.

BLANCHING ALMONDS

Blanching almonds means freeing them of their brown skins so they'll purée more smoothly when ground in the food processor, or so their surfaces can be toasted golden brown. It's easy.

In a small saucepan, bring to a boil enough water to cover the almonds by at least 2 inches. Boil the almonds hard for 2 minutes; drain them in a colander and cool under cold running water. When they are cool enough to handle, simply pop them out of their skins. That's it. Almonds could teach hazelnuts a thing or two about getting undressed expeditiously.

ABOUT TOASTING NUTS

❧*Virtually every nut benefits from being toasted just before using to heighten flavor and crunch. I prefer to toast nuts in a small toaster oven with a glass door and a timer. This way I can peep in at them, checking them often, as they burn easily. Toast nuts in small batches only as you need them.*

To toast nuts, preheat the oven to 350° F. Spread a single layer of nuts—walnuts, blanched or split almonds, raw cashews, pecans, hazelnuts, or black walnuts—in an ungreased shallow baking pan or on the toaster oven tray. Bake until the nuts are fragrant, 8 to 10 minutes, opening the oven door to check the nuts occasionally and to shake the pan. The nuts may need a few minutes more or less toasting, depending on their age and whether they are whole or in pieces. That pleasant fragrance usually indicates the precise moment the nuts are toasted to perfection.❧

Toasted Almond Soup The Inn at Long Last

I've already mentioned The Inn at Long last, in Chester, Vermont, it's "soupaholic" innkeeper Jack Coleman, and the delightful soup-only cookbook he and his former chef, Michael Brown, wrote. This is based on another from that book, but with several changes (like cutting down on the cream, adding a touch of orange peel, using rice instead of roux, substituting sherry for white wine). Innkeeper Jack notes, "We . . . assert the results are a little short of heavenly . . . On a late fall or winter night, the full, nutty flavor evokes some of the most complete feelings of well-being we know."

Our version, although it could certainly not be called low-calorie or low-fat, does save hundreds of fat grams as compared with the original—yet maintains the full and satisfying, and yes, heavenly, almondness!

If you're visiting Vermont, do visit The Inn at Long Last, on the village green in the pure New England classic

town of Chester. Write them at Box 589, Chester, Vermont, 05143; or call (802) 875-2444.

Pam cooking spray
2 quarts Chicken Stock 1 (page 19), Basic Golden Vegetable Stock (page 28), or any well-flavored chicken or vegetable stock
⅓ cup long-grain rice
½ cup blanched almonds
1 tablespoon butter
1 large onion, chopped
1 tablespoon finely chopped garlic
¼ cup dry sherry
2 tablespoons almond paste
Grated zest of 1 orange
1 cup evaporated skim milk
Salt and freshly ground white pepper, to taste
1¼ cups slivered toasted almonds (see box), for garnish
Grated orange zest, for garnish

1. Spray a large soup pot with Pam. Add the stock and bring to a boil. Turn down the heat to medium-low, and add the rice and blanched almonds. Cover, and let cook slowly for 30 minutes.

2. Meanwhile, spray a 10-inch skillet with Pam, and in it melt the butter over medium heat. Add the onion, and sauté until it starts to soften, about 3½ minutes. Lower the heat slightly, and add the garlic. Continue cooking, stirring constantly, to soften the garlic about 20 seconds. Stir in the sherry, then crumble in the almond paste a bit at a time. Remove the skillet from the heat, and whisk well to smooth it out.

3. Lower the heat under the stock to the barest possible simmer. Add the onion mixture, the orange zest, and evaporated skim milk. Let cook to blend flavors, 10 minutes more.

4. Purée the soup, in batches, in a food processor, then put through a food-mill or power strainer. Season to taste with salt and white pepper.

5. Reheat just before serving, and serve, very hot, in your most delicate cups, garnished with toasted almonds and the merest bit of orange zest.

Serves 8 as a starter

Summercorn Cashew Soup with Red Pepper

 ost Eurekans buy their natural foods groceries at the Ozark Co-operative Warehouse, based in Fayetteville, Arkansas, and one of the largest in the central United States. For some years it was connected to an excellent natural foods restaurant called Summercorn, now defunct but fondly remembered by those of us who had the pleasure of eating there. I dedicate this recipe to its memory.

The smooth variation of this soup which follows this recipe is positively voluptuous. Its color is uninspired but

that can be remedied with a bright garnish. It is best served hot.

6 to 7 cups Golden Vegetable Stock (page 28) or any well-flavored vegetable stock
1 tablespoon honey, or to taste
1 medium carrot, scrubbed and diced
8 ears fresh corn, shucked
1 to 2 tablespoons corn oil
1 medium-large onion, chopped
1 tablespoon tamari/shoyu soy sauce, or to taste
⅔ cup raw cashews
Salt and freshly ground black pepper to taste
Diced red bell pepper, for garnish
Roasted salted cashews, for garnish
Tiny sprigs of parsley, for garnish

1. In a heavy soup pot, bring the stock and honey to a boil. Add the carrot and corn on the cob. Boil 8 minutes, then remove the corn to a colander to cool. Turn down the heat under the stock to medium-low, and let simmer, covered, another 10 minutes.

2. As soon as the corn is cool enough to handle, cut the kernels from the cobs and set aside. Break the cobs in half and drop them into the stock.

3. In a 10-inch skillet, heat the oil over medium-low heat. Add the onion and sauté until very soft and limp but not browned, about 5 minutes. Turn down the heat to low. Stir in the soy sauce and cook, stirring often, about 1 minute. Remove from the heat.

4. Strain the stock, discarding the corn cobs and returning the stock to the pot. Transfer the carrot to a food processor. Add 1 cup of the hot stock and the raw cashews. Purée until very smooth, about 1 minute.

5. If you like the soup with some texture, add half the sautéed onion and half the corn kernels to the stock and add the remaining to the food processor. If you want the soup smooth, add all the onion and corn to the processor. In either case, purée until smooth, then stir the purée into the stock. Season with salt and pepper. Taste and add a little more honey or soy sauce if it needs it. Just before serving, reheat. Serve the soup hot, garnished with the bell pepper, roasted cashews, and parsley.

Serves 6 to 8 as a starter

VARIATION:

Southwestern Summercorn Soup: Omit the honey and add 1 teaspoon each cumin seeds and chili powder and a small pinch of cayenne to the sautéing onion. Garnish with a squiggle of green chili purée (follow bell pepper instructions, page 46) or a scoop of Arkansalsa (page 199).

Cream of Chestnut Soup

iss Kay, an older lady who lived around the corner from where I grew up, was my first culinary mentor after my mother. Miss Kay had her own garden, and from it I tasted raspberries off the arching briar and corn not ten minutes old. She baked from scratch: luscious fudge cake, lighter-than-air orange sponge cake with freshly squeezed orange juice. Salad would have then-exotic combinations, such as a canned pear half with a sprinkle of blue cheese artistically arranged on a bed of greens. In her home I first had lasagne, and Pepperidge Farm Bordeaux Cookies, and, one Christmas Day, chestnuts—creamed fresh chestnuts. At the time I thought, "How could anything be this good?"

Now I know the one way they can be: add to the chestnuts those other boon companions of cream, garlic, and wild mushrooms, and season with nutmeg, black pepper, and sherry. This is a soup that will transport you. Mushrooms set off the bland starchiness of the chestnuts, and the effect, when the unctuous cream is added, is magic.

4 cups Chicken Stock 1 (page 19) or
    Golden or Browned Vegetable Stock
    (pages 28 and 32) or any well-flavored
    chicken or vegetable stock
1 ounce dried mushrooms, preferably
    porcini
1 pound chestnuts, roasted, shelled, and
    skinned (page 320)
1 cup milk
4 tablespoons (½ stick) butter
1 large onion, chopped
3 cloves fresh garlic, peeled and put
    through a garlic press or finely chopped
4 ounces fresh shiitake mushrooms, stems
    removed, caps sliced
3 tablespoons all-purpose flour
Pam cooking spray
1 cup heavy (whipping) cream
3 tablespoons dry sherry
Freshly grated nutmeg to taste
Salt and freshly ground black pepper to
    taste
Finely minced fresh parsley, for garnish

1. In a small saucepan, bring 1 cup of the stock to a boil. Pour the hot stock over the dried mushrooms in a bowl and let soak for 1 hour (or if refrigerated overnight).

2. Meanwhile, slice half the chestnuts and set aside. Put the other half in a medium-size saucepan, add the milk, and barely simmer, uncovered, 15 minutes. In a food processor, purée the chestnuts with the milk, then put the purée through a food mill, fine sieve, or power strainer. Reserve. Put the remaining stock in the same saucepan over medium heat.

3. In a 10-inch skillet, melt the butter over medium heat. Add the onion and sauté until it starts to soften, about 3 minutes. Add the garlic and shiitake mushrooms, turn down the heat to low, and sauté 5 minutes more. Sprinkle the flour over the vegetables and cook, stirring often, for 1 minute. Gradually add the hot stock, stirring to smooth out any lumps. Bring to a boil, then immediately turn down the heat so the mixture simmers. Stir in the sliced chestnuts and let simmer, partially covered, 10 minutes.

4. Spray a soup pot with the Pam and transfer the sliced chestnut mixture to it. Remove the dried mushrooms from the soaking liquid and rinse them well to remove any grit. Finely chop the mushrooms, strain the soaking liquid, and add both to the soup pot. Heat over low heat.

5. Stir the chestnut purée and the cream into the hot soup. Season with the sherry, nutmeg, salt, and pepper. Heat through. Serve hot in small cups, garnished with the parsley. Watch your guests swoon. Swoon yourself.

Serves 4 to 6 as a starter

ABOUT SHELLING CHESTNUTS

🍎*You wouldn't expect a treasure like a chestnut to be easily gotten to, would you? These European nuts, starchier than most, have both a hard, dark brown shell and a hairy, inedible skin; both of which must be removed before eating. This can be done by roasting or boiling the chestnuts first. Miss Kay always boiled hers, for they came out creamier that way, but roast them if you plan to eat them unadorned.*

Whether you roast or boil the nuts, you must first cut an X with a sharp paring knife on the flat side of each chestnut.

To roast, preheat the oven to 425° F. In a skillet, toss the unshelled nuts over high heat with mild vegetable oil, allowing a teaspoon per pound, for a minute or so. Transfer the nuts to a baking sheet and spread them out in a single layer. Bake 15 to 20 minutes. Peel both the outer and inner skins while the nuts are still hot; burning your fingers is part of the experience.

To boil, drop the chestnuts into a large pot of boiling water to cover. Turn down the heat to medium-low and let simmer, uncovered, 20 to 25 minutes. Drain the nuts and shell as soon as you can handle them.

Old South Peanut Soup

hen Ned and I lived in Georgia, Savannah was our very favorite city to hide away in.

Peanut recipes abound in Savannah. We had great peanut butter pie at a couple of places and peanut butter soup more than once. This is my re-creation of one we had. I think it must be a slavery era legacy: peanuts came over with the slaves, and groundnut stew (peanuts, which grow under the ground, were called "groundnuts") is a dish commonly eaten to this day in parts of Africa.

3½ cups Chicken Stock 1 (page 19) or
    Golden Vegetable Stock (page 28) or any
    well-flavored chicken or vegetable stock
1 large onion, chopped
1 large carrot, peeled and chopped
1 rib celery with leaves, chopped
1 bay leaf
1 cup creamy peanut butter
2 teaspoons honey
1 can (13 ounces) evaporated milk or 1⅔
    cups heavy (whipping) cream
Finely chopped fresh parsley, for garnish
*Chopped dry-roasted salted or honey-
    roasted peanuts, for garnish*

1. In a soup pot, combine the stock, onion, carrot, celery, and bay leaf. Bring to a boil, then turn down the heat to medium-low and let simmer, covered, until the vegetables are very soft, about 15 minutes.

2. Strain the stock, discarding the vegetables and bay leaf. Return the stock to the pot and stir in the peanut butter (it may look curdled at first, but will smooth out), then stir in the honey and evaporated milk. Reheat. Serve hot, garnished with parsley and peanuts.

Serves 4 to 6 as a small, very rich starter

Extraordinary Mushroom Walnut Soup

ome of the most divine soups are inspired by leftovers, and in a good restaurant kitchen a person can have some pretty exquisite leftovers. In this case, the soup we concocted from the leftovers of a brandied mushroom walnut pâté was so good that we have since used it as a "planned over," serving the pâté one night and the soup the next. I would be the first to admit that the flavors sound wildly improbable, but this is simply unbelievably good (although densely caloric, alas). It is very rich and often requested. I am giving the recipe as we make it, that is, in two parts.

4 cups (see Note) Chicken Stock 1 (page 19) or Golden or Browned Vegetable Stock (pages 28 and 32) or any well-flavored chicken or vegetable stock
1 ounce dried porcini or morel mushrooms
2 tablespoons butter or mild vegetable oil, such as corn or peanut
1 large onion, chopped
2 ribs celery with leaves, chopped
2 medium carrots, scrubbed or peeled and sliced
1 parsnip, scrubbed or peeled and sliced
2 teaspoons tamari/shoyu soy sauce, or to taste
1 cup dry white wine
8 ounces domestic white mushrooms, sliced
1 tablespoon dried dill
½ teaspoon dried basil
½ teaspoon dried thyme
½ teaspoon dried oregano
1½ cups tomato or mixed vegetable juice
2 cups Brandied Mushroom-Walnut Pâté (recipe follows)
1½ cups cooked long-grain white rice
Salt and freshly ground black pepper to taste
Additional sliced fresh mushrooms, for garnish
Finely chopped fresh parsley or small dill sprigs, for garnish

1. In a large soup pot, bring the stock to a boil. In a small bowl, pour 1 cup of the hot stock over the dried mushrooms. Let soak while proceeding with the soup.

2. In a 10-inch heavy skillet, melt the butter over medium heat. Add the onion and sauté until softened, about 3 minutes. Add the celery, carrots, parsnip, and soy sauce. Turn down the heat slightly and cook, stirring often, until the vegetables start to soften, about 3 minutes more. Scrape the sautéed vegetables into the hot stock. Deglaze the skillet with a little of the wine and add the pan contents to the stock.

3. Add to the stock the remaining wine, the fresh mushrooms, dill, and herbs. Bring to a boil, then turn down the heat to very low and barely simmer, covered, 30 minutes.

4. Towards the end of this 30-minute simmering time, remove the dried mushrooms from the soaking liquid. Strain the liquid and add it to the soup. Rinse the mushrooms well to get rid of any grit, coarsely chop, and add to the soup along with the tomato juice. Simmer, covered, 15 minutes.

5. Whisk or stir the pâté into the soup ½ cup at a time, then stir in the cooked rice. Taste and add salt and pepper, plus more stock, tomato juice, or wine if needed. Heat the soup until very hot. Serve in small cups, garnishing each serving with a sliced mushroom and a little parsley.

Serves 6 to 8 as a small, very rich starter

Note: If you have more or less than 2 cups of leftover pâté, adjust the other ingredients proportionally: for every 1 cup of pâté, 2 cups stock, ¾ cup tomato juice, and ½ cup wine. Use your best judgment on the rest.

Brandied Mushroom-Walnut Pâté

his recipe makes enough pâté to work as both a soup ingredient and as a first course accompanied by crackers and crudités.

½ cup mild vegetable oil, such as corn
or peanut, or 8 tablespoons (1 stick)
butter
1 large onion, chopped
1 medium carrot, scrubbed and grated
1½ pounds domestic white mushrooms,
sliced
1 cup English walnuts, toasted (page 316)
1 heaping tablespoon peanut butter
1 heaping tablespoon light miso, or to
taste
3 tablespoons cognac
¼ teaspoon ground allspice
Several gratings of fresh nutmeg
Salt and freshly ground black pepper to
taste

1. The day before serving, in a 10-inch skillet, heat ¼ cup of the oil over medium heat. Add the onion and sauté until it starts to soften, about 3 minutes. Add the carrot and sauté until slightly softened, about 3 minutes more. Scrape the onion and carrot into a food processor.

2. Add about one-third of the remaining oil to the skillet and heat over medium heat. Add one-third of the mushrooms and sauté until the mushrooms become limp, about 7 minutes. Scrape the mushrooms into the food processor and repeat with the remaining oil and mushrooms.

3. Add to the processor the walnuts, peanut butter, miso, cognac, allspice, nutmeg, salt, and plenty of pepper. Purée until absolutely smooth. (It will be very thick.) Taste and adjust the seasoning. It may need additional miso, which gives it a salty, meaty heartiness.

4. Transfer the pâté to a crock (or, less glamorously, to a refrigerator storage dish). Cover and refrigerate overnight to ripen.

Makes about 4 cups

Loaves, Muffins

AND MORE

read is elemental. Earth, water, fire, and air, the four elements of the ancients, combine in bread. Bread has nourished humankind for time out of mind, and each kernel of the grain which makes up the bread's flour tells the same story: how the earth became our home.

Until grain was domesticated, we were in one sense visitors here. Though reverent ones, we treaded lightly and with fear, dependent on unpredictable forces we did not understand and could not control. When we learned to plant, harvest, and plant again, our relationship to all nature changed. Each kernel of grain holds the secret of those forces; holds life itself. Plant a kernel of wheat or corn or rye, and it will renew itself a thousandfold, and live again. Grind that kernel, and you have a dust that is not a symbol of death, but rather of life itself.

Combine flour with water, from which we crawled, of which we are largely made, and without which we cannot live. Add salt-of-the-earth, just a bit; salt for savor, for soul, the sharp and dangerous mineral wrested from nature yet part of nature, a rock that can be eaten, which dissolves in water only to return, unchanged and crystalline, when the water evaporates. Add yeasts, airborne vegetal travelers, which themselves make the dough "travel" (and where? Up into the air, of course!). Risings and fallings of the dough, punching downs, and the rough caresses of kneading. Mix it up and add fire. And suddenly, from those four ancient elements, bread—and just in time for supper.

In that curling steam, released from the breaking, too-hot loaf, cut into because we couldn't wait for it to cool—in that rising steam, do we glimpse eternity?

Yeast is perhaps the most enigmatic component of bread making to those new to the art. Yeasts are microscopic, mushroomlike plants which live around, in, and on us, in the air we breathe. Yeast causes the salted paste of flour and water to rise, to become bread as we know it. Yeast is alive: it is dynamic, and, until the advent of commercially grown strains in the nineteenth century, was unpredictable. (From ancient Egyptian times and even earlier until little more than a hundred years ago, people would mix their dough, set it out in a warm place, and hope that any passing airborne yeasts would stop and stay awhile; obligingly, they usually did.) Often, to those who've never made bread, yeast *still* seems unpredictable, intimidating; living yeast seems not static and adaptable, but demanding, uncertain. Dissolve in "warm but not hot" liquid, let rise "until doubled in bulk," "punch down" or "knead" the dough. These recipe directions are unlike those for any foods *except* yeast-risen breads. They are also primitive, inexact, and very physical.

Only through experience does one learn that yeast, though alive, is actually quite accommodating and unfussy. (If you are inexperienced, pick up another cookbook just on bread—Judith and Evan Jones's *The Book of Bread, Laurel's Kitchen Bread Book,* by Laurel Robertson, or, if you can find it, the very charming, but out-of-print *Uncle John's Bread Book,* all of which go into much more detail on the fine points of yeast and every other phase of bread baking than space permits here.)

Finally, though, it is yeast's very aliveness that gives the baking of bread its addictive charm, its peaceful, calming, gentle rhythms, remarked on by every home bread-baker I know. Kneading a dough that changes shape, size, and texture, punching it down, shaping it into loaves, sniffing the intoxicating aromas as it bakes—partaking in these routines, it is nearly impossible for the cook's spirits not to rise with the bread.

Yeasts follow the same life cycles we do, but in speeded-up time. They feed (mostly on carbohydrates), they grow, reproduce, and die. We don't call it life and death, though; we call it fermentation. It is the yeast on the skins of grapes that turns grape juice into wine; it is the addition of yeast to dough that makes it rise. Both transmutations happen through fermentation, one of those kitchen processes that seems, to the thoughtful cook, as magical as alchemy.

But this is a magic that moves us from awe to sustenance without pause. Bread is symbolic, yes, but bread is also bread. Bread is the staff and stuff of life, our daily bread (though we do not live by it alone). Bread heartens us, so that we may find strength to forgive those who trespass against us. We may call for it metaphorically, as in the old thirties union song whose lyrics cried out for bread and roses. We may celebrate with it; every culture has festival breads, made fanciful with fruits and nuts, eggs and cream, herbs and spices. We may contemporize bread by making it in a food processor; we may make it without added leavening or with a quick leavening (baking powder or soda) instead of yeast. But no matter how you slice it, it's still bread. For when we smell bread baking, it's simple: we know, as people have known for thousands of years, that all is well, that soon we will eat, and eat well. We know we are home.

ON KNEADING BY HAND

❧ *Call it sentiment, but I say there's a special magic in a bread's taste and texture when it is kneaded by hand that just can't be matched by a food processor or mixer with a dough hook. Don't get me wrong, I love my machines and use them continually, especially in the restaurant. But I always turn the doughs out of the machines at some point and give them at least a few kneads by hand, regardless of what the recipe says. Maybe it's the warmth of a human hand; maybe an experienced cook can bring the bread to its perfect texture only by touch; perhaps there are even good yeasts that live on skin (even just-washed skin) that contribute to the flavor. But you come taste our bread at Dairy Hollow and see if I'm not right.* ❧

YEAST BREADS

ON YEAST

There are three types of commonly available commercial yeast (leaving aside the more esoteric yeasts available for making wine, beer, champagne, etc.), two of which are used for leavening bread. These two leavening yeasts are active dry yeast (regular or quick-rise) and fresh compressed yeast.

Active dry yeast is made up of small, dry, light brown granules; the quick-rise's granules are slightly larger. Either type has a long shelf life, even stored at room temperature, as long as it is kept dry. Active dry yeast is commonly sold in individual foil packets or by the jar or in a vacuum-packed bag (once jar or bag have been opened, keep refrigerated, and, in the case of yeast from a bag, transfer to a container with a tightly fitting lid). One packet regular (not quick-rise) yeast equals 1 tablespoon yeast.

Compressed fresh yeast is always kept refrigerated or frozen, and comes foil-wrapped, in moist cubes. Both can be purchased in the supermarket.

Both yeasts are activated by contact with warm liquid, and after being activated, most often fed with honey or sugar and then flour. If the water is too hot, it will kill the yeast; if it is too cold, the yeast will awaken very, very slowly. This is why bread recipes using yeast always specify "lukewarm" liquids. Lukewarm means a temperature between 105° F and 115° F, but I have never in my life used a thermometer to test it. Just dunk a (clean) finger in the water or milk. It should be cool enough so that it is quite comfortable to the touch, but warm enough that it still registers as, well, warm. This non-scientific method has taken me through thousands of successful bread risings.

Into this lukewarm liquid, the measured amount of active dry yeast is poured, or compressed fresh yeast is crumbled. I must say I love the way compressed yeast feels in the hand—pleasantly squeaky-spongy and soft, with a texture unlike anything else in this world—but it makes no detectable difference in taste or rising time at all to the finished bread which yeast you use. Because dry is more convenient, that is the yeast we usually use at the restaurant and home.

For consistency's sake, the yeast called for in these recipes is, unless otherwise specified, regular (not quick-rise) active dry yeast. Because many bread-bakers buy in bulk, quantities are specified in teaspoons or tablespoons, not packages. Just remember that 1 packet yeast contains 1 tablespoon, and 1 tablespoon has 3 teaspoons.

About those quick-rises: I am not fond of them. I believe the bread has a superior flavor and texture when permitted to rise more slowly.

The third commercial yeast is nu-

tritional yeast, which is *not* used for leavening. It is discussed on page 31.

PROOFING

"Proofing" the yeast means dissolving it first in warm liquid and letting it sit until the liquid is foamy, before adding it to the dry ingredients. This foaminess means that your yeast is working (it *will* work unless you have inadvertently used old yeast, or too-hot water). Thus you have "proof" of the yeast's effectiveness before you begin. Yeast can be proofed in plain water, but for really showy, bubbly foaming, it needs some form of carbohydrate to feed on—a touch of honey or sugar, or dissolution in warm milk instead of water.

THE PERFECT BREADBASKET

❦At the restaurant, the amplitude and variety of our breads are commented on frequently. We try to keep our breadbaskets, lined with their pink napkins, filled to overflowing. We always have at least two selections, sometimes three. Almost invariably, one of the breads is our wonderful Skillet-Sizzled Buttermilk Cornbread (page 352), served in wedges hot from the oven. The second bread may be a biscuit but is more usually a yeast bread or roll—Whole-Wheat Butterhorns (page 346), or French Country Bread (page 328). If there's a third bread, it's a specialty bread: Herbed Mezzaluna Bread (page 336), or Rosemary Focaccia Dairy Hollow (page 337), any one of a dozen sweet tea breads, or a sweet or savory muffin, such as Deedy's Gram's Graham Muffins (page 368). It's nice to have a variety of breads to sample; it rounds out a simple meal and adds dimension to a complex one.

For at-home entertaining, a bottomless breadbasket with several breads is so unusual that it is sure to please. If the idea of making two or three breads is daunting, make just one yourself—a muffin, maybe, or cornbread, which are simple, quick, never as good bought as they are homemade—and purchase the others from a good bakery. Warm the bakery loaves slightly before serving.

Even a supermarket bread of reasonably good quality can be dressed up by toasting it and rubbing it with a garlic herb butter. Tuck the herb toasts in among your homemade offering and add a bakery French bread or raisin pumpernickel. Don't be surprised if there's not a crumb left.❦

French Country Bread

 spent years messing around trying to come up with the ultimate French-style, crisp-crusted bread, and many times came within bragging distance. But with this recipe closely adapted from Paula Wolfert's Country-Style Bread in *The Cooking of South-West France*—I've found it. I say, "Thank you, Paula." We do make enormous batches of this.

It's the simplest of breads: flour, water, salt, yeast. It's good, chewy, coarse, basic; more European than American in taste and texture. Made without fat, sugar, or milk, it has a very crisp crust, made even crisper by an in-oven spritzing with water. Thanks to a starter made a day or two ahead of time, it has the faintest tang of sourness. The length of the kneading time may seem daunting; if so, get a friend to switch off with you, or use a sturdy mixer (like a KitchenAid) with a dough hook. You'll finish the dough by hand, though, even if you use a machine.

STARTER:
1½ teaspoons active dry yeast
¾ cup lukewarm spring water
1 cup unbleached all-purpose flour

DOUGH:
1½ cups lukewarm spring water
4½ teaspoons fine sea salt
1 cup stone-ground whole-wheat flour
5½ cups unbleached all-purpose flour (see Note), approximately

Cornmeal for the baking sheet

1. One to 2 days before you plan on serving the bread, make the starter: In a medium-size bowl, dissolve the yeast in the warm water and let it proof until foamy. Stir in the flour, and mix until smooth. Cover the bowl tightly with plastic wrap, and let stand at room temperature.

2. On bread-baking day, make the dough: Transfer the starter (don't worry if it has separated) to a large bowl. Add the lukewarm water and the salt and stir well to combine. Begin adding the flour 1 cup at a time, beating well after each addition. Make sure each cup is absorbed before you add the next. If the dough is tacky after all the flour has been added, add an additional 1 or 2 tablespoons of flour.

3. Knead the dough on a lightly floured surface until it is smooth and elastic. This will take 20 minutes by hand; if you have a mixer with a dough hook, 8 to 10 minutes will do the trick. If you use a dough hook, do give the dough a few last turns by hand. You want a consistency that, in Wolfert's words, is "smooth, elastic, somewhat soft."

4. Flour the inside of a large bowl, and place the dough in it. Cover with a clean cloth, and let rise in a warm place until doubled in bulk, about 1½ to 2 hours. Punch down the dough, and knead it quickly—15 or 20 turns—then return it to the bowl and let it rise until doubled in bulk a second time. The second rising is usually a little quicker, 1¼ to 1½ hours. Punch down again, reflour the rising bowl, add the dough, and let rise a third time.

5. As the bread is on its third rise, preheat the oven to 450° F and have at hand a plastic mister, such as you use for plants, filled with spring water. Place a baking sheet as close in size as possible to that of an oven rack on the middle rack. The sheet mimics an oven floor. Sprinkle a second, smaller, baking sheet well with cornmeal.

6. When the dough has risen the third time, invert it carefully out of the bowl onto the cornmeal-sprinkled sheet, and using a razor, slash the top with two or three Xs, ¹⁄₁₆ to ⅛ inch deep. Lower the oven heat to 400°F, spritz the interior of the oven 3 or 4 times with the plant mister, and immediately slide the bread in, on its baking sheet, across the baking sheet already in the oven. Bake the bread 40 to 60 minutes, opening the oven and spritzing the inside once more, halfway through the baking. The bread is done when it is golden brown, and sounds hollow when thumped on its bottom. Cool the bread on a wire rack.

Makes 1 loaf

Note: Paula Wolfert suggests using unbleached bread flour with a 13 percent protein content. (It is the protein, or gluten, in flour that gives yeast breads their structure.) We use stone-ground, unbleached white flour and it has worked just fine; I assume its gluten content is in the range she suggests. Most flours sold as "all-purpose" in this country are within this range, but stay clear of pastry or cake flours.

INN GOOD COMPANY: DOUG STOWE AND THE MAGIC TEA BOX

Ask for tea at the restaurant, and your waiter will bring over our Dairy Hollow tea chest for you to make your selection. Chances are, you'll do some oohing and ahhhing before you choose.

The chest is made of local cherrywood and has room for twelve varieties of tea. It was made by local woodworker Doug Stowe, who uses only local hardwoods in his pieces, which range from tiny business-card holders to beds, armoires, and home entertainment centers. Doug's inlay techniques have received national and even international renown—whenever Governor Bill Clinton takes trips abroad, he buys up two or three dozen of Doug's gorgeous inlay boxes as very special from-the-state gifts for the industrialists and politicians he'll meet with.

In our tea chest, Doug created a row of inlaid cows of curly maple, with black walnut spots.

The Jones's Country Loaves from Jan Brown

an Brown adapted this recipe slightly from its source: a recipe for country bread by Judith and Evan Jones in *Food & Wine* magazine. The "collaboration" is cause for celebration. One bite and you feel nourished right down to your toes.

CAROLE'S SHOWER SUPPER

*The Jones's Country Loaves from Jan Brown

A Salad for Fall (made with beets, walnuts, apples, blue cheese) with Sesame Raisin Vinaigrette

*Lentil Dal

Buccone Dolce

This is a start-the-night-before bread. Like French Country Bread, it's also round and bakes in a steamy oven (albeit by a different, and fun, method). But it rises twice instead of three times and is not kneaded as such, which makes it coarser and heavier—perfect for peasanty soups.

Jan says "It's not necessary to knead, but kneading never hurts a good bread either."

STARTER:
1½ cups lukewarm spring water
1 teaspoon honey
1 tablespoon active dry yeast
2 cups unbleached all-purpose flour

DOUGH:
1⅔ cups lukewarm spring water
1½ cups whole-wheat flour, preferably freshly ground
5 to 6 cups unbleached all-purpose flour
1 tablespoon salt

Cornmeal for the baking sheet

GLAZE AND GARNISH:
1 large egg white, lightly beaten
1 tablespoon poppy seeds

1. Make the starter the night before you plan to make the bread: In a large bowl, mix the water and honey, and sprinkle the yeast over the top. Let stand until foamy, about 10 minutes. Add the flour and stir vigorously for about 1 minute. Cover tightly with plastic wrap, then a clean kitchen towel, and leave in a warm place overnight. It will be happiest with a 12- to 14-hour meditation.

2. The next day, make the dough: To the starter add the water, whole-wheat flour, 4 cups of the all-purpose flour, and the salt,

and stir until the mixture is smooth. Gradually stir in the remaining flour, 1 cup at a time, until the dough is smooth and elastic.

3. Oil a large bowl, add the dough, and turn to coat it. Cover with a clean cloth and let the dough rise in a warm place until doubled in bulk, about 2 hours.

4. Punch the dough down and divide it in half. Shape each half into a large round loaf. Sprinkle a large baking sheet with the cornmeal and place the loaves on it. Cover with a cloth and let the loaves rise until doubled again, 1 to 1½ hours.

5. About 45 minutes into this last rise, preheat the oven to 425° F.

6. Paint the tops of the loaves with the egg white, being careful not to disturb the rise by brushing too vigorously, then sprinkle the loaves with the poppy seeds. Place the baking sheet on the middle rack of the oven, then throw a few ice cubes onto the oven floor. (Or, if using an electric oven with a heating element on the oven floor, place 12 to 15 ice cubes in a cast-iron skillet on the bottom shelf of the oven. If your oven floor is dirty, just set a pan of water on the bottom rack.) Bake the bread for 15 minutes, throwing in a few more ice cubes after 3 minutes, then again after 6 minutes. Turn down the heat to 350° F and bake 20 minutes more. Turn off the oven and let the bread rest in the oven 15 minutes more. Cool on wire racks.

Makes 2 loaves

Frannie's Fast, Fabulous Buttermilk Bread

 letter from Frannie Lah of Norwood, Ohio, right after her and Bob's second, or was it third, visit to Eureka and Dairy Hollow in three months . . . a letter and a recipe for a great, delicious, bountiful, buttery, quick-rising, quickly made, food-processed, high-rising bread. Fancier than the breads that precede it, this is an *excellent* white bread which makes stupendous French toast, and also is a great basis for cinnamon-raisin bread.

This from Frannie: ". . . so Bob says, 'You didn't send her your recipe for buttermilk bread??? That's the best thing you make!!!' So here it is . . . This is everybody's favorite of all my breads— Bob's, my dad's, mom's, bread-and-soup-party guests, everybody. It smells outrageously good while it bakes, which I think partly accounts for its enormous popularity."

Frannie, who enjoys teaching a bread-baking class (a change of pace activity from her real life as a city prosecutor) says she always makes a double-recipe, adding "This bread freezes very well if you wrap it securely, but nothing matches eating it 20 minutes out of the oven."

¼ cup lukewarm water
1 tablespoon active dry yeast
2 cups buttermilk, preferably Bulgarian-style
4 tablespoons (½ stick) butter, plus 3 tablespoons, softened, for greasing bowl, bread pans, and brushing tops of loaves
4 to 5 cups unbleached all-purpose flour
1 teaspoon salt
¼ teaspoon baking soda
2 tablespoons sugar

1. In a large measuring cup with a good pouring lip, combine the water and yeast. Let stand until foamy. As the yeast proofs, combine the buttermilk and 4 table-spoons butter in a small saucepan, and heat over low heat until the butter melts. ("Don't let it bother you if the buttermilk curdles," says Frannie. "This bread doesn't mind.") Remove the scalded buttermilk mixture from the heat, and let stand until lukewarm. Combine with the proofed yeast.

2. In a food processor, combine 4 cups of the flour with the salt, baking soda, and sugar. Buzz with a few quick on-off spins to blend. Then, with machine running, add the buttermilk mixture through the feed tube. Process until the dough comes together, forming "a ball that whips around the work-bowl and 'dings' slightly to the sides, cleaning them," says Frannie. If the dough is too moist, add additional flour, 2 tablespoons at a time, from the extra cup. If too dry, add more but-termilk until the consistency is right.

3. Transfer the dough to a lightly floured work surface and knead it until smooth and elastic, 5 to 7 minutes. Butter a bowl with 1 tablespoon of the remaining but-ter, and place the dough in it. Cover with a clean cloth, and let rise in a warm place until doubled in bulk, about 1½ hours. Punch it down, and let it rise again, covered, again

until doubled, this time 45 to 60 minutes. Transfer the dough to a floured surface, knead it for a minute or so, then cover it, on the work surface, with a towel, for a third quick rise. ("Don't go too far away this time," cautions Frannie. "The dough is only resting for 10 minutes, not doing a full-scale rise.")

4. Divide the dough in half and form it into two loaves. Place them into standard size loaf pans buttered with a teaspoon or so of the remaining butter. Cover, and let rise again, for the final time, 45 to 60 minutes.

5. Towards the end of the fourth rise, preheat the oven to 350° F.

6. Bake the loaves until nicely golden, 35 to 45 minutes. Then turn them out onto wire racks to cool. Brush the tops with the remaining butter.

Makes 2 loaves

VARIATION:

I have sometimes made this dreamy bread substituting 1 to 2 cups of whole-wheat flour for an equal amount of unbleached all-pur-pose white.

Alex Dann's Champagne-Yeast Bread

 hen Alex and Mimi Dann, attor-ney and artist, respectively, from Memphis, Tennessee, came to stay with us late in the summer of 1987, the talk turned to food, particularly bread. Alex was a home bread-baker, and as he began to describe a yeast bread of his which used winemaker's champagne yeast, I grew so intrigued I started making notes on the spot. After returning home, Alex sent us two packages of the champagne yeast. I made the bread following from the scribbled recipe I had written that August morning. Wow!

This is a delicious bread with a silken-textured dough and an almost cakelike crumb. Oatmeal keeps it interesting and not too white-floury (you already know my prejudice here).

The champagne yeast called for in this bread can be ordered from the Winery of Overton Square, 60 Cooper Street South, Memphis, Tennessee 38104, (901) 278-2682. You will notice immediately the difference in the shape of the yeast granules and the manner in which they bubble. I know you will enjoy this bread as much as we do. A slice gives new meaning to the phrase "A toast!"

2 cups milk
2 cups spring water
2 tablespoons butter
¼ cup sugar, plus a pinch for the yeast
2 teaspoons sea salt
¼ cup lukewarm spring water
2 packages champagne yeast
1 cup rolled oats
6 to 8 cups unbleached all-purpose flour
2 to 3 tablespoons melted butter, for
  brushing the loaves

1. In a small saucepan, heat together the milk, the 2 cups water, butter, ¼ cup sugar, and the salt until the butter melts. Pour this mixture into a large bowl and let cool to lukewarm.

2. Meanwhile, in a small bowl, stir the pinch of sugar into the lukewarm water. Sprinkle the yeast over the top and let stand until foamy, 5 to 10 minutes.

3. Add the proofed yeast to the milk mixture and stir to blend. Stir in the oats, and then enough of the flour to make a smooth and elastic dough. Transfer the dough to a lightly floured surface and knead 2 minutes, no longer.

4. Butter a large bowl and add the dough. Cover with a clean cloth and let rise until doubled in bulk, about 3 hours.

5. Butter or oil three 9 × 5-inch loaf pans. Punch the dough down and knead briefly. Divide the dough in 3 pieces, shape into loaves, and place them in the loaf pans. Cover and let rise until rounded above the tops of the pans, about 1 hour.

6. About 30 minutes into this final rise, preheat the oven to 425° F.

7. Bake the loaves 10 minutes. Remove them from the oven and brush the tops with the melted butter. Return the loaves to the oven, turn down the heat to 325° F., and bake until golden, about 30 minutes. Let cool at least slightly on wire racks before eating.

Makes 3 loaves

Déjà Food: This bread makes noteworthy French toast and excellent bread crumbs; it is also good just plain toasted.

INNECDOTE

❧ *On the Friday of our first Brilliant Deductions Murder Mystery Weekend (special event weekends we hold regularly at the Inn), 18-some guests, very much in character and in costume, were milling around the lobby, beginning to sleuth. Lord Fitzoy Chillington-Worcestershire had dropped in from his ancestral home at Worcestershire-on-Thames, psychic Martina Ditsky had traveled from St. Louis sensing dark vibrations, and Petunia Petit dressed in the vintage clothing she sold at her shop, Déjà Vu, was picking a fight with her boyfriend, Victoriana buff Mitchell Frane. Things were hopping. Several guests wore prominent hats.*

A woman in search of dinner, clearly in complete ignorance of the mystery goings-on in progress, opened the door to the inn. She glanced in, looked around, and inquired, "Do you-all have a dress code?" ❧

Felicity Turner's Slightly Fanatic Dream Whole-Grain Bread

hen I met Felicity Turner, she just wasn't herself, she was Petunia Pettit, a character in one of Dairy Hollow's Brilliant Deductions Mystery Weekends. Not until the end of the weekend (during which Petunia, owner of the vintage clothing shop Déjà Vu, found the pivotal pearl-handled revolver in an alligator purse) did I learn her true identity.

Felicity's real life turned out to be easily as interesting as her character's. She now lives in Fayetteville, Arkansas, and is married to bakery-owner-turned-stockbroker Michael. The mother of two, her past includes not only a background in theater but a stint in world-class baking: she did recipe testing for Barbara Kafka, Paula Wolfert, and James Beard, as well as desserts for one of the top New York restaurants, the Quilted Giraffe. (How did she end up in Arkansas? Hey, how did *I* end up in Arkansas? We each have our stories. Call it karma. Call it kismet. Call it wanting something better and *going for it*. Anyway, here we are, she and I and plenty of other metropolitan refugees, in the Ozarks and mighty pleased with ourselves, too, I might add.)

One winter day, Felicity sent over a loaf of this bread with Sally Suze, a then neighbor who commuted regularly to and from Fayetteville. A recipe was attached; clearly Felicity knew this dense, wondrously grainy bread would appeal to me in a big way. It did. "This I devised after months of messing around trying to create my dream whole-grain bread," Felicity wrote in her note. "Clearly, I like a solid loaf. We live on this bread at our house. Both children and grown-ups eat it every day and we never seem to tire of it . . . I don't put any oil or white flour in, however some of each would probably make it more acceptable for mainstream consumption. But I am inclined to the slightly fanatic and like my bread to be pure health."

I call Felicity's bread pure delicious, in both fanatic and mainstream versions. The wheatberries called for are whole-grain kernels of wheat, available at natural foods stores.

5⅓ cups spring water, approximately
½ cup wheatberries
1 medium potato, scrubbed and diced
3 tablespoons sorghum molasses
1 tablespoon active dry yeast
2 teaspoons salt
1 cup gluten flour (high-gluten flour; available in natural foods stores)
1 cup stone-ground yellow cornmeal
5 to 6 cups stone-ground whole-wheat flour, approximately

1. In a medium-size pot, bring to a boil 3 cups of the spring water and add the wheatberries. Turn down the heat, and let simmer, covered, until the wheatberries have started to pop open and are fairly tender, 1 to 1¼ hours.

2. Meanwhile, in a small pot, bring 2 cups of spring water to a boil, and drop in the diced potato. Turn down the heat and let the potato simmer until very soft, 17 to 20 minutes.

3. When the potato and wheatberries are both tender, remove from the heat and drain, reserving the liquids and solids. Mash the potato, and combine with the wheatberries. Combine the cooking water from the potatoes and wheatberries. Measure this liquid; you will need 2⅓ cups. If the leftover cooking liquid does not equal this amount, add additional spring water. The liquid will probably still be warm from the cooking, but if you've lingered, you may need to rewarm it to get it to the requisite yeast-loving lukewarm temperature.

4. In a large bowl, combine the molasses and the 2⅓ cups lukewarm cooking water. Sprinkle the yeast over the top and let stand until foamy, 5 to 10 minutes. Add the salt and the wheatberry-potato mixture.

5. Stir in, 1 cup at a time, the gluten flour, cornmeal, and 1 cup of the whole-wheat flour. Be sure to incorporate each cup of flour before adding the next. This is a wet mixture, called a "sponge." Cover with a clean cloth, and let the sponge sit in a warm place for 1 hour. Transfer the sponge to a lightly floured work surface, and knead in enough additional whole-wheat flour (3¾ to 4¾ cups) to make a rather dry dough. ("It should be drier than most doughs, or the bread will still be wet inside, as if it were raw, when it is baked," notes Felicity. "This is important.")

6. Transfer the dough to a bowl (not necesssary to oil it, says Felicity) and let rise, covered, in a warm place until doubled in bulk, about 2 to 2¼ hours. Punch it down, form it into 2 loaves, and place it in oiled (or spray with Pam) full-size bread pans, about

4 × 8 × 2½ inches. Let the loaves rise, covered, a second time, about 40 to 50 minutes. Towards the end of this period preheat the oven to 350° F When the bread has risen, lower the heat to 325° F. and bake until the loaves are a light brown, and sound hollow when the bottoms are tapped, about 50 minutes.

Makes 2 loaves

VARIATIONS:

Mainstream Dream Whole-grain Bread: Just a little less seriously hearty than the previous loaf, but still plenty hefty, and just delicious. Add 2 tablespoons of honey to the yeast-molasses mixture. Add ¼ cup oil or melted butter to the yeast mixture with the salt. Purée the potato in the food processor, add the wheatberries, and pulse until the wheatberries are coarsely chopped. Substitute 2½ cups unbleached all-purpose flour for the equivalent amount of whole-wheat.

Herbed Mezzaluna Bread

 Dairy Hollow House original: a rich, lightly sweetened, egg and milk yeast dough (almost a traditional coffeecake dough but less sweet) is rolled out, covered with herbs and garlic, and folded over into irregular half-moon-shaped breads. (*Mezzaluna* means "half moon" in Italian.) You tear

off what you want of the finished, fragrant, lumpy loaves. They are deliberately, artistically primitive—quick, too, for the dough is made in a processor.

In these days of cholesterol consciousness, this is a bread people call "sinful." But, boy, is it good. I make this bread five or six times a year, usually on holiday or festival weekends in Eureka. There are never leftovers, and guests always beg for more. It's fun to make a great big one for a party, and let everyone break bread—person to person, heart to heart.

DOUGH:
¼ *cup plus 2 teaspoons sugar*
1 cup milk, scalded and cooled to lukewarm
2 packages active dry yeast
3 cups unbleached all-purpose flour
½ *teaspoon salt*
8 tablespoons (1 stick) butter, chilled and cut into small chunks
3 large egg yolks

FILLING:
4 tablespoons (½ stick) butter, at room temperature
1 tablespoon olive oil
3 to 4 tablespoons finely chopped combination of fresh herbs, such as rosemary, basil, savory, and parsley and/ or 1½ to 2 teaspoons dried herbs, such as basil, thyme, and oregano
5 cloves garlic, peeled and put through a garlic press or finely chopped
Pam cooking spray or additional oil
1 large egg white, lightly beaten (optional)

1. In a small bowl, stir the 2 teaspoons sugar into the warm milk. Sprinkle the yeast over the top and let stand until foamy, 5 to 10 minutes.

2. Put the remaining ¼ cup sugar, the flour, salt, and butter in a food processor. Pulse until combined. Add the yeast mixture and the egg yolks; process until thoroughly mixed, 20 to 30 seconds. Transfer the dough to a large bowl, cover tightly with plastic wrap, and refrigerate at least 4 hours or overnight.

3. Roll the dough out into a thin, large irregular circle (or 2 or 3 smaller circles). Spread the butter and drizzle the olive oil over the dough, and sprinkle with the herbs and garlic. Fold the dough in half, roll up the edges, and crimp to seal. The dough should be irregular, and flat—that's part of the charm.

4. Spray a large baking sheet with the Pam or coat lightly with oil and put the bread on it. Cover with a clean cloth and let rise until not quite doubled, about 45 to 50 minutes.

5. About 30 minutes into the rise, preheat the oven to 350° F.

6. Brush the bread with the beaten egg white for an extra-shiny top. Bake until golden, about 40 minutes (the smaller circles will bake more quickly). Serve as soon as possible, on a tray lined with a snowy white napkin. Encourage your guests to tear off hearty hunks of this. After the first piece is torn and the herby, garlicky aroma pours out, they won't really need encouragement.

Makes 1 large loaf or 3 or 4 smaller loaves; enough for 6 to 8 people

Rosemary Focaccia Dairy Hollow

ere is a second herbed bread, simpler and less rich but just as delicious as the preceding mezzalunas. It's great with any bean soup, from Italian minestrone to an Ozark-style bean soup. The dough is pulled out flat, not made into loaves or mezzalunas, then dented with the fingertips, drizzled with olive oil, sprinkled with rosemary, and served in chunky squares. There's something about its peasanty herbal flavors and salt that is simply addictive.

1¼ cups spring water
3 tablespoons dried rosemary (make sure it's strong and fragrant)
1 tablespoon honey
1 tablespoon active dry yeast
1 teaspoon salt
4 tablespoons olive oil
2½ to 3 cups unbleached all-purpose flour
1 large egg yolk
1 teaspoon water
Coarse (kosher) salt

1. Bring the water to a boil and pour it over 1 tablespoon of the rosemary in a small bowl. Let cool to lukewarm, then strain, discarding the rosemary.

2. Pour the rosemary water into a large mixing bowl. Stir in the honey. Sprinkle the yeast over the top and let stand until foamy, 5 to 10 minutes. Stir in the salt, 1 tablespoon

of the oil, then add enough of the flour to make a kneadable dough.

3. Knead the dough on a lightly floured surface until smooth and elastic, 5 to 8 minutes. Coat a large bowl with a few drops of olive oil, add the dough, and turn to coat all sides. Cover with a clean cloth and let rise until doubled in bulk, about 1 hour.

4. Coat a 14 × 12-inch baking pan with another few drops of the olive oil. Punch the dough down and put it in the oiled pan. Pat, stretch, and pull it to cover the bottom. (Don't worry about thin patches or holes; the dough will start to rise again almost immediately so you can let it relax for a few minutes and go back to it for any patch-up work.) Dimple the surface all over with your fingertips.

5. Beat together the egg yolk, 1 tablespoon oil, and 1 teaspoon water; brush this mixture over the dough. Drizzle with the remaining oil, sprinkle with the remaining 2 tablespoons of the rosemary, and a little coarse salt. Cover and let rise until doubled in bulk, about 45 minutes.

6. About 30 minutes into the final rise, preheat the oven to 350° F.

7. Bake the bread until golden and crusty, especially at the edges, about 25 minutes. Let cool slightly in the pan, then remove to a wire rack. Serve warm, cut into squares.

Makes 1 flat bread

Rabbit Hill Inn Oatmeal-Molasses Bread

ere is a wonderful, dark, crusty, fragrant bread from John and Maureen Magee's Rabbit Hill Inn, in Lower Waterford, Vermont (for more information about, and another recipe from, the inn, see page 260).

This bread is as healthful as it is delicious, with just one tablespoon of added fat, lots of oatmeal, and B-vitamin-rich blackstrap molasses. The role molasses plays is important here, making the bread as dark as pumpernickel, though with a flavor all its own. Molasses

is a key flavoring in many New England breads (such as traditional steamed Boston brown bread, or Deedy's Gram's Graham Muffins, page 368). The thick, dark syrup is a little intense on its own, but in breads like these, it is delicious, a sweetening far more dimensional than plain old sugar or even honey: sweetness with a pleasantly, very subtly sourbitter undernote of flavor.

This bread has been served at Rabbit Hill for many decades. It's great for breakfast toast: your first slice just buttered and served with your eggs, your second slice with homemade cinnamonapple jelly. It's very nice for lunch with a slice of Swiss melted over it, and as the base for an egg salad sandwich or possibly the best BLT you'll eat in your entire life.

2 cups boiling spring water
1 cup quick-cooking oatmeal
1½ tablespoons butter
1 tablespoon active dry yeast
½ cup lukewarm spring water
½ cup blackstrap molasses
2 teaspoons salt
4½ to 5 cups unbleached all-purpose flour

1. In a large bowl, pour the boiling water over the oatmeal and butter. Let stand 30 minutes.

2. In a small bowl, sprinkle the yeast over the lukewarm water and let stand to dissolve, 5 to 10 minutes. Add the yeast, molasses, and salt to the oatmeal mixture and stir well. Stir in enough of the flour to make a kneadable dough.

3. Knead the dough on a lightly floured surface until smooth and elastic, about 8 minutes. Oil a bowl, add the dough, and turn to

coat. Cover with a clean cloth and let rise until doubled in bulk, about 1½ hours.

4. Oil two 9 × 5-inch loaf pans. Punch the dough down and divide it in half. Shape the dough into loaves and place them in the prepared pans. Cover and let rise until doubled in bulk, about 40 minutes.

5. About 30 minutes into the final rise, preheat the oven to 375° F.

6. Bake the bread until crusty, about 35 minutes. Turn the loaves out of the pans onto a wire rack and let cool.

Makes 2 loaves

VARIATION:
Substitute 2 cups stone-ground wholewheat flour for an equal amount of unbleached all-purpose.

❝Chances are that an Ozarks December noontide will permit opened windows. The released aroma of freshly baked bread, cooling on the racks, will fill the house and drift through those open windows . . . [rising] to meet a robin's chirp from the gnarled, old gum tree whose last leaves slowly spiral down to join the thickened forest carpet.**❞**

—*ORIE STORM,*
THE OZARKS MOUNTAINEER,
November/December, 1987

Raisin-Pumpernickel Bread with a Secret

Ned and I only get to visit other inns in our deep off-season; January, usually, when we often take a week-long inn-to-inn driving tour. And to be candid, since we make our living indulging people foodwise, it can be hard to knock our socks off, especially at breakfast time. But when our 1992 route took us to The Inn at Brandywine Falls in Sagamore Hills, Ohio, the lavish, delectable morning repast laid out by innkeepers Katie and George Hoy did just that.

It's a sumptuous feast as ample as it is satisfying, innovative enough to fascinate, traditional enough so even the most conservative breakfaster could feel right at home. One featured player is usually this exquisite "raisin pump"— whose secret ingredient George added by mistake one day, thinking the small brown morsels were raisins when they were actually...*chocolate chips*. Good-beyond-belief. On Sundays, with raspberry preserves and Katie's Raspberry Butter, it tides guests over till 11:00 A.M. when a full-tilt glorious brunch is served.

3½ cups lukewarm spring water (substitute leftover vegetable-cooking water or vegetable stock, if available)
1¼ tablespoons active dry yeast
3 tablespoons dark brown sugar
1½ tablespoons instant coffee crystals
3 tablespoons good-quality pure cocoa powder
¼ cup blackstrap molasses
2½ cups rye flour, preferably dark rye flour
1 cup whole-wheat flour
1½ cups raisins
½ cup semi-sweet chocolate morsels
¼ cup mild vegetable oil, such as corn or peanut
1 tablespoon salt
5 cups unbleached all-purpose flour, approximately
Cornmeal, for sprinkling baking sheets
1 egg, beaten
Raspberry preserves, optional
Katie's Raspberry Butter (recipe follows; optional)

1. In a large glass or stainless-steel bowl, combine the lukewarm water, yeast, and brown sugar. Let stand until foamy, about 10 minutes. Then whisk in the coffee crystals, cocoa powder, and molasses. Add the rye and whole-wheat flours, and beat hard 100 strokes, using a wooden spoon. The dough should be the consistency of thick mud. Stir in the raisins and chocolate chips, cover with a clean cloth, and, says George, "Go take a hike."

2. After your hike (or 60 minutes later) return to the dough and stir in the oil and salt. When these have been thoroughly incorporated, begin kneading in the white flour. Some might stir in the first few cups, and then start kneading in the remainder, but, says George, "I just dump it in and go at it." Knead the dough for 8 to 10 minutes

IF YOU GET TO OHIO: THE INN AT BRANDYWINE FALLS

❦ *It's a quiet, beautifully restored farmhouse, built in 1848, a stone's throw from the Cuyahoga River's Brandywine Falls and surrounded by 33,000 acres of unspoiled Cuyahoga Valley National Park property. The house, set in a country lane on a gentle knoll, seems almost to float amidst herb gardens, while the chickens who provide eggs for the inn's breakfasts scratch amiably nearby. It simply defies belief to learn that this calm haven is less than 35 minutes from downtown Cleveland, less than 20 from Akron.*

Peaceful and bucolic though the setting is, delightful sass is added to the Brandywine experience by the outgoing, exuberant George Hoy (a former publisher) and his unflappable wife Katie (an historic preservationist). This easygoing couple exudes affability, and pleasure in the life they've chosen. Bright, warm, and people-loving, the Hoys are highly entertaining conversationalists with the magic knack of finding much in common with everyone who crosses their path—they are truly among our very favorite fellow innkeepers.*

A picture-perfect setting, innkeepers who combine intelligence and warmth, and ample quantities of glorious, indulgent food—well, in my book you've got the winning combo.

If you are thinking of visiting The Inn, write or call the Hoys at 8230 Brandywine Road, Sagamore Falls, Ohio 44067; (216) 467-1812. ❦

once all the flour has been incorporated, or until it is somewhat elastic ("Given," George adds, "that it has those raisins and chips in it.") When it is properly kneaded, you'll be able to peel the dough off your fingers.

3. Place the dough in a large oiled bowl and let rise, covered with a clean cloth, until doubled in bulk, 40 to 60 minutes.

4. Transfer the dough to a work surface and divide it into quarters. Form each quarter into a large flattened ball. Sprinkle an ungreased baking sheet lightly with cornmeal, and place all the dough balls on it. Let the breads rise, covered, until again doubled, 30 to 45 minutes, "depending on the Gods." George leaves the bread unslashed.

5. Towards the end of this rise, preheat the oven to 350° F.

6. Brush the tops of the loaves with the beaten egg. ("I just slather on with my fingers," says George. "I used to use egg beaters and brushes and all that fancy stuff—but I don't bother with that anymore, and it still tastes perfect and looks perfect when it's done."

7. Bake until fragrant, for exactly 38 minutes, assuming your oven is accurate. George thinks most people overcook their

GEORGE HOY'S THREE CARDINAL RULES FOR BREAD-BAKING

🍎*George is the bread-baker at The Inn at Brandywine Falls. One taste of any of his breads and you'll want to pay attention to anything he says on the subject.*

◆ *Don't leave out any of the ingredients. Sounds obvious, but it's easy to do.*

◆ *Don't use liquid that is too hot to dissolve the yeast; it will kill the yeast beyond regeneration. If the liquid is too cold, it will slow the action of the yeast, but it will still work (and raise the bread) eventually. Also don't let any of the dough ingredients get too hot before baking.*

◆ *Give the dough time to get up. "This varies so incredibly," says George, "and despite what the experts say, there is really no way to call it. Sometimes it'll be so anxious to go, it'll rise in a third less time than usual—even on a cold wintry day, when you'd think it wouldn't want to. Then, on a hot summer day, when by all accounts it'd be raring to go, some days it'll just lay around and not want to do anything. You just have to give it time, as much as it needs to rise fully."*🍎

bread and get it too dry. Serve with raspberry preserves and Katie's Raspberry Butter, if desired.

Makes 4 loaves

Katie's Raspberry Butter

atie deliberately makes this fruited butter without added sweetener, which allows the

raspberry flavor to come through all the more clearly. You could add a tablespoon or two of honey, but you don't need to, especially if you serve this as the Hoys do, accompanied by a glass dish of raspberry preserves as well.

It might sound like a weird combination, the raisin-pump with their morsels of semi-sweet chocolate, the raspberries both as preserves and in this butter—but it is heavenly.

1 cup (2 sticks) unsalted butter, at room temperature
½ cup unsweetened frozen raspberries, thawed

1. Combine the butter and raspberries in a food processor. Buzz until well combined, though the mixture need not be completely smooth.

2. Pack the raspberry butter into serving dishes, small crocks, or ramekins, and let chill overnight.

Makes 1 cup

Washington Penultimate Multi-Grain Granola Bread

hat a bread! Grainy and a little sweet, with a texture offering crunch (from almonds and granola) in a tender, egg-enriched dough. This cannot be called low-calorie, not with all that honey, and the nuts and eggs, and a good dollop of oil. Yet everything in it is real stuff—substantial, nutrient-dense—an indulgence, yes, but a pretty healthy one. I just love this, and use it maybe once every two weeks as the second bread in the restaurant.

My one regret is that I have misplaced the name of the kind gentleman who sent it to me, with the nicest letter (the letter, too, is gone; just the recipe remains, flour-spattered from months of hard labor in the kitchen). I do remember he was from Washington, and a devotee of our granola, printed not only in *Dairy Hollow House Cookbook* but in an early book of mine, *The Bean Book,* from way back. In fact, he said he developed the bread as a way to showcase that granola. And his original ingredient list called for "1 cup decadent granola (preferably yours)." I love stuff like this almost as much as I love this right-up-there bread itself. The only real change I have wrought in the recipe is to use real milk instead of dry-milk-plus-water.

This is best made in a heavy-duty mixer with a dough hook attachment.

¾ cup honey
3½ cups 2 percent milk, scalded
3 tablespoons active dry yeast
¾ cup rolled oats
¾ cup stone-ground cornmeal
1 cup rye flour
1 cup almonds, coarsely chopped
1 cup good granola, preferably homemade
2 cups whole-wheat flour
2½ teaspoons salt
2 eggs
⅔ cup mild vegetable oil, such as corn, peanut, or as the recipe developer suggests, canola
4 cups unbleached all-purpose flour, approximately

1. Into a medium-size bowl, pour the honey. Add the scalded milk and let stand until lukewarm. Stir in the yeast, and let stand until foamy, about 10 minutes.

2. Meanwhile, in the large bowl of a heavy-duty mixer, combine the oats, cornmeal, rye flour, almonds, granola, and whole-wheat flour.

3. When the yeast mixture is foamy,

add the salt, eggs, and oil to it, and beat well with a whisk. Pour the yeast mixture into the mixer bowl and stir manually to mix. Then using the dough hook attachment, begin adding the all-purpose flour 1 cup at a time until 3 cups have been added, forming a heavy, moist dough. When well mixed, the dough will pull away from the sides of the bowl.

4. Transfer the dough to a floured work surface. Add a little more flour and knead it in. Knead the dough slightly, 4 to 5 minutes, incorporating less flour than usual, only enough to bring the dough to barely beyond tacky.

5. Place the dough in a large oiled bowl. Cover with a clean cloth, and let rise in a warm place until not quite doubled in bulk, about 1 hour and 10 minutes.

6. Punch down the dough, and divide it in half. Form into two loaves, and place each, seam side down, in an oiled 9 × 5-inch loaf pan. Let rise a second time, again covered, in a warm place until doubled, 40 to 60 minutes.

7. During the last 10 minutes of the second rise, preheat the oven to 375° F.

8. Bake for 20 minutes, then lower the heat to 350° F and bake until crusty and deep golden brown, an additional 20 minutes. Let cool on racks, and feast.

Makes 2 large loaves

ROLLS

Homemade rolls are always special. It's not just their deliciousness, intoxicating yeasty fragrance, and cunning size. Somehow they have an atmosphere both festive and "Aw, you cared" about them, a redolence of grandmothers, home, country cooking, Sunday dinners, Thanksgivings, and Christmasses. With all these good associations, it's no wonder that rolls are frequently part of the Dairy Hollow breadbasket.

We are continually playing with new recipes, new shapes. Here are some of our current favorites.

Scotch Baps

I had never heard of a "bap" until I read Marion Cunningham's *Breakfast Book.* "This is the Scots' breakfast roll," writes Ms. Cunningham. "Crisp-crusted, soft-centered, and well-buttered, a friendlier roll you'll never meet."

It just so happened that I was in the midst of a correspondence with a very friendly Scot, Mike McIlwraith (see page 193). I dashed off a letter to him asking "What makes a bap a bap?"

Michael wrote back, "There are regional variations and these can get themselves into what purports to be 'The Original Scottish recipe.' But here is what you will find in the good hand-baker's shop. It is a simple bread dough without additive or adornment of any kind." The recipe followed, but measurements were by weight not volume.

For conversion help, I called on Peggy Pinkley, a delightful Scotswoman married to an American surgeon. Peggy, who lives in Springfield, Missouri, has both a chemist's precision and lover's sensuality about her food.

Anyway, this is our collective bap—

mine, Mike's, and Peggy's. It is so good I still haven't tried Marion's.

1¼ cups spring water, milk, or combination
¼ cup lard, margarine, or butter (lard is
*   traditional, but I use butter)*
1 teaspoon sugar
1 package active dry yeast
2 teaspoons salt
5 to 5½ cups unbleached all-purpose flour

1. Heat the water to a simmer (or milk until scalded) and, in a large bowl, pour over the shortening of your choice. Stir until the shortening melts, then stir in the sugar. Let cool to lukewarm. Sprinkle the yeast over the top and let stand until foamy, 10 minutes.

2. Stir in the salt and enough of the flour to make a soft dough. Knead until smooth and elastic, about 5 minutes. Oil a large bowl and add the dough. Cover with a clean cloth and let rise in a warm place until doubled in bulk, about 1½ hours.

3. Transfer the dough to a lightly floured surface and knead until smooth, 3 to 5 minutes. Divide it into 10 to 12 pieces. Shape the pieces into round balls, then flatten each one slightly with a rolling pin to make an oval, about 4 × 3 inches.

4. Oil a baking sheet and dust it well with flour. Place the baps about 2 inches apart on the prepared baking sheet. Dust them well with flour and let rise, covered with a clean cloth, until doubled, about 50 to 65 minutes.

5. About 30 minutes into the final rise, preheat the oven to 425° F. Dust the rolls again lightly with flour. Bake until golden and crusty, about 15 minutes. Some people dust them again with flour after they leave the oven. Eat the rolls while they are still hot.

Makes 10 to 12 rolls

CUSHIONAIRES

❧ *Cushionaires are double-insulated baking sheets: two sheets joined together with an insulating layer of air between them. I do virtually all my baking on them, for they keep cookies, biscuits, and pastries from getting brown on the bottom before the tops are done. Cushionaires ensure even browning. I can't recommend these pans highly enough. They are available in the housewares section of many department stores and discount houses.* ❧

VARIATION:

Peggy Pinkley spritzes the baps lightly with water before dusting them, both the first and second time. This not only helps the flour adhere but also adds a shine and crispness to the crust. She says that, yes, indeed, they are the premier breakfast roll in Scotland, especially with butter and a good bitter orange marmalade. But they are also eaten warmed up at teatime, or split to make a sandwich with Ayreshire bacon ("more like Canadian bacon than American bacon, which is

what we would call 'streaky,'" she said, droolingly) and tomatoes.

You may replace a third to a half of the all-purpose flour with whole-wheat; it's extremely pleasing.

Whole-Wheat Butterhorns

his is our favorite roll at the restaurant, a hearty, wheaty country cousin to a croissant, yet quite different in texture and method. These are delicious and, with our Skillet-Sizzled Buttermilk Cornbread, never cease to please.

Since they are quite rich, however, and a bit time consuming to shape, we save them for holidays and special oc-

casions, and make simpler rolls more often.

We used to make these with all whole-wheat flour but found them too heavy for a dinner roll. We also make them slightly less sweet than we used to. Here's how we do them now.

⅓ cup honey
1¼ cups milk, scalded
1 package active dry yeast
4 tablespoons (½ stick) butter, melted
3 large eggs, at room temperature, lightly beaten
2 tablespoons nutritional yeast
1½ teaspoons salt
2½ cups whole-wheat flour, preferably stone-ground
2½ cups unbleached all-purpose flour
Vegetable oil or Pam cooking spray for baking sheets
8 tablespoons (1 stick) butter, chilled, cut into small chunks
Egg Glaze (recipe follows)

1. In a large bowl, stir the honey into the scalded milk. Whisk to dissolve the honey and let stand until lukewarm. Sprinkle the yeast over the milk and let stand until foamy, about 10 minutes. Stir in the melted butter, eggs, nutritional yeast, and salt. Stir in the flours a cup at a time, alternating whole-wheat and all-purpose flours, until the dough is stiff enough to knead.

2. Knead the dough on a lightly floured surface until smooth and elastic, 6 to 8 minutes. Oil a large bowl, add the dough, and turn to coat. Cover with a clean cloth and let rise until doubled in bulk, about 1¼ hours.

3. Punch the dough down and let rise again until doubled, about 50 minutes.

4. Generously oil (or spray with Pam) 2 baking sheets with edges. This is important; some butter will melt out of the dough and you don't want the butter splashing your oven floor. Cushionaires (see page 345) are great. Punch the dough down and knead briefly. Divide the dough in thirds and roll out each piece into a ¼-inch-thick circle. Cut each circle into 10 wedges as you would cut a pie. Dot the wedges with the chilled butter, then roll up each wedge, starting from the wide end. Place the rolls about 1½ inches apart on the prepared baking sheets. Cover the butterhorns with clean cloths and let rise again until doubled in bulk, about 30 minutes.

5. About 10 minutes into the final rise, preheat the oven to 400° F.

6. Bake the butterhorns until well browned, 15 to 20 minutes. If you like, remove them after 10 minutes and brush them with the egg glaze; it makes them really pretty.

Makes about 30 butterhorns

VARIATION:
These are quite wonderful when sprinkled generously with sesame or poppy seeds before you roll them up.

Déjà Food: The butterhorns make incredible French toast. And used for chocolate bread pudding, they are heavenly!

> **"**Now, to [shape] four dozen individual rolls while dreams are still warm under one's fingers—but two definite knocks at the door interrupt [the] reverie.... There was no sound of anyone's approach, no scuffing through the leaves. I pause, waiting for another knock. Silence. I dust the flour from my hands and open the door. There stands one of our handsome Buff Orpington roosters, cocking his head at me and clucking.... It was he who had knocked ... a rooster-come-calling.**"**
>
> *—ORIE STORM,*
> *"Ozarks Daily Bread,"*
> *OZARKS MOUNTAINEER,*
> *November/December 1987*

1 teaspoon water (for a transparent, shiny gloss) or 1 whole egg with 1 teaspoon water (for a translucent shiny yellow gloss).

Egg Glaze

ny bread can get a beautifully shiny top by being brushed at some point in the baking process with either 1 egg white beaten with

Popovers

hese delicate egg-leavened breads are not distinctively Southern, although Texas-based Neiman Marcus (perhaps the ultimate Southern department store) serves them as a house specialty at their in-store restaurants.

Popovers are a one-of-a-kind bread. The first time you eat one you wonder, where's the inside? Indeed, they are hollow, with a crisp, sprightly exterior and a meltingly eggy, soft interior. They are close kin to Yorkshire pudding and to our own Dairy Hollow German Baked Pancake. They were served every Sunday at a summer camp I went to as a girl. We would absolutely gorge ourselves on them with butter and strawberry jam by the tablespoonful. They are still good that way, but they are also a festive way to round out many soup meals.

Pam cooking spray
1 cup milk
1 tablespoon butter, melted
1 cup unbleached all-purpose flour
¼ teaspoon salt
2 large eggs

1. Have all the ingredients at room temperature when you start. Preheat the oven to 450° F. Spray a muffin tin with deep cups or an extra-deep popover pan with Pam.

2. In a mixing bowl, place all the ingredients except the eggs, and whisk until smooth. Whisk in the eggs one at a time. Do not overbeat. (If you work quickly, this can be done easily in a food processor.) Pour the batter into the prepared pan, filling each cup not more than three-quarters full.

3. Bake 15 minutes. Turn down the heat to 350°F and bake 20 minutes longer, less if your muffin cups are smallish. Do not open the oven door until you are quite certain the popovers are done. Serve immediately. Popovers should exhale a breath of steam when you cut them open.

Makes 9 or 10 generous popovers

> **"In** every age, Southern bread has been a front-line weapon against poverty, hunger, and malnutrition; a litmus test for accomplished practitioners of the culinary arts; and a repeated gastronomic delight for every race, sex, age, and income level.**"**
>
> —*JOHN EGERTON,*
> *SOUTHERN FOOD*

QUICK BREADS

*B*reads leavened with baking powder or soda, instead of yeast, are called "quick" for good reason—they are. Assuming you have the ingredients on hand and have made quick bread once or twice, you can whip together a batch

of muffins or cornbread in under 5 minutes. I know—I've timed it. It's a simple matter: dry ingredients in one bowl, wet in another, combine them with a few stirs, put the batter in a pan, and bake. Half an hour or so later—*voilà*—great home-baked bread to feed the crew that will have congregated in the kitchen, following their noses to the stove.

Biscuits, due to the additional steps of cutting shortening into the flour and rolling them out, might take as much as 12 minutes—8 if you do drop biscuits, and even less for biscuits made with self-rising flour (like the luscious Charlisa's Extra-Good Sesame Drop Biscuit-Muffins, page 363).

Now, don't think I'm pointing any fingers here, but nobody is too busy to bake, not this kind of bread, anyway. And what scent other than that of baking bread can possibly evoke home and well-being so sublimely, unless it is the mingled aroma of bread baking and soup simmering? In taste as well as aroma, texture as well as flavor, nutrition as well as satisfaction, soup and bread are boon companions.

Cornbread (the Ozarks classic daily bread), muffins, and biscuits are the three quick breads we're devoting time to here—and the preceding popovers, which are not technically a quick bread, since they're not leavened by baking powder or soda, but are very speedy and so good. Any of these could be teamed up with any soup in the book and the result would not be unpleasing. However, some breads do go better with some soups than others. Popovers are magic with the Duck Soup with Sweet Potatoes (page 77), for example, as is cornbread with any bean soup, biscuits with potato or cheese soup, or a sweet muffin with a fruit soup.

The one sort of quick bread not much represented here are sweet breads, such as banana or strawberry bread, because they are rarely the best soup go-withs. However, I couldn't resist including my panettone, an Italian Christmas bread flavored with anise. It is a personal favorite, and my hand-copied recipe from a long-ago neighbor is going to fall to bits unless I put it somewhere permanent soon. Do make it, even if you think you don't like anise—it's lovely.

"A very strait-laced backwoods girl does not permit a partner to put his arm around her waist at all, but is swung by a handclasp only. The two methods of swinging are known as *biscuits* and *cornbread,* as in this old dance call: Meet your pardner / pat her on the head / If she don't like biscuits / feed her cornbread.**"**

—*VANCE RANDOLPH,*
DOWN IN THE HOLLER: A GALLERY OF OZARK FOLK SPEECH

CORNBREAD: THE SOUTHERN STAFF OF LIFE

❦ *Cornbread is the alpha and omega of Southern bread in general and of Ozark bread in particular. Corn is America's native grain. To Native Americans, corn was inseparable from life; so much so that it was considered sacred. On arriving in the Americas, Christopher Columbus was graciously given corn (along with tobacco) by the Indians who hospitably received him and his company.*

Columbus and other early explorers lost no time introducing this foodstuff to the rest of the world. By the time the first European settlers arrived in Jamestown in 1607, corn was growing in many parts of Europe.

Though somewhat familiar with corn, the first settlers in America brought with them wheat seed because they preferred the taste of wheat and knew how to cook with it. (They also brought seeds of barley and rye.) But, probably because of poor storage on the ship or soil or climate dissimilar to that of the Old World, the seed failed in the new land. Through the Native Americans' generosity, the newcomers, both at Jamestown and later, at Plymouth Rock, survived their first winters living on the dried corn the Indians shared with them.

After a few years' experimentation, American settlers, including those in the South, were able to grow wheat with success. But the South was rapidly developing into a plantation economy, based on slave labor. The currency of the land was the export and trade of highly profitable nonfood agricultural products: indigo for dye, cotton, tobacco, wood products. Wheat, fairly labor-intensive to grow and with a (then) yield of 30 to 100 times what was put in the ground, was not financially viable in such an economy—not when corn could be grown far more easily, and with an astonishing 700- to 800-fold return on its seed.

The rich plantation owners ate their share of cornbread; in the hands of a good cook (usually a slave), it was delicious. The slave-owners' abundant tables, filled with "all that could please the eye or tempt the taste," as former slave and abolitionist Frederick Douglass said, were also heaped with other breads, biscuits, and pastries made of flour imported from other parts of the Colonies—a far cry from "the close-fisted stinginess that fed the poor slave on

coarse cornmeal and tainted meat." The Ozarks, a region that was an anomaly in the South, was isolated, poor, self-sufficient in the most meager fashion, and determinedly independent. It resented the Civil War more or less entirely, and in general took sides only to the extent of being against whoever had been most recently caught stealing the chickens. The Ozarks' isolation, inland location, hilly, rocky terrain, and relatively poor soil kept the area virtually free from the taint of blood-stained inequity that was slavery: there was nothing remotely close to a plantation economy in the early days of the Ozarks. Indeed, there was hardly an economy at all, outside of that which was based on barter, a state which was to continue, to some extent, well into the 1930s. ("The Depression wasn't anything to us," I've heard more than one old-timer say with that reverse pride so much a part of this area. "Hell, we were always depressed.")*

Cornbread was the bread in the Ozarks; people grew their own corn and brought it to the nearest mill to be ground every few weeks or so. Freshly ground cornmeal, and the cornbread made from it, is incredibly good. And there are many cornbreads: from the plain, poorer-than-poor hoecakes, made of nothing more than meal and water and baked in the fire on an iron hoe,

to meltingly good egg-and-buttermilk-enriched cornbreads, to spoon bread, a cornmeal soufflé called by writer Redding Sugg the "apotheosis of cornbread" (though very good, not to my taste). In its many forms, cornbread quickly moved beyond survival food to a beloved, fully incorporated part of the diet. All over the South, but most especially, I believe, in the Arkansas Ozarks, it became mythological food, almost in the way it had been for the Indians.

Daily, ordinary food, Ozark people still rhapsodize about cornbread with pride and wonder. They write poetry about it, argue about it fiercely, in print and out, particularly over whether or not it should be sweetened. Cornbread is a living part of folk culture in a thousand ways—sayings, folk songs, square-dance calls, even contemporary local rock lyrics.

In 1988, Bob Lancaster wrote in the Arkansas Times *that Southerners could "make a filling, gratifying supper out of cornbread and not much else. Forgive the nostalgia, but my mother did it at least a thousand times that I remember—and I didn't come along until after the hard times. Cornbread and sweet milk—with a green onion on the side in season. If I had thought about it, which I don't recall ever having done, I would have supposed that this was a meal for the privileged rather than for the poor, and I would have been right."*

All right, now can we eat? ❦

Skillet-Sizzled Buttermilk Cornbread

T his is the first Southern dish I learned how to fix, back when I was still a Yankee. (Of course, some—many—would say you never outgrow this handicap, no matter how long you live in the South.) Interestingly, it is one of the most requested recipes at the inn and a house specialty: almost always on the menu. It is, to me, the perfect corn-bread—in the mid to up-per range of luxury among cornbreads, rich with eggs and buttermilk, slightly sweetened, buttery, very grainy. As often as I eat this, I never tire of it. An amazing number of peo-ple have told me it was just like what their mother or grand-mother used to make. And my old Ar-kansawyer pal Alan Leveritt, founder of both the *Arkansas Times* and *Southern* magazines, claims it is the best he has ever eaten. But I learned how to make it in New York.

In 1969 I lived for a year in a brownstone in the Fort Greene section of Brooklyn. At that time I, my then-hus-band, and the people we shared the house with were the only white people on the block. Interest in our comings and goings was intense.

We made friends with a neighbor named Freddy, a warm, outgoing, black guy, handsome of feature and limb. He was as friendly as he was good-looking, stopping by regularly to bring us news of the neighborhood, join in any meal or activity that might be going on, and to warn us of the folly of people like us (that is, white Yankee liberals) moving South, as we planned. One of his daily predictions was "They gon' *kill* you in Arkansas."

Freddy's lady friend, Viola, a large woman, was shy, quiet (at least around us), and a fabulous cook. I believe she was from Georgia. Occasionally Freddy would bring over something she had made for us, but we saw her in person only once—right before we left to go South. She fixed us a farewell dinner, brought it over, and we all ate together around the table. Better even than the fried chicken, the potato salad mayonnaise and mus-tard, and the gooey pecan pie was the corn-bread, baked in a cast-iron skillet. Viola didn't use recipes as such but cooked by feel like many—maybe most—fine home cooks.

She said she couldn't tell me how she did it. She did confess, in a soft, soft voice, to melting butter in the skillet be-fore pouring in the batter, but that, she said, was the only thing different about her cornbread. Oh, yes, and she used buttermilk. And just a little sugar.

This is my reconstruction of Viola's Fort Greene skillet cornbread, which we have been making at the inn for years now. Thanks, Viola.

And Freddy, if by some miracle you see this, they didn't kill us, buddy.

1 cup stone-ground yellow cornmeal
1 cup unbleached all-purpose flour
1 tablespoon baking powder
¼ teaspoon salt
¼ teaspoon baking soda
1¼ cups buttermilk, preferably Bulgarian-
  style
1 large egg
2 to 4 tablespoons sugar
¼ cup mild vegetable oil, such as corn or
  peanut
Pam cooking spray
2 to 4 tablespoons butter

1. Preheat the oven to 375° F.
2. In a large bowl, combine the cornmeal, flour, baking powder, and salt.
3. In a small bowl, stir the baking soda into the buttermilk. In a second bowl, whisk together the egg, sugar to taste, and the oil, then whisk in the buttermilk.
4. Spray an 8- or 9-inch cast-iron skillet with Pam. Put the skillet over medium-high heat, add the butter, and heat until the butter melts and is just starting to sizzle. Tilt the pan to coat the bottom and sides.
5. Add the wet ingredients to the dry, and quickly stir together, using only as many strokes as needed to combine. Scrape the batter into the hot, buttery skillet. Immediately put the skillet in the oven and bake until golden brown, about 25 minutes. Cut into wedges to serve.

Makes an 8- or 9-inch cornbread

VARIATIONS:
Ned's Cornbread: When we were making dinners just for guests at the inn, before we started the restaurant, Ned became a corn-

bread baker *par excellence*. He felt dissolving the soda in the buttermilk was fussy and instead he sifted it (to break up the lumps) into the other dry ingredients. It's amazing how this small change gives such a different texture; my bread is moist but also denser, his is higher and lighter, but a tad drier. The truth is they're both good. Occasionally I think he has converted me to his, then I decide, no, mine's better. Try both and see what you think.

Michael Stark's Decadent Cornbread: Michael Stark, my old friend from New Orleans, wows his many houseguests, including his mother and the singer Odetta, with his cornbread. He makes it from a mix (shame!) and uses sour cream for the liquid. Okay, Mike, take 5 minutes extra and make the beaut above from scratch with 1¾ cups sour cream instead of the buttermilk.

> **❝**An Ozarker who doesn't like cornbread is said to have gone back on his raisin', which is almost as bad as denying one's kinfolks. An Arkansas governor, at a public dinner, was admonished, 'Don't go back on your raisin', Governor!' Whereupon the governor grinned, dropped the roll he had selected, and took a corn muffin instead.**❞**
>
> —*VANCE RANDOLPH,*
> *DOWN IN THE HOLLER: A GALLERY OF*
> *OZARK FOLK SPEECH*

To Sweeten or Not to Sweeten?

❦ *That is the question among die-hard corn-bread fans. Most Southerners, men especially, say no. Here in Arkansas both Bob Lancaster (Arkansas Times) and Richard Allin (Arkansas Gazette) have, within the past few years, both written columns deriding the use of sugar in cornbread.*

But most women, who actually do the cooking, say, "Well, just a little."

If the cornmeal is absolutely freshly ground (within a day of making the corn-bread), it is sweet and no sugar is necessary. But if the cornmeal is older than that, I say definitely add sugar—just a little.

Perhaps the most sensible words on the subject of sugar in cornbread were spoken to our waiter John Mitchell by Mrs. Clark, whose husband fixes the ancient Jaguars John collects. Apparently a neighbor had brought the Clarks some cornbread, which was made without sugar. There was some discussion about how to ask her politely not to bring it again, since the family didn't care for unsweetened cornbread.

"Now, to be any good, cornbread should be just a little sweet," Mrs. Clark told John. "Just about as sweet as good sweet fresh corn, right from the garden." That settles it as far as I'm concerned. ❦

Old-Fashioned Cornbread

ith your first taste of this corn-bread, you will wonder, "Why did she bother putting this in when the other is the ultimate?" But with your second taste, as you chew, the won-derful grainy cornness, unmasked, primitive, pure and earthy, comes through. This is a poor people's cornbread, but it's very good—in fact, addictive in its own way. I've included it for that reason and three others: one, its historical merit; two, being flour-free, it is one of the few breads people with an allergy to gluten can eat; and three, crumbled and toasted in the oven, it makes the best turkey dressing.

2 cups stone-ground yellow cornmeal
1 tablespoon baking powder
¼ teaspoon salt
¼ teaspoon baking soda
1¼ cups plus 2 tablespoons buttermilk,
    preferably Bulgarian-style
1 large egg
1 tablespoon sugar
1 tablespoon mild vegetable oil, such as
    corn or peanut
Pam cooking spray
2 to 4 tablespoons butter or rendered
    bacon fat

1. Preheat the oven to 375°F.

2. In a large bowl, combine the cornmeal, baking powder, and salt.

3. In a small bowl, stir the baking soda into the buttermilk. In a second bowl, whisk together the egg, sugar, and oil, then whisk in the buttermilk.

4. Spray an 8- or 9-inch cast-iron skillet with the Pam. Put the skillet over medium-high heat, add the butter or bacon fat and heat until just beginning to sizzle, tilting the pan to coat the bottom and sides.

5. Add the wet ingredients to the dry and quickly stir together, using only as many strokes as needed to combine. Scrape the batter into the hot, greased skillet. Immediately put the skillet in the oven and bake until golden brown, about 25 minutes. Cut into wedges to serve.

Makes an 8- or 9-inch cornbread

PERFECT GO-WITHS FOR CORNBREAD

🌱 *Gumbo Zeb (page 231); most tomatoey vegetable soups, including The Soup (page 167); any bean or greens soup; and any chilled tomato soup.*🌱

Cornbread Pie à la Hippie

his is a real good, real homey Déjà-Food recipe. It's a great use for any leftover, hearty, well-flavored, beany soup or chili. We would never serve it in the restaurant, but it's an off-season home favorite. It also travels well to potluck dinners and the like. Patchwork Slaw (page 385) is a perfect accompaniment.

Pam cooking spray
4 or 5 cups hearty, thick, tasty leftover soup,
    preferably with beans and vegetables (see
    Note)
Batter for Skillet-Sizzled Buttermilk
    Cornbread (page 352) made with ½ cup
    additional buttermilk
4 to 6 ounces Cheddar cheese, shredded
    (optional)

1. Preheat the oven to 375° F. Spray a 10-inch round casserole or 13 × 9-inch baking dish with the Pam.

2. In a saucepan, reheat the soup. Taste and adjust the seasonings if needed. Pour the piping hot soup into the casserole. Spoon or pour the cornbread batter over the hot soup.

3. Bake until the bread is golden brown, 25 to 30 minutes. If using the cheese, sprinkle it over the bread about 6 minutes before it's done and continue to bake until the cheese melts. Serve very hot.

Serves 4 to 5 as an entrée

Note: If you don't have quite enough soup, you can often spell out what you have with some coarsely puréed canned whole tomatoes; just make sure the flavors are compatible.

Feather Bed Eggs

his is a divine savory pudding with cheese. It has a thousand variations printed in every church or Junior League cookbook in the South, but to my knowledge, nobody every thought of doing it with cornbread until Ned did. Boy, is this good—and, again, requested regularly by guests. More than one of our breakfast cooks has gone home and made it for her family and had it promptly become a household favorite. It's usually called something like "Overnight Breakfast Soufflé" in cookbooks; this ever-so-much-prettier name is from Marion Cunningham's *Breakfast Book*.

For breakfast at the inn, we sometimes serve this with freshly squeezed orange juice or maple-broiled grapefruit, homemade chicken sausage patties, and some sort of muffin or sweet bread (maybe Glazed Orange Muffins, page 366), coffee or tea, butter, and our own preserves.

Pam cooking spray
1 recipe Skillet-Sizzled Buttermilk Cornbread (page 352), crumbled into large chunks and left to dry overnight
Salt and freshly ground black pepper to taste
1½ cups shredded sharp Cheddar or Swiss cheese
8 large eggs
2 cups milk, or combination of milk and heavy (whipping) cream, half-and-half, sour cream, or evaporated skim milk
Dash of Tabasco or similar hot pepper sauce
Dash of Pickapeppa or Worcestershire sauce
Tiny pinch of dried dill
Tiny pinch of dried basil

1. Preheat the oven to 350° F. Spray a 14 × 11-inch shallow baking dish (see Note) with the Pam.

2. Spread the cornbread in an even layer in the prepared dish. Sprinkle lightly with salt and pepper. Pat the cheese over the top.

3. Whisk the eggs, milk, and seasonings together until blended, then pour this mixture over the cornbread.

4. Bake until the eggs are set and the

top is lightly browned and slightly puffed, about 30 minutes. Don't overbake.

Serves 6 to 8 as an entrée

Note: This can also be baked in individual ramekins. Bake about 20 minutes.

VARIATION:

Sprinkle ¾ cup diced ham over the cornbread and cheese before pouring on the egg mixture.

BRUNCH IN HIGH COTTON

*Augusta's Chilled Tomato Soup
with Basil Cream
and/or
Freshly Squeezed Orange Juice*

Feather Bed Eggs

*Char's Extra-Good Sesame
Drop Biscuit-Muffins*

Glazed Orange Muffins

Sliced Fresh Melon and Fresh
Berries

Colombian Coffee or Earl Grey
Tea

Panettone

his is a divine quick-bread version of the famous anise-flavored Italian Christmas bread: subtle but sweet, buttery, and the anise (even if you think you don't like the flavor) is the perfect seasoning. I can't speak highly enough of this. I would feel deprived if a Christmas went by without a batch.

This has no Southern pedigree but a strictly personal one. The recipe was given to me a decade-plus ago by my neighbor, Helen Cummins, who introduced me not only to the basic bread but also its dessert option—panettone served with a scoop of ice cream on top.

I love panettone with minestrone, if there's a plain bread croûte in the soup. It also works well with some nut soups and as a breakfast bread.

Butter or Pam cooking spray for loaf pans
1 large egg
2 large egg yolks
¾ cup sugar
*8 tablespoons (1 stick) butter, melted and
    cooled*
¼ cup pine nuts
¼ cup dark raisins
¼ cup chopped mixed candied fruit
1 teaspoon grated lemon zest
1 teaspoon anise seeds
*1 teaspoon anise extract (double or triple
    the amount of anise seeds if unavailable)*
3 cups sifted unbleached all-purpose flour
2 teaspoons baking powder
½ teaspoon salt
1 cup milk

1. Preheat the oven to 350° F. Butter (or spray with Pam) two 9 × 5-inch loaf pans.

2. Using an electric mixer, beat the egg, egg yolks, and sugar together until thick and pale yellow. Beat in the melted butter, then stir in the pine nuts, raisins, candied fruit, lemon zest, and anise seeds and extract.

3. Sift together the flour, baking powder, and salt. Stir half the flour mixture into the batter, than stir in half the milk. Add the remaining flour mixture and stir well. Add the remaining milk and blend thoroughly.

4. Divide the batter evenly between the prepared pans. Bake until golden brown and fragrant, about 1¼ hours. Let cool in pans 15 minutes, then turn out onto wire racks to cool completely.

Makes 2 medium-size loaves

BISCUITS

*B*iscuits have achieved a place in Southern hearts, minds, memories, breadbaskets, and culture surpassed only by cornbread. These quick-leavened little breads were not widespread in the South until two decades after the Civil War. Then, for the first time, baking powder and baking soda became available commercially. In antebellum days, the biscuits that plantation owners ate were mostly beaten biscuits, unleavened but for the air bubbles beaten into them. They were incredibly laborious to prepare. Said Mary Stuart Smith in her 1885 *Virginia Cookery Book,* "Let one spend the night at some gentleman-farmer's home, and the first sound heard in the morning, after the crowing of the cock, was the heavy, regular fall of the cook's axe, as she beat and beat her biscuit dough."

Just as important in bringing about the biscuit boom as the development of reliable leavening was a dramatic drop in the price of flour brought in from the Midwest. This was because of an essential import from Russia's Ukraine in the 1860s: durum wheat. Now, durum wheat, a high-protein wheat used for pasta and yeast breads, is not used in biscuits, for which tenderer, lower-protein spring wheat is desired. But the arrival of durum wheat brought all flour prices down. At three dollars a barrel in the 1880s, flour, as well as cornmeal, was affordable for most people. So Southerners discovered a second favorite bread, made and eaten hot on a daily basis: biscuits.

There has been a lot of mythology built up about biscuit making over the years. Some swear that no one born north of the Mason-Dixon line can turn out a decent biscuit. Hogwash. Anyone

CUSTOM-MADE BISCUITS AS YOU LIKE THEM

🍎 *The gospel according to* Dairy Hollow House Cookbook, *and still true—as eternal verities are:*

▶ *For the flakiest biscuits, handle the dough as little as possible. After the liquid has been added, stir the dough until it barely comes together, then knead with very few strokes. Roll the dough out if you must; many fine biscuit cooks simply pat it out gently with their palms.*

▶ *For high-rising tall biscuits with soft centers, roll or pat out the dough ½ inch thick. For thinner, crustier biscuits, roll or pat the dough out ¼ inch thick.*

▶ *For level tops on round biscuits, use a floured biscuit cutter and with a definite straight-down motion. Do not twist the cutter (or knife if you want to make square biscuits).*

▶ *Square biscuits have the advantage of using every scrap of dough so that rerolling is not necessary. If you do use a cutter, cut the biscuits as close together as possible to avoid unnecessary rerolling and cutting. Each rerolling toughens the dough slightly. Gather scraps and press them together gently—don't knead. The biscuits will be a little bumpy on top but far more tender than those neatly kneaded and rerolled.*

▶ *For soft-sided biscuits, place the cut biscuits close together in a shallow baking pan. For crusty biscuits, place them at least 1 inch apart on a cookie sheet.*

▶ *No matter how you like your biscuits, remember, one more time: Use a light touch!* 🍎

---

can, given the right ingredients, proper technique, understanding of the terminology and processes, and the desire to learn.

THE RIGHT INGREDIENTS

Flour: For perfect, classic, very tender biscuits, you want a soft wheat flour. The brand available throughout much of the South is White Lily, but there are also regional brands, such as Adluh and Red Brand in South Carolina. Self-rising flour, that is flour with baking powder, soda, and salt already added, are also easy to find throughout the South.

Now, a person can turn out a passable biscuit with regular unbleached all-purpose flour, but the flour to avoid absolutely is hard winter wheat flour, usu-

ally labeled "bread flour." Its protein makes a tough biscuit.

If you want whole-grain biscuits—quite addictive in their gentle, tasty heft but something many Southerners find incomprehensible—you'd best search for whole-wheat pastry flour.

Fat: A solid, saturated fat is essential for making biscuits, and that's all there is to it. Once upon a time this was lard, a fat most people now regard as just slightly more desirable than a nuclear-fuel processing plant next door. Lard is hard to come by anyway in its pure, tasty, preservative-free form. Most people these days use a hydrogenated vegetable shortening, such as Crisco. For an extra-flavorful biscuit, however, use a couple of tablespoons butter and the rest Crisco. You can use half butter and half Crisco; the flavor is excellent but the biscuits are relatively expensive and the dough tricky to handle.

Solid fat is the major ingredient responsible for that all-important aspect of the perfect biscuit—flakiness. Flakiness is the result of the pastry baking up into tiny, barely discernible layers, caused by the creation of air pockets as the fat melts during the cooking process. To ensure flakiness, the fat is incorporated into the flour just to the point at which particles are still visible; when the dough bakes, it will leave air pockets as it melts. If you cut the shortening into the flour excessively, it won't produce large enough air pockets. If you handle the dough too long—until the shortening melts instead of staying solid—there will be no air pockets at all. Also, the oven must be preheated before the biscuits go in—cold fat plus hot oven creates air pockets. If the fat melts slowly instead of rapidly, the dough will be sodden, not flaky. These same principles pertain to pie crusts as well.

All this fat means that biscuits are not a low-calorie breadstuff. Oh well.

Milk: There are sweet-milk biscuits (made with regular milk and leavened only by baking powder) and buttermilk biscuits (made with buttermilk, sour milk, or, in a pinch, yogurt thinned with water or milk, and leavened by baking powder and baking soda). Both are good. The first is a shade quicker, because of one less ingredient, and also a tiny bit plainer. Myself, I prefer a buttermilk biscuit. I believe it is somewhat more tender and moist inside and I think it has a better flavor, especially when made with a bit of butter. I especially like a buttermilk biscuit made with part whole-wheat pastry flour. However, I wouldn't turn down a sweet-milk biscuit or a white-flour buttermilk biscuit from the hands of a good cook.

Buttermilk Biscuits

uick, delectable, versatile, these biscuits give their all, wonderfully compatible with dozens of different meals, and amenable to an infinity of variations.

2 cups unbleached all-purpose flour, or 2 cups plus 2 tablespoons soft white flour (cake or pastry flour), such as White Lily, or 1 cup each unbleached all-purpose flour and whole-wheat pastry flour
1 tablespoon baking powder
½ teaspoon baking soda
1 teaspoon salt
⅓ cup solid vegetable shortening, such as Crisco, or 4 tablespoons shortening and 1 tablespoon plus 1 teaspoon butter
⅔ to 1 cup buttermilk, preferably Bulgarian-style
1 to 2 tablespoons melted butter for brushing the biscuits

1. Preheat the oven to 450° F.

2. In a medium-size mixing bowl, sift the flour, baking powder, baking soda, and salt. (If your leavenings are lump-free and you're in a hurry, you may just stir them together.) Cut in the shortening with a pastry blender or 2 knives. Particles of fat should remain; "pea size" is too big and "coarse cornmeal" is just barely too small. You want the particles almost but not quite to the point of looking like coarse cornmeal. With a few deft strokes, stir in enough of the buttermilk to make a soft dough.

3. Quickly turn the dough out onto a very lightly floured surface or (better) a marble slab. Knead with a couple of gentle strokes just until the dough comes together. This light handling ensures that the fat will not be broken down and also incorporates air into the dough—both techniques ensure high scores on the Flake-o-Meter.

4. Pat or roll out the dough ¼ to ½ inch thick (biscuits will double in height as they bake). Cut the dough into squares with a knife for the best flakiness, or with a biscuit cutter. Place the biscuits close together on an ungreased shallow baking pan for biscuits with soft sides, or at least 1 inch apart on a baking sheet for biscuits with crisper sides.

5. Bake until golden, 10 to 15 minutes. If the biscuits are not quite golden after 15 minutes, run them under a broiler briefly rather than overbake them. Some biscuit cooks swear by starting the pan on the lowest oven rack and moving it halfway through baking to the upper shelf. Brush the biscuit tops with the melted butter when they first come out of the oven. Serve hot.

Makes 12 good-size biscuits

VARIATIONS:

Food Processor Method: Place the dry ingredients in a food processor and pulse briefly to mix. Cut the shortening into 5 equal pieces and drop into the flour mixture. Process with 5 or 6 pulses, maybe more. Check the size of the fat particles between each pulse. Turn the mixture out into a bowl and proceed from there by hand. Don't try adding the buttermilk directly to the work-

bowl—if you do, it's impossible not to overblend.

Sweet-Milk Biscuits: Substitute regular milk for the buttermilk and omit the baking soda.

Drop Biscuits: These are absurdly, embarrassingly easy; not as pretty as rolled-out biscuits, but extremely flaky because they are handled less. Use ¼ cup extra buttermilk and simply stir (don't roll, don't pat) to make the dough. Drop the dough by tablespoons onto a baking sheet.

Cheese Biscuits: Reduce the shortening to ¼ cup. Add a pinch of cayenne pepper and ½ cup very finely grated Cheddar cheese to the dry ingredients with the shortening. Bake as directed, but, a couple of minutes before the biscuits are done, shake grated Parmesan cheese over them. Primo with any tomato-based soup. For biscuit appetizers, cut them tiny and fill with smoked ham and mustard butter.

Sweet Biscuits: Add 3 or 4 tablespoons sugar to the dry ingredients and a drop of vanilla to the buttermilk. Before baking, brush the tops with melted butter and dust with cinnamon and sugar. Good when used to make shortcakes and cobbler; also a good biscuit accompaniment to fruit soup.

Herb Biscuits: Combine 2 tablespoons chopped fresh parsley with 2 teaspoons to 2 tablespoons chopped assorted fresh herbs such as basil, sage, thyme, and rosemary. Use the lesser amount if the herbs are strong in flavor. Stir the herbs into the dry ingredients, then cut in the shortening and proceed as directed. Lovely with chicken and creamy soups.

Pesto Biscuits: Add 2 to 3 tablespoons pesto (page 41) with the shortening. Pesto is also great in the Cheese Biscuits variation.

Savory Biscuits: Add to the dry ingredients the herbs called for in the Herb Biscuits, 1 small onion finely chopped, 1 or 2 cloves of crushed garlic sautéed in butter, and a drop of Pickapeppa or Worcestershire sauce. Proceed as directed. Great with chicken and bean soups. If made small, they are a great base for hors d'oeuvres.

Whole-Wheat Sour Cream Biscuits: Substitute whole-wheat pastry flour for all or part of the unbleached all-purpose flour and 1½ to 1¾ cups sour cream for the buttermilk. Meltingly rich, hearty, with good whole-wheat flavor. We love these.

Glazed Cinnamon Raisin Scones: These aren't real scones but they are a great quick breakfast treat. Omit the baking soda. Add 3 tablespoons sugar and a pinch of cinnamon to the dry ingredients. Use 1 to 1¼ cups regular milk or buttermilk and 1 teaspoon vanilla. Stir in ½ cup raisins with a stroke or two after adding the milk. Drop the dough by tablespoons onto a baking sheet and bake as directed. Spoon ½ cup confectioners' sugar mixed with enough milk to make a thin icing over the scones when they come out of the oven.

> **"When an old-timer says bread, he means fresh cornbread or hot biscuits. 'I'd sooner eat a wasp's nest,' growled an elderly woodsman, when offered some ordinary bread from a city bakery.**
>
> **" 'I'd just as soon let the moon shine in my mouth as to eat light bread,' spoke up another hillman.**
>
> **"After a long silence, an old man said thoughtfully, 'Well, light bread's better than nothin'. I've tried both.' "**
>
> —*VANCE RANDOLPH,*
> *DOWN IN THE HOLLER: A GALLERY OF*
> *OZARK FOLK SPEECH*

Charlisa's Extra-Good Sesame Drop Biscuit-Muffins

ecause she's little, it might be hard to spot Char Cato in a crowd, say, at the Annual Eureka Thanksgiving Potluck or Women's Party.

But look on the table—if there's a basket of tiny, incredibly savory, rich little biscuity morsels jeweled with sesame seeds, she's there. Hunt for her; she's always worth finding. Char and I go back a long way. We are two Eurekans who can and do compliment each other regularly on our respective improvements! Charlisa is a dancer and environmentalist. Her sesame biscuit-muffins are addictive—people fight for the last one in the basket.

2 cups self-rising flour
1 cup (2 sticks) butter, at room temperature
1 cup sour cream or Crème Fraîche (page 50)
½ cup sesame seeds, lightly toasted (see Note, page 376)
1 tablespoon paprika
Pam cooking spray

1. Preheat the oven to 425° F.

2. In a mixing bowl, mix the flour and softened butter with a fork until barely blended. Add the sour cream, sesame seeds, and paprika and mix again until barely blended.

3. Spray baking sheets or mini-muffin tins with the Pam. Drop the dough by teaspoonfuls onto the pan or into muffin cups. Bake until brown around the edges, about 10 minutes. Watch closely, for they burn easily.

Makes about 48 miniature biscuit-muffins

INN GOOD COMPANY:
PAULA MARTIN

❦ *Once upon a time, a young couple who loved old houses, people, entertaining, and good food decided to open an inn. Though they did not have the vaguest idea how, they proceeded anyway. In those days we cooked, cleaned, greeted guests, and took reservations. Financial transactions were simple. We made change out of a French Market coffee can (we did have a credit card machine, too . . . it was kept in a bread box).*

These days—about a decade later—we share these and other joys and responsibilities with Paula Martin, our business manager. Without her, we would need to be kept in a bread box.

Paula has been general do-whatever-needs-doing-and-do-it-with-good-cheer person at Dairy Hollow House for quite a few years. This includes bookkeeping and a whole lot more. Although she computerized our bookkeeping, does payroll, etc., she still frequently heads up the front desk sometimes, and the odds are good that it'll be her cheerful voice you hear if you call most Mondays or Fridays. Calm and competent, she's a mother of three, married to Don Martin (the smart-alecky electrician who did all our wiring at the Main House while keeping up a running patter of jive).

An accomplished quilter, Paula brings in showstopping dahlias from her garden to grace the front desk all summer long. She takes pleasure in sharing Eureka Springs' delights and idiosyncrasies with others. Whether she's checking you in or visiting with you over the phone, Paula shares all: from where the best barbecue in town is to when you sent in your deposit to how to find the best swimming hole in a twenty-mile radius. If you call her for information about craft fairs or country music shows or walking trails, rest assured, you'll get it. Through it all, she has gently guided us towards making our business work better as a business.

"What I like about working here is meeting people," says Paula. "There really is something about our guests. We seem, as a rule, to draw people who have interesting lives at home, who are interested in Eureka in a deep, non-typical-touristy way. I've had some great conversations with guests over the years. It's fun to send people to places you know they'll like because you've taken the time to visit with them and you have a clear idea of what they're looking for." She adds, "I also like working in a small enough place that you're a big part of everything that's happening. That's not something I ever got before."

She adds one last fringe benefit. "Being able to walk through the kitchen any time and be an official taster." ❦

MUFFINS

*C*ornbread baked as muffins is as Southern as they come, and mighty good. But here at the inn, we can't resist spreading our horizons, and our butter, a little further. We make three basic muffins at Dairy Hollow. One is a dinner muffin, mostly whole-grain and a not-too-sweet companion to almost any soup or entrée. The second is a sweet muffin, infinitely varied, usually served at breakfast, but occasionally with a soup or at tea. Several times a year, we make a third muffin, Deedy's Gram's Graham Muffins, which come from Deedy Marble of The Governor's Inn in Ludlow, Vermont, our co-winners of the 1989 "Uncle Ben's Best Inn of the Year" award. These are whole-grain and molasses muffins entirely different in character from the others. They are a cholesterol-watcher's dream, for they contain no fat of any kind. Despite this, they are delicious, with a moist, almost Boston-brown-bread quality.

The big trick with muffins is not to overmix. Combine the wet ingredients in one bowl, the dry in another, then put them together with the absolute minimum number of strokes. Never, never beat a muffin batter or the muffins will be flat and tough with an unpleasant tex-

ture. I once beat a muffin batter in high school home economics class; the results were so bad that I've been a fanatic about nonbeating ever since.

Mixed Grain Muffins

*T*his is a version of Janice Carr's Mixed-Grain Muffins I most often use. Recipes evolve. This is how we make them now.

Because these muffins have a lot of baking powder in them, they do not reheat well and they're not good cold; but fresh from the oven they are unbeatable.

Pam cooking spray
¾ cup unbleached all-purpose flour
1 cup whole-wheat flour, preferably stone ground
½ cup cornmeal, preferably ¼ cup each blue and yellow cornmeal
½ cup rolled oats, ground to powder in the food processor
2 tablespoons baking powder
1 teaspoon salt
1 large egg, lightly beaten
¼ cup sugar
⅓ cup mild vegetable oil, such as corn or peanut
1 cup milk

1. Preheat the oven to 400° F. Spray 12 muffin cups with Pam or line with paper liners.

2. In a large mixing bowl, combine the flours, cornmeal, oatmeal, baking powder, and salt. Whisk together the egg, sugar, oil, and milk in a second bowl. Add the wet ingredients to the dry and combine with as few strokes as possible.

3. Spoon the batter into the prepared muffin cups, filling each one one-half to two-thirds full. Bake until browned and fragrant, 15 to 20 minutes. Serve hot.

Makes 12 muffins

Glazed Orange Muffins

his is basically a variation for Sweetness-and-Light Muffin Cakes, (page 367), but it has enough changes to present it separately. This and the lemon variation that follows are luscious, sticky, moist, and wonderful—easily my favorite of all the Sweetness-and-Light versions.

Pam cooking spray
2 cups unbleached all-purpose flour
½ to ¾ cup sugar, depending how sweet you like your muffins
2½ teaspoons baking powder
¼ teaspoon salt
1 large or 2 small oranges
¼ to ⅓ cup milk, as needed
⅓ cup butter, melted and cooled
1 large egg, lightly beaten
1 teaspoon vanilla extract
¼ teaspoon baking soda
½ cup coarsely chopped pecans, lightly toasted (page 316)

ORANGE GLAZE:
Finely grated zest of 1 orange
⅓ cup fresh orange juice
⅓ cup sugar

1. Preheat the oven to 400° F. Spray 12 muffin cups with Pam or line with paper liners.

2. In a large mixing bowl, combine the flour, sugar, baking powder, and salt. Grate the zest of the orange and juice it. Add enough milk to the orange juice to measure ½ cup plus 2 tablespoons and pour it into a second bowl. Add the butter, egg, vanilla, and baking soda and whisk until blended. Add the wet ingredients to the dry and combine with as few strokes as possible. Fold in the orange zest and pecans.

3. Spoon the batter into the prepared muffin cups, filling each one one-half to two-thirds full. Bake until golden and fragrant, 15 to 20 minutes.

4. Meanwhile, prepare the orange glaze: In a small pan, bring the orange zest and juice and sugar to a boil, stirring to dissolve the sugar. Turn down the heat and let simmer until slightly thickened, 4 to 5 minutes. Let cool slightly. The glaze should be

liquidy so that it soaks into the muffins.

5. Let the muffins cool 2 to 3 minutes, then brush the tops with the warm glaze, or drip it over them with a spoon. Serve warm. Sticky and good—real good!

Makes 12 muffins

VARIATION:
Glazed Lemon Muffins: Use the larger amount of sugar, and just 1 lemon (juice and zest) in the muffins. Substitute lemon for the orange in the glaze.

Sweetness-and-Light Muffin Cakes

delightfully light, rich, sweet, basic cake muffin, with many delectable variations. (At the inn we never do the basic recipe, always a variation.) It's the sort of cake you imagine ladies nibbling on delicately at tea, but more than once it's been the guy who requests the recipe.

1¾ cups unbleached all-purpose flour
½ to ¾ cup sugar, depending on how sweet
  you like your muffins
2½ teaspoons baking powder
¼ teaspoon salt
¼ teaspoon freshly grated nutmeg
½ cup milk
⅓ cup butter, melted and cooled
1 large egg, lightly beaten
1 teaspoon vanilla extract
Additional 2 tablespoons melted butter
  (optional)

1. Preheat the oven to 400° F. Grease 12 muffin cups or line with paper liners.

2. In a large mixing bowl, combine the flour, sugar to taste, baking powder, salt, and nutmeg. In a second bowl, whisk together the milk, butter, egg, and vanilla. Add the wet ingredients to the dry and combine with as few strokes as possible. If you like, fold in one of the additions mentioned in the Variations.

3. Spoon the batter into the prepared muffin cups, filling each one one-half to two-thirds full. Bake until golden brown, 15 to 20 minutes. Brush with the optional melted butter. Serve hot.

Makes 12 muffins

VARIATIONS:
Peach and Nut Muffins: Add a drop of almond extract to the wet ingredients. Add 3 diced unpeeled peaches and ½ cup coarsely chopped pecans or walnuts to the batter.

Ginger-Pear-Walnut Muffins: Add 2 partially mashed, diced pears, 1 tablespoon finely-minced, peeled, fresh ginger root, and ½ cup chopped walnuts to the batter.

Banana Nut Muffins: Add 2 mashed bananas, ½ teaspoon ground cinnamon, and ½ cup coarsely chopped nuts to the batter. For a very special muffin, add 1 teaspoon grated lemon zest and/or ⅔ cup diced pitted dates to the batter.

Cranberry Nut Muffins: Use the larger amount of sugar. Add 1 cup chopped cranberries and ½ cup coarsely chopped nuts to the batter. You can also add 1½ teaspoons grated orange zest.

Date Nut Muffins: Use the smaller amount of sugar. Add ¾ cup diced pitted dates (cut with the scissors dipped in sugar) and ½ cup coarsely chopped pecans to the batter.

Piña Colada Muffins: Use the smaller amount of sugar. Replace ¼ cup of the milk with ¼ cup thawed frozen pineapple juice concentrate mixed with ¼ teaspoon baking soda. Add this to the wet ingredients, then mix with the dry ingredients. Add ½ to ¾ cup shredded coconut, ½ cup coarsely chopped nuts (how about macadamias?), and, if you want, ¾ cup diced fresh pineapple to the batter.

Deedy's Gram's Graham Muffins

Somehow these good, bready muffins rich with molasses flavor say "New England." They are served at The Governor's Inn in Ludlow, Vermont, a Victorian country inn, renowned for its cuisine.

Deedy is Deedy Marble, chef–innkeeper and winner of 12 national culinary awards at last count. Visit The Governor's Inn at 86 Main Street, Ludlow, Vermont (phone 802-228-8830). And tell Deedy the Dragon said "Hey!"

Oh, by the way, graham flour is an old-fashioned name for whole-wheat.

Pam cooking spray
2¼ cups whole-wheat flour
3 cups unbleached all-purpose flour
1 tablespoon baking soda
1½ teaspoons salt
3 cups buttermilk, preferably Bulgarian-
*   style, or sour milk*
¾ cup molasses
¾ cup (packed) light brown sugar

1. Preheat the oven to 350° F. Line a 12-cup muffin tin with paper liners. Spray two small loaf pans with Pam.

2. Into a large mixing bowl, sift the flours, baking soda, and salt. In a second bowl, whisk together the buttermilk, molasses, and sugar. Add the wet ingredients to the dry and combine with as few strokes as possible.

3. Spoon the batter into the prepared muffin cups and loaf pans, filling each one two-thirds full. Bake until the muffins have risen and are fragrant and firm, 20 to 25 minutes for the muffins, 35 to 40 minutes for the small loaves.

Makes 12 muffins *and 2 small loaves*

Salad

THE GREEN PALETTE

read and soup and salad: the three play off each other. It's simple magic this synergistic triumvirate: the raw, mouth-awakening bite of garlicky, chilled fresh greens against the soothing, mellowed warmth of a soup, both set off by the hearty, earthy crunch and substance of good bread. When a salad, carefully chosen and well made, is added to a soup and bread meal, simple fare surges from hominess to feast—food to live with and on, food for the long haul.

We make many salads at Dairy Hollow. The ultimate salad, which I call The Salad, is the one I return to year in and year out and never tire of. Jan and I wrote about it at length in the *Dairy Hollow House Cookbook*. To my taste it is perfectly balanced in its blend of seasonings, which do not mask but bring out the essence of the green leaves. It's a mixed-in-the-bowl salad, put together right before it's served. Although perhaps 80 percent of our restaurant guests ask us, "How do you make that salad dressing?," The Salad can hardly be said to have a dressing as such, and what it does have is not overdone. It goes with almost any hearty, substantial, main-dish soup, particularly those in which grains or potatoes or blander starches play a major part.

The Salad will always be first in Dairy Hollow's green repertoire, but it is not our only leafy song. Some soups (the light, summery offerings and the thinner, elegant ones) need a salad with a little more ballast—perhaps a grain or potato salad for heft or a beautiful composed salad with cheese or meat for protein. We also do such salads when we serve lunches for special groups, or at our event weekends. Soups that are fairly one-dimensional, cream soups, say, also achieve new interest and appeal when paired with a salad of more texture and contrast than The Salad. And sometimes the brimming cornucopia of the seasons pours forth so irresistible a bounty of ingredients that a new salad, its ingredients sitting on the kitchen table, invents itself. This is how my favorite composed salad of recent years came to be: beautiful fresh greens and fresh beets in a colander still sparkling with water, a bowl of apples, another of new-crop walnuts, and suddenly...hey, why not put them together? What about adding blue cheese? And for a dressing, maybe something that's a little sweet, and somehow dusky and fall-like in flavor. How about one with...raisins?

HOW DOES YOUR SALAD GROW?

Deliciously, if you choose a variety of bright, intensely colored greens, including some greens that aren't green, like garnet-colored red leaf lettuce. Variety, along with freshness, is the key.

Go for at least two or three different lettuces of mild flavor: romaine,

spinach, butterhead, red leaf, oakleaf. A bitter green adds contrasting flavor that will make all the flavors sing; use arugula, radicchio, escarole, dandelion greens, or peppery watercress. These should be torn by hand, not cut with a knife. A thatch of finely slivered green or red cabbage—this you cut—can be included for crunch and contrast. Even people who think they dislike cabbage will love it this way. Very young Swiss chard or beet greens can also be finely ribboned with a sharp knife or a good pair of scissors and tossed in with the greens.

Other choices are slivered fresh herbs, herb flowers, or edible flowers (sweet pea or nasturtium blossoms) added in the very last tossing, since they are delicate. And parsley, though you may think it's a cooking cliché, is just wonderful in The Salad. Chop it very fine and toss it in the salad with the lemon juice.

THIS IS THE WAY WE WASH OUR GREENS

A friend of mine calls small imperfections and irritations "mosquitoes of life." A particularly annoying mosquito of life is biting into a beautiful, inviting salad and crunching down on grit. You wouldn't think you need to mention that salad greens need thorough washing, but after a certain number of gritty encounters, a person has to say—enough! This is the way to wash your greens.

Separate the head of lettuce into individual leaves, checking for visible dirt as you do so. Rinse each leaf quickly under cold running water. That may do it, but most likely cleaning will take more effort. Stack the leaves in a colander and rinse the whole batch a couple  more times. Perhaps you got all the grit this time? Well, check. Examine the leaves closely. Bite one. If you detect any grit, prepare for serious lettuce washing: Fill a large bowl with lukewarm—not hot—water. Add the leaves and swish them, one by one, around in the water, then lift them from the water, being careful not to stir up any gritty water in the bottom of the bowl. Put the leaves in a colander. Empty and rinse the bowl, noting the amount of grit in the bottom. Repeat, and keep repeating until there is no grit in the bottom of the bowl. Be diligent and persistent, but work quickly. Don't let the greens soak in the water, which will rob them of vitamins, flavor, and crispness. It should be a quick matter of in—swish—out.

After their final lukewarm water bath, rinse the greens with nice cold water. Let them drain briefly in the colander and get ready to dry them, unfortunately, almost as arduous as rinsing.

DRY, DRY AGAIN

A salad made with even slightly wet greens may be okay, but it will never, ever be great, for three simple reasons. Wet leaves become soggy leaves; moisture dilutes the dressing; and wetness prevents the sealant effect of the olive oil from taking place.

Here are three drying techniques I have used over the years.

1. Leaf by leaf, very carefully with a paper towel.

2. In a plastic centrifugal salad spinner, a very clever device that many salad-loving households possess.

3. The forerunner of a centrifugal salad spinner, the Ozark version, the totally silly-looking but much more effective than either of the above, to say nothing of cheaper, the New Age miracle device that should be a part of every household and generally is: a pillowcase.

A pillowcase? Yes. A flannel one is especially absorbent.

Put the dripping wet greens into a clean, clean pillowcase. Go outside. Hold the pillowcase about halfway down, closing it tightly with one hand. Whirl it around and around and around, over your head or to the side or in front of you, whatever is most comfortable. We lean over the porch and let fly and hope no guests see us (now, thank God, it is in print, so we will have a logical explanation at hand). You will see the drops of water exiting the lettuce as quickly as they can, flying off in all directions.

The sense of sheepish embarrassment, the certainty that one will be hauled off if observed in this activity, is a clear indication that one is doing it correctly.

Open the pillowcase, which should be quite damp. Pull out the lettuce, which should be quite dry. If it isn't, whirl again and open the bag again.

If you are doing a larger quantity of very wet greens, repeat, using a second, dry pillowcase.

All this said, following are some of our current favorites, starting, of course, with The Salad.

The Salad

an and I wrote up The Salad in the *Dairy Hollow House Cookbook* not as a recipe, but as nine secrets. This was because the ingredients sound unprepossessing; it is technique that makes The Salad. This time around, it is in recipe form, but otherwise identical in all particulars. Be sure to pay attention to the details, for they bring this to Olympian heights.

Quantities given here assume that salad is a major part of the meal, as in a hearty bread-soup-salad dinner. If the meal has more courses, scale portion sizes down accordingly.

*6 to 8 cups torn mixed salad greens with
    personality, such as romaine,
    buttercrunch, oakleaf, and red-leaf
    lettuces, spinach, and arugula*
1 to 3 tablespoons olive oil
3 to 4 cloves garlic, or more to taste, peeled
*Salt and freshly ground black pepper to
    taste*
1 lemon, halved
Dash of Pickapeppa or Worcestershire sauce

1. Put 4 salad plates in the freezer to chill. Assemble all the ingredients as well as

a garlic press, a big salad bowl, and a strainer for the lemon juice.

2. Wash the greens extremely well; check them over for any brown or old-looking edges. Using a salad spinner, spin the greens bone dry, then blot with towels; no moisture should cling. At least 75 percent of salad mediocrity comes from not-quite-fresh greens that are not quite washed and then not completely dried.

3. Pour the oil into a large salad bowl. I don't like a lot of oil on my salad. At home I use ½ to 1 teaspoon per person and am most happy with the results. A tablespoon per person is standard and what people, theoretically, are used to, but I think it overwhelms the freshness and delicacy of the greens. At the restaurant I use a bit more than I use at home but still less than the classic amount. Play with the amount of oil, as with all the ingredients, the first few times you make The Salad until you get it just right for you.

4. Put the garlic through the garlic press into the olive oil. Into the bowl, put the well-rinsed bone-dry salad greens. Toss the greens, gently but with vigor, until each leaf glistens with olive oil. The oil seals in the greens' moisture and flavor, so that the ingredients will not immediately penetrate the leaves and for a few moments the greens will exist in a sublime state: lightly coated, yet crisp.

5. Sprinkle the glistening greens with ½ to 1 teaspoon salt, several hearty grinds of pepper, the juice of half of the lemon squeezed through the strainer to catch the seeds (if it's a particularly large or juicy lemon, don't squeeze out every drop), and a small shake of Pickapeppa or Worcestershire sauce. Toss the greens a couple of times and taste. You may well need the juice of the other lemon half, a dash more salt, or an extra grind of pepper. Come on, add it, hurry up, time's a-wasting!

6. Quickly get your salad plates from the freezer, divide the salad among the plates, and immediately serve.

Serves 4 to 8

CHILLING OUT

🌿*At any restaurant (our place, too) getting the hot dishes to the table still piping hot is of paramount importance. But in my heart of hearts I know getting The Salad to the table not more than thirty seconds after it's tossed, with the plates still cold, is even more essential. Heaven forbid someone should send their food back because it wasn't hot enough, but if they did, it could be reheated. The Salad, however, is at its height only very briefly, and after the moment has passed, it's passed and nothing in the world will bring it back. Moral: Everyone should be sitting down and ready to eat before you start tossing The Salad. And get the salad plates out of the freezer only as the salad is completed.*🌿

GREAT NEWS ON THE "DRESSING FOR SUCCESS" FRONT

❦ *If you're a devotee of homemade vinaigrettes, mayonnaises, and so on, and possess a food processor, you're in incredible luck. In recent years, I have learned (from Peggy Pinkley, of Springfield, Missouri) a wonderful trick that makes the emulsifying of oils a breeze.*

Most salad dressings, as you probably know, are basically made of two components: the seasonings (comprised of the vinegar or lemon juice and any spices, mustards, herbs, garlic, and so on that are added to it) and the oil. As you will immediately recognize from having seen hundreds of oil-and-vinegar dressings over the years, these two components do not readily blend, but tend to separate. Emulsification is the process by which oil is absorbed bit by bit into the seasoning mix, making for a smooth and homogenous dressing. Whether by hand, in a blender, or food processor, the seasoning ingredients are first beaten. While in motion, the oil is dripped in bit by bit. Gradually the mixture thickens and smooths into one unified whole.

Food processors made this much easier, since the seasonings could be buzzed until combined, then whirl merrily along as you stood there patiently dripping in the oil. Now, even that last part has been simplified.

Examine your processor. Cuisinart processors, and every other brand I've examined, have a hollow cylindrical plastic pusher, open on the top, closed on the bottom, which slides down into the feed tube. In the closed bottom of the pusher, right in the center is a tiny hole. It is this hole that makes your processor a simply magic emulsifying tool.

Here's how. You put your seasoning ingredients in the workbowl, and start buzzing. Measure out your oil in a spouted measuring cup. Fit the pusher in place, in the feeder tube. With the machine still running, pour into the hollow plastic pusher as much of the measured oil as will fit (the capacity of the pusher will vary with the model and brand; ours holds ⅔ cup). This is the magic part: the centrifugal force of the machine will pull the oil down through that little tiny hole, in a thin stream, slowly and consistently. This, one, leaves you free to do other kitchen tasks while the dressing is being made and, two, assures that just the right amount of oil will be added, slowly, to the dressing. All you have to do is refill the pusher tube when it's run out of oil.

By the time all the oil has been absorbed, you'll have a luscious, creamy-textured, perfectly emulsified dressing. ❦

COMPOSED SALADS

The Salad is, literally, tossed together. Composed salads, by contrast, are carefully placed, arranged salads of great beauty. Usually they begin with a few whole green leaves, and are topped by more greens, torn by hand (never cut with a knife—but you learned that at your mother's knee, right?) into bite-size pieces. On this are arranged the ingredients of the day: fresh, just-cut-from-the-cob corn in summer, perhaps, or marinated cooked beets in winter, or fresh asparagus, steamed and chilled, in spring. Lastly, if the ingredients have not been previously marinated in a vinaigrette of some sort, a bit of an appropriately seasoned dressing is spooned on, or sometimes passed at the table. The salad may be sparked with herbs, or perhaps sesame seeds, garlic, ginger, or any number of things.

Composed salads are elegant, wonderful dishes, innovative and ever-changing. They're ready to adapt to the season, the menu, the cook's imagination—to some extent, even the table setting. They're so pretty that they become an integral design element in a dinner, as much as a vase of flowers or a centerpiece (maybe more so, if you hold with the "form follows function" dictate).

Here are some new composed salads from Dairy Hollow, beautiful in form, delectable in function.

A Salad for Fall

Celebratory with the pure, clear flavors of the harvest, this is my current favorite composed salad. The flavors are simply magical together, and it is so pretty. I fed this to Jan Brown, who liked it so much that the following Thanksgiving she stayed home and made it (and just it) for herself.

The dressing is on the sweet side but is not cloying, like so many sweet dressings. It has some zing and intrigue. I would not choose this or the two salads that follow, however, if I were planning an entrée with a sweet note.

4 or 5 small or 2 or 3 large fresh beets
Sesame-Raisin Vinaigrette (recipe follows)
1 head red leaf lettuce, leaves separated, thoroughly washed and dried
½ head romaine lettuce, leaves separated, thoroughly washed and dried
1 small red onion, sliced paper thin
3 ounces good-quality blue or Roquefort cheese, crumbled
1 crisp Granny Smith apple, cored and cut into tiny matchstick-size pieces
½ to ¾ cup walnut pieces, toasted (page 316)

1. Steam or boil the beets until just barely tender, about 15 to 20 minutes for small beets, 30 to 40 minutes for large. Let cool, then peel; cut into ¼-inch dice. Place the beets in a bowl and toss with 2 to 3 tablespoons of the vinaigrette. Chill. This can be done hours in advance or just before you put the salad together.

2. Arrange a few whole lettuce leaves on chilled individual salad plates or a large platter. Tear the remaining greens into bite-size pieces and place over the whole leaves. Arrange the beets, onion, and blue cheese over the greens. Sprinkle the apple over, and distribute the walnuts. It is appealing if the walnuts are still a bit warm. Drizzle the salad portions with the vinaigrette or pass it at the table.

Serves 4 to 6

VARIATION:
Instead of dicing and marinating the beets, just grate them, cooked, directly over the plated salad greens. Substitute a ripe, but still slightly firm, pear for the apple.

Sesame-Raisin Vinaigrette

 his must be made in a food processor.

½ cup cider vinegar or other fruit vinegar, such as blueberry
2 tablespoons honey
⅓ cup dark raisins
¼ cup sesame seeds, toasted (see Note)
½ teaspoon salt
¾ cup peanut oil
¼ cup toasted sesame oil

▶ Place all ingredients except the oils in a food processor and process until the raisins are chopped to a dark paste. Put the machine's pusher tube in place. With the machine running, add both oils, through the little hole in the pusher tube, and process until emulsified. You will have some vinaigrette left over, but it keeps very well in the refrigerator. (If it thickens when refrigerated, thin it with a little additional vinegar.)

Makes about 1¼ cups

Note: In a small heavy skillet, toast the sesame seeds over medium heat until they begin to pop, are golden brown, and give off fragrance. Stir the seeds and shake the pan while they toast, for they burn if left unattended. This should take 2 to 4 minutes, max.

Déjà Food: A little of this vinaigrette stirred into mayonnaise makes a wonderful dressing for chicken salad. It's also a delicious spread for a curried egg-salad sandwich, or a turkey, bacon, and lettuce sandwich.

Spinach and Red Leaf Lettuce Salad

imilar in concept to the previous, this plays a sweet dressing and dice of fresh fruit against the crunch of toasted nuts and crisp greens, and the zing of onion. The raspberry dressing makes the salad quite distinctive—just delicious and the perfect color for the Christmas holidays. Red-skinned pears makes it even prettier. In fact, we developed this salad for our first Christmas at the restaurant. We also like its vibrancy of color and flavor on Valentine's day.

*1 head red leaf lettuce, leaves separated,
   thoroughly washed, dried, and torn
   into bite-size pieces*
*1 pound fresh spinach, tough stems
   removed, thoroughly washed and
   dried*
*Raspberry Vinaigrette (recipe
   follows)*
*1 cup raw cashews, toasted
   (page 316)*
1 red onion, sliced paper thin
*1 slightly firm ripe pear, preferably
   red-skinned, cored and finely
   diced*

 Combine the lettuce and spinach and place it on 4 to 6 chilled individual salad plates. Drizzle lightly with bright ribbons of the vinaigrette. Divide the cashews, onion, and pear among the plates. Pass the remaining vinaigrette at the table.

Serves 4 to 6

Raspberry Vinaigrette

es, raspberry and garlic sounds bizarre, but the combination works very well. The berries are very tart and acidic.

*¾ cup thawed frozen unsweetened
   raspberries*
¼ cup raspberry vinegar
1 clove garlic, peeled
2 tablespoons honey
½ teaspoon salt
*1 cup mild vegetable oil, such as corn or
   peanut*

1. In a food processor, purée the raspberries then press the purée through a fine sieve to remove the seeds. You should have ¼ cup seedless purée.

2. In the food processor, place the raspberry purée and remaining ingredients except the oil, and process until blended. Put the machine's pusher tube in place. With the machine running, add the oil through the little hole in the pusher tube, and process until emulsified. Taste for seasonings; you may wish to add a little more honey.

Makes about 1⅓ cups

Mexican Corn and Avocado Salad

beautiful composed salad of fresh, summery flavors, as pretty to look at as it is delicious, and full of the good Southwestern tastes we know and love: cumin, cilantro, tomatoes, onions, and avocado. The sweetness of the corn and the jícama is balanced by the slight spiciness of the dressing.

4 ears fresh corn, or 2 cups frozen corn
*   kernels*
Cilantro Vinaigrette (recipe follows)
3 ripe avocados
1 lemon
1 head red leaf lettuce, leaves separated,
*   thoroughly washed, and dried*
½ head romaine lettuce, leaves separated,
*   thoroughly washed, and dried*
¼ head red or green cabbage, finely
*   shredded*
1 small sweet white onion, such as Walla
*   Walla, finely diced*
2 ripe tomatoes, finely diced, or 1 each red
*   and yellow bell peppers, cored, seeded,*
*   and diced*
½ cup peeled and finely diced
*   jícama*
8 slices bacon, cooked crisp and coarsely
*   crumbled (optional)*
Alfalfa sprouts, for garnish
Chopped fresh cilantro and parsley, for
*   garnish*

1. If using fresh corn, shuck the ears and steam over boiling water about 5 minutes. Let cool slightly, then cut the kernels from the cobs. If using frozen corn, run hot water over the kernels in a colander until thawed and bright yellow. Toss the corn with 2 tablespoons of the vinaigrette and chill.

2. Pit and peel the avocados, then cut into fine dice. Juice the lemon and toss the avocados with the lemon juice to keep them from darkening.

3. Arrange a few whole lettuce leaves on 4 to 6 chilled individual salad plates or a large platter. Tear the remaining greens into bite-size pieces, combine them with the cabbage, and mound on top of the whole leaves. Scatter the corn, onion, tomatoes or bell peppers, avocados, jícama, and optional bacon over the greens. Drizzle the salads with vinaigrette and garnish with alfalfa sprouts, cilantro, and parsley. Pass the remaining vinaigrette at the table.

Serves 4 to 6

VARIATION:

Entrée Mexican Corn and Avocado Salad: Add a mound of diced cooked chicken, a good sprinkle of grated very sharp Cheddar cheese, and/or additional crumbled bacon on top of the cabbage and greens. For a vegetarian entrée salad, omit the chicken and bacon and add diced tofu or cooked kidney or pinto beans, chick-peas, or black-eyed peas.

ABOUT VINAIGRETTE

❦Vinaigrettes are essentially simple dressings. Vinegar and seasonings are combined, and oil is drizzled in while the mixture is being beaten or whisked by hand, or whirled in a food processor. The oil emulsifies, thickening the mixture.

But this simple basic can go in a thousand directions depending on the ingredients. The vinegar can be herbal or balsamic, red wine or white, even made from fruit like raspberry or strawberry. Or you can use lemon or lime juice instead. The seasonings? Un-

limited. Basil, oregano, rosemary, or garlic make a vinaigrette French, Italian, or Continental. Sesame and ginger take it East and do so beautifully. Cilantro plus chilies take it south of the border; cilantro plus curry take it to India. Even the oil affects a vinaigrette's character: olive, toasted sesame, or a full-flavored nut oil all add impact, while corn and peanut oil are pretty neutral.

If you want a thicker, creamier vinaigrette, make a mayonnaise by adding an egg to the vinegar before you drizzle in the oil.❦

Cilantro Vinaigrette

Citrus juice sparks this vinaigrette's taste with a special freshness that vinegar cannot match. If possible, make it a day or two ahead of time to allow the flavors to blend.

⅓ cup strained fresh lime or lemon juice, or red wine vinegar, if you prefer the taste
4 cloves garlic, peeled
2 tablespoons chopped fresh cilantro, or to taste
2 tablespoons chopped fresh parsley
2 teaspoons chili powder
1½ teaspoons ground cumin
¼ teaspoon dried oregano
⅛ teaspoon cayenne pepper, or to taste
¾ teaspoon salt
Freshly ground black pepper to taste
1 cup mild vegetable oil, such as corn or peanut

► Place all ingredients except the oil in a food processor and process until combined. Put the machine's pusher tube in place. With the machine running, add the oil through the little hole in the pusher tube, and process until emulsified. Taste for seasoning; you may need to add a little more cayenne pepper or extra cilantro. Refrigerate at least 1 hour but preferably overnight.

Makes about 1 cup

Avocado and Orange Salad

gain, contrast—melting tender avocado, juicy orange, crisp greens, crunchy cashews, and a great dressing. A wonderfully fresh-tasting salad, with surprises in every bite.

1 head red leaf lettuce, leaves separated, thoroughly washed, dried, and torn into bite-size pieces
1 pound fresh spinach, tough stems removed, thoroughly washed and spun dry
Orange-Scallion Vinaigrette (recipe follows)
1 cup raw cashews, toasted (page 316)
2 or 3 ripe avocados, pitted, peeled, and cut into ½-inch dice
2 juicy navel oranges, peel and white pith removed, cut into segments, then into ½-inch pieces

▶ Combine the lettuce and spinach

and place on 4 to 6 chilled individual salad plates. Drizzle lightly with the vinaigrette. Divide the cashews, avocadoes, and oranges among the plates. Pass the remaining vinaigrette at the table.

Serves 4 to 6

Orange-Scallion Vinaigrette

¼ cup fresh lemon juice
¼ cup fresh orange juice
3 scallions, trimmed and coarsely chopped
1 to 2 tablespoons honey
1 teaspoon finely grated orange zest
½ teaspoon tamari/shoyu soy sauce
1 cup mild vegetable oil, such as corn or peanut
1 tablespoon toasted sesame oil (optional)

▶ Place all the ingredients except the oils in a food processor and process until combined. Put the machine's pusher tube in place. With the machine running, add the oils through the little hole in the pusher tube and process until emulsified. Taste for seasoning; you may need to add a little more honey or soy sauce.

Makes 1½ cups

Composed Salad of Asparagus and Snow Peas

ur predilection for sesame and Oriental touches shows up in this light, spring salad, elegant and festive. We served it at our first dinner in the new restaurant dining room.

25 to 40 asparagus spears, tough ends trimmed (the larger the spears, the fewer you'll need)
25 fresh snow peas, trimmed
Sherried Sesame Vinaigrette (recipe follows)
1 head red leaf lettuce, leaves separated, thoroughly washed, and dried
8 to 12 fresh cherry tomatoes
1 to 1½ cups alfalfa seed sprouts
2 yellow bell peppers, cored, seeded, and diced
5 scallions, trimmed and thinly sliced

1. Steam the asparagus and snow peas separately over boiling water until just barely crisp-tender. Cool quickly under cold running water and drain well. Toss the asparagus and snow peas separately with enough of the vinaigrette to coat lightly. Chill.

2. Arrange a few whole lettuce leaves on 4 to 6 chilled individual salad plates or a large platter. Tear the remaining leaves into bite-size pieces and place them on the whole leaves. Arrange the asparagus, snow peas, and cherry tomatoes on the lettuce and spoon a little vinaigrette over the top. Add a puff of alfalfa sprouts and sprinkle with the bell peppers and scallions. Pass the remaining vinaigrette at the table.

Serves 4 to 6

Sherried Sesame Vinaigrette

1 piece (2 inches) fresh gingerroot, peeled and finely chopped
2 cloves garlic, peeled
¼ cup light miso paste
⅓ cup rice wine vinegar
¼ cup sweet sherry or mirin (sweet Japanese rice wine)
2 tablespoons tamari/shoyu soy sauce
2 tablespoons honey
2 tablespoons tahini (ground sesame seed paste) or creamy peanut butter
Tiny pinch of cayenne pepper
⅔ cup peanut oil
2 tablespoons toasted sesame oil
¼ cup sesame seeds, toasted (see Note, page 376)

▶ Place all ingredients except the oils and sesame seeds in a food processor and process. Put the machine's pusher tube in place. With the machine running, add the oils through the little hole in the pusher tube, and process until emulsified. Add the sesame seeds and combine with a few on/off pulses.

Makes 1¾ cups

GRAIN-BASED SALADS

*I*t was almost audible, the sigh of relief, when carbohydrates began again to get their due as nutritional building blocks instead of diet spoilers. (But, hey, our bodies knew it all along, didn't they? Why do you think people say, "Boy, I've really got a craving for pasta," as opposed to, say "a craving for haddock"?)

Grain salads are hearty and delicious. They pair well with light, chilled soups; they travel well to picnics and potlucks (where, in my experience, they are always the first things eaten). They're also excellent leave-in-the-fridge-and-take-a-nibble-anytime foods, good for the hottest days of summer.

One of the grain salads listed here, the bursting-to-overflowing Dairy Hollow House Pasta Salad, could as well have been listed under the entrée salad section; you can serve it with, or as, the main course. The other salads are usually accompaniments.

Tabouleh

*T*he widespread popularity of this wheat salad has not diminished its appeal. I like this version, not far removed from the classic but with the seasonings turned up in volume. It's easy to make and incredibly refreshing, zinged with fresh lemon and fresh mint. I prefer whole-grain cracked wheat to the smaller, more refined bulgur wheat. Steer clear of instant tabouleh mix, which is quick but less than tasty. With a tiny bit more kitchen time, you can make tabouleh from scratch and get infinitely more flavor for less money.

3 cups well-salted any well-flavored vegetable stock, boiling
1½ cups cracked whole-grain wheat (from natural foods store) or bulgur wheat
2 to 4 tablespoons olive oil
Juice of 2 to 3 lemons
3 cloves garlic, peeled and put through a garlic press
3 to 4 tablespoons finely chopped fresh mint
3 to 4 tablespoons finely chopped fresh parsley
½ teaspoon dried oregano
Salt and freshly ground black pepper to taste
2 or 3 ripe tomatoes, chopped
1 cucumber, peeled, quartered lengthwise, seeded, and cut into chunks
1 small red onion, finely chopped
1 green bell pepper, stemmed, seeded, and diced
1 red bell pepper, stemmed, seeded, and diced
Salad greens, for serving

1. In a large mixing bowl, pour the boiling stock over the wheat. Let stand until all the liquid has been absorbed, about 2 hours. Add the olive oil, juice of 2 lemons,

the garlic, fresh and dried herbs, salt, and pepper; toss to coat and combine. Taste and adjust the seasoning, adding more lemon juice, salt, and pepper if needed. Chill to allow the flavors to blend, at least 3 hours but preferably overnight.

2. Just before serving, fold in the vegetables. Serve on a bed of salad greens.

Serves 6

SUNDAY NIGHT SUPPER IN
AUGUST

❦

Gazpacho Rosa

Tabouleh

Sliced Fresh Peaches with
Brown Sugar and Yogurt

❦

Wild Rice Salad Vinaigrette with Peas

 e never use convenience foods at the restaurant and only rarely at home. But one day the market was out of my beloved Uncle Ben's con-

verted rice, and Ned brought home a box of their wild rice mix. I wound up using it in a salad in the tabouleh idiom and liked it so much I've been making it ever since. Don't add salt, for the mix is salty enough. (And, yes, I was quietly making this years before we won the Uncle Ben's "Best Inn of the Year" award.)

1 cup Uncle Ben's converted white rice
1 box (6 ounces) Uncle Ben's Original Long Grain and Wild Rice Mix
5 cups any well-flavored vegetable or chicken stock
⅓ cup olive oil
1 tablespoon Garlic Oil (page 41)
Juice of 1 to 2 lemons
¼ cup finely chopped fresh parsley
Freshly ground black pepper to taste
1 bunch broccoli, cut into small flowerets, stems reserved for other use
1 package (10 ounces) frozen peas
2 or 3 ripe tomatoes, chopped
1 small red onion, finely chopped
1 green bell pepper, stemmed, seeded, and diced
1 red bell pepper, stemmed, seeded, and diced
Salad greens, for serving

1. Cook the converted rice and wild rice mix separately according to the package directions, replacing the water with stock and omitting the butter. Remove from the heat and combine in a large bowl. Let cool.

2. Add to the rice the olive oil, garlic oil, juice of 1 lemon, the parsley, and pepper; toss to coat and combine. Taste and adjust the seasoning, adding more lemon juice or seasonings, if needed. Chill.

3. Meanwhile, steam the broccoli flowerets over boiling water until crisp-tender.

Cool under cold running water and drain well. Run hot water over the peas until barely cooked and drain well.

4. Add the vegetables to the rice and toss to combine. Chill for at least an hour. Serve on a bed of salad greens.

Serves 6 to 8

Dairy Hollow House Pasta Salad

s popular as pasta salads have been in the last decade, one would think everybody would have a recipe for one by now. But every time we serve this, whether at the restaurant or at home, we get asked for the recipe. It is delicious and hard to stop eating. I don't think I've picnicked for years without taking along a bowl of this.

This is of the "more is more" school—more herbs, more vegetables, and more garlic make this more delicious. It's very, very flavorful and colorful, yet has pasta's comforting plainness. With chunks of cheese and chick-peas added, it's a full meal.

One thing it is not "more of" is dressing. I don't like a dressing of any type which you have to shake off the salad. Too much oil drowns out flavor;

just a bit enhances it. In a pasta salad, especially, excess dressing is greasy. This pasta salad is lightly, tastefully dressed.

You can use fewer vegetables than those I've listed here, or cut back on the fancy stuff if you like. It's good with just the seasonings and a few vegetables. But doing the whole number is not hard; despite the long list of ingredients, it goes together in a flash. You prepare the pasta and seasonings, then, when that's well underway, the vegetables. Finally you toss all together with the finishes.

Necessarily, this recipe yields a large quantity—it takes a lot of pasta to balance all the other ingredients that make the salad so luscious.

PASTA AND DRESSING:
Salt
2 pounds sturdy-shaped pasta, such as bow ties, tubes, or curlicues (some can be spinach, tomato, carrot, and/or beet pasta)
Marinade from 1 jar (6½ ounces) marinated artichoke hearts (see Finishes list)
4 to 6 tablespoons olive oil
3 tablespoons red wine vinegar, or more to taste
Juice of 1 lemon
6 cloves garlic, peeled
¼ cup chopped fresh basil leaves or 2 teaspoons dried basil
¼ cup chopped fresh parsley
2 teaspoons dried oregano
⅛ teaspoon crumbled dried rosemary
Freshly ground black pepper to taste

VEGETABLES:
4 carrots, peeled, cut into 1 x ⅛-inch
square strips, blanched 2 minutes, well
drained
1 zucchini, scrubbed, cut into ½-inch
cubes, blanched 30 seconds, well drained
1 bunch broccoli, separated into bite-sized
flowerets, stems peeled and julienned,
blanched 3 minutes, well drained
¼ head cauliflower, separated into small
flowerets, blanched 2 minutes, well
drained
1 package (10 ounces) frozen peas,
"cooked" by pouring boiling water over
them, well drained
1 cup cherry tomatoes, preferably red and
yellow, stemmed
2 red bell peppers, stemmed, seeded, and
diced
2 green bell peppers, stemmed, seeded, and
diced

FINISHES:
Marinated artichoke hearts from 1 jar
(6½ ounces)
15 to 20 Kalamata olives, pitted and
coarsely chopped
1 can (15 ounces) chick-peas, drained well
12 to 18 ounces mild firm cheese, such as
mozzarella or Fontina, cut into ¼-inch
cubes
6 ounces feta, cut into ½-inch cubes or
coarsely crumbled

1. Fill your largest soup pot with water and bring it to a boil. Salt the water, add the pasta, and cook until tender but still firm to the bite.

2. Meanwhile, drain the marinade from the artichoke hearts into a food processor. Add the oil, vinegar, lemon juice, garlic, and herbs and process until smooth.

3. Drain the pasta well, cool under cold running water, and drain well again. Transfer the pasta to a large bowl, pour the dressing over it, and toss to combine. Season with salt and pepper. Taste, and amend to your liking with additional olive oil, vinegar, or seasonings.

4. Add the blanched and fresh vegetables to the pasta and toss to combine.

5. To finish, coarsely chop the artichoke hearts and add with the olives; toss again. Taste for seasoning and chill.

6. Just before serving, add the chick-peas and cheeses. Toss to combine, then serve.

Serves 14 to 16 as a side dish or 10 to 12 as an entrée

Patchwork Slaw

The Curried Vinaigrette in the recipe on page 387 is just too good. Inspired by it, we wondered how this fabulous dressing would work in a slaw? Of course, it couldn't be just *any* slaw. What developed has proven to be a four-star favorite. I can't tell you how many guests have told me, "I don't like curry and I don't like slaw, but this is great!" As if this wasn't enough, we even got a rave on this dish in *Gourmet* magazine: "Coleslaw is treated with grace and imagination and served as a course on its own—coarsely chopped, frilly red and white cabbage with a curry vinaigrette, sometimes garnished with a mustard blossom, sometimes with a sage flower. It is fiery and delicious."

Its secrets are simple. One, a great dressing; two, rather than being thrown together as most coleslaws are, this is arranged with the attention usually given a composed salad; three, the ingredients are not permitted to sit in the dressing so long that they become soggy; and four, it is a lovely, festive salad—the mix of red and green cabbage with other bright offerings from garden and orchard make it as delicious as it is colorful. Pretty as a double wedding ring or lone star quilt hung on a line to dry, this is one slaw that's as at home at a dressy dinner as at a picnic.

1 head green cabbage, core and outer
    leaves removed, very thinly sliced
1 crisp red apple, cored and cut into tiny
    dice
¼ red onion, very finely diced
3 carrots, scrubbed or peeled and grated
⅔ cup Curried Vinaigrette (facing page),
    plus additional for serving
1 tablespoon honey
½ teaspoon salt
¼ head red cabbage, core and outer leaves
    removed, very thinly sliced
3 tablespoons finely minced fresh parsley
1 large red bell pepper, cored, seeded, and
    finely diced (optional)

   1. Not more than 1 hour before serving, in a large bowl toss the green cabbage, apple, onion, and half the grated carrots together with ⅔ cup of the vinaigrette, honey, and salt. Taste and adjust the seasoning with additional salt or honey if needed.
   2. Immediately before serving, divide the slaw among chilled serving plates. Scatter a line of the red cabbage over the top of each serving; sprinkle on the parsley and red pep-

per. Serve immediately, passing extra dressing at table.

Serves 8 to 10

VARIATION:

Creamy Patchwork Slaw: Decrease the Curried Vinaigrette by 3 tablespoons and add ¼ cup crème fraîche, plain yogurt, or sour cream to the tossed part of the slaw. This is luscious.

Curried Lentil Salad with Vegetables

aking the dressing will require a trip to a spice store, but you will have enough curry spice mix left for several batches of the divine mayonnaise, or for curried rice or vegetables.

Pam cooking spray
1 pound lentils, rinsed and picked over
Enough well-flavored vegetable stock to
    cover lentils by 1½ inches
1 cup Curried Vinaigrette (recipe follows)
3 ears fresh corn
1 medium red onion, very finely chopped
1 green bell pepper, stemmed, seeded, and
    finely diced
2 ripe tomatoes, diced
Salt and freshly ground pepper to taste

1. Spray a heavy pot with the Pam. In it put the lentils and pour in enough vegetable stock to cover. Bring to a boil, then turn down the heat to medium-low and simmer, covered, adding stock as needed, about 45 minutes (or up to 2 hours if the lentils are old), until tender but still holding their shape. Drain well, reserving the liquid to use as stock in another recipe. Let cool to room temperature.

2. Combine the lentils with the vinaigrette and chill deeply.

3. Shuck the corn and cut the kernels from the cobs. Steam over boiling water for 2 minutes and let cool.

4. Add the corn, onion, bell pepper, and tomatoes to the lentils and toss to combine. Season to taste with salt and lots of freshly ground pepper. You can serve the salad right away, but it's even better after chilling for several hours or overnight.

Serves 8

Curry Spice Mix

⅓ cup coarsely ground black pepper
¼ cup ground cumin
3 tablespoons dry mustard
3 tablespoons ground turmeric
3 tablespoons best-quality curry powder
1½ tablespoons ground cardamom
1½ tablespoons ground coriander
1 tablespoon ground mace
1 tablespoon freshly grated nutmeg
1 tablespoon ground cinnamon
1 tablespoon ground cloves
1½ teaspoons cayenne pepper

► Combine all the spices and store in a tightly covered jar. If stored in a cool, dark place, it will keep for about a year. Use the mix anywhere curry powder is called for in this or any other cookbook. We make it by the quart at the restaurant.

Makes about 1½ cups

Curried Vinaigrette

⅓ cup cider vinegar
3 tablespoons light brown sugar
3 tablespoons honey
2½ to 3½ tablespoons Curry Spice Mix (above)
1½ teaspoons salt
1 cup mild vegetable oil, such as corn or peanut

► Place all the ingredients except the oil in a food processor. Put the machine's pusher tube in place. With the machine running, add the oil through the little hole in the pusher tube and process until emulsified. The vinaigrette will be thick and a deep golden brown by the time all the oil has been absorbed.

Makes 1⅓ cups

THE ENTRÉE SALAD PLATE TO GO WITH A COLD SOUP

❦*Long hot summer days, the still air shimmering with heat, the leaves hanging exhausted and dusty on the trees . . . Still, hunger, though made desultory by the heat, makes its old eternal rounds. But who wants to cook, or indeed eat, if the choices are heated or overly substantial or labor-intensive? Enter the chilled soup and salad-plate meal.*

At its simplest, it's composed of a cup of any one of the chilled soups in this book—many of which are made in a flash—and two or three takeout-style prepared salads (one a protein-rich entrée type, like a marinated shrimp, egg, or chicken salad) from a deli or haute *deli. These salads are arranged attractively on assorted greens with, perhaps, a garden-ripe tomato, its red heart still warm with sun, sliced and fanned out on a chilled plate. Got a sprig of fresh basil or cilantro? There's your garnish. Serve a glass of chilled white wine, icy, sweating beer, lemonade in a frosty glass, or iced tea fragranced with lemon and a sprig of mint perched on the glass. Add bread from the bakery or the store (you could do* Charlisa's Extra Good Sesame Drop Biscuit-Muffins *(page 363) in even less time than it'd take to go to the store) and a wedge of melon, or maybe some sherbet for dessert, and there you have it.*

Now this scenario is very nice if you live in a part of the world where there are well-stocked haute *delis, and if price and calorie count (both usually sky high at such establishments) are of no object. But in a place like Eureka Springs, fancy takeout isn't available. At home in the summertime we, like lots of other people around town, make our own more substantial salads to have on hand for chilled-plate meals, as well as for the impromptu picnic, or snack, or maybe sandwich filling.*

Curry, always a pleasant flavor in hot weather, finds its way into our lentil salad, our Patchwork Slaw *(page 385), and our egg salad.* White Bean Salad *(page 390) is simple and fresh flavored, Greek in feeling. Fruit combines with poultry, austere tofu with a silken, indulgent vinaigrette (a creamy vinaigrette with lots of garlic and fresh dill is great on tofu),*  *cheeses with vegetables. Store-bought tortellini (now those we can get around here, will wonders never cease?) goes with red peppers, garlic, broccoli, and the dressing described in the* Dairy Hollow House Pasta Salad *(page 384). We enjoy garden cukes coolly marinated in yogurt or sour cream spiked with garlic or dill, tomatoes nestled in neat slices overlapped with fresh herbs, mixed vegetables bathed in a lemon-sparked dressing. Our home-style chilled plates would probably feature just one prepared salad of this type, a protein-rich one, though occasionally we might second it with a very simple vegetable preparation.*

If you live in a place where you have a choice of a hundred takeout items, duck liver here, lobster there, might you not think this limited selection a little drab? Au contraire. *Add the pretty bed of greens, the sliced tomato (with maybe sliced red and yellow bell peppers), a scoop of the chosen salad or two, perhaps a few overlapped slices of a good cheese—wonderful. And consider the true garnish for that icy cup of soup and good bread—a view from the front porch looking into the July-lush green of Dairy Hollow; a slow-moving glider with its cushions wrapped in an old quilt; a day off, or even just a few minutes to sit on a busy day, some lemonade or iced herbal cooler, and a pileated woodpecker hammering congenially on the big black walnut tree—the good life.*

Here are some of our favorite chilled entrée-type salad plates. I have no doubt you could think of a thousand more.

▶ *The salad: red leaf lettuce with a scoop of curried egg salad and sliced fresh tomatoes garnished with a puff of sprouts. The bread:* Frannie's Fast, Fabulous Buttermilk Bread *(page 331). Pass the chutney (homemade or bottled) to spread on the bread—really excellent with the*

curried egg salad. The Soup: Chilled Summertime Zucchini Soup (page 165). Curried Egg Salad is simply your favorite egg salad (mine is hard-cooked country eggs, a little minced onion and celery, mayonnaise, salt, and freshly ground black pepper) with curry powder to taste.

▶ *The salad: romaine with a scoop of* Curried Lentil Salad with Vegetables *(page 386) or* White Bean Salad *and sliced red pepper. The bread: sesame seed whole-grain pita breads, from a natural foods store. The soup: chilled* Celery and Tomato Soup Aurore with Brandy *(page 122), or* Augusta's Chilled Tomato with Basil Cream *(page 265). Pass unsweetened yogurt at the table; it's wonderful with this salad.*

▶ *The salad: butterhead lettuce with a scoop of* Chicken Salad with Orange-Mint Dressing *(page 390), sliced fresh orange, sliced red onion, a few Greek olives, and wedge of feta cheese. The bread: French bread from a bakery, or* French Country Bread *(page 328). The soup:* Chilled Avocado Soup Mexique Bay *(page 109).* 🌱

White Bean Salad

nother bean salad with clear, fresh tastes. We serve it often as part of the entrée salad plates at the restaurant's special luncheons.

*1 pound dried navy beans, washed and
    picked over*
Pam cooking spray
*Enough well-flavored vegetable stock to
    cover the beans by 1½ inches*
*1 whole head garlic, cloves separated and
    peeled*
2 bay leaves
1½ teaspoons dried oregano
1½ teaspoons dried basil
4 ribs celery, finely chopped
2 medium red onions, finely chopped
*5 cloves garlic, peeled and put through a
    garlic press or finely chopped*
*1 large bunch fresh Italian (flat-leaf)
    parsley, finely minced*
½ cup olive oil
Juice of 3 to 4 fresh lemons
Salt and freshly ground pepper to taste

1. The night before you plan to make the salad, soak the beans in water to cover overnight.

2. The next day, drain the beans and place them in a large heavy pot that has been sprayed with Pam. Add enough stock to cover, the head of garlic, bay leaves, oregano, and basil. Bring to a boil, then turn down the heat to medium-low and let simmer, covered, until very tender but still holding their shape, about 1 hour. Drain the beans well (save the liquid for use as stock in other recipes), and place them in a large mixing bowl.

3. Add the remaining ingredients to the warm beans and toss well. Chill at least 4 hours. Taste and adjust the seasoning just before serving, adding more lemon juice, salt, or pepper if needed. Chopped fresh basil is quite good tossed in the salad just before serving.

Serves 8 to 10

Chicken Salad with Avocado and Orange-Mint Dressing

his is a beautiful, elegant salad, the most formal of all the entrée salads here. If you have a gazebo to eat it in, so much the better!

Pam cooking spray
1 chicken, cut up
1½ to 2 quarts boiling water or any well-
    flavored vegetable stock
1 whole head garlic, cloves separated and
    peeled
1 potato, scrubbed and quartered
1 rib celery with leaves, split lengthwise
6 to 8 black peppercorns
1 tablespoon celery seeds
Zest of ½ orange
2 oranges, peel and white pith removed, cut
    into segments
1 ripe avocado, pitted, peeled, and diced
½ ripe cantaloupe, rind and seeds
    removed, diced
4 scallions, trimmed and thinly sliced
Orange-Mint Dressing (recipe follows)
Salt and freshly ground black pepper to
    taste
Salad greens, for serving
Fresh mint sprigs, for garnish

1. Spray a large heavy pot with the Pam, and in it place the chicken. Pour over the boiling water or stock to barely cover and add the garlic, vegetables, peppercorns, celery seeds, and orange zest. Let simmer, covered, until the chicken is cooked through, about 40 minutes. Remove the chicken from the pot and let cool.

2. Strain the poaching liquid and return 2 cups of it to the pot. Boil the stock until reduced to 3 to 4 tablespoons of thick syrupy broth. (The time this takes depends on how high your heat and how wide your pot is.) Reserve this broth for the dressing.

3. Remove and discard the skin and bones from the chicken and cut the meat into large pieces. Chill.

4. In a large mixing bowl, combine the chicken, orange segments, avocado, cantaloupe, and scallions. Add the dressing and toss to coat. Season with salt and pepper. Marinate in the refrigerator no longer than 4 hours (the fruit will get mushy if marinated longer; see Note).

5. To serve, make a bed of greens on a large platter or on individual salad plates. Mound the chicken salad on top and garnish with mint sprigs.

Serves 4 to 6 as an entrée

Note: To prepare this further ahead of time, marinate the chicken in the dressing up to 8 hours in the refrigerator and combine with the fruit and scallions just before serving.

Orange-Mint Dressing

3 to 4 tablespoons reduced chicken
    poaching liquid (see step 2 of the chicken
    salad recipe)
1 large egg
¼ cup fresh orange juice
1 teaspoon grated orange zest
3 tablespoons white wine vinegar
2 tablespoons honey
Juice of 1 lime or lemon
1 to 2 cloves garlic, peeled
Salt and freshly ground black pepper to
    taste
1 cup mild vegetable oil, such as corn or
    peanut
2 tablespoons chopped fresh mint, or to
    taste

► Place all ingredients except the oil and mint in a food processor and process until combined. Put the machine's pusher tube in place. With the machine running, add the oil through the hole in the pusher tube, and process until emulsified. Taste and adjust the seasonings. Add the mint and process with on/off pulses until just combined; the mint should not be puréed.

INDEX

T